1986

P9-ARF-195

Mass Media & the First Amend- ment

Mass Media & the First Amendment

An Introduction to the Issues, Problems, and Practices

Maurice R. Cullen, Jr.
Michigan State University

wcb

Wm. C. Brown Company Publishers
Dubuque, Iowa

wcb

Book Team

Susan J. Soley, Editor
Julia A. Scannell, Designer
Laura J. Beaudoin, Production Editor
Faye Schilling, Visual Research Editor
Mavis M. Oeth, Permissions Editor

Wm. C. Brown Company Publishers, College Division

Lawrence E. Cremer, President
Raymond C. Deveaux, Vice President/Product Development
David Wm. Smith, Assistant Vice President/National Sales Manager
David A. Corona, Director of Production Development and Design
Matthew T. Coghlan, National Marketing Manager
Janis Machala, Director of Marketing Research
Marilyn A. Phelps, Manager of Design
William A. Moss, Production Editorial Manager
Mary M. Heller, Visual Research Manager

Photo credits—chapter openings

Chapter 1 (Stanley Forman, *Boston Herald American*) "Collapse of Fire Escape"
Chapter 2 (Culver Pictures, Inc.) H. V. Kaltenborn
Chapter 3 (Wide World Photos, Inc.) Anthony Kiritsis
Chapter 4 (© The *Cincinnati Enquirer*) Larry Flynt
Chapter 5 (Bill Fitz-Patrick, The White House) Jimmy Carter
Chapter 6 (Don Black) Nelson Rockefeller
Chapter 7 (Wide World Photos, Inc.) Myron Farber
Chapter 8 (Wide World Photos, Inc.)
Chapter 9 Jay Shelledy
Chapter 10 (Stanley Forman, *Boston Herald American*) "The Soiling of Old Glory"
Chapter 11 (© Don Fontaine, The Springfield News Papers) "A Fight for Life"
Chapter 12 (Bill Wunsch, The *Denver Post*)
Chapter 13 (UPI)

Contents

3 Reporting the News   65

4 Mass Media Audiences   103

5 Mass Media and Government: The Executive Branch   139

6 Mass Media and Government: The Legislative Branch   163

7 Mass Media and Government: The Judicial Branch   193

8 Mass Media Controls: Sex and the Mass Media   231

9 Mass Media Controls: Libel and Privacy   263

10 Other Controls 293

13 Mass Media and Future Shock 417

Tables

Preface

The news media have frequently served high and noble purposes throughout American history. On occasion they have also allied themselves with questionable causes that have tarnished their special place in the social-political system. As with other democratic institutions, the news media are operated by human beings. And human beings are good and evil, weak and strong, and many things in between. These truths are frequently raised in discussions of why the media sometimes fail to live up to their potential in the democratic order. They also serve as *excuses* for failure. Because of these realities, it is essential for Americans to remain in touch with how the news media are working and how they affect the daily lives of media consumers.

Among those who analyze the place of media in society, many believe that the media are out of touch, that they no longer provide the positive, creative input that the nation needs to meet new challenges. Questions of credibility reflect the reigning media problem of our time.

The purpose of this book is to explore the roots of the free press concept in the United States and to determine what the press was meant to be, what it is in present-day America, and what the future is likely to hold. It also tells *why*.

This text offers an alternative approach to the multitude of introductory books that currently crowd the marketplace. It is not a how-to-do-it production manual nor is it a guide to employment opportunities. It is an issues-oriented book based on actual case studies that reflect the pros and cons of media activity. It also attempts to apply fair evaluations to media performance, as shaky as that exercise can sometimes be. These elements provide topical springboards for understanding, for thinking, and for discussion.

Unlike other texts now in use, the First Amendment to the United States Constitution is the guiding theme throughout this volume. It is critic, evaluator, judge, and friendly adversary. The chapters explore all essential topics: mass media responsibility fitted to the historical traditions of the First Amendment; mass media performance as a measure of its responsibility; media impact on audiences; the issues involved in the media's relationships to government and the clashes between the two that have become dangerously commonplace. Also included are the various "popular" issues such as the place of sexually oriented content in the mass media, libel and the right of individual privacy, and the different forms of controls over media content. It explores ethical issues, the media as "business," and what the future holds via dynamic changes in media technologies. Throughout the chapters, photographs, illustrations, and easy-to-follow charts and graphs underscore the many tempers of mass media activity.

The particular strength of this text is the thrust of the First Amendment as a gauge of media performance, an ingredient that other texts ignore or treat peripherally. No discussion of current media issues and problems can be meaningful without considering what the mass media *should be,* or at least *might be.* As a measuring device, the First Amendment offers sufficient flexibility to meet the challenges of the time, *any* time.

This text is designed for the student of the mass media, beginning or advanced, who has not yet bent over the critical media issues of the day. It is especially for the student who is beginning a program of mass media studies—journalism, telecommunication, advertising, public relations, and other publicly oriented mass media. It has application to majors drawn from other academic disciplines who recognize, or need to recognize, the dynamic role played by the media in our society. As lifelong consumers of mass media information, all present-day students share a vital stake in how and why the media operate as they do.

Today's students have been exposed to mass media content to a greater degree than any generation in history. Hence, most have established attitudes about media performance based on their own experiences and those of their parents, associates, teachers, and others. This text is designed to build on earlier experiences in the development of reasoned adult viewpoints.

Finally, a concerted effort has been made here to provide evidential balance in presentations of major issues. Even so, some course instructors and some students might still disagree with one position or another as presented. That is the nature of controversy and the mass media are embroiled in many. But if this text succeeds in bringing the issues forward for open discussion in a scholarly climate, the purposes of scholarship will be served. And that's what this book is really about.

Acknowledgments

It is a rare researcher who has nobody to thank in the production of a volume of this scope and magnitude. I have several. To Professor Henry T. Price, of the University of South Carolina—Columbia, Professor Delbert McGuire, of Colorado State University—Ft. Collins, and Professors John Paul Jones and Charles C. Russell, of Cornell University—New York, I owe more than I could hope to pay. Each took on the manuscript at several points in its development and again upon its completion. Each contributed meaningfully to the final version. Professor George A. Hough III, chairperson of the Michigan State University School of Journalism during most of the time it took to complete this project, offered suggestions and encouragement as needed and juggled my teaching schedule to provide sufficient blocks of time to complete this text. Erwin P. Bettinghaus, Dean of the College of Communication Arts and Sciences at Michigan State, lent support from the outset and came through with cogent comments based on his own textbook productivity.

Special appreciation must go to Professor E. Jerry McCarthy, of the Michigan State University College of Business, who freely shared his vast experiences as a leading author of textbooks. The office staff of the School of Journalism at Michigan State aided this project substantially via steering me clear of potholes in manuscript production. Thus I am grateful to Virginia Brenner and Robyn Meadows. Pat Vermeer contributed in a major way by organizing the search for illustrative matter and seeking permissions, a sometimes nerve-wracking activity. Hence, I owe her much.

My wife, Mary Maloney Cullen, has to be one of the most demanding editors of all time. She not only read every draft of every chapter produced but offered incisive commentaries on all aspects. She also ordered me into the study to work when taking a walk or sharpening pencils seemed more enticing than juggling research findings. The contributions of my four teenage offspring, Mary Pat, Kathleen, John, and Maureen, may have been the most significant of all. They willingly kept the four stereos at subblast levels when they heard the clack of the typewriter rattling through the house. Such sacrifice must not pass unnoticed.

Realistically, accolades need go to my students in Journalism 110, Journalism in a Free Society. Over the years I tested out with them new material, new media crises, issues, and successes that became sharpened on the whetstone of open discussion and debate. This book is theirs as much as it is mine.

Maurice R. Cullen, Jr.
School of Journalism
Michigan State University

A Note on Sexism

Particular efforts have been made in the preparation of this volume to avoid derogatory references to feminine and masculine genders. The author recognizes that in modern society sexist references to either are insulting to both and certainly have no place in a textbook geared to men and women students.

At the same time, the English language offers no generic singular for "they" or "them." The sole option is to use combinations of singulars such as "she and he," "his or her," "she or he," and so forth. Unfortunately, usage of such combinations becomes unwieldy, especially when repeated frequently, and interrupts reading flow. In some cases the problem can be corrected by simply restructuring the sentence and, where that has been workable in this volume, it has been done. In others where revision does not effect a solution, the singular pronoun "he" or "his" has been employed. It has been employed *only* in its traditional function of serving as the accepted singular of "they" or "them" and *not* as the *masculine* singular as such.

Mass Media & the First Amendment

News in Pictures

Historical Background to the First Amendment

1

Upon completing this chapter you should know—

the origins and significance of early English and American roots of the First Amendment

how and why governments have tried to control freedom of expression by arrests, trials, torture, and executions, and those who suffered because of it

how and why courageous individuals attempted to speak out on public issues in spite of various forms of intimidation, and who they were

details of the Zenger case and why it has earned a place in the history of freedom of expression

the role of truth as a defense in libel

Chapter Objectives

Divine Right   Kings ruled because God favored them; thus, they and their appointed officials were held to be above popular criticism and such criticism was treated as a crime. (p. 5)

Treason   An attempt to overthrow government by force. (p. 7)

Sedition   An attempt to stir up public opinion against government. (p. 7)

Seditious Libel   An attempt to stir up public opinion against a specific government official or officials. (p. 7)

Prior Restraint   Government determination *before* publication of what may or may not be published; censorship. (p. 8)

Key Terms

This is true liberty, when free-born men,
Having to advise the public, may speak free.

Euripides, fifth century B.C.,
Greece

The English Roots

The ongoing struggle for freedom of speech and press in America has its roots
in sixteenth- and seventeenth-century England.[1] In those times, authorities
looked disapprovingly on the notion that a private citizen should be able to
speak out on the actions of government. A ruler was lord and master in those
times. His authority was granted by the "divine right" of God; this was an
important factor, for the ruler and his ministers were thus held to be above
public criticism. Anyone who took exception to the rule usually found himself
facing charges of treason, and that customarily brought imprisonment, torture,
mutilation, or death. Yet, in spite of such dreadful consequences, some noble
souls made the effort. A few cases in point follow.

Divine Right

In 1579, John Stubbe, a writer, and Hugh Singleton, his printer, produced a
pamphlet that questioned the appropriateness of a rumored marriage between
Queen Elizabeth I and a French nobleman. Stubbe expressed his loyalty to
the queen, but he questioned the logic of such a union between leaders of these
two frequently embattled nations. Elizabeth became enraged that a common
person would dare to comment on government matters openly and in print.
The two were arrested for treason and sentenced to lose their right hands.
Stubbe's hand was removed and he saluted his queen with the other. At the
last moment, Singleton's sentence was set aside.

**Early Struggles
for Freedom of
Expression**
John Stubbe

In 1584, William Carter was hanged, disemboweled, and quartered for
high treason after printing pro-Catholic pamphlets in a country then governed
by Protestants.

William Carter

Printer John Twyn found himself in trying circumstances with the crown
when, in 1664, authorities searched his house without a warrant and carried
off corrected proofs of a book he had been setting into type. Titled *A Treatise
on the Execution of Justice*, the book, among other revolutionary notions,
insisted that government was accountable to the people, who in turn possessed

John Twyn

the right to revolt and seize the government should it fail them. They arrested Printer Twyn, who, in a blaze of courage, refused to identify the author. The court found *him* guilty, and so he was hanged, drawn, and quartered for the crime of printing someone's opinions.

Through history with the *old* New York Times

Jehovah Resting After 6-Day Task

Woman Created From Rib Of Adam

Cain Is Accused In Killing Of Abel

Noah Builds Ark; Sees A Long Rain

Methuselah Dies; Judean Was 944

Moses, On Sinai, Gets 10-Pt. Plan

Solomon Offers To Sever A Child

Plague Of Locusts Besets Egyptians

Ten Chores Set For Greek Hero

Achilles Is Shot In Trojan Battle

Penelope Joyful After Long Wait

Homer Dies At 89; Poet Wrote 'Iliad'

Boy Slays Goliath With A Slingshot

3 Kings Report Sighting Of Star

Rome In Flames; Nero Plays Violin

World Conquered By Genghis Khan

Marco Polo Tells Of Trade Mission

World Is Round, Genoan Declares

A Maid In France Burned At Stake

Pocohantas Saves A White Settler

Holland Settlers In $24 Land Deal

Tea Ship Is Sunk; Indians Blamed

French Are Urged To Consume Cake

Guillotine Busy In French Dispute

Blaze In Chicago Is Linked To Cow

Twenty years ago, copy editors at the *New York Times* amused themselves for a time by testing their skill against the great events of the past. The result was this collection, reprinted from *Times Talk*, the in-house publication, for February 1961. (The New York Times Company, Reprinted by permission.)

In 1693, William Anderton, another printer, refused to name the author of two books that he had printed, which, the court said, *tended* to incite rebellion. Anderton was hanged for treason.

From time to time other courageous individuals took their chances against government by composing philosophical essays on the subject of freedom of expression. In the summer of 1644, William Walwyn, a religious and political writer, composed and had printed *The Compassionate Samaritane*. Published anonymously (for safety) and without license, the pamphlet admitted that certain forms of licensing were necessary but not to the extent of crushing "dissenting discussion" unharmful to the state. Henry Robinson, another pamphleteer of that period, endorsed free expression as being an essential ingredient of private enterprise and property. The best known of the pamphleteers was poet John Milton, whose famed *Areopagitica*, published on November 24, 1644, spoke for the right of open exchange of conflicting ideas. Milton argued that "though all the winds of doctrine were let loose to play upon the earth, so truth be in the field, we do injuriously by licensing and prohibiting to misdoubt her strength. Let her (truth) and falsehood grapple; who ever knew truth put to the worse, in a free and open encounter?" While Milton's essay has much to recommend it, especially in the passages most often quoted, he expressly called for certain limitations. In the main he would extend the privilege of free and open debate to intellectuals of his own Puritan sect but not at all to "Popery, and open superstition" or to the "impious or evil," which "no law can possibly permit." In fact, he skirted the matter of freedom of the press entirely and a few years later even became a censor of newsbooks.* Even so, *Areopagitica* certainly supported a loosening of the bonds that had long muzzled freedom of expression in the British system.

As the seventeenth century grew to a close, some enlightened legal minds began to view oral and printed criticisms of government actions as something less than treasonous. By definition, treason involved efforts to overthrow government *by force*, that is, by *armed force*. So, in time, the crime became "sedition," or the crime of stirring up public opinion against authority. Thus "seditious libel" became the crime of criticizing a government *official*. While a lesser crime, penalties often remained as severe as before. For example, nineteen-year-old John Mathews was hanged for sedition in 1720 for printing the claims of James III to the throne.

*It is evident that Milton supported free exchange of ideas primarily among scholars and Puritan leaders. In a later essay, he urged these "approved" intellectuals to write in Latin "which the common people understand not." And he certainly did not favor granting freedom to the "journalists" of his time.

Until 1695, English authorities possessed the right of "prior restraint," that is, the right to *censor* what went into a publication before it was printed and distributed to readers. Parliament abolished the practice that year for various reasons, but mainly because it had become nonenforceable. Now citizens could be as daring as they wished, provided they were willing to endure the fury of government *after* publication.[2] The move would have great significance in colonial America.

The American Roots

English law came to the American colonies along with other social and political institutions as Britain expanded her control overseas. The colonies were administered by officials appointed by the crown. As in England, government officials in America viewed printing with suspicion and even alarm. In 1671, Sir William Berkley, who governed Virginia for thirty-eight years, summed up the views of many of the king's representatives in the New World:

> But I thank God we have not free schools nor printing; and I hope we shall not have [them] these hundred years. For learning has brought disobedience and heresy and sects into the world; and printing has divulged them and libels against the government. God keep us from both.[3]

Even so, in the American colonies, Britannia "ruled" rather loosely, sometimes leaving the colonists to their own designs in organizing local governments and colonial legislatures. Three thousand miles of ocean separated the two, making communication between America and London agonizingly slow. The only medium of communication, sailing ships, took months to make a single crossing. In time, this isolation created local pride among colonists who carved their livelihoods out of the wilderness. Ultimately, they organized profitable business and trade activities distinctly their own. They also founded free schools for their children and, by the beginning of the War of Independence, they had opened nine colleges, an important and unique development among English colonies.

Discontent began to brew with the wars against the French and accompanying British affronts to colonial troops. British generals outranked American generals, British captains outranked American captains, and so on up and down the lines of command. Holding the provincials at Fort Louisburg through an ugly and idle winter, during which illness and death decimated the American ranks, did not win loyalties for Britain.

Bostonians wrote of the trials of their sons in the North, and newspapers and pamphlets began to speak of the *American* army and *American* rights. When the soldiers came home, they and their families turned sullen faces to a city bordering on economic collapse. Newspaper content began to reflect the woes of the times.

The Press Responds

Another factor in the development of the American press was that, as time passed, an increasing number of American colonists were native-born, had never seen the mother country, and became dedicated to furthering local economic and social interests. Among other benefits, their commitments to "home and hearth" increased their feelings of personal independence as a people, and newspapers began to reflect that as well.

Thus, when Parliament passed the Stamp Act in 1765, notably without consulting colonial legislatures as had been the practice, newspapers and broadsides immediately resisted, due mostly to the fact that printers were among those hardest hit by the act.* In less than a dozen years, the "patriot movement," led by its press, embroiled all of British North America in the greatest affront to authority the monarchs of Europe had ever known. Inspired by the humanist writings of John Milton, John Locke, and other English thinkers, colonists took control of their legislatures in the name of the people, and British governors became powerless to deal with them.

Passage of the Stamp Act

At one point Samuel Adams editorialized in the *Boston Gazette*:

The Press Takes Sides
Samuel Adams in the Gazette

> Curs'd Prudence of interested, designing Politicians who have done their utmost to have the Liberties of Millions of honest and loyal American citizens sacrificed to their own Ambitions and Lust of Dominion and Wealth . . . hungry Wolves— ye insatiable Vultures—ye devouring Monsters. . . . See what is already the Consequence of your impudent Temerity—a whole Continent awakened— alarmed.[4]

An astounding attack considering the laws of seditious libel of the time!

In time, the Loyalist press became overwhelmed and intimidated by the radicals to the extent that many shut down rather than suffer midnight visits by the Sons of Liberty. With few exceptions, the remaining press turned bland.

Invective and insult against government officials became standard fare by anticrown editors and contributors. Matters became so bad that Governor Francis Bernard of Massachusetts wrote Lord Halifax that the *Boston Gazette* (for one) "has swarmed with libells of the most atrocious kind. These have been urged with so much vehemence and so industriously repeated, that I have considered them as preludes to action."[5]

Governor Bernard Evaluates the Press

*The law placed a sizeable tax on paper, which made it more expensive to purchase by printers. In addition, printers who published newspapers also had to pay taxes on each issue of the paper and on each advertisement run.

Prosecutions for seditious libel evolved in colonial New York almost as soon as Britain wrested control of Manhattan Island from the Dutch. One Peter Chocke, for example, dared to characterize his governor as the worst in the colony's history. The court ruled his words so "highly criminall" that he was hauled before the highest tribunal in the province to answer for his sins.

In Maryland in 1686, John Coode, tried on charges of sedition and blasphemy, denounced the punishments available to citizens of that colony who dared speak their minds: they included "Whipping, Branding, Boreing through the Tongue, Fine, Imprisonment, Banishment, or Death."[6]

*The First
American Newspaper*

In 1690, Benjamin Harris founded what may loosely be called the first newspaper in America. His *Publick Occurrences, Both Foreign and Domestick* appeared in Boston on September 25 of that year. It never appeared again. Harris, who had already spent two years in an English dungeon for violating publishing regulations, had failed to secure a proper license for his venture. Worse yet, he carried objectionable quips and comments and even criticized the conduct of England's Indian allies for having recently butchered some French captives.[7] The boot of authority came down hard; official Massachusetts had no need of critics.

Thomas Maule

In 1695, that same province became embroiled in a landmark sedition case which, in some ways, became the blueprint for the trial of John Peter Zenger. Thomas Maule, a tough, determined Salem man, published a book that questioned the conduct of both civil and religious leaders in Boston. Authorities had him arrested and his books burned. At his trial, where he served as his own defense counsel, Maule added insult to injury by repeating in court what he had written in the book. Waving off warnings to keep a civil tongue in his head, Maule replied that he had spoken the truth and, since he had already been imprisoned five times and whipped twice for speaking his mind, he feared no one. The court then reindicted him to include these verbal outrages as well. Maule gallantly attacked the evidence against him, comparing his trial with the recent Salem witch-hunts, which still terrified the public conscience. He brazenly urged the jury to judge the law and not merely the fact of publication as was the practice. Amazingly for that time period, the jury ruled in his favor. But with it all, freedom of expression, per se, was not a vital issue in the trial, not even to Maule himself. That would come at another time. Nonetheless, his year in jail stood as his personal memorial to individual freedom.[8]

Government Pressures against the Press

Growth of the American press was snaillike in those years. Newspapers came into existence, some to die off quickly, others to prosper under the watchful eye of government. Most were dull journals that excited few and generally steered out of harm's way. Most printers were the same. A notable exception

Benjamin Franklin launched his journalism career on brother James's *Courant* both as printer's apprentice and secret author of the Silence Dogood letters. (The Bettmann Archives, Inc.)

was James Franklin, elder brother of Benjamin, whose *New-England Courant* shattered the serene, strict world of Puritan Boston. "There can be no such thing as public liberty without freedom of speech," Franklin told his readers as he ignored the licensing requirement and got away with it. His newspaper avoided direct criticism of the king's officials in favor of ridiculing in brilliant satire the religious power structure of the Bay Colony. But government eventually recognized certain dangerous tendencies in this free spirit and sent him to jail for a month for contempt. Further, he was forbidden to publish the *Courant*, "Except it be first Supervised, by the Secretary of this Province"— a classical definition of censorship. Jail seemed to temper Franklin's pen and he eventually moved to Rhode Island where, in 1732, he founded the short-lived *Rhode Island Gazette.*[9]

These and other cases like them were minor incidents compared with what was to come as the colonists, growing impatient under the heavy hand of arbitrary government, sought greater freedom to express their opinions orally and in print.

Franklin's New-England Courant

From MONDAY February 4. to MONDAY February 11. 1723.

The late Publisher of this Paper, finding so many Inconveniencies would arise by his carrying the Manuscripts and publick News to be supervis'd by the Secretary, as to render his carrying it on unprofitable, has intirely dropt the Undertaking. The present Publisher having receiv'd the following Piece, desires the Readers to accept of it as a Preface to what they may hereafter meet with in this Paper.

Non ego mordaci distrinxi Carmine quenquam,
Nulla venenato Litera onista Joco est.

LONG has the Press groaned in bringing forth an hateful, but numerous Brood of Party Pamphlets, malicious Scribbles, and Billlogsgate Ribaldry. The Rancour and bitterness it has unhappily infused into Mens minds, and to what a Degree it has sowred and leaven'd the Tempers of Persons formerly esteemed some of the most sweet and affable, is too well known here, to need any further Proof or Representation of the Matter.

No generous and impartial Person then can blame the present Undertaking, which is designed purely for the Diversion and Merriment of the Reader. Pieces of Pleasancy and Mirth have a secret Charm in them to allay the Heats and Tumors of our Spirits, and to make a Man forget his restless Resentments. They have a strange Power to tune the harsh Disorders of the Soul, and reduce us to a serene and placid State of Mind.

The main Design of this Weekly Paper will be to entertain the Town with the most comical and diverting Incidents of Humane Life, which in so large a Place as Boston, will not fail of a universal Exemplification: Nor shall we be wanting to fill up these Papers with a grateful Interspersion of more serious Morals, which may be drawn from the most ludicrous and odd Parts of Life.

As for the Author, that is the next Question. But tho' we profess our selves ready to oblige the ingenious and courteous Reader with most Sorts of Intelligence, yet here we beg a Reserve. Nor will it be of any Manner of Advantage either to them or to the Writers, that their Names should be published; and therefore in this Matter we desire the Favour of you to suffer us to hold our Tongues: Which tho' at this Time of Day it may sound like a very uncommon Request, yet it proceeds from the very Hearts of your Humble Servants.

By this Time the Reader perceives that more than one are engaged in the present Undertaking. Yet is there one Person, an Inhabitant of this Town of Boston, whom we honour as a Doctor in the Chair, or a perpetual Dictator.

The Society had design'd to present the Publick with his Effigies, but that the Limner, to whom he was presented for a Draught of his Countenance, descryed (and this he is ready to offer upon Oath) Nineteen Features in his Face, more than ever he beheld in any Humane Visage before; which so raised the Price of his Picture, that our Master himself forbid the Extravagance of coming up to it. And then besides, the Limner objected a Schisin in his Face, which splits it from his Forehead in a strait Line down to his Chin, in such sort, that Mr. Painter protests it is a double Face, and he'll have Four Pounds for the Pourtraiture. However, tho' this double Face has spoilt us of a pretty Picture, yet we all rejoiced to see old Janus in our Company.

There is no Man in Boston better qualified than old Janus for a Couranteer, or if you please, an Observator, being a Man of such remarkable Opticks, as to look two ways at once.

As for his Morals, he is a chearly Chistian, as the Country Phrase expresses it. A Man of good Temper, courteous Deportment, sound Judgment; a mortal Hater of Nonsense, Foppery, Formality, and endless Ceremony.

As for his Club, they aim at no greater Happiness or Honour, than the Publick be made to know, that it is the utmost of their Ambition to attend upon and do all imaginable good Offices to good Old Janus the Couranteer, who is and always will be the Readers humble Servant.

P. S. Gentle Readers, we design never to let a Paper pass without a Latin Motto if we can possibly pick one up, which carries a Charm in it to the Vulgar, and the learned admire the pleasure of Construing. We should have obliged the World with a Greek scrap or two, but the Printer has no Types, and therefore we intreat the candid Reader not to impute the defect to our Ignorance, for our Doctor can say all the Greek Letters by heart.

His Majesty's Speech to the Parliament; October 11. tho' already publish'd, may perhaps be new to many of our Country Readers; we shall therefore insert it in this Day's Paper.

His MAJESTY's most Gracious SPEECH to both Houses of Parliament, on Thursday October 11. 1722.

My Lords and Gentlemen,

I Am sorry to find my self obliged, at the Opening of this Parliament, to acquaint you, That a dangerous Conspiracy has been for some time formed, and is still carrying on against my Person and Government, in Favour of a Popish Pretender.

The Discoveries I have made here, the Informations I have received from my Ministers abroad, and the Intelligences I have had from the Powers in Alliance with me, and indeed from most parts of Europe, have given me most ample and current Proofs of this wicked Design.

The Conspirators have, by their Emissaries, made the strongest Instances for Assistance from Foreign Powers, but were disappointed in their Expectations: However, confiding in their Numbers, and not discouraged by their former ill Success, they resolve once more, upon their own strength, to attempt the subversion of my Government.

To this End they provided considerable Sums of Money, engaged great Numbers of Officers from abroad, secured large Quantities of Arms and Ammunition, and thought themselves in such Readiness, that had not the Conspiracy been timely discovered, we should, without doubt, before now have seen the whole Nation, and particularly the City of London, Involved in Blood and Confusion.

The Care I have taken has, by the Blessing of God, hitherto prevented the Execution of their trayterous Projects. The Troops have been incamped all this Summer; six Regiments (though very necessary for the Security of that Kingdom) have been brought over from Ireland; The States General have given me assurances that they would keep a considerable Body of Forces in readiness to assist.

Biting satire of Puritan morality was standard fare in James Franklin's *New-England Courant*. (The Bettmann Archives, Inc.)

One of the most notable cases in colonial America's struggle for freedom of expression involved William Bradford, who, in 1685, founded the first printing press in Philadelphia, the third in America, and the first outside Massachusetts.[10] Shortly thereafter he agreed to print an almanac for a client, which contained terminology frowned upon by certain members of the council. The council ordered him to appear before them and gave him a tongue-lashing and warned him not to print anything without gaining the council's approval—in advance. Three years later, Bradford found himself in similar circumstances. This time the client's work contained critical barbs aimed at the council itself. Enraged at the spunk displayed by the printer, the governor himself delivered a second lecture.*[11] But words alone were not sufficient to stem the passions that drove William Bradford. A year later he found himself in a jail cell on a charge of seditious libel in what appears to have been the first such criminal action involving freedom of the press in America. Bradford had published a series of tracts authored by two dissenting Quakers, which reeked of heresy. Pennsylvania was a Quaker stronghold just as Massachusetts was for the Puritans. One of the tracts attacked various ministers of government; hence, authorities arrested the two authors along with Bradford. A panel of magistrates, six of whom had been assailed in the offensive tract, convicted all three "without All Hearing or Tryal." Bradford's hackles were up and he demanded his right to trial by jury. The court agreed and returned him to jail for another six months to await his fate.

Role of the Jury

Under the legal system then in vogue, a jury involved in such a case could rule only on the *fact* of publication, that is, it could determine only whether or not the defendant actually wrote or printed the libelous statement. Jurors did not have the authority to find the defendant innocent because the statement was true as they may in modern times. In fact, common interpretation of the law recognized that the greater the truth in libel, the greater the libel. That is what Bradford and his cohorts faced.

In the trial that followed, William Bradford became the first American charged with seditious libel to demand that the jury be permitted to weigh not only the fact of publication, but the guilt or innocence of the accused as well, "for the Jury are Judges in Law, as well as in matter of fact."[12] Even with that, however, Bradford did not base his defense on the truth of what he had printed, but on the court's inability to prove that he had, in fact, set the type and printed the offensive publication. When the court ordered that the "form," or full frame of type, be presented as evidence, so the story goes, a sympathetic juror nudged it with his cane, sending the type frame crashing to the floor, the type scattering in all directions. So much for the court's "evidence!"[13]

*Among other things, the governor warned him: "Sir, I have particular order from Governor Penn for the suppression of printing here, and narrowly to look after your press, and I will search your house, look after your press, and make you give in five hundred pounds security to print nothing but what I allow, or I'll lay you fast."

Imprisoned to await yet another trial, Bradford finally gained release at the intervention of New York Governor Benjamin Fletcher, who happened to need a printer of his own. Bradford seized the opportunity to escape his tormenters and on April 10, 1693, he became the official printer for New York.[14] He was soon to learn, however, that he had only exchanged one set of publishing rules for another. Yet, in time, he warmed to his new prosperity. In fact he even became something of a company man to the point where he would one day defend the established order with as much fervor as he had opposed it.[15]

The Role of the Printer

Many printers in early America invested enormous amounts of time, energy, and personal courage in support of their right to speak their beliefs. Though one of the best-paid workers in town, the printer's income was rarely in line with the investments made in hours, sweat, and worry. The amount and duration of daylight limited the workday, especially in winter when darkness came early. The poor quality of artificial light, mostly from candles or lanterns, made typesetting a painful exercise at best, even in a shop as well organized as Bradford's. All supplies and equipment—inks, type, paper, and presses—had to be imported from Europe. Hence, early American printers frequently used worn-down type crowded onto pages to save paper, which made reading a nightmare. Because of type shortages, the printer frequently used a variety of type faces and sizes in a single publication, which created even more visual problems for the reader.

The Colonial Newspaper

Launching a newspaper created many pitfalls. By and large, the journals carried outdated foreign news, philosophical essays, bad poetry, letters to the editor (sometimes authored by the printer himself), and advertising, which promoted all manner of goods and services from wet nurses to cannon balls, beeswax to frocks. Cure-alls exploited the childlike fancies and superstitions of subscribers left to struggle without adequate medical knowledge. But most advertising came from legitimate businesses that had interesting, even vital, things to sell.[16]

Importance of the Printer

William Bradford toiled at his press at a point in history when the trade, worldwide, stood at its lowest aesthetic level. This fact must be considered when evaluating the printer's contributions to the social, political, and religious development of America. Without question the printer played a major role in these developments, and the deplorable working conditions that he faced each day are a testimony to his dedication.[17] The printer held an important position in the community, more so than other tradesmen, which must have contributed to his feeling of personal independence. Since he used postal services more than most, it was not uncommon to find a printer also serving as postmaster. The print shop thus became a gathering place for townspeople, and a place

The Diffusion of Printing Through the Original Thirteen Colonies, Louisiana, Florida, Maine, Mississippi, The Middle and The Far West

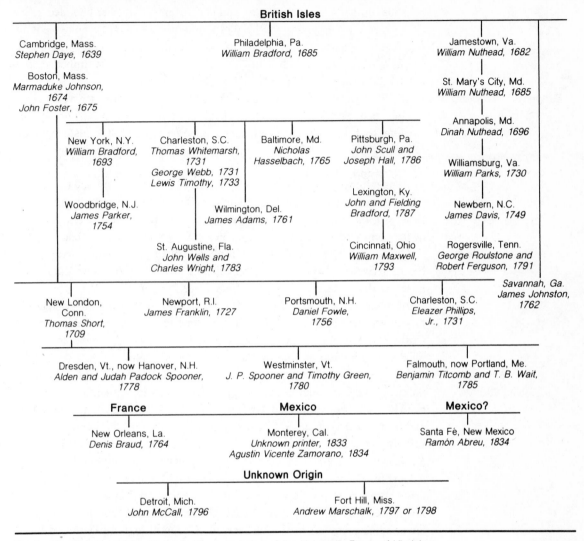

British Isles

Cambridge, Mass.
Stephen Daye, 1639

Boston, Mass.
Marmaduke Johnson, 1674
John Foster, 1675

Philadelphia, Pa.
William Bradford, 1685

Jamestown, Va.
William Nuthead, 1682

St. Mary's City, Md.
William Nuthead, 1685

New York, N.Y.
William Bradford, 1693

Charleston, S.C.
Thomas Whitemarsh, 1731
George Webb, 1731
Lewis Timothy, 1733

Baltimore, Md.
Nicholas Hasselbach, 1765

Pittsburgh, Pa.
John Scull and Joseph Hall, 1786

Annapolis, Md.
Dinah Nuthead, 1696

Williamsburg, Va.
William Parks, 1730

Woodbridge, N.J.
James Parker, 1754

Wilmington, Del.
James Adams, 1761

Lexington, Ky.
John and Fielding Bradford, 1787

Newbern, N.C.
James Davis, 1749

St. Augustine, Fla.
John Wells and Charles Wright, 1783

Cincinnati, Ohio
William Maxwell, 1793

Rogersville, Tenn.
George Roulstone and Robert Ferguson, 1791

Savannah, Ga.
James Johnston, 1762

New London, Conn.
Thomas Short, 1709

Newport, R.I.
James Franklin, 1727

Portsmouth, N.H.
Daniel Fowle, 1756

Charleston, S.C.
Eleazer Phillips, Jr., 1731

Dresden, Vt., now Hanover, N.H.
Alden and Judah Padock Spooner, 1778

Westminster, Vt.
J. P. Spooner and Timothy Green, 1780

Falmouth, now Portland, Me.
Benjamin Titcomb and T. B. Wait, 1785

France

New Orleans, La.
Denis Braud, 1764

Mexico

Monterey, Cal.
Unknown printer, 1833
Agustin Vicente Zamorano, 1834

Mexico?

Santa Fé, New Mexico
Ramón Abreu, 1834

Unknown Origin

Detroit, Mich.
John McCall, 1796

Fort Hill, Miss.
Andrew Marschalk, 1797 or 1798

Wroth, *The Colonial Printer*, Reprinted by permission of the University Press of Virginia.

where gossip made the rounds, sometimes finding its way into print.*[18] Increasingly, then, the colonial American printer became one to be reckoned with—even by government.

*With his shop also a place for social lingering, the enterprising printer sometimes offered for sale a variety of items having nothing to do with books, broadsides, and newspapers. Benjamin Franklin sold coffee, patent medicines, wine, spectacles, Rhode Island cheese, and lottery tickets, along with his printing services. Such practice was common in early America.

The Zenger Case

John Peter Zenger's arrival in the New World was inauspicious, even depressing, at least to him. One of a pathetic group of immigrants from the war-torn Upper Palatinate in Western Germany, he arrived in New York in 1710 with his mother, younger brother, and two sisters. His father had died at sea. So now, at thirteen and as the head of the family, he sought employment and was fortunate indeed to find a position as apprentice to William Bradford, the colony's only printer. This became a union of immense importance in America's struggle for press freedom.

Zenger and Bradford

In 1725, Bradford established a short-lived partnership with young Peter Zenger, as he preferred to be called. He also established the *New-York Weekly Gazette*, that colony's first newspaper. For some reason lost to history the two failed to get along, and soon Zenger was on his own and in desperate financial straits.

Zenger took on odd jobs of various kinds, married, and set up his own printing business. That did little to improve his ability to earn a living because Bradford, the official printer, received all of the government work plus most of the commercial volume. Even so, Peter Zenger's stock was about to rise.

Governor Cosby

On August 1, 1732, William Cosby, a strutting patrician of Anglo-Irish blood, arrived in New York as the colony's new governor. New York would never be the same: neither would John Peter Zenger.

After governing the island of Minorca in the Mediterranean—and almost bringing on war between England and Spain due to his greed and ineptness—Cosby had gone home, mended his fences, pulled strings, and, incredibly, had plucked the juiciest of plums—the governorship of New York.*

Immediate Confrontation

Upon arriving, Cosby immediately confronted Rip Van Dam, a dedicated political figure and senior member of the council, and demanded that he turn over half the salary he had lawfully earned as acting governor during the eighteen months preceding Cosby's arrival. Van Dam refused and Cosby filed suit. Because of Van Dam's immense popularity among the people of New York, Cosby decided to ignore trial by jury and designated the Supreme Court a court of equity and placed the suit before the three justices. That infuriated large numbers of people who had long embraced trial by jury as one of the few protections they had from tyrants. James Alexander and William Smith, outstanding members of the bar, served as counsel for Van Dam and immediately challenged the governor's authority to establish such a procedure with-

---

*Cadwallader Colden, a prominent New Yorker and member of the council, later commented on Cosby's appointment: "How such a man, after such a flagrant instance of tyranny and robbery [the Minorcan affair], came to be entrusted with the government of an English colony and to be made chancellor and keeper of the king's conscience in that colony, is not easy for a common understanding to conceive." Colden also stated flatly that Cosby had come to New York "to repair his fortunes." Cadwallader Colden, *History of William Cosby's Administration as Governor of the Province of New York . . . through 1737*, New-York Historical Society *Collections*, 1935, pp. 283–86.

out the assembly's approval. Supreme Court Chief Justice Lewis Morris agreed, declaring that "if judges can be so intimidated as to not dare to give any opinion but what is pleasing to a governor and agreeable to his private views," the people must surely suffer. Then, in utter contempt for the law, Cosby removed Morris from the Supreme Court and appointed a lackey, James Delancey, chief justice. He also refused to name a replacement for Morris, thus holding the number of justices at two, both of whom were firmly in the Cosby camp.

Turning to other matters, the new governor took a tour of his new domain. *Cosby's Excesses* In the process, he nullified a deed with the Mohawk Indians that protected certain of their lands from settlement for as long as the tribe existed, and he collected handsome profits from new settlers. He made other land grabs as well. "Cosby Manor," for example, contained a section twenty miles by ten miles, which now encompasses the City of Utica. He also demanded one third interest in each land patent sold, which further affronted many New Yorkers. And to keep the opposition down, Cosby summoned to meetings of the council only those members who were willing to overlook his appetite for greed. This turned even more citizens against him. In short order, many New Yorkers began to find truth in the words of Rip Van Dam: "We are Tenants at Will to Governors, and exposed to be fleeced by them from Time to Time at their Pleasure."

Finally the opposition group—or the "popular party," as the rebel faction *The "Popular Party"* soon called themselves—set about braking the governor's criminal activities. That, in turn, required revealing the man's crimes to as many as possible as frequently as possible. But Cosby maintained tight control of William Bradford's *Weekly Gazette*, the only newspaper in the province. And Bradford, knowing where his fortunes lay, would certainly not open his pages to attacks on the administration. The fire of his early combats with arbitrary authority had been stifled beneath a pile of government printing contracts. So James Alexander and other opposition leaders sought out the only person who could assist them. They offered Peter Zenger financial, moral, and editorial support *Birth of* if he would publish a paper to air their grievances. Zenger agreed. On *Zenger's Journal* November 5, 1733, he published the first issue of the *New-York Weekly Journal containing the freshest Advices, Foreign and Domestic*, the first politically independent newspaper in America.[19] The newspaper war, also a first, was on.*

*The only real confrontation between colonial American newspapers prior to this developed between James Franklin's *New-England Courant*, which lashed out at the Puritan leadership in Massachusetts in pungent satire, and the *Boston News-Letter* and the *Boston Gazette*, which carried Puritan responses, more comic relief than heated journalistic debate in which government, per se, was rarely a target.

THE

New-York Weekly JOURNAL

Containing the freſheſt Advices, Foreign, and Domeſtick.

MUNDAY November 12, 1733.

Mr. *Zenger.*

INſert the following in your next, and you'll oblige your Friend,

CATO.

Mira temporum felicitas ubi ſentiri quæ velis, & quæ ſentias dicere licit. Tacit.

THE Liberty of the Preſs is a Subject of the greateſt Importance, and in which every Individual is as much concern'd as he is in any other Part of Liberty: therefore it will not be improper to communicate to the Publick the Sentiments of a late excellent Writer upon this Point. ſuch is the Elegance and Perſpicuity of his Writings, ſuch the inimitable Force of his Reaſoning, that it will be difficult to ſay any Thing new that he has not ſaid, or not to ſay that much worſe which he has ſaid.

There are two Sorts of Monarchies, an abſolute and a limited one. In the firſt, the Liberty of the Preſs can never be maintained, it is inconſiſtent with it; for what abſolute Monarch would ſuffer any Subject to animadvert on his Actions, when it is in his Power to declare the Crime, and to nominate the Puniſhment? This would make it very dangerous to exerciſe ſuch a Liberty. Beſides the Object againſt which thoſe Pens muſt be directed, is their Sovereign, the ſole ſupream Magiſtrate; for there being no Law in thoſe Monarchies, but the Will of the Prince, it makes it neceſſary for his Miniſters to conſult his Pleaſure, before any Thing can be undertaken: He is therefore properly chargeable with the Grievances of his Subjects, and what the Miniſter there acts being in Obedience to the Prince, he ought not to incur the Hatred of the People; for it would be hard to impute that to him for a Crime, which is the Fruit of his Allegiance, and for refuſing which he might incur the Penalties of Treaſon. Beſides, in an abſolute Monarchy, the Will of the Prince being the Law, a Liberty of the Preſs to complain of Grievances would be complaining againſt the Law, and the Conſtitution, to which they have ſubmitted, or have been obliged to ſubmit; and therefore, in one Senſe, may be ſaid to deſerve Puniſhment. So that under an abſolute Monarchy, I ſay, ſuch a Liberty is inconſiſtent with the Conſtitution, having no proper Subject in Politics, on which it might be exercis'd, and if exercis'd would incur a certain Penalty.

But in a limited Monarchy, as *England* is, our Laws are known, fixed, and eſtabliſhed. They are the ſtreight Rule and ſure Guide to direct the King, the Miniſters, and other his Subjects: And therefore an Offence againſt the Laws is ſuch an Offence againſt the Conſtitution as ought to receive a proper adequate Puniſhment; the ſevera Conſtil

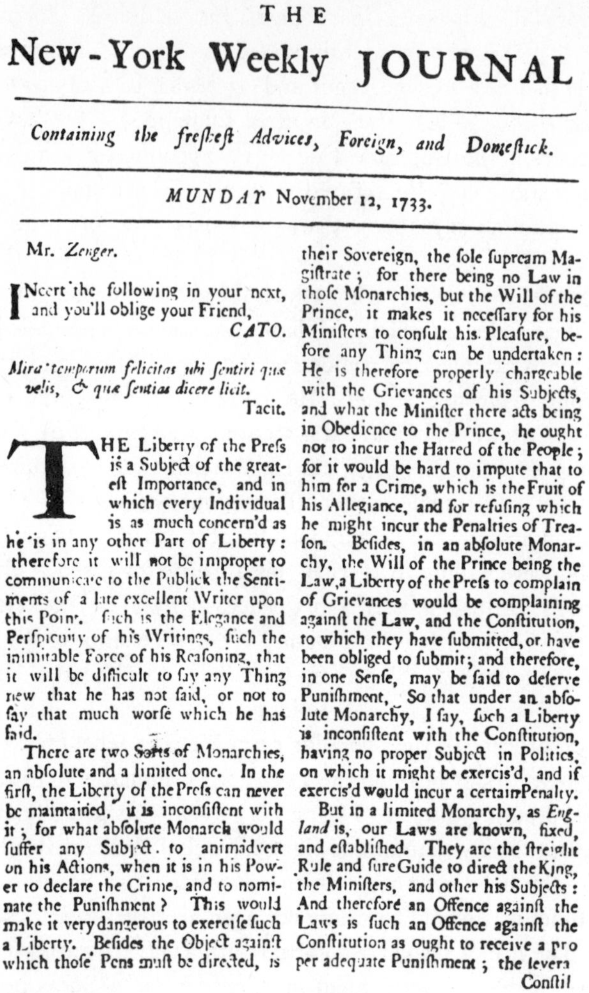

Peter Zenger's appeal to uphold freedom of the press, November 12, 1733. (The Bettmann Archives, Inc.)

James Alexander: Force behind the Resistance

It has been suggested that some popular party leaders had strong personal reasons for wishing the governor away.[20] To some extent that is likely, especially where position and sagging family fortunes were at stake. Yet such individuals of reputation and influence as Gerardus Stuyvesant, a wealthy merchant; Philip Livingston and William Smith, noted attorneys; scientist and political leader Cadwallader Colden—all of them outside the governor's ring of intimates and all without personal axes to grind—had much to lose by alienating themselves from the most powerful figure in the province, but alienate themselves they did. All this suggests that, initial personal considerations aside, the popular party leaders were men of substance whose courage held fast.

James Alexander emerges as the principal mover behind the newborn *New-York Weekly Journal*. He served as its editor in chief, editorial writer, and the first great champion of press freedom in American history. He was one of the more influential of the Cosby opponents and for strong moralistic reasons. The fact that Cosby's court ultimately disbarred him because of his defiance of authority did not begin his opposition. Disbarrment came as a *result* of his opposition.

As for Peter Zenger's part in all this, he must certainly have felt the powerful hand of the governor hovering over him, eager to strike him down with his other enemies. As a working printer, he also must have been familiar with the workings of seditious libel. Yet the offer presented by Alexander and other opposition leaders seems to have been grasped quickly and for understandable reasons. Zenger had fallen on hard times. Bradford controlled the printing business in New York. Besides that, Zenger had difficulty coping with the English language, was a poor writer, and, as even Alexander complained, was only passable as a printer. He also had a large family to support. Hence, the offer of cash in hand, and probably a good deal of it, must have been irresistible.

Zenger's Motives

The *Journal*, which sold for three shillings per quarter, was a four-page paper, only adequately printed but sufficient to deliver to the public a record of Cosby's greed and administrative incompetence as compared to the image of the governor created by Bradford's *Gazette*. The paper became instantly popular, so much so that shortly after its first issue, Zenger polled his readers about making it a semiweekly publication. The writing, vivid and razor sharp, attacked the enemy in one screed after another. Many of the articles were satirical pieces that infuriated Cosby and his followers. Widespread support for Zenger, the popular cause, and the *Weekly Journal* were tied to exciting issues over and above the money dispute with Rip Van Dam. The people grew restless. Angry at the governor's excesses, they found their voices through Zenger's paper and the editorial wizardry of James Alexander and other fallen leaders who, in print, labeled Cosby an "idiot" and a "Nero," among other choice selections. They also demanded that London order him home. This was dangerous business considering the seditious libel laws of the time and the authority of government officials to strike back with painful swiftness.

Popularity of the Journal

James Alexander's ideas about the preservation of liberty are reflected in all his writings for the *Journal*. A student of the liberal philosophy of Locke, Swift, Addison, and Steele, he read avidly the famed "Cato's Letters" of Thomas Gordon and John Trenchard, English libertarians enormously popular in the American colonies at that time. In a letter to Peter Zenger (which is appropriate to any age including our own), Alexander warned that threats to a nation's freedoms from within are more dangerous than armed invasion from outside "by being the hardest to remove. . . . For every nation undone

Alexander's Views on Liberty

by foreign invaders, ten have been undone by their own nature." The real culprit is greed for power among a nation's leaders: "An unrestrained power of one man, or a few over all, is so monstrous, that it turns men that have it into monsters." Hence, even a good man is not to be trusted with it. "Men change with their Stations and power of any sort rarely alters them for the better; but, on the contrary, has often turned a very good man into a very bad." He further cautioned that those in power be watched carefully for breaches of the public trust. If passed over, Alexander felt that these breaches would be followed by more, since, according to human nature, repetition somehow makes violations acceptable.[21]

The first American printing press, brought to America by Stephen Day and established at Harvard in 1640. (The Bettmann Archives, Inc.)

Historical Background to the First Amendment

The second issue of the *Journal* carried the first of two installments on freedom of the press, both authored by Alexander under his favorite "Cato" pseudonym: "The liberty of the press is a subject of greatest importance, and in which every individual is as much concerned as he is in any other part of liberty," the essay read. It went on to score the excesses of government authority with many obvious references to Cosby himself. The essay also warned citizens to be wary of those who urge controls on press criticism of government, calling the press "a curb, a bridle, a terror, a shame and restraint to evil ministers." All liberty would be lost, he went on, were freedom of the press suppressed. "No nation ancient or modern ever lost the liberty of freely speaking, writing or publishing their sentiments but forthwith lost their liberty in general and became slaves. LIBERTY and SLAVERY! how amiable is one! how odious and abominable the other!"[22]

Alexander on Press Freedom

Controls on Press Criticism

Freedom of the press rang out more than any other *Journal* theme. In one part of the paper, the writers assailed the excesses of Governor Cosby while in another they justified their actions in doing so. Cosby's position became indefensible to a growing number of citizens and the *Journal* gleefully beat the drum.

Cosby finally moved to indict the *Journal's* writers for seditious libel. He selected four particularly offensive (to him) issues of the paper and presented them to the grand jury as the basis for his charges. The grand jury refused to act. The assembly also refused to cooperate and the council agreed only that the four issues were indeed crammed with seditious utterances and should be burned at high noon by the official hangman. At the appointed hour, a Cosby supporter arrived with the copies of the paper but no government official came to witness the symbolic execution, including the hangman. The papers were burned by a common workman. Cosby, it appears, had lost again.

Cosby Takes Action

Finally the frustrated governor went after Zenger himself. The printer had published and circulated the offensive pieces and his name had appeared in every issue of the paper. Under the law that was sufficient for arrest. On Sunday, November 17, 1734, the warrant was served; Zenger was charged with printing and publishing "Several Seditious Libells" in the *Journal*, which tended "to raise factions & tumults among the people of this Province enflaming their minds with a Contempt of his Majesties [*sic*] Government and greatly disturbing the peace thereof."[23] A classical definition of seditious libel! Zenger was placed in a cell on the third floor of city hall.

Zenger's Arrest

In the issue of the *Journal* immediately preceding Zenger's arrest—and perhaps knowing that the move would be made—the paper's writers summed up matters in succinct terms:

Without freedom of Thought there can be no such Thing as Wisdom, and no such Thing as public Liberty; without Freedom of Speech, which is the right of every man, as far as by it he does not hurt or controul the Right of another; and this is the only check it ought to suffer, and the only bounds it ought to know.[24]

The warrant issued by the council and signed by Chief Justice Delancey constituted a gross violation of Peter Zenger's rights in two important ways: first, the council's authority in so moving was in serious doubt; secondly, that body presented no evidence to support its actions and offered Zenger no opportunity to defend himself. Such "trivia" failed to deter the governor and his circle, however.

For several days Zenger was not permitted to communicate with anyone. And while the following Monday passed without an issue of the *Journal*, the intrepid printer found means to bring out an issue the following week.

Public Opposition to the Trial

Cadwallader Colden wrote of the "aversion to this prosecution" among "all sorts of people" and wondered why the Cosby faction insisted on taking on such an unpopular cause. Indeed, it was sufficiently unpopular for the grand jury, comprised of private citizens, to refuse to indict Zenger, at which point his supporters prepared for his release. Then Attorney General Richard Bradley filed an "information,"* charging the *Journal* printer with publishing and disseminating libelous utterances: *Journal* numbers 13 and 23 were cited as particularly offensive.[25]

On April 15, James Alexander and William Smith, representing the defendant, challenged the commissions of Supreme Court Justice Delancey and Justice Frederick Philipse on various points. Delancey remained aloof, refusing to even consider the objections. He then disbarred both Alexander and Smith[26] and appointed young and inexperienced John Chambers as defense counsel for Zenger. The defendant's hopes must have sagged with two of the finest legal minds in the land silenced by the enemy and a man unknown to him appointed by his opponents to defend him.

Enter Andrew Hamilton

The change in defense counsel bothered Alexander and Smith. They feared that Chambers, while a competent attorney, did not share their total dedication to the Zenger cause.[27] They needed a seasoned legal mind to present the defense with Chambers or, better yet, to take charge. They decided that Andrew Hamilton of Philadelphia would more than fill their needs. Nearly eighty years of age, Hamilton was a powerful political figure and a lawyer of vast reputation even beyond the boundaries of his home province. When Hamilton saw how the cards had been stacked against Peter Zenger, he agreed to help in spite of a painful recurrence of gout, and he would do so without charge. His addition to the Zenger defense staff would also be kept secret—for the moment.[28]

---

*The "information" was a legal device that permitted authorities to file charges against a suspect without formal jury indictment, a distasteful strategy that set even more people against Cosby.

An artist's version of the trial of Peter Zenger in New York, 1734. (The Bettmann Archives, Inc.)

The jury* trial began on August 4, 1735. People from all walks of life pressed into the courtroom to witness the struggle. A great deal was at stake and people knew it: if Zenger were acquitted, the Cosby forces would be marked as losers—hardly in keeping with a governor's image—which would likely curb his greed. But if the printer lost, the opposition party would fall apart.[29]

The defense scored a significant psychological point at the outset with the unexpected appearance of Andrew Hamilton.[30] James Alexander had prepared a brilliant defense, which Hamilton followed with dramatic skill. The prosecution centered its case on the two issues of the *Weekly Journal*, numbers 13 and 23, which contained "a false, scandalous and seditious Libel," the attorney general intoned, and which were calculated "to create Differences among Men, ill blood among the people and oftentimes great Bloodshed between the Party Libelling and the Party Libelled." That was an exaggeration in the extreme. Nonetheless, Hamilton seized upon a single word in the indictment, a word around which Alexander had built the case for Zenger: the word was "false."

*While a jury was not required to bring charges against Zenger in the "information," the law required that he be *tried* before a panel of his peers.

Hamilton, a native Scot, clearly outstripped the thirty-two-year-old Delancey in experience and knowledge of the law. Following a feeble opening speech by Chambers, Hamilton (perhaps even to Chambers' surprise) rose and informed the chief justice that he would share the defense of Peter Zenger. He then announced to the court that it had no need to prove the printer guilty of publishing the offensive material. Indeed, he admitted in open court that Zenger had printed and disseminated the two issues in question. The Zenger forces were stunned. According to accepted legal practice, all the prosecution need do was to prove the *fact of publication* and the defense counsel had just admitted it! There remained nothing for the prosecution to *prove*!

Attorney General Bradley then dismissed his witnesses and prepared to charge the jury to return a verdict of guilty. But then, in dramatic tones, Hamilton cautioned Bradley that the case was far from over:

> I hope it is not our bare Printing and Publishing a Paper that will make it a Libel: You will have something more to do before you make my Client a Libeller; for the Words themselves must be libellous, that is, *false, scandalous and seditious** [as the law actually read] or else we are not guilty.

Hamilton pressed his point:

> The word *false* must have some Meaning or else how came it here . . .? I will agree that if he [Bradley] can prove the Facts charged upon us, to be false, I'll own to them to be *scandalous, seditious* and a *Libel*. . . . and Mr. Attorney has now only to prove the Word *false*, in order to make us Guilty.

Then, recognizing that his logic was falling on unwilling ears, Hamilton bowed to the bench, turned to face the jurors, and began one of the most meaningful courtroom orations in American history.

"Then, Gentlemen of the Jury, it is to you we must now appeal, for Witness, to that Truth of the Facts we have offered, and are denied that Liberty to prove." He went on to say that the statements published in the *Journal* "are notoriously known to be true; and therefore in your Justice lies our Safety. And as we are denied the Liberty of giving Evidence, to prove the Truth of what we have published, I beg leave to lay down as a standing Rule in such Cases, *That the suppression of Evidence ought always to be taken for the strongest Evidence.*"†

Thus the question of the rights of juries became the focal point of Hamilton's defense. (In line with that, the issue of the *Journal* published just two days before the trial carried an editorial on the same subject—the right of juries to judge both the fact of publication and the law as well.)

*Italics in original document.

†Italics in original document.

Historical Background to the First Amendment

Magazines struggled for recognition in early America but did not yet enjoy the successes enjoyed by newspapers. (The Bettmann Archives, Inc.)

Hamilton compared lawless power of public officials to a river overflowing its banks; "it is then too impetuous to be stemm'd," and would destroy everyone. Liberty is "the only Bulwark" against it. He attacked "Informations, set on Foot by Government to deprive a People of the Right of Remonstrating" against the arbitrary actions of men in power. Finally, he charged the jury to do its duty by striking a blow for liberty, "the liberty both of exposing and opposing arbitrary Power by speaking and writing Truth."

Andrew Hamilton then limped to his chair. Chief Justice Delancey charged the jury in a brief, ungainly oration and the jurors retired. Less than ten minutes later they returned and foreman Thomas Hunt announced the verdict of acquittal. The room erupted in cheers and Delancey, pained by the sudden outburst, attempted to quiet the crowd but to no avail. Peter Zenger had won! That was worth cheering about.

119,265

The ordeal of John Peter Zenger was a substantial contribution to the eighteenth century story of resistance to overbearing government authority in colonial America, which ultimately brought on the American Revolution. But in fact, the case contributed little or nothing towards establishing press freedom in its own time. In fact it received little publicity beyond New York at the time. The significance of the case centers on three vital points: (1) a popular party won out over governmental authority thus serving notice that Americans, feeling increasingly daring as their country grew in strength and numbers, would not heel eternally at every command of the British Crown; (2) for the first time truth served successfully as a defense in a seditious libel case; (3) the first philosophical statement on press freedom in the United States would soon develop as a result of the trial. The case itself, judged by American rather than English experiences, emphasized the relationship between political freedom and freedom of the press. It also provided guidelines against judicial abuses later incorporated into the Eighth Amendment to the United States Constitution. Change came about because *the times were right for it*. It was William Cosby's misfortune to encounter a populace growing increasingly impatient with imperial high-handedness. Social, political, and economic factors created the climate. The previous generation would have produced no such confrontation.

Significance of the Zenger Case

Critics of the Trial

Certainly not everyone agreed with the jury's decision, including some who opposed the wily ways of the governor with as much vigor as those close to Peter Zenger. Their view, generally, was based on the fear that a totally free press would mean that every citizen's deepest secrets would be exposed on the pages of scandal sheets, and that the old view of "the greater the truth, the greater the libel" made good sense. It must also be remembered that freedom of the press as it exists in the United States at present, did not then exist anyplace in the world. The concept was new, revolutionary, at the very least radical, and some were slow to accept such notions.

Two critics of the Zenger acquittal, both lawyers and anti-Cosby people, took the time to put their views on paper, and what they wrote was published in the *Barbadoes Gazette* in July 1737 and reprinted in the *American Weekly Mercury* in Philadelphia. They succeeded in raising the hackles of the man who had led the editorial war against William Cosby. James Alexander took pen in hand and challenged the two dissenters in what became the first philosophical statement on press freedom in American history. This statement is one of the most important even to the present time. Published in the *Pennsylvania Gazette*, and for a time thought to be the work of Benjamin Franklin, it warned readers that "Republics and limited monarchies derive their strength and vigor from a popular examination into the actions of magistrates," and that abuses of free speech and press should be suppressed. But, he asked rhetorically, "to whom dare we commit the care of doing it? An evil magistrate, entrusted with a power to punish words, is armed with a weapon the

Alexander Responds

most destructive and terrible. Under the pretense of pruning off the exuberant branches, he frequently destroys the tree." He saluted the Zenger case as a *cause célèbre*: "The liberty of the press in that Province depended on it." The essay concludes stirringly: ". . . A free constitution and freedom of speech have such a reciprocal dependence on each other that they cannot subsist without consisting together."[31]

With it all, however, the Zenger case was a political, but not a legal, victory. In the years that followed the trial, printers continued to suffer at the hands of despots, private and public, who continued to view the shackling of free expression as sound policy.

The Case in Perspective

In 1742, Thomas Fleet, printer of the *Boston Evening Post*, found himself facing an irate governor's council after stating in print, and, as it turned out, accurately, that British Prime Minister Sir Robert Walpole would soon be arrested for botching the war against Spain. After thoroughly berating Fleet for his "scandalous and libellous Reflection," the council dropped the case for fear the jury of Fleet's fellow townsmen would refuse to convict him.[32]

Later Cases

The First Permanent Newspaper in Each Colony in Order of Establishment, 1704–1800

Colony	First Permanent Newspaper	Year	By Whom Established
Massachusetts	The Boston News Letter	1704	John Campbell
Pennsylvania	The American Weekly Mercury	1719	Andrew Bradford
New York	The New York Gazette	1725	William Bradford
Maryland	The Maryland Gazette	1727	William Parks
South Carolina	The South Carolina Weekly Journal	1732	Eleazer Phillips, Jr.
	The South Carolina Gazette	1732	Thomas Whitemarsh
Rhode Island	The Rhode Island Gazette	1732	James Franklin
Virginia	The Virginia Gazette	1736	William Parks
North Carolina	The North Carolina Gazette	1751	James Davis
Connecticut	The Connecticut Gazette	1755	James Parker
New Hampshire	The New Hampshire Gazette	1756	Daniel Fowle
Georgia	The Georgia Gazette	1763	James Johnston
New Jersey	The New Jersey Gazette	1777	Isaac Collins
Vermont	The Vermont Gazette	1780	J.P. Spooner & Timothy Green
Florida	The East Florida Gazette	1783	Charles Wright for John Wells
Delaware	The Delaware Gazette	1785	Jacob A. Killen
Maine	The Falmouth Gazette	1785	Benjamin Titcomb & Thomas B. Wait
Kentucky	The Kentucke Gazette	1787	John & Fielding Bradford
Tennessee	The Knoxville Gazette	1791	George Roulstone & Robert Ferguson
Ohio	The Centinel of the North-Western Territory	1793	William Maxwell
Louisiana	Moniteur de la Louisiane	1794	Louis Duclot
Mississippi	The Mississippi Gazette	1800	Benjamin M. Stokes

Wroth, *The Colonial Printer*, Reprinted by permission of the University Press of Virginia.

In 1747, New York Governor George Clinton ordered James Parker, a public printer, to omit certain objectionable statements from the assembly's minutes published for public perusal. Parker ignored the order and printed the statements in his newspaper. In 1756, he came under official wrath again when his paper questioned editorially how certain members of the assembly had gained their seats. Damning the article as "a high Misdemeanor and a Contempt of the Authority of this House," the politicians in question wrung pledges of good behavior from Parker and his associates before their anger cooled.

Hugh Gaine, printer of the *New York Mercury*, suffered censure in 1753 for publishing the governor's speech to the assembly without permission.[33]

In 1754, authorities arrested Daniel Fowle as the suspected printer of a satirical pamphlet that spoofed a debate in the Massachusetts House on an unpopular tax bill. While no author was listed on the offensive publication, officials took aim at Fowle, his brother, their apprentice, and a fourth individual. The latter three went free, but Fowle was jailed incommunicado and was moved from a dank dungeon to "improved" quarters among "Murderers, Thieves, Common-Cheats, Pick-Pockets &c" only when he caught a "prodigious cold." The House dropped the case when it accurately gauged the depth of public support behind Fowle.[34]

In 1758, a justice of the peace, Samuel Townsend, sent a letter to the New York Assembly asking that financial assistance be given to some poverty-stricken persons on Long Island. The speaker of the House termed the letter "insolent" and ordered Townsend to appear before that body to answer for his crime. He refused. The assembly cited him for contempt, arrested him, and found him guilty of a "high Misdemeanor and a most daring Insult." After spending time in jail, Townsend apologized for his misdeed, promised to behave, and finally gained his freedom.[35]

Inclusion of other cases would only belabor the point that the Zenger case was only a beginning. It in no way altered the course of freedom of speech or press in eighteenth-century America. The *status quo* held fast long after the trial had ended. Even with the founding of the United States, press criticism of government officials remained a thorny issue. The administration of President John Adams, who helped make the American Revolution a reality, created the detestable Alien and Sedition Acts, which gave government the authority to silence—even jail—those who dared to question the policies or behavior of officials.*

---

*The most prominent case under that legislation involved Matthew Lyon, a Revolutionary War veteran and member of Congress. The court sentenced him to four months in jail and a $1,500 fine for accusing President Adams, in a letter to the editor, of "ridiculous pomp, foolish adulation, and selfish avarice."

In CONGRESS, July 4, 1776.

A DECLARATION

By the REPRESENTATIVES of the

UNITED STATES OF AMERICA,

In GENERAL CONGRESS ASSEMBLED.

AMERICA: Boston, Printed by JOHN GILL, and POWARS and WILLIS, in Queen-Street.

The sentiment of independence. (The Bettmann Archives, Inc.)

"Zenger's paper," as the opposition called it, did become the blueprint for the journals of the stormy decade preceding the outbreak of the American Revolution.[36] Indeed, the case itself took on new dimensions in those turbulent years, possibly due to a reissue of the Zenger story around 1770. Hamilton's courtroom arguments on truth as a defense in seditious libel cases were quoted frequently by Whig leaders and their newspapers. On March 19, 1770, the Boston Sons of Liberty, commemorating the repeal of the hated Stamp Act in 1766, offered toasts to "the Memory of Andrew Hamilton, Esq.," to "Zenger's Jury," and to "A total Abolition of the Star-Chamber Doctrine of Libels."[37] The Zenger trial had demonstrated dramatically the impact of civil disobedience in correcting abuses of government. Whig leaders were quick to adopt this instrument throughout the 1760s and 1770s. Again,

Zenger Remembered

Historical Background to the First Amendment

printers and writers led the way. The thundering verbal assaults of Sam Adams, James Otis, Isaiah Thomas, and other penmen of the patriot cause took much from the Zenger experience and put it to good use. Their newspapers were remarkably similar to the *Weekly Journal* in style and content. Many years later, Gouverneur Morris, a descendant of Lewis Morris and signer of the Declaration of Independence, expressed his view of the Zenger case and its place in history: "The trial of Zenger in 1735 was the germ of American freedom, the morningstar of that liberty which subsequently revolutionized America."[38]

Sam Adams and Press Freedom

The *Boston Gazette*, the revolutionary paper for which Sam Adams was chief editorial writer, commented on press freedom many times. An example, stated in many ways over and over again:

> There is no liberty in this Country, which is more dear than that of the press . . . for if it is destroyed, what else to boast of is gone in an instant. Arbitrary Ministers (and none but such) are Enemies to this Liberty, because it has ever been a Check upon their Tyranny.[39]

Summary

Assigning the press the responsibility of public overseer of the actions and performances of those entrusted with running the government is something that the Founding Fathers understood. They had learned the lessons of history, lessons that are summed up in three brief reflections:

1. The constitutional guarantees of freedom of speech and press are rooted in the cases and trials of many believers in the right of freedom of personal expression and of those who spoke out in defense of those rights.

2. The individual citizen possesses the right of free speech and press no matter how unpopular the message or that everyone else might disagree with it. As John Stuart Mill wrote of it, "Mankind would be no more justified in silencing that one person than he, if he had the power, would be justified in silencing mankind."[40]

3. Thomas Jefferson spoke of the *necessity* of the American people to "keep up" with the workings of government as their greatest protection against tyranny. And to the news media he cautioned: "Cherish, therefore, the spirit of our people and keep alive their attention. Do not be too severe upon their errors, but reclaim them by enlightening them. If once they become inattentive to the public affairs, you and I, and Congress and Assemblies, Judges and Governors, shall all become wolves."[41] Therein lie the historical bases of the First Amendment, its charge to the individual citizen, its charge to the mass media. The remainder of this volume will explore how well and how poorly this charge is operating.

1. Information on the "English Roots" comes from Frederick S. Siebert, *Freedom of the Press in England, 1476–1776* (Urbana: University of Illinois Press paperback, 1965), pp. 88–95, 193–97, 264–75, 366–67.

2. Arthur M. Schlesinger, *Prelude to Independence: The Newspaper War on Britain* (New York: Caravelle paperback, 1965), p. 62.

3. Frank Luther Mott, *American Journalism* (New York: Macmillan, 1941), p. 6.

4. Harry Cushing, *The Writings of Samuel Adams* (New York: Putnam, 1908), I, p. 7.

5. Bernard to Lord Halifax, Aug. 14, 1765, in Edmund S. and Helen M. Morgan, *The Stamp Act Crisis* (New York: Collier, 1963), p. 240.

6. Leonard Levy, *Freedom of Speech and Press in Early American History: Legacy of Suppression* (New York: Harper Torchbook, 1963), p. 23.

7. Mott, *American Journalism*, pp. 9–10.

8. Levy, *Freedom of Speech and Press*, pp. 32–34.

9. Isaiah Thomas, *The History of Printing in America* (Albany: J. Munsell, Printer, 1874), II, p. 217.

10. Mott, *American Journalism*, p. 24.

11. Douglas C. McMurtrie, *A History of Printing in the United States* (New York: R. R. Bowker Co., 1936), II, pp. 1–9; Levy, *Freedom of Speech and Press*, pp. 24–25.

12. Levy, *Freedom of Speech and Press*, p. 27.

13. Mott, *American Journalism*, p. 24.

14. McMurtrie, *A History of Printing*, p. 136.

15. Irving G. Cheslaw, "John Peter Zenger and THE New-York Weekly Journal," (New York: Zenger Memorial Fund monograph, circa 1951), p. 12.

16. Maurice R. Cullen, Jr., "The Boston Gazette, A Community Newspaper," *Journalism Quarterly*, Spring 1959, p. 204.

17. Lawrence C. Wroth, *The Colonial Printer* (Charlottesville: University of Virginia paperback, 1964), p. 14.

18. Wroth, *The Colonial Printer*, pp. 187–90.

19. Cheslaw, "John Peter Zenger," pp. 3–7.

20. Information on "James Alexander: Force Behind the Resistance," "Zenger's Motives," and "Popularity of the Journal" from Cheslaw, "John Peter Zenger," pp. 9–12; James Alexander, *A Brief Narrative of the Case and Trial of John Peter Zenger*, S. N. Katz, ed. (Cambridge: Harvard University Press, 1963), pp. 2–5.

21. James Alexander Papers, File No. 6, New York Public Library.

22. *New-York Weekly Journal*, 12 November 1733, New York Public Library.

23. Alexander, *A Brief Narrative*, p. 48.

24. *New-York Weekly Journal*, 12 November 1733.

25. Cadwallader Colden, *History of William Cosby's Administration as Governor of the Province of New York . . . through 1737*, New-York Historical Society *Collections*, 1935, p. 323; Cheslaw, "John Peter Zenger," p. 15.

26. Cheslaw, "John Peter Zenger," p. 15.

27. Information on the change of counsel and Alexander's fears from Cheslaw, "John Peter Zenger," p. 17; Alexander, *A Brief Narrative*, p. 21.

28. Cheslaw, "John Peter Zenger," p. 17.

29. McMurtrie, *A History of Printing*, pp. 145–46.

30. Unless otherwise indicated, details of the trial are from the official transcript as it appears in James Alexander's *A Brief Narrative of the Case and Trial of John Peter Zenger*, S. N. Katz, ed., pp. 41–105. It is also included in other editions.

31. *Pennsylvania Gazette*, 17 November 1737, 8 December 1737; reprinted in The *New-York Weekly Journal*, 19 December 1737, 9 January 1738.

32. Schlesinger, *Prelude to Independence*, pp. 63–64.

33. Ibid.

34. Levy, *Freedom of Speech and Press*, pp. 39–40.

35. Ibid., p. 47.

36. Vincent Buranelli, *The Trial of John Peter Zenger* (New York: New York University Press, 1957), p. 60.

37. Schlesinger, *Prelude to Independence*, p. 116.

38. Buranelli, *John Peter Zenger*, p. 63.

39.   The *Boston Gazette*, 15 July 1765, 17 July 1765, Boston Public Library.
40.   John Stuart Mill, "The Case for Freedom," *Voice of the People*, Reo M. Christenson and Robert O. McWilliams, eds. (New York: McGraw-Hill, 1962), p. 263.
41.   Thomas Jefferson, "A Founding Father's Various Views," *Voice of the People*, Reo M. Christenson and Robert O. McWilliams, eds. (New York: McGraw-Hill, 1967), p. 119.

For Further Reading

Alexander, James. *A Brief Narrative of the Case and Trial of John Peter Zenger*. Edited by S. N. Katz. Cambridge: Harvard University Press, 1963.

Buranelli, Vincent. *The Trial of John Peter Zenger*. New York: New York University Press, 1957.

Cullen, Maurice R., Jr. "The Boston Gazette, A Community Newspaper." *Journalism Quarterly*, Spring 1959, p. 204.

_____. "Benjamin Edes: Scourge of Tories." *Journalism Quarterly*, Summer 1974, p. 213.

Levy, Leonard. *Freedom of Speech and Press in Early American History: Legacy of Supression*. New York: Harper Torchbook, 1963.

Schlesinger, Arthur M. *Prelude to Independence: The Newspaper War on Britain*. New York: Caravelle paperback, 1965.

Siebert, Frederick S. *Freedom of the Press in England, 1476–1776*. Urbana: University of Illinois Press paperback, 1965.

Wroth, Lawrence C. *The Colonial Printer*. Charlottesville, Va.: University of Virginia paperback, 1964.

News in Pictures

Mass Media Responsibility 2

Upon completing this chapter you should know—

Chapter Objectives

Upon completing this chapter you should know—

the major First Amendment issues debated in the creation of the United States Constitution

the force and nature of the modern American press, which makes it the only private business in the nation whose right to exist is guaranteed by the Constitution

the nature of and issues involved in media "responsibility" along with appropriate examples

the findings of the Hutchins Commission, the Twentieth Century Fund, and other organizations and persons dedicated to improving press performance

Key Terms

Press Freedom Limited or absolute? The right to have unlimited access to information vs. qualified or limited access. (pp. 37–38, 40)

The Right to Know The public's need for information to fully participate in a democratic society. (pp. 38, 41)

Responsibility The gauge by which the news media provide democratic peoples with information. (p. 42)

Without freedom of thought there can be no such thing as Wisdom, and no such thing as public liberty; without freedom of speech, which is the right of every man, as far by it he does not hurt or control the right of another; and this is the only check it ought to suffer, and the only bounds it ought to know.

Cato (Thomas Gordon and
John Trenchard) 1720, England

The Constitution of the United States

During the summer of 1787, American political leaders got together to formulate a plan that would replace the rickety Articles of Confederation and, it was hoped, place the infant nation on solid footing for the future. They created the Constitution of the United States, a remarkable statement of faith that is with us today, though a bit battered about the edges. British Prime Minister William Gladstone called it "the most wonderful work ever struck off at a given time by the brain and purpose of man."[1]

The purpose of the Constitution was to create order out of chaos before the infant ship of state sank as many thought it would. It would also unite the thirteen states in support of the whole, though it would require the agony of civil war before real unity would be achieved. The nation was filled with hope.

The American "Press" in 1787

In that collection of youthful, brilliant minds, even the most imaginative could not predict the impact their labors would have on future generations. This was especially true in the cause of freedom of the press, which they all more or less supported. Thirty-five newspapers existed at the close of the War of Independence, most of them drab little sheets exciting to neither eye nor intellect. But they were *free,* free to write what they wished and that was unique in the entire world at the time. Those newspapers, a handful of almanacs, and occasional pamphlets constituted the "mass media" of 1787. The press enjoyed broad support because of its contributions to the anticrown onslaughts beginning with passage of the Stamp Act in 1765.

Freedom: Limited or Absolute?

With the war won and independence a frightening fact, the framers of the Constitution determined that a free press must not only continue to be free, but that its existence must be guaranteed by law. They did not speak of limited freedom, freedom for certain persons, or for particular kinds of information at the expense of others. They drafted no rules. They must not have wanted any limitations on freedom. Therefore, it must be assumed that freedom was to be total, not limited. It was that important!

Democracy and the Press

In the new nation, the people would rule (as appalling as that seemed back then) and they would do so through their elected representatives. That radical alliance would succeed only if the proprietors of government, *the people,* kept up with the ideas and actions of those representatives. A free and dedicated press was essential to the success of the system. The press would keep an eye on the workings of government officials—local, state, and national. It would report its observations and opinions to the people. The people would read their press, discuss and debate the issues, and inform their representatives of their views and wishes. The press would also keep government informed of public sentiment. To fulfill its mission, the press had to be free of the clutches of government, of its power, and of its influence.

Thomas Jefferson's View

Thomas Jefferson spelled it out: the people must have information "through the channel of the public papers, and to contrive that those papers should penetrate the whole mass of the people." Hence, the two-way flow of information between people and government was a vital part of the whole. It was not to be interfered with. Jefferson again:

> The basis of our governments being the opinion of the people, the very first object should be to keep that right; and were it left to me to decide whether we should have a government without newspapers, or newspapers without a government, I should not hesitate a moment to prefer the latter. But I mean that every man should receive these papers, and be capable of reading them.

Press Responsibility

Jefferson then called for the education of all the people at public expense so that all could attain basic literacy in order to read the newspapers and act accordingly. As one-sided as the press had been up to that point (and would continue to be) it is certain that Jefferson also meant for journalists to act in the public interest in fulfilling their functions. Those functions would be pivotal to everything else, the axle about which the wheel would turn.[*2] If the press failed, the plan failed.

So thoroughly did the framers of the Constitution support this people-press-government connection that debate broke out over whether the Constitution really needed written guarantees. Was a bill of "rights" necessary at all? To Alexander Hamilton, all "rights," including freedom of press and speech, were logical extensions of natural rights. To possess natural rights, as

Alexander Hamilton's View

*Along with others, Jefferson would learn that this ideal would not be embraced by all journalists at all times. In his own presidency he encountered a biased press, which brought him close to despair. In 1807, he wrote: "Nothing can now be believed which is seen in a newspaper. Truth itself becomes suspicious by being put into that polluted vehicle."

all people did, was to possess *all rights*. There was no need to put them to paper. In Hamilton's view, the Constitution itself was a bill of rights. Therefore, as he saw it, it would be repetitious to tack on guarantees of what was already guaranteed. Government was not to interfere with the free exercise of civil liberties in any way: "We the people. . . ." said it all![3]

Jefferson disagreed. He felt that such guarantees should be included in a fully developed bill of rights if only to insure that they would be honored and observed for all time to come. He also felt that some states would refuse to ratify the Constitution without formally written guarantees, so important had they become to the people.[4] Thus, actual guarantees for the "four freedoms," so-called, were carried into the First Amendment to the Constitution. Simply stated, uncluttered, it reads:

> Congress shall make no law respecting an establishment of religion, or prohibiting the free exercise thereof; or abridging the freedom of speech or of the press; or the right of the people peaceably to assemble, and to petition the Government for a redress of grievances.[5]

First Amendment Debates

The very simplicity of the statement has served as something of a battleground of interpretation and debate throughout the 200 years since the First Amendment was created. The primary issue in the free press arena has to do with how one views and interprets the word "free." The United States has undergone staggering changes since 1787 and so has the press. The changes in the country at large have also changed the mass media of communication and the way in which the public views them. For one thing, the print media—newspapers and magazines primarily—have grown from those thirty-five mini-newspapers to some 17,500 dailies and weeklies, in addition to a vast assortment of magazines and journals, some of them with circulations in many millions. More importantly, the print media are moving into fewer and fewer hands, which creates real fear in many observers that the much-needed "objectivity" of the press is being eroded.

Broadcast Journalism

Broadcast journalism exploded into the information business in the 1930s and today enjoys a place of eminence and authority in a social spectrum that would amaze Jefferson and Hamilton. Broadcasting has created even more questions, more doubts, more disenchantment among those who seriously wonder what ever happened to the people-press-government continuum that was to make American democracy work. Seemingly, if any of the three were to falter, the remaining two would die on the vine. Yet today, "people" and "government" stand together and glare at the "press" with toe-tapping impatience and fire away as if it were the enemy.

Part of the problem with modern media is that the press has become big business, whether newspapers, television, magazines, or combinations of these. Some critics complain that the Constitution protects only one aspect of private business. It is the mass media of communication that some say have their collective eyes more on profits than on their constitutional obligations. The actions of some corporate media leaders tend to support the claims.

The Media as Business

It is true that "the press," as such, is private enterprise and, due to its unique social role among other businesses, enjoys significant advantages that others do not. Its economic power alone, critics point out, makes the press avoid publishing stories that might reflect negatively on its balance sheets. Or it might slant certain kinds of stories in favor of a big advertiser. Or it might overlook excesses in other community-based businesses because it is part of community business itself, and businesses typically stick together.

The many questions from modern critics come down to one essential point. Have the mass media watered down their place in the people-press-government connection and become dedicated to their own interests before those of the people? The answer is both yes and no.

Meaning of "Free" Press

The Liberal View

The question of interpreting the word "free" reflects an even broader sphere of debate. In modern times, "free press" seems to mean what one wants it to mean. There are many extremes of interpretation, with considerable gray areas in between. Liberals of the stamp of the late Supreme Court Justice William O. Douglas tend to see freedom of the press as absolute, no holds barred. No topic, no person, no cause is too lofty or lowly for exploration and commentary in and by the news media. Nothing is too base beyond the legal bounds of libel and invasion of privacy. Even "good taste" is open to personal interpretation. "Freedom" means precisely that: there are no limits.

The Conservative View

To others, freedom of the press has *reasonable* limits inherent in the word itself. It is limited to information of genuine public concern—pending legislation, public speeches, inoffensive interviews—news that does not open to the light of day the negative aspects of public actions or the private moonlight dabblings of elected officials or anyone else. To those of this mind, "freedom" does not protect the rights of magazines, newspapers, and motion pictures to portray sexual exploits in living color, to use gutter language, to vivify the sordid aspects of human behavior as such. Those holding to this view find the root of their argument in the First Amendment itself: "Congress shall make no laws. . . ." That clearly states that the press is free to report to the people the business of government—*period*! Others select positions of interpretation within these extremities. Thus, the debate is not so clearly drawn.

How one interprets the First Amendment depends on any number of personal attitudes and influences that serve as a kind of psychological sorting bin of personal perceptions and viewpoints. Some citizens have no interest whatever in the Bill of Rights. They do not read newspapers or catch the evening news on television. They do not vote, do not debate or even discuss issues, and do not care that they don't. That is also a privilege of freedom. But, fortunately, others don't feel that way, and they want to develop informed opinions in matters that affect their lives. How are their opinions developed? It might depend on where in the United States they live, where they stand on the social-economic ladder, whether they are labor or management or neither, the length and quality of their education, where they go to church if they go at all, whether they served in the armed forces, their age, their political party preference if they have one, their height, their weight, the style of their hair, the cut of their clothes, and on and on.

Diversity of People

How one interprets the First Amendment also determines how he or she sees the press and that applies to private citizens as well as to the publisher, editor, and reporter. Some restrict "the press" to the *New York Times*, the *Christian Science Monitor*, the *National Inquirer*, or the *Hometown Gazette*. Others consider it to be *Time, Newsweek, Playboy,* or *Cosmopolitan.* Still others find it in the credible, fatherly image of Walter Cronkite. What the press *is* to the individual American is a private judgment that he or she makes. That's why the newsstands and the television tube offer such vast varieties of information packages. Therein also lies the seed of much controversy between the press and the American people.

Diversity of "Press"

We hear and read much about the public's "right to know" because it is an age-old maxim. Some outstanding reporting has brought many compelling social and political issues into the open in its name. But many journalistic sins have been committed under the same label. The public does have the right to know and the news media are charged with telling them. But responsibility also requires that we consider the public's right to know *what*? How much? What kinds of things do they *need* to know to function in a democratic society? For example, does the public have the right to know the name of a rape victim in a news story? The name of a first-time juvenile offender? Some states have passed laws prohibiting such usage. What of the reporter who writes a story based on stolen government documents? He did not steal them but he read them and writes about them. Does the public have the right to know about the private lives of their neighbors? Is a reporter being responsible if he breaks into a private home and conceals himself in a closet and observes how an average American family spends its day and then writes a story about it? Is it responsible journalism for a newspaper to provide its readers with all the

The Public's Right to Know *What*?

blood and gore that might accompany a murder case or an automobile accident? Who is being served in such cases? It is not the intention here to make judgments but to reflect on questions that are raised over and over again by private citizens and by others who consider themselves bona fide press critics. Some of them are journalists. Such questions also enter the decision-making process of reporters, editors, and publishers, who sometimes disagree on the answers. There are no yardsticks to show the way, no measures of good and bad, right or wrong. It's probably instinct or "feeling" that decides if stories of questionable value or taste are used or eliminated. One gauge might be, Is the story clearly meant to inform or is it clearly meant to increase the paper's circulation or the television station's ratings? But even that measure fails under the individual's personal notions of what press freedom is and how responsibility applies to him. In any case, press "responsibility" and the public's "right to know" can be a good marriage as seen, say, in the Watergate events and the controversy over publication of the Pentagon Papers. It can also create upheaval in and out of the press, because to serve one does not always mean that the other is also served.

| "Responsibility": A Recent Concern | One reason why journalism has had trouble serving these two ends is that "responsibility," as such, is pretty much a latter-day concern of the news media. In fact, most of the history of news gathering in the United States has, with a few exceptions, been marked by irresponsibility. The Penny Press, the first newspapers for the masses and forerunners of the modern big dailies, started in the 1830s as offshoots of the Industrial Revolution. The first truly *mass* circulation newspapers, they were sold on streetcorners by hawking newsboys for a penny or two. Because of the low cost to the reader, circulations soared far beyond the stuffy old established papers, and dollar-minded advertisers eagerly paid the bills.

The founders of the first penny papers saw their offspring primarily as instruments of entertainment. Their contents reflected this. They were the first newspapers to write of the fates and foibles of the common people on a grand scale. These were not "important" stories in the sense that the public was uplifted—or could uplift itself—because of their revelations. They brought few sweeping social reforms. They failed to dent the evils of an industrial system that drew vast wealth for the few from the labors of the impoverished many, though the impoverished kept circulations booming. They were "interesting" papers and the common people read them and recognized themselves in them and sometimes even laughed at themselves. They sold well and that was sufficient. And when exciting fare became scarce, enterprising reporters were not above creating exciting yarns that were passed off as real. With some notable exceptions, this mode of zany journalism characterized the entire nineteenth century. Indeed, the century closed with the wildest display of journalistic irresponsibility in history—the dynastic circulation wars of Joseph Pulitzer and William Randolph Hearst. Sensationalism and exaggeration were the earmarks of this "Yellow Journalism."[6] Truth took a thrashing and circulations rose to unprecedented heights.

Police Office

Margaret Thomas was drunk in the street—said she never would get drunk again "upon her honor." Committed, "upon honor."

William Luvoy got drunk because yesterday was so devilish warm. Drank 9 glasses of brandy and water and said he would be cursed if he wouldn't drink 9 more as quick as he could raise the money to buy it with. He would like to know what right the magistrate had to interfere with his private affairs. Fined $1—forgot his pocketbook, and was sent over to bridewell [a jail].

Bridget McMunn got drunk and threw a pitcher at Mr. Ellis, of 53 Ludlow st. Bridget said she was the mother of 3 little orphans—God bless their dear souls—and if she went to prison they would choke to death for the want of something to eat. Committed.

Catharine McBride was brought in for stealing a frock. Catharine said she had just served out 6 months on Blackwell's Island, and she wouldn't be sent back again for the best glass of punch that ever was made. Her husband, when she last left the penitentiary, took her to a boarding house in Essex st., but the rascal got mad at her, pulled her hair, pinched her arm, and kicked her out of bed. She was determined not to bear such treatment as this, and so got drunk and stole the frock out of pure spite. Committed.

Bill Doty got drunk because he had the horrors so bad he couldn't keep sober. Committed.

Patrick Ludwick was sent up by his wife, who testified that she had supported him for several years in idleness and drunkenness. Abandoning all hopes of a reformation in her husband, she bought him a suit of clothes a fortnight since and told him to go about his business, for she would not live with him any longer. Last night he came home in a state of intoxication, broke into his wife's bedroom, pulled her out of bed, pulled her hair, and stamped on her. She called a watchman and sent him up. Pat exerted all his powers of eloquence in endeavoring to excite his wife's sympathy, but to no purpose. As every sensible woman ought to do who is cursed with a drunken husband, she refused to have anything to do with him hereafter—and he was sent to the penitentiary.

Dennis Hart was fighting in the street. Committed.

John Movich, of 220 Mott st., got drunk and disturbed his neighbors. Committed.

An example of the penny press presenting news that was interesting to readers regardless of its importance. The police column was standard fare in the *New York Sun* in the 1830s. (*New York Sun*, July 4, 1834.)

Ochs and the New York Times

As a direct challenge to the excesses of Pulitzer and Hearst, Adolph Ochs rescued the bankrupt *New York Times* without fanfare and put it on the road to eminence in American journalism, a position that it enjoys even now. Ochs created a motto for the revitalized *Times* that summed up its aims and substance: "All The News That's Fit To Print." To Ochs that meant that news *not* fit to print would not make it with the *Times*. Ochs saw to it that all facts were reported fairly and accurately, without embellishments or distortions. It became a newspaper that readers could believe, a newspaper of record. That's what responsibility meant to Adolph Ochs. So the century turned and the First Amendment moved into new times, staggering but still on its feet.

Pulitzer Reforms

By this time, Joseph Pulitzer had wearied of his circulation combats with archrival Hearst and began to contemplate the real meaning of American journalism. He recognized that if matters continued on the present course, journalism would make a mockery of the constitutional guarantees that protected it. He also recognized that the establishment of a professional school of journalism might assist in providing future journalists with professional skills, along with badly needed development in the arts and sciences, for the benefit of the profession. Even better, it might develop workable, high-level guidelines for responsible performance, which had not developed to the degree that journalism itself had developed. In that connection, he wrote in 1904:

> Nothing less than the highest ideals, the most scrupulous anxiety to do right, the most accurate knowledge of the problems it has to meet, and a sincere sense of moral responsibility will save journalism from a subservience to business interests, seeking selfish ends, antagonistic to public welfare.[7]

The Muckrakers

There were other stirrings as well. As the century turned, a small group of journalists, most of them magazine writers, took a studied look at the promise of the American democracy itself. They were appalled at what they found: corporate and governmental corruption of the worst sort, the peddling of contaminated meat and milk to the poor, the horrors of the tenements, child labor, death and disease in the mines—all manner of social wrongs. They began writing about what they had seen and Theodore Roosevelt hung upon them the negative label, "muckrakers," meaning people who preferred to look down at filth than up at the glories of western civilization. The muckrakers embraced the label as they went after the social evils. Journalism had begun creating its own conscience. All that activity and more culminated in 1923 in the adoption of the *Canons of Journalism Ethics* by the American Society of Newspaper Editors, the first formal guidelines of journalistic responsibility in American history. The thrust of the ASNE code is found in these passages:

> The right of a newspaper to attract and hold readers is restricted by nothing but considerations of public welfare. The use a newspaper makes of the share of public attention it gains serves to determine its sense of responsibility, which it shares with every member of its staff. A journalist who uses his power for any selfish or otherwise unworthy purpose is faithless to a high trust.[8]

The *Canons* received rousing approval around the country. But in spite of their display window idealism, tacky journalism continued to thrive. The Roaring Twenties brought a new form of sensationalism in the Jazz Journalism of the new tabloid newspapers, so-called because of their abbreviated, booklike format.[9] But soon the name tabloid, or tab, reflected the racy content that outstripped the worst of the Yellow sheets. Minor stories with sexual overtones became standard fare in the tabs, one of the most notorious being the exploits of fiftyish millionaire Daddy Browning and his sixteen-year-old heartthrob whom he affectionately dubbed "Peaches." If it titillated, stunned, or terrified, it was hot copy. Faked photographs called composographs, columns of advice to the lovelorn, gangsters portrayed as heroes, bathtub gin and the speakeasies, and the ups and downs of flapper morality all became fair game in the tabloids in a decade that changed the face of the nation.

The Carnival Revisited
Renewed Sensationalism: The "Tabs"

On January 12, 1928, a reporter for the *New York Daily News* attended the executions of murderess Ruth Snyder and her hapless cohort-lover Judd Gray at Sing Sing Prison. By official order, no photographs would be allowed in the death chamber: indeed, cameras would be banned. But an enterprising reporter for the *News* taped a small camera to his leg and covered it with his trousers. When Mrs. Snyder had been strapped into the chair and the current opened full force, he snapped up his camera and tripped the shutter. The resulting photograph appeared on the front page of the *News* on Friday, January 13 and again on Saturday. Beneath the full-length picture, the paper included the following cutline in its Saturday issue:

The Daily News *and the Snyder-Gray Execution*

> WHEN RUTH PAID HER DEBT TO THE STATE!—The only unofficial photo ever taken within the death chamber, this most remarkable, exclusive picture shows closeup of Ruth Synder in death chair at Sing Sing as lethal current surged through her body at 11:06 Thursday night. Its first publication in yesterday's EXTRA edition of the NEWS was the most talked-of feat in history of journalism. Ruth's body is seen straightened within its confining gyves, her helmeted head, face masked, hands clutching, and electrode strapped to her right leg with stocking down. Autopsy table on which body was removed is beside chair.

The *New York Daily Graphic*, probably the most offensive of the tabs, failed to get a picture but made a circulation pitch to its readers in another way. On the day of the execution, the *Graphic* offered a sizzling promise:

Don't fail to read tomorrow's *Graphic*. An installment that thrills and stuns! A story that fairly pierces the heart and reveals Ruth Synder's last thoughts on earth; that pulses the blood as it discloses her final letters. Think of it! A woman's final thoughts just before she is clutched in the deadly snare that sears and burns and FRIES AND KILLS! Her very last words! Exclusively in tomorrow's *Graphic*.

This photo of Ruth Snyder appeared on the front page of the *News* on January 14, 1928. (New York News, Inc. Photo.)

The point in recounting portions of the sordid aspects of news gathering and dissemination in America is to emphasize that in the almost 300-year history of journalism in America, "responsibility" is a mere teenager, and a young one at that. Many practitioners still do not know quite how to handle unfettered freedom and we continue to see questionable examples of press performance issued in the name of the public's right to know. Hence, the debate launched in the first administration of George Washington carries on as it probably always will. There are hopeful signs but increasingly, American citizens have become and continue to become disenchanted with the Fourth Estate.

"Responsibility": A Teenager

The Hutchins Commission

In 1947, the Commission on Freedom of the Press completed a three-year analysis of the news media and their obligations to the American people.[10] The commission, headed by Robert M. Hutchins, chancellor of the University of Chicago, was also concerned about the personal sense of responsibility of media owners and managers in trying to develop public opinion on important issues and events. Taken together, the commission determined that the media are "probably the most powerful single influence" on public opinion in the United States. The commission also found that freedom of the press in America is in considerable danger and for three fundamental reasons:

1. The importance of the press has greatly increased with the development of the news media over the years. But along with that development there has been a sharp decrease in the number of people who can express their views through the media. In brief, the American people are permitted less personal participation in the media as the media have grown in importance.
2. Those relatively few who are able to use the news media (editors, publishers, etc.), have failed to provide adequate services to the people in line with the needs of a democratic society.
3. Those who control the news media have periodically engaged in practices that society condemns and that, if continued, will eventually bring on outside controls of the news media.

Findings of the Commission

"Outside controls" would likely destroy freedom of the press and make meaningless the entire First Amendment. When one freedom falls all freedoms are apt to fall with it.

The Hutchins Commission also indicated that (as of 1947) freedom of expression was not in immediate danger of being lost. By its very position in the public arena, the report reads, freedom of the press has always been in danger and probably always will be. The basic problem was that, compared with earlier times, the relationship of the news media to society was new and more complicated than ever before. Thus, the report indicates, the modern press must recognize its powerful role in the democratic process. In that pursuit, it must identify and adhere to selfless goals vital to maintaining and advancing a free society.

Press "Credibility" Issue

The concerns raised by the Hutchins report have to do with the credibility of the press as a contributing, constructive force in the American democratic experience. Again, it was the belief in the necessity of freedom of expression in the newborn democracy that made the founding fathers incorporate that provision into the United States Constitution. It is also clear from their personal writings that a free press is necessary to keep an appraising eye on the performances of public officials and to report their doings, good and not good, to the people. One easily senses the urgency with which the framers of the Constitution proclaimed that the press must be free if the people are to be free. One also senses their insistence that the press perform to the best of its abilities and be dedicated to the highest levels of service. Against the ringing declarations of Jefferson, Hamilton, and others in support of press freedoms comes a piercing clash by the founder of another nation who saw all this in a different context:

Lenin's View of Press Freedom

> Why should freedom of speech and freedom of the press be allowed? Why should a government which is doing what it believes to be right allow itself to be criticized? It would not allow opposition by lethal weapons. Ideas are much more fatal things than guns. Why should any man be allowed to buy a printing press and disseminate pernicious opinion calculated to embarrass the government?[11]
>
> Nikolai Lenin
> USSR

Government Accountable to the People

While the Soviet government is accountable to nobody, the American government is accountable to the people through the press. That was the plan in 1787 and it is still the plan today. Thus, the press must reveal all of the truths all of the time without playing favorites and without constraints, self-inflicted or otherwise. The performance record indicates that all of these responsibilities have not been pursued all of the time. "Credibility" means *believability, reliability,* and *trust* between individuals. In a healthy marriage, husband and wife trust each other; they share credibility. The American press has major credibility problems.

Report of the Twentieth Century Fund

The Hutchins report was published in 1947, certainly far enough in the past for the news media to have shored up their underpinnings and donned the cloak of responsibility. Yet a second study, sponsored by the task force of the Twentieth Century Fund and released in 1972, strongly suggests that matters have not improved. Indeed, they have worsened.[12]

Members of the task force looked carefully into the relationship between the modern press and government. They came away with the impression that in America "press freedom might be more fragile than is widely assumed— and that its role in American democracy is so crucial that the nation cannot afford to risk its erosion." The report emphasized that the constitutional provision of free press exists for the *people,* not for the press alone, just as the remaining three "freedoms" are vested in the people. Because of the peculiarity of the functions involved, freedom of the press is vested in the news media in the *name* of the people. This is because each person cannot be his own collector and evaluator of information as he participates in the democratic process. In the words of Supreme Court Justice Hugo Black, the press exists so that it can "bare the secrets of government and inform the people. Only a free and unrestrained press can effectively expose deception in government." It is presumed, therefore, that the most effective weapon against *deception* is *truth.* But according to the findings of the task force, an impressive number of Americans *do not believe their press.*

Freedom Is for the People

Justice Black

The basic problem, the study indicates, is that when the press is attacked by government, the public should view it as an attack on themselves since the constitutional guarantee of free press is for the *people.* But the people, or large numbers of them, rarely see it that way. In fact, the task force found that many Americans disapprove of the press revealing "truths" that are critical of government. The report found "that many, if not a majority, of the people believe that the press is being either irresponsible or unpatriotic when it publishes material that the government feels should not be made public."

Attacks on Press = Attacks on People

The report also indicates that public disillusionment with the news media might be tied to public disillusionment with all of the various institutions designed to represent them.* Thus, the news media are the "victims" as well as the "recorders" of events. "If the press reports dissent," the study states, "it is held to be the vehicle of dissent."† But if the press fails to report, it is not performing its constitutional duty "to serve as the bulwark against arbitrary government."

In sum, the task force states that the American people must recognize, as the Founding Fathers did, that a free press is essential to a free people. "In the last analysis, the public has the most to lose from a whittling away of the safeguards that have, since the founding of the nation, preserved and protected the invaluable tradition of a free press." It is essential, the study goes on, that

Summation by the Task Force

---

*A national survey by the Louis Harris organization in December 1977 found that many Americans feel that leaders in their most important institutions are out of touch with those they are supposed to lead or help.

†This is a latter-day extension of the "kill the messenger" concept of ancient times. If a messenger arrived to report bad news to the king, the messenger was slain as the *bearer* of bad news although he did not create the bad news. He only upset the king.

the press resist all efforts by government to in any way weaken that freedom. At the same time, the news media must act *responsibly* in providing all pertinent information to the people—regardless of the personal preferences or biases of publishers, editors, and reporters—so that they might be attuned to and participate in the business of government. "It is this above all that will make the maintenance of a free press not a cherished cliché but the cornerstone of a free society."

The Marquis Childs Study

The root of the problem of disaffection between press and people has many branches, some of them buried deeply in the public psyche. Credibility problems are chief among them. In 1976, Pulitzer Prize journalist Marquis Childs published the results of a study he had completed for the Ford Foundation on public attitudes toward the press. It was based on interviews with many newspaper editors and television executives around the country. He found widespread "uncertainty about the extent of credibility and commitment in their audiences." As he traveled about the country, he noted significant neg-

Public Support for Nixon Attacks

ative public reaction to "monopoly control" over the news "by a handful of men in New York" as well as the problem of slanted or biased news. That the press in the United States is in danger is reflected in the public support given the Nixon administration when it tried to curb the press. Childs was especially astonished to learn that so many Americans, youth particularly, failed to understand the origin or meaning of the First Amendment. "Failure to understand its importance will open the way to demogogues and demogogic laws." He went on to say: "If we are to keep an independent press in the last years of this century, we shall all have to do a great deal more than we have done thus far."[13]

Table 2.1   Average Number of Hours Devoted to News Programs by the Three U.S. Television Networks, 1970–76

	Regularly Scheduled News Programs	Sponsored News Specials	Network Sponsored News Specials	Total News Hours
1970–71*	289	72	25	386
1971–72	310	62	13	385
1972–73	326	72	25	423
1973–74	318	62	33	413
1974–75	313	43	44	400
1975–76	318	73	20	411

Source: Nielsen Television Index, A.C. Nielsen Company.

Note: This table focuses on network television news programming from 1970 to 1976, showing the total averaged hours of regularly scheduled news for all three networks. About 80 percent of these figures are the standard evening news programs; the remaining 20 percent are sponsored news specials and network-sustained news specials which are usually scheduled on short notice in response to news events. A news-programming peak in the 1972–1973 season is probably due to the end of U.S. involvement in Vietnam and to coverage of the presidential election year.

*Seasons run from September thru April of years given.

Media critic Ben Bagdikian shares Child's concerns. He warns that "the First Amendment will survive only if it is a *living principle** in the minds of the people" and "there is doubt that this is true in the United States today. An appalling number of Americans, including judges, legislators, doctors and some of the most powerful leaders in our society, give lip service to the Bill of Rights but are hostile or indifferent to the actual exercise of those freedoms." With those attitudes among national and community leaders, it is little wonder that press freedom is being eroded. Bagdikian points out that when President Nixon decided to snap the "critical" segment of the press back into line, he told John Dean, "One hell of a lot of people don't give one damn about this issue of supression of the press." It would appear, then, that he moved with the confidence that many Americans would approve. Bagdikian also refers to a Gallup Poll of American high school juniors and seniors in which the following question was posed: "Would the nation be better off, in your opinion, if every news article sent out of Washington was checked by a government agency to see that the facts are correct?" Sixty-three percent answered *yes*![14]

Presidential Assaults on the Press

If public disenchantment with the news media is reflected in what the above surveys and individuals indicate, the press and the American public have reason for concern. When no less a personage than the vice-president of the United States undertakes repeated verbal assaults on the press—over national television—as Spiro Agnew did in 1969, it is fair to assume that he does so with the blessings of the administration. It is also fair to assume that the power of the presidency itself is being harnessed in an effort to abuse a vital provision of the Bill of Rights, which the president has sworn to uphold and defend. Worse yet, many Americans applauded these tactics in 1969 as many do now. While it is true that no president in history, including Thomas Jefferson, has enjoyed a totally harmonious relationship with the press in the rip and bump of political activity, no administration in modern times has gone after the press as the Nixon administration did. Along with including the names of certain journalists on his "enemies list," Richard Nixon attempted to use antitrust laws against the three major television networks in an effort to bring them into line. For example, White House Press Secretary Ron Ziegler informed Dan Rather of CBS that since the networks were anti-Nixon "they are going to have to pay for that, sooner or later, one way or another." Seven months after the antitrust suit against the networks was filed by the Nixon people, White House Chief Counsel Charles Colson told CBS Vice Chairman Frank Stanton: "We'll bring you to your knees in Wall Street and

*Italics mine.

on Madison Avenue."[15] Other "unofficial" steps were taken against the press including employment of government agents, such as the Federal Bureau of Investigation, to harass and intimidate reporters.

Press Shortcomings a Factor

A major point to this is that the press is not entirely blameless in its increasing encounters with government and in the growing disapproval of the American people. As the task force determined, the news media's "irresponsible scrambling for reader and viewer attention has only led many to look with skepticism at what they see on their television screens and to doubt what they read in their papers."[16] As stated earlier, recent polls indicate that large numbers of Americans have become disenchanted with their press. It is especially so with newspapers, since news is the mainstay of the print media and not a sideline as it is with broadcasting. Secondly, newspapers are not government regulated as broadcasting is by the Federal Communications Commission. Hence, most of the criticism is aimed at the print media.

Marquis Childs found that current press critics are better educated, are more directly and personally involved in public affairs, and are better attuned to and versed in public issues and problems than ever before. Many of them, perhaps most, do not believe much of what they read. If disenchantment continues to grow, disaffection will result. Should that develop, it is not difficult to predict what would happen to the free press in the United States. Clearly, if press freedom is to thrive, the mass media must cultivate the support of the people who, in the final sum, will determine what is to be free and what is not. Perhaps the press needs fewer mimeographed codes of ethics-for-all and greater direct, personal dedication to public service of the caliber found in other professions.

Table 2.2 Measurements of Public Confidence in Television and Newspaper Leadership, 1973–1976

	1973		1974		1975		1976	
	Number	Percent	Number	Percent	Number	Percent	Number	Percent
			Confidence in the people running television					
Total Sample Size	1,504	—	1,484	—	1,490	—	1,499	—
Total Number Responding	1,480	100.0%	1,464	100.0%	1,451	100.0%	1,464	100.0%
"A great deal"	278	18.8	347	23.7	265	18.3	279	19.1
"Only some"	875	59.1	861	58.8	853	58.7	779	53.2
"Hardly any"	327	22.1	256	17.5	333	23.0	406	27.7
			Confidence in the people running the press					
Total Sample Size	1,504	—	1,484	—	1,490	—	1,499	—
Total Number Responding	1,477	100.0%	1,463	100.0%	1,442	100.0%	1,463	100.0%
"A great deal"	346	23.4	383	26.2	354	24.6	424	29.0
"Only some"	911	61.7	821	56.1	823	57.0	776	53.0
"Hardly any"	220	14.9	259	17.7	265	18.4	263	18.0

Source: National Opinion Research Center.

History has dramatically portrayed the chaotic results of public dissatisfaction with the institutions of freedom that fail to meet their responsibilities to the people. A case in point of recent date: the destruction of democracy in pre-World War II Germany by a group of fanatics who managed to *convince* the people that freedom was their greatest enemy.[17] Under the leadership of President Paul Von Hindenberg, the infant German republic had weathered the internal upheavals of the 1920s and had begun to tidy up its affairs, economic and otherwise. Then, by cleverly manipulating democratic processes, Adolf Hitler became the minority party chancellor under Hindenberg on January 30, 1933. Hitler and his National Socialists, or Nazis, could not tolerate the existence of a free press that might object to the ghastly plans they had in mind. Hence, almost immediately the new chancellor and his followers set about destroying press freedom in Germany. They began by convincing the people that the privately owned newspapers, magazines, radio, and other media were operated by dedicated enemies of the state, many of them Jews, and that only Hitler could save Germans from internal and external enemies and return the country to world power. Only the government, in the person of Hitler, could offer truth.

*Freedom: Their
Greatest Enemy*

Following the historic Reichstag fire, rigged by Nazis and blamed on Jews and German Communists, Hitler convinced the aged and ill Von Hindenberg that all would be lost to the nation's enemies if drastic measures were not taken immediately. He then thrust a piece of paper at the president and demanded his signature. Hindenberg signed. With that simple gesture, seven sections of the German constitution were eliminated, all of them legal measures that protected individual and civil liberties. In a moment, freedom of the press and speech and the right of public assembly were wiped away. Police were given the right to invade the personal privacy of citizens at will, to violate the mails, to tap telephones, and to search private homes and businesses as they wished.

Loss of Civil Liberties

"After the party came to power in 1933 . . . many of those (newspaper) concerns, such as the Ullstein House, which were owned or controlled by Jewish interests, or by political or religious interests hostile to the Nazi Party, found it expedient to sell their newspapers or assets to the Eher concern. There was no free market for the sale of such properties and the Eher Verlag was generally the only bidder. In this matter the Eher Verlag, together with publishing concerns owned or controlled by it, expanded into a monopoly of the newspaper publishing business in Germany. . . . The party investment in these publishing enterprises became financially very successful. It is a true statement to say that the basic purpose of the Nazi press program was to eliminate all the press which was in opposition to the party."

Statement made by Max Amann, Reich leader for the press and head of Eher Verlag, the Nazi publishing firm, during the Nuremberg trials.

The "new order" also imposed the death penalty for "disturbing the peace" by armed persons (though not applicable to Hitler's storm troopers). A wave of terror swept the nation as disciplined Nazis arrested and jailed suspected enemies of the state. Diehard propagandists convinced millions of peasant and middle-class Germans of the imminent takeover of the country by Bolsheviks unless they vested total authority in Adolf Hitler. The Nazi press, the only press remaining, was harnessed to the cause. Public officials who opposed the Nazis were arrested, some of them members of the Reichstag even though it was illegal to arrest a member at all. All political parties other than the National Socialists were disbanded.

*Nazi Press
Stood Alone*

Leading American commentator H. V. Kaltenborn reporting on the problems in Nazi Germany. (Culver Pictures, Inc.)

Total control of the mass media was essential to Hitler's plan for the future of Germany. In line with that, he created the Reich Press Law, passed on October 3, 1933, which made the practice of journalism a "public vocation" regulated by the government. The law stipulated that each employee must be a German citizen of Aryan descent and not married to a Jew. Editors published only what Propaganda Minister Josef Goebbels permitted them to publish. Thus, in nine brief, stormy months, Adolf Hitler had succeeded in making the free press of Germany the enemy of the people. And with passage of the Reich Press Law, no voices of dissent remained. It is clear that what Hitler was about to unleash on the world had the impressive support of the German people for there was no free press to throw light into darkened corners.* The roots of suppression appear ageless even in the present decade.

The Press under Fire

Out of the Senate hearings into the financial dealings of Bert Lance, then the director of the Office of Management and Budget in the Carter administration, came a barrage of criticism of the news media from various quarters. The charge was that the media had been unduly abusive to Lance, and that they had railroaded him back to Georgia. Lance supporters on the Senate Governmental Affairs Committee endorsed the "railroading" theory. "Media overkill" was charged. Some wondered how much attention the case would have received by the media if, at the same time, there had been a bonafide crisis in the Middle East, a black dissident seizure of the South African government or an explosion of a new-fangled Soviet bomb.

Public officials have long vocalized their objections to the severity of press coverage of political figures and activities. So these charges came as no surprise to the press. As CBS viewed it, the media reported only what took place, nothing more.[18] In the course of the hearings, Senators Abraham Ribicoff, Charles Percy, and other committee members threw all manner of charges at Lance, some of them vague and unsubstantiated, and the press reported these statements and veiled suggestions of evil-doing as part of the overall coverage. Out of all this came complaints from segments of public and private sources that the media had treated Lance unfairly. Fair or not, there seems to be a consensus that press inquiries into the public and private activities of government officials are becoming more rigorous.

The Press and Government Investigations

*It is interesting to gauge how thoroughly and rapidly Hitler and his henchmen conned the German people out of their legal rights. On November 12, 1933, a special election or "plebiscite" was held throughout the country to determine to what extent the people had embraced the new order. The results showed that ninety-two percent of the registered voters cast ballots in favor of the Nazi regime, the only party on the ballot since all other parties had been liquidated. Incredibly, 2,154 of the 2,242 inmates of the concentration camp at Dachau voted for the fascist government that had put them there.

Reporting the crimes of Watergate might have launched this brand of journalistic crusading or perhaps it was born of distrust of government resulting from the Vietnam War. Whatever, the disclosures of the drinking habits and nocturnal activities of former Congressman Wilbur Mills brought about his downfall as it should have done. Journalists generally agree that the public does have the right to know about the total behavior of elected officials; this private behavior might have a vital impact on professional behavior. Yet many members of the Washington press corps had been aware of Mills's shortcomings—and those of others—for years but were hesitant to expose them for fear of cutting off sources of information. Public officials feel extremely vulnerable to publicity that might in any way mar their images before the voters. It's the nature of the job. Then came the sizzling story of Congressman Wayne Hays, who kept his personal mistress on the government payroll in return for personal favors. After that the press went after those public officials who might have dabbled in handouts from a wealthy South Korean rice peddler. These and other exposés might well have motivated an already-aggressive press corps to new levels of probing. Thus, the probings and the questions became more demanding and the cries of foul play more strident and frequent. To public officials, these activities are the frantic efforts of journalists, by-passed by the excitements of Watergate, out to carve reputations for themselves at anyone's expense. To the press, the personal and public lives of government officials *are* the people's business, and thus the price one pays for entering public life. As President James Garfield once said, "Authority should do no act that will not bear the light."[19] Harry Truman was more direct: "If you can't stand the heat, stay out of the kitchen!" The press tends to agree. Many other Americans do not.

The Press as Official Critic

Within the democratic order, it is considered the responsibility of social institutions to gather and evaluate commentaries and criticisms for the purpose of improving their services to the public. Traditionally, the press, one of the most powerful of all social institutions, has upheld its First Amendment right to evaluate and criticize the working of government at all levels. At times, particularly since Watergate, it has done so as if government were not the "friendly adversary" of historical tradition but the *enemy*.

Press Critics

Former United States Senator J. William Fulbright, who admits to having received a "good press" throughout his years of public service, referred to the press as "the vanguard" of a new aggressiveness. "If once the press showed excessive deference to government and its leaders, it has become excessively mistrustful and even hostile." What was needed, he wrote, was remedial planning to rebuild public faith in government, to shore up weaknesses. What was not needed was the constant rumble of the drum of doom to seek out and punish transgressors, most of whom were guilty of no more than bad judgment.

"Public" vs. "Private"

"My own view is that no one should get everything he deserves—the world would become a charnel house."[20]

CBS commentator Eric Sevareid seemed to agree. Speaking of press coverage of the Bert Lance hearings, he said that "some media overkill" had taken place and that Lance was probably guilty only of "a boundless faith in himself."[21]

Journalistic "Truth"

Press critics also charge that the press does not present an "objective" view of issues and events. It presents only part of the story and, thus, truth is abused. It also thrives on media events, or minor happenings blown out of proportion. Certainly "truth" is an elusive ideal for anyone in any area of interest on any level of activity. If "truth," or "objectivity," means total truth or total objectivity and nothing less—every fact associated with an event, every person, every mechanical action, each thrust of nature, each name, each print in the sand—it is rarely, probably never, achievable. A trial court seeks to determine "the truth, the whole truth, and nothing but the truth." Yet it bases its judgments on the evidence and arguments presented, not on those *not* presented. The daylong telecasts of the Ervin Committee hearings into the Watergate mess throughout the summer of 1973 produced an amazing number of facts, truths, half-truths, mistruths, speculations, wizardry, weeping, posing, and posturing. But it was not the *totality* of Watergate.

No matter how dedicated to digging out the truth, the journalist is strapped: he is strapped by space limitations in the newspaper or air time at the television station; he is strapped by budget limitations that won't pay him overtime while he pursues truth or will not permit him to travel to seek it out; he is strapped by deadlines that are ruled by a clock. He is even strapped by himself in his personal notions about what is important and what is not, whom he should interview and whom he can pass up. But even with these constraints placed upon him, the dedicated reporter can approach truth in terms of the accuracy of whatever portion he does cover, call it "truth-accuracy" or anything else.

Cornelius Ryan

The late Cornelius Ryan, a veteran journalist and war correspondent, produced several award winning books on major battlegrounds of World War II, which personalized and redramatized what happened there. Ryan based his recounts on military documents, histories, memoirs, maps, and other documentary evidence available to him. More impressively, he also based his stories on personal interviews with thousands of participants, friend and foe. While no one of his books—nor all together—purports to portray the total truth of a single military action, Ryan could boast of "truth" in the accuracy and objectivity of that which he did present. Other authors have done the same. Hence, one may surmise that truth is served when personal bias is reasonably laid aside and the reporter gives the reader what he or she must know as the

Accuracy as Truth

basis for gaining knowledge and/or making decisions. That is "truth-accuracy" rather than "truth-totality." It is worthwhile and it is attainable. It becomes even more vital in terms of the common good when *many* media seek it out and present it to the public. At that point the audience moves even closer to truth via variety, for there is safety in numbers.

The critical problem with all this is that not every reporter or editor or publisher pursues truth-accuracy and delivers it to the public as such. Heavy hands sometimes come into the action and the square may eventually be

Eugene McCarthy on Press

formed into a circle. Former United States Senator Eugene McCarthy expressed the view that press freedom is an extension of free speech and free speech "is a derived right based not on the right of anyone to say anything he wishes to say, under any circumstances, but rather on the need for information and truth." And, again, since truth is elusive, members of a democratic society are best served by permitting those who have something to say to *say it* or write it. That is so others may accept or reject it. But, he continues, the news media must *carry* it or the public loses its option to accept or reject. Thus, McCarthy concludes, standards must be devised by the media to insure that the public is served.[22]

Critics of press performance frequently complain that the news media readily, even gleefully, serve as critics of all democratic institutions but do not willingly submit to criticism themselves. In fact, when criticized, the news media frequently treat it "as a matter of high drama," as Professor James Carey puts it:

> The criticism of the press in America, as sporadic, as inadequate, as ill-intentioned as it often is, is a tribute to the importance of the press in American life, an importance felt not only by government officials but by the community generally. The proper response is not to retreat behind slogans and defensive postures but the encouragement of an active and critical tradition and an important body of professional critics.[23]

Self-Criticism

When the Hutchins report was released in 1947, it advanced various recommendations through which the news media might render more directly and responsibly their services to the American people. One of the recommendations was that "members of the press engage in vigorous mutual criticism." While supporting the notion that government should "not be invoked" in correcting press shortcomings, the commission agreed that criticism must be encouraged and carefully weighed. "If the press is to be accountable—and it must if it is to remain free—its members must discipline one another by the only means they have available, namely public criticism."[24] Former Senator Fulbright said it another way: "For a start, journalists might try to be less thin-skinned. Every criticism of the press is not a fascist assault upon the First Amendment."[25]

Much could be said about criticism of specific press shortcomings and the press has them to be sure: the slanting of news; exclusion of those stories that are personally offensive to management—worse, offensive to friendly outside interests; placing cash inflow over the public welfare. But with all its warts, the free press is the most vital asset the nation possesses because it helps to span the void between people and government and all the other interest areas beyond and between. The evolvement of community press councils offers hope for constructive dialogue between the public and its press, especially in matters of local concern. The advent of quality, critical journals such as the *Columbia Journalism Review,* the *Washington Journalism Review,* and others offers constructive commentaries on media performance by critics who are of and for the press. Evidence also indicates that some who bear major responsibility for gathering and disseminating news are willing to listen to "friendly critics," many of them on the community level.

Friendly Critics

The Need for Mutual Understanding

Certainly the media have internal needs and problems that critics frequently ignore or know nothing about. For example, the media must remain financially solvent to fulfill their First Amendment responsibilities. To hold its place in the *people-press-government* connection, the press *must* remain financially independent. The sole option is government control of media. The news function and the business function in a newspaper or broadcast outlet can and does coexist for the betterment of both. But when the latter is emphasized to the neglect of the former, the public is not being served. This problem is most pronounced on some small dailies and weeklies that avoid controversy at all costs for fear of unsettling their readers. In many instances their readers *should* be unsettled. An even greater problem develops when a newspaper or broadcast station passes over an important story because it might irk big advertisers or the local political power structure. A prime example is the Bay of Pigs fiasco when President John Kennedy pressured the *New York Times* to hold the story. The *Times* obeyed!

In any case, impatient critics are vocal and sizeable because old ways and entrenched practices of the press are slow in changing. Veteran journalist William L. Chenery commented: "The newspaper as an institution has been neither better nor worse than any other institution of a democracy."[26] That is supported by the Harris survey cited earlier. It also does not say much for newspapers or other institutions of the American democracy. Because all newspapers are community oriented (even the metropolitan press), and because they are highly visible to consumers of information (even more than radio or television), criticism of newspapers is increasing. And that is what newspapers must deal with; they can no longer remain aloof.

No Better, No Worse than Others

Norman Isaacs's Rules

Norman E. Isaacs, a renowned journalist and outspoken advocate of high standards, wrote some years ago: "What we need are good newspapers. And this is the best newspaper promotion in the world. Just plain *good* newspapers." Isaacs then offered ten fundamental measures of what a *good* newspaper is.*

1. It is *honest* and will print the news without taking sides, as objectively as possible;
2. It will not crimp on news space in order to sell more advertising;
3. It is *just*: it does not pretend that everything it prints is 100 percent accurate though it tries to do so. If it makes a mistake it will admit it and attempt to rectify it. It will give equal prominence to a story of the man who has been cleared as it did to the story that he was accused;
4. It is *courageous* in the sense that it will not look for a fight but will take one on if it is important to do so;
5. It is *clean*—not prudish—but clean. It will not seek out cheap sex stories for the purpose of selling more copies. It is a newspaper that does not have to apologize for entering the homes of its readers;
6. It is a *growing* newspaper in the sense that it continually strives for excellence;
7. It is *readable* in an appealing visual way, one that looks tidy and neat;
8. It *leads* rather than follows on the high road of public service. It is not the organ of selfish interests;
9. It has *manners* and is courteous to its readers regardless of their station in society;
10. Most important, it has a *conscience*. It is dedicated to the service of the reader, of the community, of the state and the nation. It has principles, ethics and morals. It is conscience that makes a newspaper different from other industrial organizations, that gives it its individual character, that makes it perform above and beyond the call of duty.[27]

E. B. White Calls on *Esquire*

A moving example of the application of high principle took place in 1976, not by a powerhouse publication but by a journalist of vast accomplishment, E. B. White, who for many years was a prime editorial mover behind the *New Yorker* magazine.[28]

The giant Xerox Corporation had arranged with *Esquire* magazine to produce a print media "special" along the lines of its established television specials. For openers, they invested $175,000 in the project and paid former *New York Times* editor and writer Harrison Salisbury $55,000 to write the epic. Xerox also provided *Esquire* with $115,000 in advertising.

*Condensed in the interest of space.

White read the first installment and took immediate exception to the entire plan. In a letter to Xerox, he indicated that it is "ominous and unhealthy when a corporation underwrites an article in a magazine of general circulation." To White, the issue was not the company trying to influence *Esquire's* editorial policy or opinion. The issue was that people would wonder why a large corporation would invest so much money in a magazine article. White asked why a respected journalist of Salisbury's reputation would agree to such an unlikely arrangement. He also asked why the magazine would permit a commercial corporation—Xerox—to pick up the tab when publications are supposed to finance their own stories and thus maintain their editorial independence. These are reasonable questions that require considered responses.

"The press in our free country is reliable and useful," White wrote Xerox, "not because of its good character but because of its diversity. As long as there are many owners, each pursuing his own brand of truth, we the people have the opportunity to arrive at the truth and to dwell in the light." White emphasized the crucial role of owners of the media in the ongoing struggle to keep the press an independent instrument of democracy:

Need for Diversity in Media

> For a citizen in our free society, it is an enormous privilege and wonderful protection to have access to hundreds of periodicals, each peddling its own belief. There is safety in numbers: the papers expose each other's follies and pecadillos, correct each other's mistakes and cancel out each other's biases. The reader is free to range around in the whole editorial bouillabaise and explore it for the one clam that matters—the truth.

White pointed out that when a major corporation underwrites an article in a magazine, the ownership of that magazine diminishes, the identity of the publication blurs. "Whenever money changes hands, something goes along with it. . . . It would be hard to resist the suspicion that *Esquire* feels indebted to Xerox, that Mr. Salisbury feels indebted to both, and that the ownership, or sovereignty, of *Esquire* has been nibbled around the edges."

Xerox thanked E. B. White for responding as he did. The company also cancelled its plans to do more magazine specials. This was thoughtful criticism from one who devoted his life to the principles of freedom of the press and who is sufficiently devoted to it to share his views with a well-intentioned industrial giant. E. B. White made his point. It hardly hurt at all.

The meaning of freedom of expression has become a matter of personal interpretation. It is personal because it is based on many *personal* variables. Just as people differ on compelling public issues, they differ in interpreting what freedom itself means. Their interpretations of press responsibility depend on the media content they absorb and what they accept and reject as appropriate reading or viewing.

Mass Media Responsibility

Thus, content itself becomes the measure of responsibility. That, in turn, contributes to public confidence in the media or to media credibility problems. Selecting what goes into a publication or a newscast is at the nub of it all. If the publisher or news director seeks to genuinely inform the people and labors responsibly in that pursuit, he will probably have consumer support. If he seeks first to entertain, to titillate, or to shock in order to create sales, some will delight in it while others will seek their information from other sources.

Over the years journalism practitioners have become concerned about performance and, in their zeal to serve the public, have enacted various codes of ethics for guidance. Private interests such as the Hutchins Commission and the Twentieth Century Fund have gone a few steps further by researching troublesome areas and making recommendations to help the media solve them. The fact that a large segment of the population is increasingly critical of press performance suggests that they are disenchanted and want improvements. What is particularly vexing to many critics is the press's seeming inability to critically evaluate itself in the interest of providing a more meaningful product. The media serve as critics of all social institutions except their own. That fact alone is sufficient to create so-called credibility gaps.

The problems, with little variation, are as old as American journalism itself. Yet the most strident efforts to achieve responsibility have been made in this century, most of it in recent times. If that tide continues to rise, the press, and the people, will be the better for it.

Notes

1. Alistair Cooke, *America* (New York: Knopf, 1974). p. 125.
2. Thomas Jefferson, "A Founding Father's Various Views," *Voice of the People*, Reo M. Christenson and Robert O. McWilliams, eds. (New York: McGraw-Hill, 1967), p. 119.
3. Catherine Drinker Bowen, *Miracle at Philadelphia* (Boston: Little, Brown, 1966), p. 245.
4. John Hohenberg, *Free Press/Free People* (New York: Columbia University Press, 1971), pp. 59–61.
5. Cooke, *America,* p. 147.
6. For details on Yellow Journalism see Edwin Emery, *The Press and America* (Englewood Cliffs, N.J.: Prentice-Hall, 1972), 3d ed., pp. 349–75.
7. As quoted in Fred S. Siebert, Theodore Peterson and Wilbur Schramm, *Four Theories of the Press* (Urbana, Ill.: University of Illinois Press paperback ed.), p. 83.
8. As quoted in John L. Hulteng, *The Messenger's Motives; Ethical Problems of the News Media* (Englewood Cliffs, N.J.: Prentice-Hall, 1976), p. 19.
9. Information on tabloids from Emery, *The Press and America,* pp. 552–62.
10. The Commission on Freedom of the Press, *A Free and Responsible Press* (Chicago: University of Chicago Press, 1947), pp. vii, 1–3.
11. From a Lenin speech in Moscow, 1920 as quoted in The *Quill,* September, 1976, p. 13.
12. The Twentieth Century Fund. *A Free and Responsive Press* (New York, 1972), pp. 48–49.
13. Marquis Childs, "Criticism and Control of the Press." *Intellect,* March 1976, p. 415.
14. Ben H. Bagdikian, "The Child in Jeopardy," The *Quill,* September 1976, pp. 33–35.
15. Paul Laskin, "Shadowboxing With the Networks," The *Nation,* June 14, 1975, p. 714.
16. The Twentieth Century Fund, p. 6.
17. Information on Germany and Hitler from William L. Shirer, *The Rise and Fall of the Third Reich* (New York: Simon and Schuster, 1960), pp. 194, 245, 211–12.

18. CBS Evening News, Thursday, 22 September 1977.
19. As quoted in The *Quill*, September 1976, p. 35.
20. "Fulbright on the Press," *Columbia Journalism Review* November 1975, pp. 39–45.
21. CBS Evening News, Friday, 23 September 1977.
22. Eugene McCarthy, "Sins of Omission," *Harpers*, June, 1977, pp. 90–92.
23. James W. Carey, "Journalism and Criticism: The Case of an Undeveloped Profession," *Readings in Mass Communication,* Michael C. Emery and Ted Curtis Smythe, eds. (Dubuque: Wm. C. Brown Company Publishers, 1977), p. 78.
24. The Commission on Freedom of the Press, p. 94.
25. "Fulbright on the Press," pp. 39–45.
26. William L. Chenery, *Freedom of the Press* (New York: Harcourt, Brace, 1955), p. 156.
27. Norman E. Isaacs, "Conscience and the Editor," *The Responsibility of the Press,* Gerald Gross, ed., (New York: Fleet, 1966), pp. 134–45.
28. E. B. White example from "What E. B. White Told Xerox," *Columbia Journalism Review,* September/October, 1976, pp. 52–54.

Bagdikian, Ben H. "The Child in Jeopardy." The *Quill*, September 1976, pp. 33–35.
Bowen, Catherine Drinker. *Miracle at Philadelphia*. Boston: Little, Brown, 1966.
Childs, Marquis. "Criticism and Control of the Press." *Intellect*, March 1976, p. 415.
Hohenberg, John. *Free Press/Free People*. New York: Columbia University Press, 1971.
Laskin, Paul. "Shadowboxing with the Networks." The *Nation*, June 14, 1975, p. 714.
McCarthy, Eugene. "Sins of Omission." *Harpers*, June 1977, pp. 90–92.
Siebert, Fred S.; Peterson, Theodore; and Schramm, Wilbur. *Four Theories of the Press*. Urbana: University of Illinois paperback, 1969.
The Commission on Freedom of the Press. *A Free and Responsible Press*. Chicago: University of Chicago Press, 1947. The "Hutchins Commission" report.
The Twentieth Century Fund. *A Free and Responsive Press*. New York, 1972.
"What E. B. White Told Xerox." *Columbia Journalism Review*, September/October 1976, pp. 52–54.

For Further Reading

News in Pictures

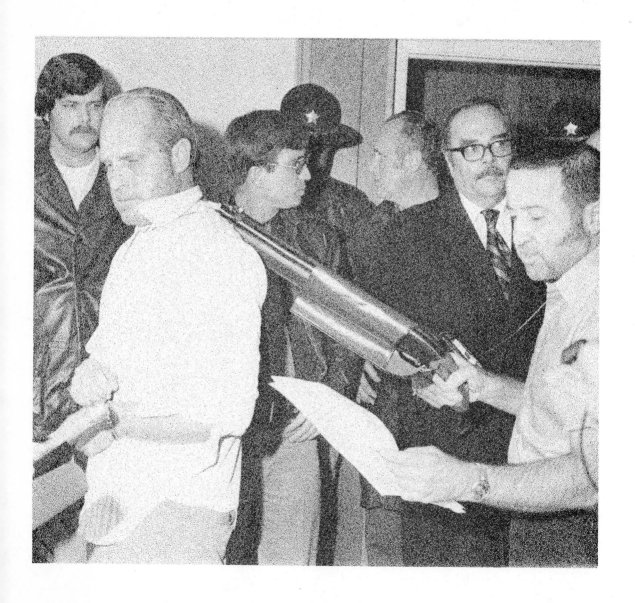

Reporting the News 3

Upon completing this chapter you should—

know how to define "news" and the purpose and function of "gatekeepers"

be able to provide various examples of responsible and less than responsible news reporting and why they are so

be able to discuss the issue of what the public *needs* from the mass media as opposed to strictly entertainment content, e.g., puffery, trivia, portrayals of violence, titillation, and so forth

There can be no such thing as public liberty without freedom of speech.

James Franklin, 1721, Colonial
Massachusetts

News Defined

The principal product of the press is "news," a confusing label at best. It is appropriate, at this point, to attempt to define news; attempt in the sense that the task proves to be a daring one.

What is "news?" On the surface it would appear a simple word to define. So would "holy" or "good" or "big" or "smelly," except that each means different things to different people. One might say that news is what happens at a particular time and place. However, many things happen at particular times and places and they are hardly "news." One might conjecture, then, that news is what happens at a particular time and place and is of interest to those who are not aware of it only when it is related to them.

News Is Many Things to Many People

The *American Heritage Dictionary* defines news as: "Recent events and happenings, especially those that are unusual or notable." Its second definition reads: "Information about recent events of general interest, especially as reported by newspapers, periodicals, radio or television."[1] *American Heritage Dictionary* thus differentiates between news that is circulated by a medium (or media) of communication and news that is not. Yet it calls both "news." It is a significant difference in that *most* of the events of any given day, worldwide and local, are not reported by the news media at all. Indeed, they may be known only to a few or even one.

Most consumers of news would probably agree that news, as such, is timely, meaningful information that comes to them through recognizable transmission systems such as newspapers, magazines, or broadcast outlets. But "news" is by no means limited to those carriers. Person-to-person communication is as old as the human race itself. As media historian Edwin Emery points out, exchanges of news existed far back into ancient times: "Newspapers did not create news," he writes, "news created newspapers."[2]

News Is More than News Media

Even today a vast assortment of news is exchanged daily in the same manner: two people chatting at the bus stop; teacher to students; mother to child. The consumer of information tends to *absorb* the kinds of messages that have the most direct meaning to him or her. That's why the mass media of communication offer *variety* in news, to please or interest as many as possible. Hence, there is truth in the definition of Morton Mintz, a reporter for the *Washington Post*. "News, like beauty, is in the eyes of the beholder. News, to strip the point of euphemism, is what we say it is."[3]

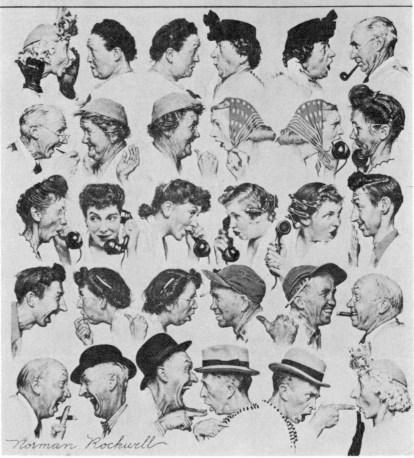

"The Gossips" by Norman Rockwell.

Another consideration: most consumers of the mass media do not recognize that the media are also largely responsible for the information consumers do *not* receive. In brief (if brevity is possible given the topic), various "gate-keepers," or persons operating between the occurrence of an event and publication of information about that event, shape it in any number of ways. The newspaper reporter at the scene may decide that the event is of no interest to *his* readers. So he lets it go unreported. Or he might decide to give it a particular slant to emphasize one aspect he considers most important. He then calls the story in to his paper where the rewriteperson may alter the original version to suit his requirements. The story then goes to the copy desk where it is edited to fit what space is available in the paper. That could mean reducing its length. Ultimately, the story is published and goes to the reader. But that does not happen until the story passes the tests of various persons, each of whom makes subjective judgments concerning what is and is not important. If those judgments are based on fairness and a desire to serve the public, the public *is served*, since no medium can realistically carry all the news available each day. But if judgments are based on the personal biases of any or all of the gatekeepers, the opportunity for the public to decide what is important is greatly diminished.

Reprinted by permission of the Chicago Tribune-New York Times News Syndicate, Inc.

With these factors in mind, then, it would be fair to say that "news" is information of any kind, which comes to an individual directly or through the communications media, and which that individual considers important enough to note.

Eric Sevareid's "Rules"

In his farewell broadcast for CBS on November 10, 1977, commentator Eric Sevareid shared his memories with his audience. In what *New York Times* columnist James Reston called "a news event of more than passing interest," Sevareid took his leave after thirty-eight years with the network. But he left the audience with something of himself, his personal "credo," an assortment of self-devised and self-imposed rules that had guided him along the way.

Eric Sevareid (CBS News Photo).

Given the significant problems of credibility that haunt the American press today, Sevareid's rules might be considered and absorbed by others who strive for excellence in the service of the press:

> Not to underestimate the intelligence of the audience and not to overestimate its information.
> To elucidate, when one can, more than to advocate.
> To remember always that the public is only people, and people only persons, no two alike.
> To retain the courage of one's doubts as well as one's convictions in this world of dangerously passionate certainties.
> To comfort oneself, in time of error, with the knowledge that the saving grace of the press, print or broadcast, is its self-correcting nature. And to remember that ignorant and biased reporting has its counterpart in ignorant and biased reading and listening. We do not speak into an intellectual or emotional void.[4]

Journalism as Routine

At various times in its history, American journalism has created moments of splendor when it has basked in the light of public approval. In recent times, coverage of the latter part of the Vietnam War, the Pentagon Papers story, and the Watergate blight serve as media monuments. But mostly the press is operated routinely by men and women who work for large and small dailies, weeklies, semi-weeklies, and all the rest. They dig out and write up what become the nuts and bolts of the business, day in and day out. Most of them are far removed from the recognized news centers of the world—the oil cartels of the Mid-East, the Kremlin, the Great Wall, the Dallas Cowboys, and backstage at the Morosco. By and large, working journalists plug away at what they do because they enjoy it and consider it worthy, knowing, or at least hoping, that others think so too. As Eric Sevareid reflected, this is serious business. It's giving the public what it needs as well as what it wants, even if the public doesn't want what it needs. To paraphrase Thomas Jefferson, the effort must be made or the game is over. That applies to the smallest weekly and the most renowned daily, to the tank-town radio station and the corporate network. The First Amendment applies to all media. Journalism is a job that is frequently exhausting, demanding, endless, discouraging, sometimes dangerous, and usually taken for granted. But this is what the press is supposed to be. Many consider it a high calling.

Nuts and Bolts

Donald Barlett and James Steele comprise a two-man investigative reporting team for the *Philadelphia Inquirer.*[5] Among other awards for journalistic excellence, they have won the Pulitzer Prize, two George Polk awards, and two Sigma Delta Chi Distinguished Service Awards. Barlett and Steele spe-

Barlett and Steele

cialize in "public records" reporting, which means they keep an eye on government performances by checking the records. Glamorous? Not to hear them tell of it.

"It requires weeks, indeed months, of painstaking labor which can only be classed as drudgery," they say. "It is slow, tedious, often boring work that no amount of Hollywood ingenuity could make exciting." But their findings are often dramatic.

Among other impressive projects, Barlett and Steele spent several months analyzing the effectiveness of the court system in coping with Philadelphia's spiraling crime rate. The system improved because of them. Their efforts required careful examination of more than a thousand court cases. The work was hard and monotonous but essential for people to know. They also investigated a major American-financed housing project in the Republic of South Korea, supposedly constructed for that nation's poor. After Barlett and Steele had finished pouring over endless State Department files, they found that President Park Chung Hee had doled the quarters out not to the poor of his country but to the supporters of his dictatorship who held high positions in the government and the armed forces of South Korea.

Summaries of Five Series By Barlett And Steele

CRIME AND INJUSTICE

A seven-month, seven-part investigation of the operations of Philadelphia's criminal courts. The investigation disclosed broad patterns of discrimination in the administration of justice: robbers were more likely to be sent to jail than rapists, persons under 30 were more likely to receive jail terms than persons over 30, and blacks who committed violent crimes were more likely to receive longer jail terms than whites who were convicted of similar offenses. The investigation, in which more than 1,000 cases were studied, was built around the first comprehensive computer study of a criminal justice system ever made by a newspaper.

AUDITING THE IRS

A six-month, seven-part study disclosing the IRS's annual failure to collect billions of dollars owed the U.S. Treasury and the Treasury's adoption of tax enforcement policies favoring the wealthy. In addition to documenting the gradual erosion of IRS tax collection efforts, the series focused on the cases of high-income taxpayers who had successfully escaped payment of millions of dollars in taxes owed the government.

THE SELLING OF AN OIL CRISIS

A seven-month, multi-part study on the energy crisis in 1973. The series documented the expansion of the American oil industry abroad at the expense of the American consumer and long-standing federal mismanagement of oil policy matters by the federal government. Ranging from the oil fields of Texas to the oil capitals of Europe, the investigation disclosed, among other things, that at the same time American oil companies were accusing American consumers of being energy wastrels, they were urging Europeans and Asiatics to use more oil.

FOREIGN AID: THE FLAWED DREAM

A seven-month, six-part investigation of the $9-billion-a-year American foreign aid program. In an investigation extending from Bangkok, Thailand to Lima, Peru, the series found that the American aid program was punctuated with profiteering, waste, corruption and deception, and was often aggravating the very problems it had been enacted to help solve.

THE SILENT PARTNER OF HOWARD HUGHES

A seven-month, seven-part investigation of the relationship between the late recluse's business empire and the federal government. Contrary to the image of Hughes as an enterprising capitalist, the series showed that his organization rests mightily on the federal government and is nourished by federal dollars. Since 1965, the series disclosed, Hughes's companies have received more than $6 billion, or $1.7 million a day, in contracts from nearly a dozen different federal agencies and departments.

In the city of Long Beach, California, a series of minor political scandals brought about the dismissal of the city's planning director on charges of bribery.[6] Word of the scandals spread throughout Southern California and ended up on the desk of the metropolitan editor of the *Los Angeles Times*. The editor looked into it, then assigned reporters Mike Goodman and George Reasons to go to work on it. As the two reporters began digging, they noted that major stories dealing with the scandals had been ignored by the local daily newspaper, the *Long Beach Independent Press-Telegram*, a Knight-Ridder publication. So they began investigating the newspaper itself. In short order, they uncovered evidence that Daniel H. Ridder, editor-publisher of the paper, had killed stories dealing with the city's Economic Development Corporation (EDC), an agency in which the paper's leadership was deeply involved. Although the EDC was funded with government grants, it functioned without open meetings or public records, which was a violation of the law.

Donald Barlett and James Steele (Photo by Joan Ruggles, March 1977 issue of the *Quill*, published by the Society of Professional Journalists, Sigma Delta Chi).

Yet this was public business and EDC was accountable. They also found that Ridder and two of his executives helped create "a powerful machine" that committed the city to financial involvement in the Queen Mary liner fiasco and other public projects. These projects were undertaken without voter approval. The manipulating was done by setting up various city-linked agencies; Ridder and his two executives served on the governing boards of six of the agencies. In brief, the story of Long Beach's scandals included a major part played by the local newspaper.

A Paper's Political Ties

Government in the Dark

Goodman and Reasons kept digging and uncovered other stories: a Long Beach city employee had "looted" a public building; an expensive Centrex telephone system had been installed in a city-owned building without benefit of a legal contract; city officials had steered public funds to a firm that promoted Grand Prix races in spite of assurances that public monies would not be involved. Eventually a federal investigation was ordered on the basis of fraud related to the city's poverty programs. The efforts of Goodman and Reasons bore fruit when a new city manager was brought in, charged with undertaking a thorough housecleaning. In this case the First Amendment and the people were served.

A Martyr to the Cause

Don Bolles, a forty-seven-year-old reporter for the *Arizona Republic,* a daily newspaper in Phoenix, had been investigating land fraud and other conflict of interest cases in Arizona. On the night of June 6, 1976, he received word from an informer who said he had information related to the reporter's investigation. Would Bolles meet with him? It appeared routine enough, and Bolles agreed. When Bolles arrived, he parked his car in a lot and went to the appointed place. While he talked with the informant another man planted a bomb beneath his car. When Bolles returned and turned on the ignition, the car exploded in flames. As Bolles lay dying on the street, witnesses heard him mumble the words "Adamson," "Emprise," and "Mafia." He died in a hospital ten days later. As it developed, "Adamson" was the man who planted the bomb. Upon arrest, he turned on his partners in exchange for a twenty-year prison sentence. The other two received the death penalty.[7]

Awards for Excellence

The *Columbia Journalism Review (CJR),* which serves as an evaluator of press performance, frequently singles out journalists, big-time and small-time, who have served the public interest in special ways. A few of their case histories should help to place the reportorial function in perspective, regardless of the size of the publication or broadcast outlet.

Jim Raglin and Michael Holmes of the *Lincoln* (Neb.) *Evening Journal* were cited by *CJR* for uncovering alleged sales of private insurance programs by army personnel to army recruits. Allegations indicated that civilian representatives of the insurance firm were illegally assigned use of army office space, army telephones, and army time to conduct their business.[8] Len Ackland, business writer for the *Des Moines Register,* developed a two-part series that brought to light practices of discrimination by money lenders in home mortgages in Des Moines.[9] Andrew Houlding, of the *New Haven* (Conn.) *Journal-Courier,* investigated illegal wiretapping in the New Haven area. His series resulted in fifty-two civil suits against thirty-six defendants including the Southern New England Telephone Company. Suits were also filed against four agents of the FBI and several former police chiefs.[10] *Time* magazine was cited for a major story on "The American Underclass," a report on the hopelessness of millions of Americans "stuck more or less permanently at the bottom."[11] Four *Post-Newsweek* television stations in Florida were cited for their "Nobody Ever Asked Me" programs, which gave viewers the opportunity to present their personal views on the broadcasting needs of their communities. The live programs were aired through an entire evening of prime time and the stations provided free telephone service for viewers who wished to participate.[12]

Don Bolles (Courtesy of *Arizona Republic*).

Washington Post newsroom (The *Washington Post*).

A sampling of *some* Pulitzer Prize winners from a single year also reflects how the news media work routinely in the public interest: the *Lufkin* (Tex.) *News* was awarded a Pulitzer for their investigation of the death of a local young man at a Marine Corps training base. The paper's revelations led to reforms in Marine Corps recruiting and training methods. Margo Huston, of the *Milwaukee Journal,* was recognized for her compelling series of the plight of the aged. Acel Moore and Wendell Rawls, of the *Philadelphia Inquirer,* received the prize for their coverage of conditions at the Farview (Pa.) State Hospital.

The National Magazine Award for 1977 went to *Philadelphia Magazine* for an article, "Forgotten Children," which exposed the appalling conditions in a state institution for the retarded.[13]

Some Labor without Fanfare

To catalog the names and deeds of only *recent* award winners—selected by journalism reviews such as *CJR,* or the Pulitzer Prize committee, or professional societies and state press associations—would require a sizable volume. There is also a small army of newspeople, especially reporters for small dailies and weeklies and local radio and TV stations, who go about their duties in a fair, responsible manner but are rarely—sometimes never—singled out at all. Nonetheless, a great number of journalists labor day after day to keep their audiences informed about matters that directly affect them and the institutions that chart their lives. But given those laudatory efforts in the public interest, there still remain highly vocal critics in and out of journalism. They complain that much of the press is not responding to what the First Amendment is all about. Hence, a view of the other side of press performance is in order.

Editors at Odds with Public's Needs

A recent Louis Harris survey indicates that the nation's press leadership has badly miscalculated the public's interest in the various categories of news. Harris tapped the views of a cross section of 1,533 adults from the general public, eighty-six top editors and news directors, and seventy-six reputable reporters and writers in the United States. Among other revelations, Harris found that 34 percent of media executives believe that the public is "very interested" in national news. But Harris found that a much higher 60 percent of the public say they have "high interest" in national news. Similarly, 27 percent of the news executives believe that the public has "high interest" in state news. Yet a substantially higher 62 percent of the public say they are "very interested" in events at the state level. These same discrepancies are reflected in other news categories as well, including energy news, science news, business and financial news, and columns and commentaries. In the sports category, a substantial 75 percent of the news people think the public is "very interested" in sports news while only 35 percent of the people expressed that much interest.[14]

If the Harris survey truly reflects the realities of news popularity, and that is likely, the reading and viewing public is being shortchanged in categories of information that it feels it must have. Problems of mass media credibility, discussed in the preceding chapter, are directly linked to mass media content which, in turn, is an integral part of mass media performance. How well or how poorly the press performs is gauged by the public in terms of the total package it gets from the media.

The Four Functions of the Press
The Four Functions Work Together

If we are to accept the traditional notion that the four functions of the press are to inform, to instruct or educate, to mold public opinion, and to entertain, it is essential that they not be segmented as if each functions in isolation from the whole. They function simultaneously, as do the workings of a clock. For example, the entertainment function is not fulfilled only through the comics section. It is fulfilled in the simple act of *reading* the news or watching it on television. Yet a good many modern news executives appear to view the functions as four separate entities, and that view is increasingly mirrored in media content. Entertainment content for entertainment's sake—light, breezy pieces that offer little if any substance—is in many instances taking over news that informs, instructs, and influences the opinion-forming process.

As Harris determined, many judgments made by news executives on media content are frequently wide of the mark. This is puzzling since the press also has access to survey research as do all commercial enterprises with something to sell. The answer seems to be that independent research firms such as the Harris organization present findings that do not jibe with what the news media believe the public wants to view and read. So, the findings are ignored. The Harris findings indicate that in certain categories the gap between the two is substantial. And since other studies, including the one by the Twentieth Century Fund, suggest that the news media not only have credibility woes rooted in content but that they are increasing, it appears logical to ask the media, What are you doing wrong? Better yet, Why are you doing it?

What the reader or viewer *sees* provides the basis for judgments on the value of the messages offered by the media and their *personal* relevance. If the messages are irrelevant—too lofty, too violent, too trivial—the medium that carries them also becomes irrelevant. Hence, it is essential to review the content of the press to determine the kinds of messages the reader or viewer sees, where the problems rest, how they have come to be problems, and why they remain so.

"Rip and Read" Journalism

Even with the many improvements and advances in techniques and technology in the last thirty years, broadcast journalism, radio especially, is still mired in the "rip-and-read" method of delivering news to the public. Not all, but too many, still cling to this stagnant practice. It's a simple, inexpensive procedure, which makes it attractive to those who use it. For example, "ripping" a national or international story from the Associated Press teletype is accepted practice since the station pays for the service. Thus, the news editor feels entitled to use it as he wishes. (Even so, many stations in competitive broadcasting markets prefer to rewrite major wire stories if only to avoid a "sameness" with other stations.)

Nonnews

In other cases, local television stations may subscribe to syndicated filmed or taped feature services that treat a variety of "nonnews" subjects. On a given evening, say, a small station in Michigan might supplement its local fare with some items selected from the syndicated material. Thus, the viewer is treated to a feature dealing with a rodeo winner in Oklahoma, a bathing beauty in Savannah, a state fair in Wyoming. The question must obviously arise, how well are the Michigan viewers being served via doses of trivia from Oklahoma, Savannah, and Wyoming? The practice is common.

Another questionable practice in the rip-and-read school of broadcast journalism frequently occurs when the local broadcast station is owned by the local newspaper, in which case the announcer might read the news directly from the newspaper without benefit of alterations. This even happens when the broadcast station has no ties whatever with the local newspaper. Many television and radio executives denounce the practice as unprofessional, but it goes on nonetheless. A case in point: a reporter for the *St. Louis Globe-Democrat* took a day off to go fishing. As he sat bobbing about in his boat, line dangling in the water, he turned on his portable radio to catch the early news. One story in particular caught his attention not so much for what it said but for *how* it was said. It was, word for word, the exact story he had filed with his newspaper editor the evening before. Not a word had been changed. "I nearly fell out of the boat," he said.[15] When news content reflects a dismal "sameness" in the eyes and minds of the audience, the audience has a problem, but the news media have a greater one. A news outlet, print or broadcast, cannot have a credibility crisis and blame it on the public. That's arrogance at its worst. It also does critical harm to First Amendment guarantees.

The St. Louis Fisherman

Manipulating the News

Network Sameness

The corporate leaders of the three major television networks, CBS, NBC, and ABC, all headquartered in New York City, have been charged at various times with scheduling the content of their nationwide evening shows on the basis of the stories clustered on the front page of the *New York Times* each morning. For the last fifteen years, prime time television news on all three networks has consisted largely of what one critic calls "a predictable muchness—earnest, responsible, muted." And what appears on the tubes are "three look-alike, sedately animated versions of the *New York Times.*"[16]

Sameness in news content goes beyond even the questionable tactics outlined here. It also includes categories of news that seem to appear and reappear regardless of the medium carrying them. As one Washington-based observer commented, "Why is it that such a high percentage of news is negative not merely in content but in tone: is it catering to a human need for bad news, or is it creating such a need?"[17] Part of the answer, if not all, appears to be a kind of "negative revolution" in the press along with an onslaught of trivia.

As stated earlier, news executives seem to be caught in a peculiar bind between giving the public what it wants and giving it what it needs to function in a democratic society. To concentrate on what media consumers *want* is acceptable if it is also what they *need to know.* If the latter is not the major consideration in formulating news content, the public is not much better served than are those in totalitarian states where content is strictly determined by government, prior to publication. There it's called censorship, which is a dirty word in the American press system. The end results are not far apart, however. In the American scheme of things, if content is not based on what the people *need* then it is trivia, i.e., the kind of content intended to amuse or horrify or entertain primarily for the emotional charge it offers. It need not have basic value of any kind.

"Trivial" news wins out over "honest" news. (Illustration by Marcus Hamilton, from the October 1977 issue of the *Quill,* published by the Society of Professional Journalists, Sigma Delta Chi.)

The news media have always had room for news of fundamental human interest, even for chitchat, if it genuinely informs the audience of, say, the drama of human relationships. The issue is not one of presenting only news stories that shake the earth—stories of wars, pestilence, and sin in high places—versus secondary or even minor news stories. The issue is one of news versus nonnews or, more appropriately, "junk news." The bust size of a Hollywood starlet (along with an appropriately angled photograph) might be stirring to some, but it is hardly *news*. Yet the sentimental portrayal of a gnarled old World War I veteran rescuing a child's kitten from a garage fire is *news*. It is minor news, but it is *news* that portrays strong human involvement, which, in turn, reminds readers that the world is not all wars, pestilence, and sin in high places—or busty starlets for that matter. That dimension has always been well received in the news media and by consumers of news. Even within the strict time constraints of television newscasts, CBS occasionally finds time for Charles Kuralt's award-winning "On the Road," which is based soundly on the identity between human beings.

"Trivia" in the news media is something else again. Syndicated columnist Sydney J. Harris called for the establishment of an annual award to be given to the newspaperman or woman who "most consistently avoided running a popular topic into the ground."[18]

Manufacturing the News

A *Saturday Review* editorial titled, "Manufacturing the News," questions whether the news media really give Americans the vital information they need to participate in debates over crucial major issues. The editorial cited a statement by Secretary General Kurt Waldheim on the efforts of the United Nations to reverse the trends in the arms race. Waldheim pointed to the potential dangers of spiraling competition between nations for military spending which, in coming years, would reach $300 billion. The statement was worthy of coverage both in terms of its content and the man who made it. But it didn't impress the news media. Even in New York, the home of the United Nations, the media gave far greater coverage to the city council's efforts to control pornography than to Waldheim's effort to contain a destructive international threat which, if unchecked, could one day make the earth "as barren as Mars." The *Saturday Review* rankled: "Are we to believe that the issue of human survival is less important than whether a massage parlor should be located 300 or 500 feet from a residential neighborhood?"[19]

In a bit of comic relief, television journalist Joanne Shore offers an example of how nonnews, or trivia, mixes with the heavy stuff on the evening news:

> Good evening, this is Larry Kane for "Action News." The Philippines were wiped out by a tidal wave this morning and a Manayunk man was killed along with 337 other passengers aboard a 747 Jumbo Jet that crashed into the Empire State Building. But the big story on "Action News" tonight is in North Philadelphia where a seventeen-year-old girl won a $2,000 lottery.[20]

Ron Powers, former television critic for the *Chicago Sun-Times,* won a Pulitzer Prize for his analyses of television performance.[21] Now critic-at-large for WMAQ-TV, Chicago, he offers keen insights into the trivia problem as it exists within one of Chicago's major television outlets.

The Critic at Work

To arrive at his conclusions, Powers observed the content of one evening's hour-long local news program. The lead story, comparable to a page one banner headline story in a newspaper, contained filmed closeups of grim-faced policemen wearing sunglasses and toting loaded shotguns as they warily crept toward a school building that reportedly concealed a murder suspect. The television cameras reflected the excitement and tension on the faces of spectators. Then the police charged the school building! More tension on the faces! A brief wait and the police came out hauling a man with them!

When the coverage ended, the anchor revealed to his emotionally upended viewers that, as things turned out, the man was not the murder suspect at all. He was just an innocent person who happened to be in the school. The station's news team, Powers pointed out, knew that fact before the evening news went on the air. But the anchor kept it from the audience because the film footage provided a dramatic opener. The story was a nonstory; it was junk. The viewers had been cheated!

Following that, Powers went on, the weatherman clowned around with a forsythia bush via trick camera work, while his off-camera colleagues yucked it up for the folks at home. Then a reporter did a segment on a swim program at the South Shore YMCA in which an inspired instructor teaches children to swim by throwing them into the deep end of the pool. All of that and more, one hour's worth, was presented with copious chucklings and elbow-in-the-ribs humor, all of which suggests that, across the board, there were few problems in Chicago, or the world, that day.

More Hijinks

Powers has seen it elsewhere too. Station WMAL-TV in Washington ran a film clip in which reporter Betsy Ashton read a report dealing with a will of the late Howard Hughes—while seated in a cemetery. At KTTV, Los Angeles, the coanchor persons took turns reading the *lead* stories on the evening news. One was about a pending bill in the Tennessee legislature promoting a state fossil and another about a misprint in a newspaper piece about a "Mary Hartman" joining the planning commission. At WKYC-TV, Cleveland, comedienne Judy Carne made a sudden appearance in the news room during a broadcast and started playing with the newsman's ears.

Yucking It up on the Air

The onrush of trivia is by no means restricted to television. It is reflected increasingly in the pages of the garish tabloids that are sold in supermarkets, and in standard papers that have changed content and makeup in hopes of coping with circulation losses. It is reflected in gossip-oriented magazines of recent vintage in the style of *People* and a variety of others. Even the relatively staid *New York Times* now advertises itself as offering "a lot more than news." The *Times* has also launched a chitchat publication of its own called *Us,* along the lines of *People.*

Trivia and the Print Media

The grinding out of trivia. (Illustration by Becky Iobst, *Washington Journalism Review*.)

Why Trivia?

Why trivia? Is there really a national preoccupation with lightweight amusement as opposed to hard information that people must have if they are to maintain democratic order? The answer appears to depend on one's view. Without doubt, it is a media issue of significant proportions that is likely to be with us for some time.

Media observer Cable Neuhaus states his position succinctly: "What is occurring is that media analysts and 'product packagers'—people professionally disposed toward advertisers and revenues—are increasingly aiming their mass journalism at Joe Sixpack. There is profit in it. The trivialization of the news has begun—with a vengeance."[22]

Losses in Newspaper Circulations

According to Fergus Bordewich, another media observer, 61.3 million Americans once purchased a newspaper each day, an all-time high.[23] But by 1977, 2.5 million people had stopped doing so. The circulation losses affected 287 daily newspapers that cover cities having populations of over 100,000—the big cities. To counter those losses, some newspaper editors and publishers have been reaching out for ways and means of stemming the tide. The same thing is happening to television stations where competition for viewers and the advertising dollar are keen. In both media, the target is *content*. And the question is, Can content be altered or "packaged" in new, sufficiently compelling ways that will attract and hold desired audiences? While many media executives insist that "marketing" the news pays off, others insist that better journalism is the only solution to the problem.

Changing News Content

For example, in the newspaper industry, survival is tied directly to circulation, the number of readers who regularly purchase newspapers. Total paid circulation is the barometer that determines how much the paper will receive in advertising income. The higher the circulation, the higher the income. Problems arise when advertising falls off for whatever reason, and the newspaper's management is stuck with producing and distributing the high circulation newspaper. The cost per copy does not pay for production and distribution. Therefore, to maintain a reasonable balance between the two, some news executives are "consigning their papers to the well-scrubbed hands of professional consultants who insist that the market alone ought to determine what is news." In short, the news media should market news just as other products are marketed—cosmetics, cars, diapers, or beer. For that to work one must offer to the people what they *want* even if it is not what they need. And if a newspaper is to remain competitive, it must provide the reader with more appealing "products" than the opposition does. To many news executives, that strategy calls for greater emphasis on *content that entertains* rather than on hard news whose basic function is to inform.

Marketing Content

News, Diapers, and Beer

Surveys indicate two other important changes: (1) newspapers are losing advertising income to television; (2) the number of newspaper readers in the eighteen to thirty age group is declining and that age group includes those who are most dissatisfied with the traditional newspaper format. Other factors behind changes in readership and advertising income include possible increases in illiteracy among the young; increased unemployment; the problems of distributing newspapers in urban areas with their guarded high-rise apartment buildings; high crime rates; and the increased mobility of the American people. Finally, there is the major problem of increasing production costs, especially among metropolitan papers.

Current Newspaper Problems

What are the options available to newspapers? Raising the price per copy to help meet increasing expenses has traditionally been resisted by readers accustomed to a low purchase price. Some habits are not easily changed and this is one of them. The *Boston Globe* serves as a prime example. When that popular paper raised the price of its Sunday edition from fifty to seventy-five cents to meet increased costs, it lost 98,000 paying readers in a single stroke.

Solutions?

Dilemma of the Boston Globe

And advertisers are increasingly wary of paying high rates for space in newspapers whose circulations are falling off. So newspapers, feeling the pinch at both ends—circulation and advertising income—are turning to new strategies in an effort to shore up sagging financial bases.

Problems of Broadcasters

Broadcasting news is feeling pains of its own. Television stations and networks also rely on audience numbers for their income. In this case, advertising rates are based on survey estimates of how many viewers watch what and when. Competition for viewers with other stations and other media is heavy. Thus, television is also looking for ways to develop and hold audience support.

Table 3.1 Cost Per Copy Increases among Daily and Sunday Newspapers in U.S., U.S. Territories, and Canada, 1966-1975

	1966	1967	1968	1969	Daily Newspapers 1970	1971	1972	1973	1974	1975
Number of Daily Newspapers Selling at:										
3–9 Cents	636	449	251	151	88	54	43	31	31	13
10 Cents	1,212	1,392	1,589	1,680	1,606	1,481	1,407	1,316	832	433
11–14 Cents	1	2	2	9	8	23	36	29	12	6
15 Cents	4	5	9	19	146	290	350	476	938	1,237
16–19 Cents	0	0	0	0	0	0	0	0	2	1
20 Cents	2	2	3	3	5	5	4	4	42	157
21–24 Cents	0	0	0	0	0	0	0	0	2	0
25 Cents	0	0	0	0	1	1	1	1	4	13
30 Cents	0	0	0	0	0	1	1	2	0	1
Average (Mean) Price (Cents)	8.6	9.0	9.5	9.7	10.2	10.7	10.9	11.3	12.7	14.3

					Sunday Newspapers					
Number of Sunday Newspapers Selling at:										
1–9 Cents	23	17	9	6	2	1	1	0	2	0
10 Cents	140	120	104	91	90	79	79	74	64	37
11–14 Cents	1	0	0	0	0	0	0	0	0	0
15 Cents	171	173	160	145	116	94	90	89	68	61
16–19 Cents	0	0	0	0	0	0	0	0	0	0
20 Cents	166	161	161	160	140	126	127	97	66	49
21–24 Cents	0	0	1	0	0	0	0	0	0	0
25 Cents	58	81	101	128	163	183	194	222	203	173
30 Cents	5	5	17	16	30	47	46	56	49	62
35 Cents	1	3	11	26	35	43	42	51	112	157
40 Cents	0	1	0	0	3	6	8	10	27	37
45 Cents	0	0	0	0	0	0	0	0	3	3
50 Cents	0	0	1	1	4	6	5	7	23	51
55 Cents	0	0	0	0	0	0	0	0	0	1
60 Cents	0	0	0	0	0	0	0	0	1	4
75 Cents	0	0	0	0	0	0	0	0	1	1
Average (Mean) Price (Cents)	16.0	16.8	18.1	19.1	20.5	21.8	21.8	22.7	25.8	29.1

SOURCE: "Facts About Newspapers," 1979, American Newspaper Publishers Association.

More than a dozen consulting firms are in active business in the United States for the purpose of providing the communications media with content tailored to the desires and interests of their particular audiences. They are not particularly interested in *needs* but in the blend of content that will seize and hold audience attention. The firms employ market research techniques to determine what is popular among a mass audience and what is not.

When a newspaper or broadcast outlet accepts the assistance of a media "doctor," as the firms are sometimes called, all facets of the medium, within and without, are carefully picked over and explored. The market researchers survey the medium's audience in terms of age, average income, social class, and education. They also take a careful look at the newspaper or broadcast station itself: the news budget; staff numbers (how many, how effective—in the case of television, how "popular"); equipment; corporate structure; and the thinking of management. When all the data are in, the researchers feed them to the computer. The results in hand, they then make recommendations for changes in content (and sometimes in personnel) based on what is high and what is low on the audience preference list.

As Robert Scheer, of the *Los Angeles Times,* puts it, the result is that news "must be continually sliced up, wrapped, renamed, and resold with the emphasis on product differentiation, e.g., Eyewitness News, Action News, Newscenter 4."[24] The public gets what the researchers *say* they want. Media executives say that the system works and that it pays off financially. Others are disturbed at the trends, whether they pay off at the cash register or not. Cable Neuhaus commented:

> It is harder now than ever before to locate serious, dispassionate (for the moment forget interesting) news coverage. The vaguely amusing and the hideously voyeuristic have ascended to a level of acceptance whereby they are in danger of perceptibly redefining news and standards of news coverage.[25]

The media packagers pressure editors to de-emphasize stories that are not widely read (but which might be important) in favor of those that are heavy in entertainment content (even if less important or unimportant). A case in point is the *Detroit News*. With circulation losses of more than 65,000 in two years, the paper's leadership called for an increase in "fine examples" of rapes, robberies, and auto accidents on page one.

Page one, traditionally the billboard for the major news events of the day, has, in many cases, become the showcase of what the disenchanted call "blatant trivia." It includes stories that titillate, horrify, amuse, or tug at the heartstrings. But their importance or relevance is questionable in terms of the major world, national, regional, state, and local events on which citizens are supposed to base decisions.[26]

While addressing a meeting of CBS affiliates, a usually composed Walter Cronkite commented on these matters in straightforward, concerned terms:

> There is no newsman worth his salt who does not know that advisers who dictate that no item should run more than 45 seconds, that there must be a film story within the first 30 seconds of the newscast, and that it must have action in it— a barn burning or a jack-knifed tractor-trailer will do—that calls a 90-second film piece a ''mini-documentary,'' that advises against covering city hall because it is dull, that says the anchorman or woman must do all voiceovers for ''identity''— any real newsman knows that sort of stuff is balderdash. It's cosmetic—pretty packaging—not substance.[27]

Alternative Solutions   Again, many news people and media observers protest that employing scientifically marketed trivia in place of badly needed information is not the solution to the circulation and advertising problems of America's mass media. Speaking of the newspaper industry, Fergus Bordewich offers an alternative:

> The need . . . is to create newspapers that more people will read. But few editors are talking about reporting more news and analyzing more deeply the news they do report; few are talking about developing more effective ways of explaining the complexities of politics, the urban crisis, the environment, science, or economics to their readers.[28]

An Optional Course   In this squabble over giving the public what it wants or what it needs, it is certain that many media outlets seem to be leaning more toward entertainment than toward the other functions of the press. But at least one study suggests that public demand for meaningful information continues to hold fast. The recent findings of the Newspaper Readership Project confirm that consumers of broadcast and print journalism are generally the same people, "that hard news is what they most want, and that younger citizens are less trivia-minded than some had deduced."[29]

Making Quality Work   One who resists gimmickry in making news interesting and attractive to the audience is James L. Snyder, for many years the man in charge of the number one news station in Washington, D.C. A veteran of twenty-six years in television news, Snyder is respected by reporters for being dedicated to providing them a professional atmosphere in which to work, financial support for meaningful investigative projects, and his personal guidance and expertise. The result: Snyder has produced one of the best news operations anywhere. He downplays murders, blood and guts tragedies, and other trappings that monopolize the content of other stations. "I don't have any magic formulas," Snyder said. "What we've done here is hire the best reporters and put them to work." In line with his insistence that the news be meaningful to his viewers, Snyder set up a three-hour, live show in prime time to hear the complaints of viewers and to respond constructively to them.[30]

Walter Cronkite (CBS News Photo).

Other cases-in-point: after suffering sizable circulation losses prior to 1970, the *Los Angeles Times* increased its circulation by 82,000 between 1970 and 1975 in spite of the fact that the population of Los Angeles declined by 80,000 over the same period. It succeeded by giving reporters the time and space to develop in-depth, total coverage of important events, not by watering down the product in the interest of entertainment alone. The *Philadelphia Inquirer* and the *Long Island* (N.Y.) *Newsday* did much the same thing. Again, they reversed dropping circulations by overtly seeking readers via heavier diets of good writing and analytic reporting—not fluff. As for journalistic "breeziness," Bordewich commented: "Many papers are becoming so breezy you can hear the whistling through the holes where the news might have been."[31]

William H. Hornby, executive editor of the *Denver Post,* fears that "marketing" news content on the basis of what is popular will cause the press to overlook its constitutional mandate to give the people what they need to know to function in a democratic society.[32]

How the
L.A. Times *Did It*

The observations of Marquis Childs, referred to in chapter 2, determined that many Americans, young people especially, do not understand the origin or meaning of the First Amendment. A study completed by the National Assessment of Educational Progress found that nearly all teenagers could identify the president of the United States by name, but fewer than half could give

The State of the First Amendment

the name of *one* of their elected senators or name their representatives in the House of Representatives. This federally sponsored survey tested 145,000 teenagers in 1970, 1972, and 1976 "to chart their political knowledge and attitudes." In line with the findings of Marquis Childs, the survey determined that the ability of seventeen-year-olds to explain the basic concept of democracy—government by the people through majority rule—declined over the time period from 86 percent to 74 percent. In the thirteen-year-old category, the ability to explain those concepts fell from 53 percent to 42 percent.[33]

If the future of the American democratic system rests in the hands of today's youth, as it surely must, the nation might be hard pressed to find capable, effective leaders in the years to come. That is especially significant if the press relinquishes, in whole or in part, its vital position in the people-press-government connection; the hub of the wheel needs to be strengthened, not weakened. As Neuhaus noted, "Better, as a nation, that we should suffer some earnest boredom than a blizzard of cuteness that makes us smile. And makes us dullards."[34]

Packaged Violence

Violence as a form of marketable news seems to be at the top of the best-seller charts of marketing recommendations. It is especially recognizable in two categories that increasingly receive major local and national coverage by all the news media: terrorism and murder. It is not so terrible that coverage is provided to such events but rather *how* the events are sometimes covered. Critics in and out of the media have labelled them "media events," i.e., events that are ballooned out of importance to attract audiences and, thus, sell newspapers or broadcasting time.

Covering Terrorist Activities

As a major news event, terrorism is a relative newcomer at least in its current form. A major concern of law enforcement people is that unreasonable press coverage might tend to popularize acts of terrorism among other deranged or dissident individuals or groups. They also fear that overblown coverage might encourage someone involved in a terrorist act to hold out longer or to go to lengths not originally planned. These possibilities pose potential disaster for those caught up in them. Psychologist Robert A. Baron, of Purdue University, says that seeing detailed accounts of terrorist activity on television not only gives "unstable people the idea of doing the same, but also teaches them exactly how to go about it—it cuts out trial and error."[35] At the same time, these incidents qualify as news and must be covered. Again, it is not the news media's coverage of terrorism that creates the problems, it is *how* it is covered. A few actual examples highlight the finer points involved.

In 1977, Anthony Kiritsis, a frustrated Indianapolis land developer, made a hostage of Richard Hall, president of a mortgage company. Two days later, police trailed the pair to Kiritsis's apartment and waited for the terrorist to make his next move. More than sixty hours later, he emerged with a loaded shotgun wired to Hall's neck, the muzzle resting at the base of his skull. A hastily arranged pressroom was set up so that Kiritsis could address his grievances to newspaper and television reporters. When all was ready, Kiritsis shoved Hall into the room bellowing, "Get those goddamned cameras on! Get those cameras on! I want the people to see this man!" He then launched into a bitter verbal assault on the mortgage company, his rantings flavored with obscenities. The three local television stations carried it live and before long the networks were hooked into it. The terrorist raged on: "I'm a goddamned national hero and don't you forget it!" Through all the haranguing, Hall stood stiffly, the gun muzzle brushing his neck. Eventually, Hall was released and Kiritsis arrested and jailed.

Terrorism in Indianapolis

Public and media reactions to the event were mixed. One Indianapolis television station eventually returned to regular programming in the belief that continued live coverage would only encourage others to "hold up" television stations. The general manager of another local station elected to stay with it because: "As responsible journalists, we couldn't walk away from the story." Most of the 250 viewers who wrote to the station disapproved of the decision. The third local station announced at one point that it would discontinue coverage but, feeling that the terrorist was about to give up, decided to hold on. Of the thirty or so letters received by that station, most criticized the foul language. And what if Kiritsis had shot his victim to death on live television? The news director of the third station replied: "I was nervous about that. But it was the biggest breaking story in the country at the time."[36]

Mixed Reactions

Steven Yount, news director of an Indianapolis radio station later wrote that the news media "made a mistake" in covering the Kiritsis story as they had. It was a mistake in three parts: (1) the media gave the kidnapper everything he wanted, which made hostages of the reporters; (2) the media portrayed Kiritsis as the helpless victim of big business rather than a gun-wielding kidnapper who held a man's life in his hands; (3) because they agreed with a police request not to report anything that might upset Kiritsis, reporters became part of a police plan to fool a kidnapper rather than remaining independent servants of the people. Yount also emphasized that the media must cover crimes as *crimes,* that news like the Kiritsis situation "cannot be written off as excusable forms of social protest."[37]

Response from a Broadcaster

Anthony Kiritsis (Wide World Photos).

In March 1977, a dozen terrorists who identified themselves as Hanafi Muslims, rivals of the much larger Black Muslim group, seized three Washington, D.C., buildings and 134 hostages whom they held for thirty-eight gruelling hours. It was evident from the outset that Hanafi Muslim leaders sought publicity just as Anthony Kiritsis had. The news media obliged by coming out in packs. (The *Washington Post* sent twenty-six reporters.) Television cameras and crews popped up everywhere. At one point a television

camera panned down a street where police were unloading a truck, and the reporter breathlessly informed his viewers that the boxes were filled with ammunition. As it turned out, the boxes contained only food. A police sergeant on the scene commented that making such an irresponsible statement on live television might have had tragic results had the Hanafi Muslim leadership heard it.[38]

The actions of the Hanafi Muslims on this occasion certainly qualified as a news event, which the media are entitled to cover. Again, it is *how* such an event is covered that may place innocent hostages in danger. As *Time* magazine commented, "The terrorists made dramatically clear what has become all too obvious: anybody with a cause and a gun, be he mad or madcap, fanatic or eccentric, can seize and hold national attention by kidnapping and threat-

ening to kill innocent victims." Dean George Gerbner, of the Annenberg School of Communication, University of Pennsylvania, called the coverage a "media event." He charged that press handling of the Hanafi Muslims's takeover was "an act of terrorism" designed to build newspaper circulations and broadcast ratings. "Cameramen began covering cameramen covering the story," he said.[39]

Reprinted by permission of the Chicago Tribune-New York News Syndicate, Inc.

The debate continued from both sides. Delayed news coverage—or worse, no coverage at all—would create wild rumors, for it could hardly be kept secret that a person or group had seized a building and hostages. As Richard Simon, formerly of the Los Angeles Police Department, said, "If truth is not good, it's better than rumors, which are generally horrible."[40]

Police View

Maurice R. Cullinane, Washington, D.C. police chief, would like to see greater cooperation between law enforcement people and the press in dealing with terrorists. He believes that the press can cover such events thoroughly and without police interference and still not endanger the innocent or plant terrorist ideas in the minds of other social or mental misfits. To accomplish that, he urges that police and press get together and develop workable strategies acceptable to both.[41] At least one newsman appears ready to support the idea. Charles Fenyvesi, a reporter on the staff of the *National Jewish Monthly* and one of the hostages taken by the Hanafi Muslims, has seen the workings of terrorism from the inside. Fenyvesi urges journalists to adopt a "Life Over Scoop" posture when covering terrorist activities, warning that their actions could "stoke, stir or trigger" terrorists into killing people.[42]

An Eyewitness's View

On October 6, 1975, a twenty-three-year-old drifter named Ray "Cat" Olsen held ten hostages in a New York City bank for eight hours, demanding that authorities release Patty Hearst and jailed members of the Symbionese Liberation Army. He also demanded $10 million in gold. Olsen eventually surrendered and released the hostages.

Other Cases

On January 7, 1976, a forty-year-old man named Miklos Petrovics made hostages of two employees in a Culver City, California bank. He demanded that the bank's air be filtered through bird seed, that the bank manager "cleanse himself in the ocean," and that "everyone join hands, walk to the ocean and meditate."

On March 7, 1977, twenty-five-year-old Cory Moore disarmed a police captain in Warrensville Heights, Ohio, demanded that President Carter apologize for black oppression in America, and that "all white people leave the planet within seven days."[43] As authorities tried to reason with the terrorist, a mobile television unit zeroed in on positions where police sharpshooters had been secretly placed. The reporter informed his viewers of that fact—on live television! He did not know that Moore had a television set with him and when he saw the sharpshooters, he screamed with rage, "Everything's off right now!" Eventually he released the police captain and was taken into custody.

There have been other terrorist acts in the United States and there are likely to be more. As for press coverage of those events, Stuart H. Loory, managing editor of the *Chicago Sun-Times,* urges that the press "start thinking about the ways people like terrorists are using us. We have become part of the story."[44]

The Son of Sam Case

As bad as terrorist activities in the United States have been, thus far the country has been spared bloodbaths. But the archtypical study in marketable human slaughter has to be the case of New York's Son of Sam, a classic "media event."[45]

The murders in New York of six young victims and the wounding of seven others in little more than a year began on July 19, 1976. The story was seized by local and then national media in a manner and style reminiscent of the Jazz Journalism of the Roaring Twenties. The worst journalistic offenders were easily the *New York Daily News* and the *New York Post.* The *Post* had been recently purchased by Australian newspaper tycoon Rupert Murdoch and converted from a journal of commentary to a jazzed up tabloid in the tradition of the old *New York Daily Graphic.*

The Daily News and the Post

The New Yorker Responds

Throughout the period that preceded the arrest of a suspect, the *Daily News* and the *Post* raged repeatedly about the killer on the loose, demanding increased police action and terrifying the people of New York in an onslaught of sensationalism that Americans had not witnessed in generations. It became so bizarre that the *New Yorker* magazine composed a high-level editorial evaluation of the performances of the city's news media, giving particular attention to those two papers. The *New Yorker* allowed that the case was newsworthy and that the press was entitled to report it. But in the matter of *how* it was covered, the magazine judged that the sensationalism employed, particularly by the *News* and the *Post,* made a bad situation worse for residents of the city:

> By transforming a killer into a celebrity, the press has not merely encouraged but perhaps driven him to strike again—and may have stirred others brooding madly over their grievances to act. He has a public reputation now and must live up to it.

Breslin's Anniversary Gift

The *New Yorker* added that "the right of the press to report the news has been asserted by the tabloid press's reporting more nonnews than this city has seen since the Mad Bomber was captured in 1957." The editorial offered a compelling example in the person of Jimmy Breslin of the *Daily News.* On the first anniversary of the slaying of Son of Sam's initial victim, Breslin wrote as if addressing the then-unidentified killer. The following, written in third person, is excerpted from the Breslin piece as quoted in the *New Yorker:*

> Is tomorrow night, July 29, so significant to him (Son of Sam) that he must go out and walk the night streets and find a victim? Or will he sit alone and look out his attic window and be thrilled by his power, this power that will have him in the newspapers and on television and in the thoughts and conversations of most of the young people in the city?
> I don't know. Nobody else does either. For we deal here with the night wind.

The Post *Keeps Up*

The *New York Post* also remembered the first anniversary of Son of Sam's initial strike. This tabloid devoted its centerfold to the story, including photographs of the street where the first victim had lived, the office from which police tried to coordinate their search for the killer, another victim who had been wounded a few months before, a civilian patrol unit in Pelham Bay, and a clock in the police squad room.

The coverage intensified as the number of victims increased. Among other items on the case, the *Post* ran a front-page appeal to Son of Sam to surrender—to the *Post* of course.

David Berkowitz Arrested

At 10:30 P.M. on August 10, 1977, twenty-four-year-old David Berkowitz was arrested as a suspect in the case.[46] The following day the *Post* came out with a large headline in red ink that read "CAUGHT!" accompanied by a photograph of the suspect beneath. A subhead read, "Son of Sam Was On Way to Kill Again." The *Post* also quoted Berkowitz as saying, "I wanted to go out in a blaze of glory," suggesting, as the *New Yorker* observed in a second editorial, that the "blaze" was the idea of a grossly irresponsible newspaper. Not until the first sentence of the accompanying article did the

Caricature of David Berkowitz as a media "event." (Illustration by Kenneth Stark, from the November 1977 issue of the *Quill*, published by the Society of Professional Journalists, Sigma Delta Chi.)

Post qualify its private trial and conviction of the suspect with the line, "The man police say is the Son of Sam."

The *Post* also ran ten pages of copy of the arrest beneath another red headline, "Inside the Killer's Lair," with a story describing the interior of the suspect's apartment which, though sealed by police, had been broken into by three newspaper photographers. Five photographs highlighted that story.

The *Post* also carried a story that suggested that various persons were out to kill Berkowitz, which, if nothing else, might have convinced another deranged mind that somebody should.

There is no need to include further *Post* coverage of the arrest except for one gem that was probably the most accurate arrangement of words of all: Another headline—"Post Sells a Million." The story's lead read: "The *Post* sold more than a million copies yesterday—the highest since June 6, 1968—the day Senator Robert Kennedy was shot." This was true except that the date was incorrect. The *Post* had gone all-out to sell newspapers—and succeeded.

At the *Daily News* building, Jimmy Breslin was as dedicated to convicting Berkowitz in print as the rival *Post* was. "His name was [*sic*] David Berkowitz and he told cops he was the .44 killer who used the name 'Son of Sam'," Breslin wrote in spite of the fact that the suspect had not yet been charged with any crime.

When Rupert Murdoch was asked in an interview if Berkowitz had been *convicted* by the New York press, he replied directly, "Yes and that's bad."[47]

Television Coverage

While the *Post* and the *Daily News* were far ahead of New York's other news media in celebrating the arrest of David Berkowitz, television stations tried their best to compete. Though there was a substantial amount of other worthwhile news to be covered that first day following the arrest, New Yorkers were hard pressed to find it. In what *Saturday Review* called "an example of a news team more concerned with garnering ratings than with gathering news," WABC-TV offered two and one-half hours of special coverage of the arrest, including film coverage of Berkowitz's arraignment.[48] With considerable drama, reporter Rose Ann Scamardella informed viewers that she and her crew had "managed to get in a back door" to the precinct house and get close enough to the suspect to see his "cold, very blue, piercing eyes." She filled out the remainder of her segment of the show by reflecting on her emotional state as a result of her experiences that memorable day. She had been "shaken" by it all.

Leading Questions

Another WABC-TV reporter interviewed patrons at one of many discotheques on Long Island. His question: "What do you think would have happened if (Berkowitz had) walked into the disco with a machine gun?" "I don't know," came one response. "The place would have been a mess."

Other reporters from both print and broadcast media spread out in a frenzied effort to uncover hot copy of their own. The search included goading survivors of Son of Sam's bullets into making vengeful statements, such as,

"What would you do if you had Berkowitz in this room with you now?" Reporters even interviewed each other in order to pad out the thrill aspect of the Son of Sam story.

Jim Frisinger, a Michigan journalist, attempted to assess the media coverage as it developed around the country. He ended up wondering, with the great media splash evident everywhere, if David Berkowitz could get a fair trial anywhere in the country. "The most striking aspects of the coverage," Frisinger wrote, "was its failure to adhere to the most fundamental professional standards. There was flagrant disregard of the accused's rights to presumed innocence and a repeated failure to attribute to sources the 'facts' and 'evidence' in the case."[49]

Two journalists in Wisconsin questioned why, in what was really a local story, did television networks give it ten or more minutes on the evening news. And why, they wondered, was it necessary for the news media to scrounge out a picture of Berkowitz's graduation class and to interview his neighbors. "It was hysteria for sure," they concluded, "and a blatant way for unprofessional journalists to capitalize on a tragedy."[50]

Sensationalized coverage of the Son of Sam tragedy, or any others, is not calculated in the long run to win friends for the news media, especially at a time when they are already suffering critical losses in the popularity polls. It only furthers the already-critical problems of credibility and makes the First Amendment appear to be little more than a license to commit mayhem for the sake of profit. As Carll Tucker of The *Saturday Review* wrote:

> Newsmen in a free society must balance the obligation to report the facts against the necessity to excite an audience. When news organizations start opting for hype in the guise of news, they risk the fate of the boy who cried wolf: when a real crisis comes, nobody will take them seriously.[51]

© Tony Auth, The *Philadelphia Inquirer*.

News Packaging Defended

One defender of the marketing, or packaging, of news is Philip Meyer of the Knight-Ridder newspapers. Meyer, a specialist in applying social science research methods to journalism, feels that the conflict between market research and the ideal of press responsibility to the public is "more imagined than real," that marketing need not result in "flashy graphics, chopped-up news summaries and fluffy entertainment in place of solid information about public affairs."

As evidence, Meyer points to the decline in newspaper readers in the total population of the United States even though the national population has increased. He points out that the "success" reflected by newspapers that have opted for light, breezy news and flashy designs for their pages is not supported by research findings. In brief, the drastic changes are not working. Indeed, Meyer emphasizes, research findings indicate that people want *news* in their newspapers and prefer traditional page designs to the newer, splashy layouts.

The Globe's *New Designs*

He cites the *Boston Globe* as an example. When management decided to consider new designs for its pages, the *Globe* leadership undertook a survey to tap reader preferences. They offered readers five different formats to be rated in preference from one to five. The newer "splashy" designs came in last while the paper's current format was rated second. The first choice of those surveyed was a design more conservative than the present one, similar to the look abandoned by the paper two years before. Meyer adds:

> This case illustrates the kind of thing that hard research data are most likely to show. If you are really desperate to innovate, you will have to go beyond (research) data. Helping editors to take that dangerous leap into the unknown may be the real function of the newspaper doctors.[52]

It should seem obvious from recent significant developments in technology within the mass media that the operation of the American press and the gathering and disseminating of meaningful information is undergoing, and will continue to undergo, dramatic changes. Johannes Gutenberg revolutionized printing in the fifteenth century when he introduced movable type. Then came high-speed presses that created mass circulation journalism, and the inventions of the telegraph and the linotype machine—all brought radical changes to the information media in their own time. Presently, computerized typesetting, electronic editing, and other developments have made relics of equipment and systems that were essential only a few years ago.

It also seems apparent that survey research, for better or worse, will be an important part of the process of communication. That need not terrify anyone who is dedicated to a free press in a democratic society. In the final equation, the human element is present and needs to keep a rein on the communication process. If the behavioral sciences can help deliver an improved, low cost product to the American people, all to the good. If, however, the marketing people sell media the notion that they must cater to the lowest common denominator, if media's future is to be dedicated to junk news, nonnews, and trivia for the sake of hiking sales, nothing will be won and much will be lost. In its broadest application to the mass media, technology can be a valuable asset if it is tempered by human elements within the media—the publishers, editors, reporters, and audience, who absorb, interpret, consume, and apply it—with the proviso that the horse not run off with the rider. The performance of the communications media in the years to come—what they do and, more importantly, how they do it—will determine the shape and hue of their image in the public mind. It will also determine to what extent they will be supported and believed by the American people. The media already face credibility problems and the First Amendment has grown weary from abuse. Will the media solve their problems or create more?

Summary

"News" is many things to many people. What we take from the mass media constitutes the bulk of information that comes to us each day. Other news comes from our neighbors, business or professional associates, friends, and even enemies.

Since the news media cannot logically carry all news with each issue or telecast, they become the sole determiners of what readers and viewers do *not* receive. That process involves various professional people who are in positions of accepting or rejecting, in whole or in part, what information comes to them.

Reporting the news is largely a routine exercise—checking records and files, attending meetings of governmental and other bodies, interviewing people who have interesting or vital things to say. At times, a single story may take days, weeks, even months to complete. But if it is what the public needs to know, it is worthwhile.

While most journalists labor in relative obscurity, save for the by-line if they get one, some do extraordinary things and are singled out.

As we have seen, not all news is good news. Major media surveys indicate that the public is not getting the news it needs as the First Amendment requires. Studies also indicate that the public preoccupation with trivial news is on the increase. That, in turn, adds to existing media credibility problems among those who are serious about their need for the hard information they require to function in the democratic order. Much of the issue stems from economic problems and the employment of media analysts to solve them. The analysts probe local readers and viewers to determine reading or viewing preferences. Then plans are formulated to serve those interests. The results are frequently large doses of what is termed "junk news." It might be junk, say concerned publishers and news directors, but it seems to sell.

The insane antics of terrorists and mass killers are certainly newsworthy. But the extent to which some reporters and editors seek to serve public appetites has become a major media issue. The New York print and broadcast media's preoccupation with the Son of Sam slayings and associated matters has been roundly criticized in and out of the media. Critics indicate that such fare is not only exaggerated but potentially dangerous because it terrifies the citizenry and even goads the killer into seeking more victims.

Again, most reporting in the American press is done routinely, honestly, and with reasonable objectivity. It is done by men and women who take pride in and enjoy what they do. They receive few public accolades for services rendered. In spite of that brand of quiet dedication, elements of the media increasingly conduct themselves in the mood and temper of a Barnum and Bailey broadside. Obviously some media consumers relish that, but others seriously wonder about it and what the First Amendment has come to mean. They obviously care about it.

Notes

1. © 1979 by Houghton Mifflin Company. Reprinted by permission from *The American Heritage Dictionary of the English Language.*

2. Edwin Emery, *The Press and America* (Englewood Cliffs, N.J.: Prentice-Hall, 1972), 3d ed., p. 2.

3. Morton Mintz, "Professionalism in the Newsroom," *Nieman Reports,* December 1972/March 1973, p. 5.

4. Eric Sevareid, "Elucidation," CBS Evening News, November 30, 1977.

5. Information on Barlett and Steele from Donald L. Barlett and James B. Steele, "So Much for the Glamorous Life of an Investigative Reporter," The *Quill,* March 1977, p. 19.

6. Information on the Long Beach, Calif. example from Dewayne B. Johnson, "Scandals in City Hall; Government by Newspaper," The *Quill,* June 1977, p. 25; Tom Willman, "Ridder's Long Beach 'Production' Comes with 'Horsefeathers'," The *Quill,* December 1977, p. 6.

7. "Notables: Zenger Award," The *Quill,* January 1977, p. 9; "2 Guilty in Bolles Case," The *State Journal,* Lansing, Michigan, November 7, 1977, p. 4–A.

8. *Columbia Journalism Review,* November/December 1977, p. 17.

9. *Columbia Journalism Review,* September/October 1977, p. 7.

10. *Columbia Journalism Review,* October/November 1977, p. 7.

11. *Columbia Journalism Review,* November/December 1977, p. 14.

12. *Columbia Journalism Review,* January/February 1978, p. 22.

13. The *Quill,* May 1977, p. 10.

14. Louis Harris, The Harris Survey, New York: Chicago Tribune—New York News Syndicate, January 9, 1978. Also see "Press Underplay News, Overdoes Sports: Readers," *Editor & Publisher,* January 21, 1970, p. 33.

15. "St. Louis Blues: Now the Hourly Plagiarism . . . ," *Columbia Journalism Review,* September/October 1973, p. 35. Reprinted from the *St. Louis Journalism Review.*

16. Thomas Griffith, "Revving Up the Television News," *Time,* August 22, 1977, p. 58.

17. Larry McMurtry, "Spectrum: News Without End, Amen," *Washington Journalism Review,* October 1977, p. 4.

18. Sydney J. Harris, "Let's Have an Award for Avoiding Trivia," *Detroit Free Press*, January 26, 1977, p. 15–A.
19. Editorial, "Manufacturing the News," *Saturday Review*, June 25, 1977, p. 4.
20. Joanne Shore, " 'Happy Talk:' All the Non-News Fit to Air," *Columbia Journalism Review*, November/December 1972, p. 35 (reprinted from the *Philadelphia Journalism Review*).
21. Ron Powers, *The Newscasters: The News Business as Show Business*, St. Martins Press, Inc.
22. Cable Neuhaus, "Trivialization of the News Punches Its Way to the Top," The *Quill*, October 1977, p. 34.
23. Information on "Losses in Newspaper Circulations" and "Current Newspaper Problems" from Fergus M. Bordewich, "Supermarketing the Newspaper," reprinted from the *Columbia Journalism Review*, September/October 1977, p. 24.
24. Robert Scheer, "Pretty Picture News Successful (Financially)," The *State Journal*, Lansing, Michigan, July 3, 1977, p. 1–E.
25. Cable Neuhaus, "Trivialization of the News," p. 34.
26. Fergus M. Bordewich, "Supermarketing the Newspaper," p. 24.
27. As quoted in Robert Scheer, "Pretty Picture News Successful," p. 1–6.
28. Fergus M. Bordewich, "Supermarketing the Newspaper," p. 24.
29. Publisher's Notes, "Frivolous Journalism," *Columbia Journalism Review*, January/February 1978, p. 18.
30. William J. Mitchell, "Ch. 4 Shift Portends TV News Revolution," *Detroit Free Press*, January 23, 1978, p. 3–A.
31. Fergus M. Bordewich, "Supermarketing the Newspaper," p. 24.
32. Philip Meyer, "In Defense of the Marketing Approach," *Columbia Journalism Review*, January/February 1978, p. 60.
33. "Ain't Democracy a Kind of Pizza?" *Detroit Free Press*, February 2, 1978, p. 1–B.
34. Cable Neuhaus, "Trivialization of the News," p. 34.
35. "Terrorism and Censorship," *Time*, March 28, 1977, p. 57.
36. Phil Bremen, "Television's Dilemma: Stay on the Air—Or Bail Out?" The *Quill*, March 1977, p. 8.
37. Steven Yount, "Kidnaping Is Kidnaping," The *Quill*, May 1977, p. 4.
38. Louise Sweeney, "Police, Media, and Terrorism," *Christian Science Monitor*, December 5, 1977, p. 46.
39. "The 38 Hours: Trial By Terror," *Time*, March 21, 1977, p. 14.
40. "Terrorism and Censorship," *Time*, March 28, 1977, p. 57.
41. Louise Sweeney, "Police, Media, and Terrorism," p. 46.
42. "Weighing Lives Against Press Freedom," The *Quill*, December 1977, p. 23.
43. These "Other Cases" from "America's Manacing Misfits," *Time*, March 21, 1977, pp. 18–20.
44. "Terrorism and Censorship," *Time*, March 28, 1977.
45. Information on Son of Sam from "The Talk of the Town," The *New Yorker*, August 15, 1977, p. 21.
46. Information on the arrest of David Berkowitz from "The Talk of the Town," The *New Yorker*, September 5, 1977, p. 19.
47. "Rupert Murdoch on 'Son of Sam,' " The *Quill*, November 1977, p. 16.
48. Information on "Television Coverage" from Carll Tucker, "The Night TV Cried Wolf," © *Saturday Review*, October 1, 1977, p. 56, All Rights Reserved.
49. Jim Frisinger, "Son of Sam = David Berkowitz?" The *Quill*, November 1977, p. 14.
50. Ray Mueller and Paul O'Connor, "Embarrassed By 'Son of Sam' Coverage," The *Quill*, November 1977, p. 8.
51. Carll Tucker, "The Night TV Cried Wolf," p. 56.
52. Philip Meyer, "In Defense of the Marketing Approach," p. 60.

For Further Reading

Barlett, Donald L., and Steele, James B. "So Much for the Glamorous Life of an Investigative Reporter." The *Quill*, March 1977, p. 19.

Bordewich, Fergus M. "Supermarketing The Newspaper." *Columbia Journalism Review*, September/October 1977, p. 24.

Bremen, Phil. "Television's Dilemma: Stay on the Air—Or Bail Out?" The *Quill*, March 1977, p. 8.

Editorial. "Manufacturing the News." *Saturday Review*, June 25, 1977, p. 4.

Griffith, Thomas. "Revving Up the Television News." *Time*, August 22, 1977, p. 58.

Johnson, Dewayne B. "Scandals in City Hall; Government by Newspaper." The *Quill*, June 1977, p. 25.

McMurtry, Larry. "Spectrum: News Without End, Amen." *Washington Journalism Review*, October 1977, p. 4.

Meyer, Philip. "In Defense of the Marketing Approach." *Columbia Journalism Review*, January/February 1978, p. 60.

Mintz, Morton. "Professionalism in the Newsroom." *Nieman Reports*, December 1972/March 1973, pp. 5–13.

Neuhaus, Cable. "Trivialization of the News Punches Its Way to the Top." The *Quill*, October 1977, p. 34.

Powers, Ron. "Eyewitless News." *Columbia Journalism Review*, May/June 1977, p. 17.

Shore, Joanne. " 'Happy Talk:' All the Non-News Fit to Air." *Columbia Journalism Review*, November/December 1972, p. 35.

"Terrorism and Censorship." *Time*, March 28, 1977, p. 57.

"The 38 Hours: Trial By Terror." *Time*, March 21, 1977, p. 14.

Tucker, Carll. "The Night TV Cried Wolf." *Saturday Review*, October 1, 1977, p. 56.

"Weighing Lives Against Press Freedom." The *Quill*, December 1977, p. 23.

Willman, Tom. "Ridder's Long Beach 'Production' Comes with 'Horsefeathers.' " The *Quill*, December 1977, p. 6.

Yount, Steven. "Kidnaping Is Kidnaping." The *Quill*, May 1977, p. 4.

News in Pictures

Mass Media Audiences 4

Chapter Objectives

Upon completing this chapter you should recognize—

the unique problems of news gathering in the United States among the publics the media serve

how media consumers "see" press freedom

how the media reflect negative images of audiences by the use of stereotypes

Key Terms

The "Uniqueness" of the United States Press in the World It is unique in its size, composition, content, coverage, and the diverse audiences it serves. (p. 105)

Demographics How the media serve their audiences is determined on the basis of their income, education, needs, wants, and other "demographic" factors. (p. 107)

Stereotyping The utilization by media of devices that place various groups in "typical" social slots for easy identification and utilization. (p. 114)

The liberty of the press is a subject of the greatest importance, and in which every individual is as much concerned as he is in any other part of liberty.

New-York Weekly Journal,
November 12, 1733

The Causes and Effects of Media Activity

In a very real sense, one cannot consider any mass media issue without directly considering and involving the audiences of the media. Audiences reflect both the causes and effects of media activity. Hence, they are the principal judges of media performance, which is why they play a dominant role throughout this study. At the same time, it is appropriate to look carefully at this great mass of humanity in a special way—in terms of their many parts and what large numbers of them "get" from the media, how they "get" it, and how they are reflected in the media along the way.

The mass media in the United States cover a vast assortment of events on local, area, state, regional, national, and international levels. They disseminate their findings among more than 200 million people in a country that is roughly 3,000 miles wide and 2,000 miles north to south. That activity is unique, for it does not happen anyplace else in the world. Yet it is only one aspect of the uniqueness of the American mass media. That freedom of the press is a constitutional guarantee, even though the press functions as the adversary of government, is another unique aspect. The media also comprise a massive sector of private enterprise. It is the only sector of private business that enjoys constitutional protection. And the media offer all manner of editorial viewpoints and biases with which audiences must grapple.

The Media Have Many "Audiences" *

Uniqueness of the American Media

For example, there are newspapers of many shades of opinion and editorial direction to choose from. These extend from the *Manchester* (N.H.) *Union-Leader,* a staunchly conservative publication that strikes at the roots of liberalism at every opportunity, to the liberal *Los Angeles Times.* In between, some 1,750 daily newspapers circulate 60,977,011 copies to readers each day. There are also 650 Sunday newspapers with a combined circulation of 51,565,334 copies per week. Weekly newspapers, biweeklies, semiweeklies, triweeklies, and other forms circulate all over the nation to the tune of

Diversity of the Media

*Other aspects of media audiences are treated in chapter 11.

38,006,868 copies per issue. Still other papers serve minorities, foreign language interests, religious denominations, labor unions, professional associations, high school and college students, and many other segments of society. A vast assortment of magazines, general and specialized in content, have circulations in many millions.[1] There are also the seemingly endless outlets of broadcasting that reach every part of the land. That reveals much about the diversity of the mass media; it tells even more about the diversity of the audience being served. Yet, when one thinks about the American press, as such, one tends to conjure up an image of his local newspaper or perhaps of the anchorperson on his local television station. The mass media in the United States are considerably more complicated and awesome than that. So are the American people.

Emphasis on Local Issues

Despite the media's emphasis on national and international news, the American people are primarily concerned with local issues and events that affect them directly. Newsworthy developments in New York City might not have a sizeable impact on people in the Southwest who have other kinds of problems to cope with. The reverse would also hold true. Agricultural communities have different interests and problems than industrial centers. Communities supported by the fishing industry on both coasts have problems and needs considerably different from the miners of West Virginia. The United States is a nation of countless local communities—towns, cities, counties, states. Its population has many foreign roots, races, religions, and economic

Table 4.1   Statistical Changes in U.S. Population between 1900 and 1975

Year	Total Population	% of Population by Community Size			% of Population by Region				Total Households	Median Age of Population	% of High School Graduates among Population over 17
		Urban	Suburban	Rural	North-east	North Central	South	West			
	(millions)								(millions)		
1900	76.1	19%	21%	60%	28%	35%	32%	6%	16.0	22.9	6%
1905	83.8	—	—	—	—	—	—	—	17.9	—	7
1910	92.4	22	24	54	28	32	32	8	20.2	24.1	9
1915	100.5	—	—	—	—	—	—	—	22.5	—	13
1920	106.5	26	26	48	28	32	31	9	24.5	25.3	16
1925	115.8	—	—	—	—	—	—	—	27.5	—	24
1930	123.2	30	27	44	28	31	31	10	30.0	26.5	29
1935	127.4	—	—	—	—	—	—	—	31.9	—	41
1940	132.1	29	28	43	27	30	32	11	35.2	29.0	49
1945	139.9	—	—	—	—	—	—	—	37.5	—	47
1950	151.7	29	35	36	26	29	31	13	43.5	30.2	57
1955	165.3	—	—	—	—	—	—	—	47.8	—	63
1960	180.7	28	41	30	25	29	31	16	52.8	29.4	63
1965	194.3	—	—	—	24	28	31	17	57.3	28.1	76
1970	204.9	28	45	26	24	28	31	17	62.9	27.9	76
1975	213.6	—	—	—	23	27	32	18	71.1	28.8	74

Source: U.S. Bureau of the Census.

Note: Definitions for community size are as follows: urban—100,000 or more population; suburban—2,500 to 99,000; rural—under 2,500.

bases. For these reasons, the United States does not have national newspapers as many European countries do. The nation is too big, the people too diverse. The television networks serve the country on a coast to coast basis, to be sure, but the total news output by all three networks combined, per day, accounts for only a tiny fraction of the total news available. Therefore, the people devote their attention to news that affects them most. And that tends to be information on local issues and events.

No Truly "National" News Media

Mass Media Audiences

The omnipresence of the mass media in America is readily accepted, if not always appreciated, by virtually everyone. While every citizen in the nation could probably launch into discussion about the media, in basic or advanced terms—how he sees them, perhaps even the intricacies of how they function— it is clear that people know more about the media than the media know about people *as people*. The media tend to "see" their audiences in terms of "demographics": numbers, genders, economic, and social factors. These data project to media leaders a kind of collective "face," whose nose presses against the outside of the television tube or whose eyes flit about the pages of the newspaper or magazine.

Demographics

While the media depend on "people" for economic survival, they profess to know relatively little about real-life human beings beyond the statistical variables that chug up media engines. Mass media audiences are comprised of human beings of all manners, ages, colors, genders, and viewpoints. Audiences are comprised of the *individual* multiplied many times, then forming into various units or groups. When a television viewer watches the evening news, he does so alone regardless of how many persons are in the room with him. It is his single experience, *his* mind, *his* eyes. The same applies to other forms of media consumption. The man or woman who buys a daily newspaper does so by personal choice just as one casts his or her ballot in the isolation of the polling booth. But individuals also ally themselves with others based on common interests or bonds. Most people belong to one or more identifiable groups via employment, church membership, veterans organizations, fraternal lodges, the professions, and so forth. Thus, initially, the individual functions alone in developing opinions based on his attitudes, his station in life, and other personal considerations. But he functions with others in exchanging ideas and opinions, perhaps even refining his own views in the process. The differences between the two functions are important. Every politician with an eye on public office clearly recognizes the distinction. That's why the candidate shakes *each* hand, kisses *each* baby. He acts out one-to-one communication in hopes of molding many individuals into a large body of support. But he must begin with the individual, who listens and watches by himself. The mass media tend to overlook the individual in favor of the masses and have suffered because of it: marketing the news is a prime example.

Audiences = Individuals and Groups

Table 4.2   Demographics: Characteristics of Daily Newspaper Readers in the U.S. (1979)

| | Percent Who Read Daily Newspapers | | |
Characteristics of Readers	All Adults	Male Adults	Female Adults
Total Adult Population	70	72	69
Age			
18–24 years	60	64	57
25–34 years	66	68	65
35–44 years	73	73	73
45–54 years	79	81	78
55–64 years	75	77	73
65 and older	72	72	72
Education			
College graduate	79	81	77
1–3 years of college	75	76	73
High school graduate	73	72	73
Some high school	66	69	64
Grammar school or less	57	58	56
Household Income			
$35,000 and over	84	85	82
$25,000–$34,999	79	79	79
$20,000–$24,999	76	76	76
$15,000–$19,999	72	70	73
$10,000–$14,999	67	68	66
$5,000–$9,999	62	62	62
Under $5,000	50	50	50
Employment Status			
Employed	71	73	70
Full time	72	73	69
Part time	71	71	71
Not employed	68	68	68
Occupation			
Professional, technical	78	79	76
Managerial, administrative	80	82	76
Clerical, sales	73	78	71
Craftsman, Foreman	69	69	—
Other employed	65	62	63
Marital Status			
Married	74	47	73
Single	64	66	62
Widowed/Divorced, or Separated	64	65	63
Number of People in Household			
1	61	64	59
2	72	72	71
3–4	71	72	71
5 or more	71	74	69
Race			
White	72	73	71
Black	59	62	56
Other	56	62	50
Locality type			
Metropolitan central city	72	74	69
500,000 and over	71	75	68
50,000–499,999	72	73	70
Suburban	72	73	71
Nonmetropolitan	66	65	66
Geographic Region			
Northeast	79	81	77
North central	75	76	74
South	62	63	62
West	67	69	65

SOURCE: Simmons Market Research Bureau.

Table 4.3 Demographics: Characteristics of Sunday/Weekend Newspaper Readers in the U.S. (1979)

Characteristics of Readers	Percent Who Read Daily Newspapers		
	All Adults	Male Adults	Female Adults
Total Adult Population	69	69	68
Age			
18–24 years	62	65	59
25–34 years	68	67	70
35–44 years	74	73	75
45–54 years	74	74	74
55–64 years	72	72	71
65 and older	65	68	63
Education			
College graduate	81	80	82
1–3 years of college	76	78	75
High school graduate	72	72	73
Some high school	63	63	62
Grammar school or less	49	49	48
Household Income			
$35,000 and over	84	84	83
$25,000–$34,999	80	80	79
$20,000–$24,999	76	75	78
$15,000–$19,999	71	67	74
$10,000–$14,999	64	63	64
$5,000–$9,999	59	59	59
Under $5,000	47	44	49
Employment Status			
Employed	72	71	72
Full time	71	71	72
Part time	72	76	70
Not employed	65	63	65
Occupation			
Professional, technical	79	79	79
Managerial, administrative	81	82	79
Clerical, sales	77	80	75
Craftsman, Foreman	69	69	—
Other employed	62	62	63
Marital Status			
Married	71	71	72
Single	66	67	66
Widowed/Divorced or Separated	62	63	61
Number of People in Household			
1	59	60	59
2	70	70	69
3–4	70	69	71
5 or more	71	72	69
Race			
White	70	70	70
Black	61	61	61
Other	60	65	56
Locality type			
Metropolitan central city	74	76	73
500,000 and over	75	77	74
50,000–499,999	72	75	71
Suburban	74	75	73
Nonmetropolitan	54	53	55
Geographic Region			
Northeast	73	76	71
North Central	73	73	72
South	63	62	64
West	68	70	66

SOURCE: Simmons Market Research Bureau.

Individual media consumers are also highly selective in what they read in the print media or view on television. Some place sports news at the top of their preference list but have little or no interest in political news. Others hold to the reverse order. Certainly no newspaper can hope to publish an issue that, in its total content, has maximum appeal to each and every reader. The same applies to broadcasting content. There is too much happening each day and media decision makers have their own ideas about what is important and what is not. Therefore each news medium attempts to present content that will appeal to readers on a broad front, something for everyone but hardly *everything* for everyone. But even recognizing the complex problems that the media face in this regard, many consumers complain that local news of consequence to them is being neglected in favor of news from far away, that much of what the news media carry is irrelevant to them. As the report of the Twentieth Century Fund indicates, many people even wonder why press freedom is touted so vocally by the media when it has relatively little to do with their own lives.

The Freedom of Information (FOI) report of the Society of Professional Journalists, Sigma Delta Chi, indicates that the press has not been effective in bringing to the people its case of what press freedom really means. Indications are that "the press has failed to explain to the public that when it is acting to protect freedom of expression, it is seeking to protect and enhance freedom in general." Scott Aiken, chairperson of the Society's Freedom of Information Committee, warns that members of the press must be clear in their own minds that the struggle for freedom of information is not being fought for their own benefit. Ultimately, it is meant to protect and nurture the democratic system as provided by the First Amendment. "And we must then convey that important message to the public."[2]

Another equally important issue is again associated with the "localness" of newspapers and broadcast stations. If the First Amendment requires that the news media give the public everything it has related to an important issue, it clearly cannot be the right of publishers and editors to hold back information in the interest of "protecting" their audiences from social or political evils. Yet some news outlets avoid certain classifications of news for a variety of reasons including fear of offending their readers. Omitted stories might relate to suicides, rapes, offenses committed by "respectable" members of the community, or information dealing with the scandalous private lives of office-holders. Without question, the media should be accountable to their audiences for what they reveal. Perhaps even more, they should be accountable for what they do not reveal.

In local matters, news of politics and government head the priority list. Government officials, elected and appointed, make the community gears turn, and citizens need to have complete, uncolored information about the machinery if they are to participate in the democratic process as the Constitution provides. They need all of the truth that can be found. The *public* must decide what is relevant and what is not.

Table 4.4 Demographics: Characteristics/Preferences of Television Audiences, 1960–1975

Characteristics of Audience	Average Viewing Hours per Week			
	1960	1965	1970	1975
Household Size				
1 to 2 members	33:01	32:50	36:31	37:26
3 to 4 members	39:20	45:13	49:03	50:36
5 or more members	49:49	52:09	59:03	56:46
Children under 18 years				
None	N/A	34:05	39:00	38:41
1 or more	N/A	49:08	55:46	53:12
Income Level				
$5,000 or less[a]	42:42	38:26	42:55	42:17
$5,000 to $15,000	44:36	44:27	45:35	48:03
$15,000 or more	41:12	40:44	43:20	46:52
Education Level				
Grade School	N/A	41:14	48:14	46:53
High School	N/A	43:03	49:50	48:21
1 or more years of College	N/A	39:33	40:22	40:27
County Size[b]				
Urban ("A" and "B" counties)	41:14	42:17	46:54	45:41
Rural ("C" and "D" counties)	37:31	40:53	42:58	43:56
National Average Viewing Hours	40:02	41:52	45:41	45:07

SOURCE: Nielsen Television Index, A. C. Nielsen Company.

NOTE: All data are as of November of each year. (a) Income levels for 1975 were changed to $10,000 or less, $10,000 to $15,000, and $15,000 or more. (b) County-size categories are defined by A. C. Nielsen Company as follows: "A" counties: All counties not in the 25 largest metropolitan areas. "B" counties: All counties not in the "A" category, with populations of over 150,000 or in metropolitan areas over 150,000. "C" counties: All counties not in "A" category, with populations of over 35,000 or in metropolitan areas over 35,000. "D" counties are all other counties.

Emmett K. Smelser, executive editor of the *Palladium-Item* in Richmond, Indiana, wrote of this responsibility to the public:

Some Evaluations

> If it is our role as journalists to provide readers with the greatest amount of accurate information so they may intelligently guide their lives and choose their government, we cannot decide for readers what they should or shouldn't know. Nor, whether we agree with them or not, should we decide for them that an illicit love affair should have no bearing on their assessment of a man's character.[3]

Ken Gjemre, journalist and critic, wrote of the avalanche of national political news that seems to glut newspapers at the expense of important local stories:

> Political chicanery comes and goes, elections come and pass, corrupt alliances form—break up—reform, almost totally unreported at the state, county, city and local level. The background of candidates, in-depth interviews, quotes that reveal the real person are not the newstuff of the city editor or ownership of local media.[4]

As to the *why* of the problem, syndicated columnist Jerry terHorst says that the news media may be keeping a good deal of news from their audiences. "Some of the least covered stories of significance are the result of media dereliction, neglect, and the lack of perception."[5]

Table 4.5 Demographics: Characteristics of Magazine Readers, 1966

Family Characteristics	Percentage Distribution of All U.S. Families	Percentage Distribution of Expenditures on Magazines
Region		
Northeast	26.5%	30.5%
North Central	27.0	26.0
South	29.0	23.0
West	17.5	20.5
Race		
White	88.5	94.0
Nonwhite	11.5	6.0
Market Location		
Metropolitan Areas		
Central Cities	33.0	33.5
Urban Fringe	29.0	35.0
Other Areas	6.5	7.0
Outside Metropolitan Areas		
Urban	15.5	12.5
Rural	16.0	12.0
Education Level of Head of Household		
Grade School or less	29.5	13.5
Some High School	18.0	13.5
High School Graduate	29.0	30.0
Some College	10.0	15.5
College Graduate or higher	13.5	27.5
Family Income (before taxes)		
Under $3,000	16.0	3.5
$3,000 to $5,000	15.0	7.5
$5,000 to $7,500	21.0	15.5
$7,500 to $10,000	19.0	21.0
$10,000 and over	29.0	52.5
Occupation of Head of Household		
Professional/Technical	12.0	24.0
Managerial/Official	12.0	18.5
Clerical/Sales	11.5	12.5
Foreman/Craftsman	16.0	15.5
Operative	16.5	11.5
All other	32.0	18.0
Age of Head of Household		
Under 25	6.5	5.0
25 to 34	18.0	20.0
35 to 44	20.5	24.5
45 to 54	19.5	21.5
55 to 64	15.5	15.5
65 and over	20.0	13.5
Family Size		
One member	19.5	12.0
Two members	28.5	28.5
Three members	16.5	19.0
Four members	15.0	18.5
Five members or more	20.5	22.0

SOURCE: National Industrial Conference Board (1967).

Alan Barth, of the *Washington Post,* wrote that only a public that knows a great deal about what its government might like to conceal from it can be self-governing. He offers a timely quote from former Supreme Court Justice Hugo Black:

Hugo Black and Press Freedom

> In the First Amendment the Founding Fathers gave the free press the protection it must have to fulfill its essential role in our democracy. The press was to serve the governed, not the governors. The government's power to censor the press was abolished so that the press would remain forever free to censure the government. The press was protected so that it could bare the secrets of government and inform the people.[6]

New generations that move into the adult stream of community life are better educated than their predecessors, more articulate, more impatient with things as they are, and also more critical of their press when it fails to perform to expectations. In a recent Harris survey, 1,520 adults across the nation gave "prestige estimates" of various vocational occupations. Journalists were ranked among the bottom five along with salespeople.[7] As Eric Sevareid said of it, "It is the press that makes the community weather and sounds the notes of the day."[8] The *press*!

How Journalists Rate with Other Professions

As stated earlier, mass audiences are comprised first of the individual and second of groups of individuals brought together due to common interests. The social, fraternal, or business aspects of the individual's life has little bearing on the *act* of absorbing media messages, though these associations might well influence the interpretation of facts after they are initially received. In the case of certain "specialized" audiences, other forces, which do not apply to most media audiences, come into play for certain compelling reasons. The messages received and the images projected have initial, profound impact on groups as a whole. These groups find themselves reflected in or characterized by the messages and images, frequently in uncomplimentary terms. These specialized audiences see themselves as *victims* of the mass media. As groups they are becoming increasingly disgruntled and vocal about it. They are victims of "stereotyping."

Special Audiences

Victims of the Media

Stereotyping is by no means new to the mass media. As a practice, it is as old as the human race itself. It has remained because it is a simple device to apply to human groups, whether ethnic, racial, or sexual, for rapid identification and association by audiences. The stereotype of the Irish-American may be

Stereotyping

portrayed as a police officer or political hack who likes whiskey and usually shows it; the Italian-American speaks out of the corner of his mouth, devours garlic, and is tied to criminal elements; the black is lazy, stupid, and equipped with a natural sense of rhythm that makes him want to dance; the Jewish-American talks with his hands, is physically noncombative, and is possessed by an insatiable drive to acquire money. There are other stereotypes easily recognized by media audiences. Any of these examples can be easily debunked by presenting overwhelming numbers of exceptions that prove that people are people, good and bad, clean and unclean, intelligent and brainless. But stereotyping remains in spite of torrents of evidence to the contrary.

Stereotyping: The Easy Way Out

Those who employ stereotypes do not pursue truth. They pursue the easiest, most direct way of creating and manipulating categories of characters for quick recognition by audiences. To introduce a character who is out of a stereotyped cubicle takes effort, creativity, and time. For example, to depict an Irish-American as a well-adjusted, skilled physician who speaks English without a brogue and who is a respected community leader takes more effort, creativity, and actual performance than to portray him as a police officer who likes whiskey. Similarly, to present an Italian-American as a professor of philosophy at a major university who wears tweeds, smokes a pipe, and is idolized by his students requires much ground breaking. Why not simply cast the part as a stereotypical white Anglo-Saxon Protestant and simplify matters? Viewers or readers would have nothing to figure out. The performer would clearly fit the desired stereotype.

Stereotyping Defined

Webster's New World Dictionary of the American Language defines stereotype as "an unvarying form or pattern; specifically, a fixed or conventional notion or conception, as of a person, group, idea, etc., held by a number of people, and allowing for no individuality, critical judgment, etc."[9] Many persons in and out of the media find it convenient to fall back on stereotyping to help sort new friends or ideas into predetermined slots. But those within the media bear the greatest responsibility for employing and projecting stereotypes of millions of Americans (and have prospered in doing so), thus reinforcing them in the public mind. Stereotypes make fun of individuals or entire groups. Perhaps the most obvious vehicle for stereotyping is the political cartoon, which exaggerates a subject's prominent nose, or exceptional height, or large teeth. The idea is to get a laugh out of the news. As one journalist puts it, "They [stereotypes] constitute a journalistic shorthand, a means whereby to bridge the difficult communication gap between news disseminators and their audiences. They are thus tempting. They are also insidious, destructive of individuality and sometimes gross distorters of reality."[10] When the media employ stereotyping, they simultaneously exploit and denigrate the group portrayed. Actually, they exploit them *in the act of* denigrating them.

Groups respond to stereotyping, sometimes bitterly. Three recognizable groups that are probably the most frequent victims of mass media stereotyping are the elderly, women, and racial and ethnic minorities.

Statistics indicate that older people watch more television than any other American age group. The A. C. Nielsen Company has determined that the country's almost 23 million elderly watch television between four and seven hours *more* each week than average viewers do. The elderly are also a clearly identifiable minority and, like other minorities before them, they have begun demanding their rights—more positive portrayals of the elderly in the media and less negative stereotyping.[11] The problem has extended into the Congress of the United States. Some representatives and a coalition of the elderly have complained that the media, television in particular, pay too much attention to the "Pepsi generation" and not enough to older media consumers. Representative Claude Pepper, seventy-seven, chairperson of the House Select Committee on Aging, asks: "Are we so victimized by our own stereotypes that we only recognize as elderly those television characters who are toothless, sexless, humorless, witless and constipated?"[12]

The Media and the Elderly

Maggie Kuhn and young and old Gray Panthers at nuclear protest in Washington, D.C., October 1979. (© Julie Jensen.)

Claude Pepper (House Aging Committee).

America's elderly watch television to pass the time. Too frequently there is little else for them to do. Yet there are few programs that address their particular needs and interests because advertisers gear their sales pitches to eighteen- to forty-nine-year-olds. The programs that offer character portrayals of the elderly are frequently insulting and repugnant.

**The Elderly
Respond to Media:
The Gray Panthers
and Johnny Carson**

Americans sixty-five and older represent a $6 billion market and close to two million of them have incomes in excess of $15,000 per year. But even though they have the wherewithall and the leisure time to indulge themselves, advertisers largely ignore them.[13]

In hopes of bringing pressures to bear on the industry, a group of oldsters formed an organization called the Gray Panthers, which has come down hard on the media's use of stereotypes. A major target has been the popular "Tonight Show," in which Johnny Carson dresses up as an old woman named Aunt Blabby. Lydia Bragger, seventy-four, who heads the Panther's Media Watch Task Force, reported that "Johnny Carson seems to have a hangup about prunes and old people. I think he's scared to death of getting old."[14]

Johnny Carson as "Aunt Blabby." (The National Broadcasting Company, Inc.)

Representative Pepper agrees: "Is Johnny Carson's repertoire so limited that he cannot afford to sacrifice Aunt Blabby, his sick parody of the elderly woman?" Representative Thomas J. Downy, D–N.Y., at twenty-eight the youngest member of Pepper's House Committee, urges older Americans to boycott products that offer offensive advertising. He cites an example of a lemonade drink that depicts two old men playing checkers absentmindedly.[15]

Table 4.6 Average Daily Household Use of Television in U.S., by Sex and Age of Viewers and Time of Day, 1955–1975

Time of Day and Viewer Characteristics	1955	1960	1965	1970	1975
Early Day (10 a.m. to 1 p.m.), Monday through Friday					
Households Using Television	16%	21%	19%	22%	21%
Men	12	14	15	16	19
Women	53	59	55	59	60
Teenagers	4	4	5	4	6
Children	31	23	25	21	15
Afternoon (1 to 4 p.m.), Monday through Friday					
Households Using Television	17	21	25	28	27
Men	14	18	16	16	17
Women	52	62	64	66	63
Teenagers	6	5	5	5	7
Children	28	15	15	13	13
Early Fringe (5 to 8 p.m.), Monday through Friday					
Households Using Television	42	48	42	52	52
Men	19	23	26	28	30
Women	27	34	36	38	39
Teenagers	13	12	10	10	10
Children	41	31	28	24	21
Prime (8 to 11 p.m.), Monday through Sunday					
Households Using Television	62	61	59	62	61
Men	32	32	32	32	34
Women	39	42	42	42	42
Teenagers	11	10	10	11	11
Children	18	16	16	15	13
Late Fringe (11 p.m. to 1 a.m.), Monday through Sunday					
Households Using Television	N/A	30*	31*	28	29
Men	N/A	37	39	39	41
Women	N/A	49	50	49	45
Teenagers	N/A	6	7	8	9
Children	N/A	8	4	4	5
Average Hours of Use per Day	4:51	5:06	5:29	6:32	6:26

SOURCE: Nielsen Television Index, A. C. Nielsen Company.

NOTE: Data are as of November of each year.

*11 p.m. to midnight only.

The proportion of television viewers who describe themselves as "super-fans" has declined in all age groups since 1960. Viewers surveyed in 1970 also reacted with greater negativity to television advertising. (The rising percentage of viewers willing to pay to do without advertising may be an encouraging sign for pay-television systems.) Finally, although television's educational role (or at least, potential) is still strongly endorsed by the public, its role as a "babysitter" has dropped sharply—or at least viewers are more reluctant to admit such a use of the television set. Concern about sex and bad language on the screen has increased more than 100 percent, while the concern about smoking, drinking, and other adult themes has increased more than 400 percent.

On the other side of the issue, Fred de Cordova, producer of the "Tonight Show," says: "Nowhere in the television area is there a fairer and more complimentary view of the older generation than appears with us."[16]

Why Do Elderly Complain?

What do the elderly object to about Johnny Carson? An example of his barbed wit aimed at them: "The Gray Panthers are a group of older people and they're very militant. They went on a college campus today and gave the sign of the clenched prune."

Lydia Bragger responded heatedly: "Isn't that stupid. Just another prune joke. Old people are not the only ones to get constipated." She adds that Aunt Blabby is "the embodiment of many negative, stereotyped images in one silly old lady."

Aunt Blabby is not the only target of America's elderly who are out to eradicate cruel stereotypes. Others have been the character of the Fernwood Flasher (Grandpa) on "Mary Hartman, Mary Hartman," categorized by the Panthers as a "dirty old man;" Fred Sanford, portrayed by Redd Fox as "crotchety;" Mother Jefferson, of "The Jeffersons" as "meddlesome," and the Major on "Soap" as "senile."

Positive Images of the Elderly

Positive images of the elderly on television are more difficult to find. Exceptions are the grandfather and grandmother on "The Waltons;" Hermoine Baddely who played Mrs. Naugatuck on "Maude;" Mother Dexter on the now-defunct "Phyllis"—all of them feisty and in command of their lives, persons able to care and give and be without having to be propped up by younger generations.

The Elderly and Media Violence

Other negative aspects of television and the aged have little to do with questionable character portrayals of old people as such. After ten years of study, George Grebner, of the Annenberg School of Communications, the University of Pennsylvania, is convinced that many Americans, especially older people, are living lives of irrational fear due to "an exaggerated sense of danger and vulnerability. Exposure to TV violence has a lot to do with generating fear of victimization."[17]

The elderly have also pointed their guns at the motion picture industry for its use of stereotypical old characters. One elderly person commented on the portrayals of the elderly in *The Sunshine Boys*, which co-starred senior citizen George Burns: "I think its a putdown of older people. It makes them out to be cranky, petty-minded jerks."

Roy Hemming, editor of *Retirement Living*, a magazine geared for older people, tends to agree. "As played by Walter Matthau and George Burns, each character has a warm, lovable core—but most of the time the emphasis is on how advancing age has made one or the other of them anile, irritable, forgetful, selfish, generally out of touch with the world, and dependent on the forbearance of suffering relatives to see them through day-to-day life. . . . To me, *The Sunshine Boys* is no ray of sunshine in an era where retirees are disproving such stereotypes."[18]

On the positive side, the elderly have become a booming market for some print media publishers. Senior citizens also read and some magazine editors have pooled their efforts to standardize their formats in order to attract national advertisers. The elderly have long been overlooked by the print media although they comprise one of the largest media audiences in the nation. And their numbers continue to multiply. By 1985, about 50 million Americans will be fifty-five years of age and older. Senior citizens also carry impressive clout as consumers, a fact that many print advertisers have ignored until recently. The images of the elderly frequently portrayed by the media have helped create negative images of this group, which is probably why advertisers have typically aimed their appeals at younger audiences.[19]

The Elderly as
a Media Market

The Public Broadcasting Service (PBS) also offers hope for better treatment of senior citizens. The nation's first daily television series geared specifically to the needs and interests of older Americans debuted on public television in November 1977. "Over Easy," supported by the Administration on Aging, offers entertainment and information of special interest to older people. The show is hosted by Hugh Downs, former host of the "Today" show. Goals of the series include "the fostering of positive attitudes about aging in the society as a whole . . . , and dispelling myths and stereotypes which blind old and young alike to the realities of aging." Programming includes information on nutrition, health and medicine, management of money, consumerism, and many other appropriate topics.[20]

*Positive Programming
for Elderly*

In New York City, the Department for the Aging gave $80,000 to produce nine weekly television programs titled "Getting Along," along with $185,000 for national evaluation and dissemination of the series. Also broadcast over PBS, "Getting Along" featured older people who spoke for themselves. The average age of cast members was seventy-five. The series won two Academy Awards. In line with that, a group of commercial television executives who had contributed to sensitive television portrayals of older people met with a group of senior citizens to discuss mutual problems. The panelists were shown excerpts from prime time commercial television shows that portrayed older people positively. The showing was followed by a discussion of media use of stereotypes, the code of the National Association of Broadcasters, and the activities of special interest groups.[21]

"Getting Along"

The plight of senior citizens, as reflected in the mass media, is far from rosy and that circumstance is likely to hold for some time. But some changes have come, small, perhaps, but better than most elderly had hoped for.

Second-class status for women is deeply imbedded in many cultures, even to the point where life itself is in the balance. In India the death rate among baby girls is significantly greater than for baby boys because, when food is scarce, parents tend to feed what they have to the male babies to enable them

**The Media
and Women**

to survive and care for the parents in their old age. For centuries, some Asian cultures engaged in the practice of tying women's feet together to force them to take dainty steps. Others burned widows at the stake with their dead husbands, to whom they literally "belonged." While these and other barbaric customs seem to be on the ebb, others remain. For example, in some African countries, the clitoris of young women is cut off and the labia are stitched up and remain so until marriage to insure that virginity is kept inviolate for the husband-to-be.

U.S. Lags in Equality for Women

While sexism in the United States is considerably more subtle than some of the examples above suggest, sexism in many, sometimes brutal forms is with us yet. The United States is notably behind in the drive to achieve true equality between the sexes both legally and in actual practice. Socialist and other countries that have the official policies and the determination to achieve full equality have made significant advances in opening employment and educational opportunities to women. The Scandinavian countries, in the vanguard of these advances, attempt to *force* their mass media not to treat women "as sex objects or as hysterical housewives getting all excited at the smell of clean clothes." These nations, along with Australia, New Zealand, and still others, are "attempting to use mass media as instruments of social change rather than as a force that perpetuates traditional attitudes."[22]

Table 4.7   Proportion of Male and Female Employees by Race, Ethnicity, and Job Category for 40 Television Stations for 1975

		White		Black	
		Males	Females	Males	Females
Officials		747	223	49	45
and	Row	68.34	20.40	4.48	4.12
Managers	Column	15.33	13.45	7.13	8.75
	Total	9.14	2.73	0.60	0.55
Professionals		1302	441	169	127
	Row	60.31	20.43	7.83	5.88
	Column	26.71	26.60	24.60	24.71
	Total	15.92	5.39	2.07	1.55
Technicians		2047	89	256	23
	Row	81.10	3.53	10.14	1.11
	Column	42.00	5.37	37.26	5.45
	Total	25.04	1.09	3.13	0.34
Sales		173	96	36	8
Workers	Row	55.81	27.74	11.61	2.58
	Column	3.55	5.19	5.24	1.56
	Total	2.12	1.05	0.44	0.10
Office		145	777	75	291
and	Row	10.08	54.03	5.22	20.24
Clerical	Column	2.97	46.86	10.92	56.61
	Total	1.77	9.50	0.92	3.56
Craftsmen		347	28	21	1
	Row	83.61	6.75	5.06	0.24
	Column	7.12	1.69	3.06	0.19
	Total	4.24	0.34	0.26	0.01

SOURCE: *Window Dressing on the Set: Women and Minorities in Television,* A Report of the United States Commission on Civil Rights, August 1977, p. 141.

Women
Stereotypes
in the Media
A Place in the Kitchen

In a review of recent research findings in sex stereotyping, Dan G. Drew and Susan H. Miller found that stereotyped images of women continue to be presented in television commercials and programs, magazine advertisements, textbooks, and magazines.[23] One study found that in television commercials, women were more likely than men to be associated with kitchen, bathroom, and personal hygiene products. Another study found that women in television commercials are associated with domesticity and submissiveness, while men were portrayed in more worldly and dominant roles. The same imagery was reflected in an analysis of magazines in which no women were portrayed in professional or high-level business roles. Most were depicted as homebodies.

In regular television programming involving both children and adults, another study determined that males were cast in serious roles more often than women. Males were portrayed as more powerful, intelligent, rational, and stable than women, while women came across as more physically attractive, fair, sociable, warm, happy, peaceful, and youthful than males.

In an analysis of soap operas, researchers discovered that 58 percent of the men were cast as professionals compared to only 19 percent of the women.

Television programs geared for children also portrayed women in stereotypical roles with males appearing more knowledgeable, aggressive, independent, logical, and less emotional than women.

Asian American		Native American		Spanish Origin		Row Total
Males	Females	Males	Females	Males	Females	
8	3	0	0	14	4	1093
0.73	0.27	0.00	0.00	1.28	0.37	100.00
12.50	3.57	0.00	0.00	7.78	4.30	13.37
0.10	0.04	0.00	0.00	0.17	0.05	13.37
17	25	0	2	55	21	2159
0.79	1.16	0.00	0.09	2.55	0.97	100.00
26.56	29.76	0.00	22.22	30.56	22.58	26.41
0.21	0.31	0.00	0.02	0.67	0.26	26.41
24	5	9	0	61	5	2524
0.95	0.20	0.36	0.00	2.42	0.20	100.00
37.50	5.95	69.23	0.00	33.89	5.38	30.87
0.29	0.06	0.11	0.00	0.75	0.06	30.87
3	0	1	0	3	0	310
0.97	0.00	0.32	0.00	0.97	0.00	100.00
4.69	0.00	7.69	0.00	1.67	0.00	3.79
0.04	0.00	0.01	0.00	0.04	0.00	3.79
7	51	1	7	21	63	1438
0.49	3.55	0.07	0.49	1.46	4.38	100.00
10.94	60.71	7.69	77.78	11.67	67.74	17.59
0.09	0.62	0.01	0.09	0.26	0.77	17.59
1	0	2	0	15	0	415
0.24	0.00	0.48	0.00	3.61	0.00	100.00
1.56	0.00	15.38	0.00	8.33	0.00	5.08
0.01	0.00	0.02	0.00	0.18	0.00	5.08

Drew and Miller also found evidence of sexual bias in news content, such as sparse coverage of women's liberation news in two American and two British newspapers analyzed. In addition, a content analysis of news photographs in the *Los Angeles Times* and the *Washington Post* determined that men dominated the photographs, and that women were typically presented as spouses and socialites rather than as professional persons.

Women Stereotypes and the News

These analyses raise a serious question of whether or not stereotypical images affect the gathering and reporting of news about women. For example, a reporter might direct the content of his story to information that supports a stereotype of women and dismiss information that shows women to be successful in a profession or business as unimportant or not true to life.

Gaye Tuchman, a sociologist and vice president of Women in Society, points out that television's basic product is not programming, which changes day by day.[24] The basic product is the audience, which television "sells" to advertisers; an audience *developed* on the basis of demographics (age, sex, educational and social levels, etc.) and not merely *found*. An important part of developing audiences is to teach them to *want* advertised products that will make them as attractive as the characters that appear on their sets. Part of the process, Tuchman says, is teaching a way of life, accepting a society dominated by males and the stifling void of a class system. Television teaches acceptance of American life as it is—not as it could be.

Typecasting of Female Roles

Tuchman has also found that for women to get major roles in television programs, they (like racial minorities) are consigned to comedy programs. In action-adventure programs, the woman is either assisted by a white male or needs such assistance to protect her from the rigors of her work. In these programs, women are the victims of criminal acts, not the perpetrators. Even in comedy, victimization of the woman occurs usually as the butt of jokes. In portrayals where a man and a woman converse, the man is likely to dominate the dialogue. In soap operas, male dominance is reflected in the use of camera closeups; the camera remains fixed longer on the male than on the female.

Women and the USCRC Report

A report of the United States Civil Rights Commission (USCRC) revealed that, because of television's enormous consumption of program content and the intense competition between networks, television dramas "have little time to develop situations of characters, necessitating the use of widely-accepted notions of good and evil."[25] There is insufficient time available to develop and project the thoughts and feelings of the characters or to create dialogue that reflects human relationships. "To move the action along rapidly, the characters must be portrayed in ways which quickly identify them. Thus, the character's physical appearance, environment, and behavior conform to widely accepted notions of the types of people they represent." So we have the wife and mother portrayed at the kitchen sink, at the market, or at the dressing table as if these were the only activities she is interested in or capable of performing.

Typical Roles for Women and Men

Meanwhile, the husband and father is portrayed as hacking out new frontiers from his skyscraper office; making a business deal on the ninth green at the country club; consulting with the Secretary of State over the feasibility of the neutron bomb.

The USCRC survey, which extended over a five-year period between 1969 and 1974, also determined that of 5,624 major and minor drama characters portrayed on television, 65.3 percent were white males (the largest number of all the characters); 23.8 percent were white females; 8.6 percent were nonwhite males and 2.3 percent were nonwhite females.

The advertising industry is a major conduit of stereotyped women. And women, individually and in groups, have been objecting strongly in recent years to portrayals of themselves as the housewife grinning triumphantly through a grease-caked oven because she has finally found the right cleaner; the properly-attired young wife hurrying to pretty up before hubby comes home; the happy family scene with dad and the kids yucking it up at the table while mother labors over breakfast preparations.

Sexism and Advertising

The National Organization of Women (NOW) monitored commercials of WABC-TV, New York City. Based on 1,241 commercials observed, they found that women were typically portrayed either as sex objects or home-makers-mothers. Particular role aside, women came over as "dependent, un-intelligent, submissive creatures who were adjuncts of men."

Report from NOW

One of the most pointed of the sex object commercials was National Airlines' "Fly Me!" campaign. It featured an attractive young woman dressed as a stewardess, who purred over the television tube (and from the pages of newspapers and magazines), "I'm Cheryl! Fly me!" Despite complaints lodged with the company and efforts to have the commercial banned, National Airlines welcomed a 19 percent increase in passengers the following year.

Sexism in the Air

The same promotional approach was later adopted by Continental Airlines under the slogan, "We Really Move Our Tail For You!" Continental executives insisted that no sexual suggestion was intended in the slogan, that the phrase was only "part of the currency of American casual speech" such as "Shake a leg!" or "Get a move on!" But, according to Continental stewardesses, the company provided them with appropriate rejoinders for passengers who might ask, "Will you move your tail for me?" Responses included, "Why, is it in the way?" and "You bet your ass!"

The National Advertising Review Board (NARB) looked into the matter of sexism in advertising and concluded: "The problem is real. To deny that a problem exists, in fact, is to deny the effectiveness of advertising."

Newspapers have traditionally relegated women to a special page or section appropriately labeled. Content has included wedding and engagement announcements complete with mug shots of the fortunate maidens. And the copy beneath usually reads, "Mr. and Mrs. Theodore Carport are happy to announce . . . ," indicating that a terrible weight had been finally lifted from their shoulders. Otherwise, members of one or another women's clubs are portrayed clustered about the silver service as "Mrs. Gerald Honeygrup pours."

Other content, typically, has been aimed at women as housewives in the form of recipes, tips on cleaning stubborn stains, and all the rest. There have been promising signs of improvement in this area as some editors have recognized the need for providing probing stories on women as women, their achievements, and their opportunities for personal growth. Where it has happened it has been based on management's awareness of the need to recognize the equality of women in American society and their particular interests and contributions beyond the kitchen and the bedroom. But across the board, women remain in the women's section. They rarely get up front.

Another View

One media observer, John B. Sisk, suggests that sexual stereotyping is likely to be with us for some time to come.[26] "The stereotype, like the role or cliché, is an economical organizer of information and therefore effectively a form of censorship." He indicates that those caught up in the sexual revolution see themselves as "breaking out of an individuality-denying cultural prison to

Table 4.8   Male-Female Majority and Minority Employees in U.S. Printing/Publishing, Newspaper, and Motion Picture Industries

	Printing/ Publishing Industry		Newspaper Industry		Motion Picture Industry		All U.S. Industries	
	1966	1973	1971	1973	1966	1973	1966	1973
All Employees	100.0%	100.0%	100.0%	100.0%	100.0%	100.0%	100.0%	100.0%
Male	69.1	65.5	77.6	74.7	70.2	60.6	68.5	63.2
Female	30.9	34.5	22.4	25.3	29.8	39.4	31.5	36.8
White Employees	N/A	90.0	93.2	92.4	N/A	83.6	88.6	84.2
Male	N/A	59.4	72.2	69.0	N/A	50.9	59.6	53.7
Female	N/A	30.6	21.0	23.4	N/A	32.7	29.0	30.5
All Minority Employees	N/A	10.0	6.8	7.6	N/A	16.4	11.4	15.8
Male	N/A	6.1	5.4	5.8	N/A	9.7	7.9	9.5
Female	N/A	3.9	1.4	1.9	N/A	6.7	3.5	6.3
Black Employees	4.8	6.6	4.7	5.1	5.1	7.9	8.2	10.6
Male	3.1	3.9	3.8	3.8	3.7	4.8	5.7	6.3
Female	1.7	2.7	.9	1.3	1.4	3.1	2.5	4.3
Spanish-Surname Employees	1.7	2.7	1.7	1.9	4.5	6.4	2.5	4.1
Male	1.2	1.8	1.4	1.5	3.3	3.7	1.7	2.6
Female	.6	.9	.3	.4	1.2	2.6	.8	1.5
Asian Employees	N/A	.5	.2	.4	N/A	1.6	.5	.8
Male	N/A	.3	.2	.2	N/A	.9	.3	.4
Female	N/A	.2	.1	.1	N/A	.7	.2	.3
American Indian Employees	N/A	.2	.2	.2	N/A	.5	.2	.4
Male	N/A	.1	.1	.1	N/A	.3	.1	.2
Female	N/A	.1	.0	.0	N/A	.2	.1	.1

Source: Equal Employment Opportunity Commission (1968, 1975).

discover the infinite variety of their own potential as autonomous beings. Yet it is hard to escape the belief that in proportion as people become preoccupied with their sexuality, they become alike, not different." He cites the major magazines as a collective example, a mass medium virtually up to its neck in the effort to eradicate stereotypical images, be they *Ms., Cosmopolitan,* and *New Woman* or *Penthouse, Playboy* and *Gallery.*

Table 4.9 Professional Job Titles Reported by Eight Television Stations Organized by Job Function, Sex, Race, and Ethnicity

	White Males	White Females	Black Males	Black Females	Asian American Males	Asian American Females	Spanish Origin Males	Spanish Origin Females
On-the-Air Professionals								
News Anchor	1							
News Correspondent Anchor	2		1	1				
Executive Editor and Chief Correspondent	1							
News Correspondent and Reporter	48	9	4	7			1	1
Investigative Street Reporter	1							
Street Feature Reporter	1							
Weather-Ecology Reporter	1							
Sports Director	1							
Sports Announcer/Reporter	1							
Sports Announcer/Photographer				1				
Producer/Reporter	7							
Producer/Talent			1					1
Talent	7	3	1	1			2	
Announcers	8	1	1					
Local News Trainee				1				
Producers								
Senior Producer	2	1						
Producer	22	14	2	1		1		
Film Producer	2							
News Producer	3	2						
Sports Producer								
Contributing Producer	2							
Segment Producer	1							
Consulting Segment Producer	1							
Field Producer		1						
Promotion Producer							1	
Producer-Director	8	2	1					
Producer-Reporter			1					
Temporary Producer-Director	1							
Associate Producer	6	17	2	4		1	1	1
Assistant Producer		1						
Associate Producer-Writer		1						
Associate Producer-Researcher		1						

Source: U.S. Civil Rights Commission Report.

*Data reported here reflect job titles provided by all eight stations. However, one station limited its list of on-the-air professionals to staff announcers.

In each grouping, the competition for faithful readers is ferocious, thus requiring the content of each to outdo the others in "liberating" readers. The articles pour forth in abundance: how to be a sexual dynamo; how to learn the intricacies of sexual play; how to improve your odor; how to dress attrac-

Stereotypes Beget Stereotypes?

tively—women's magazines, men's magazines. The editorial aims of each group seem to be dedicated to eradicating social stereotypes within its readership to be replaced by sexual stereotypes within its readership. Hence, in this view, certain specialized publications are advancing the cause of human stereotypes as they seek to abolish them. It thus remains a major media problem.

The Media and Minorities

In the early days of commercial television in the United States, members of minority groups were all but excluded from participating in television programming. In infrequent appearances, they were cast in clearly defined stereotyped roles for rapid recognition by the overwhelmingly white audience. Blacks came across as tap dancers and slapstick comics, Indians as painted savages who collected white scalps and grunted a good deal. Mexican-Americans were depicted as marauding, unclean banditos who waylaid the Gringos from cowardly ambush. For reasons already mentioned, stereotyping served programmers effectively because the roles portrayed had been portrayed so frequently in the pretelevision media. So large audiences readily responded to their portrayals. Seeing a stereotyped minority on the tube was akin to greeting an old friend—or enemy.

Black Stereotypes
"Amos 'n' Andy"

"Amos 'n' Andy" Moves to Television

The first "minority" program came to radio in 1929 in the form of "Amos 'n' Andy" a weekly series set in New York's Harlem. It was a show *about* blacks if not *for* blacks. But the two leading roles were played by white men who projected recognizable black stereotypes with which listeners could easily identify. The show became a major hit. In 1953 "Amos 'n' Andy" was transplanted to television as other radio programs were doing. Only now the characters would be played by black actors and actresses. Television executives became concerned about how an almost all-white viewing audience would accept a show cast with black faces. That had never happened before. To boost the odds in favor of acceptance by whites, the black performers were coached to play the old black stereotyped roles rather than to act as they themselves perceived the roles to be. In short, they were not permitted to play blacks as blacks really are but as nonblacks thought them to be. From the outset, white viewers supported the show; blacks did not. Black leaders aimed

The Frito Bandito

The Frito-Lay campaign was launched in 1967. It was built around the "Frito Bandito" who was a reincarnation of the Hollywood film stereotype of Mexicans: he had a Spanish accent, a long handlebar mustache, a huge sombrero, a white suit tightly covering a pot belly, and he used a pair of six-shooters to steal corn chips from unsuspecting victims. The Bandito sold a lot of corn chips, but he also resurrected the image of the Mexican bandit, one of many negative Mexican stereotypes offensive to the Chicano community. The Mexican American Anti-Defamation Committee called the campaign "probably the most subtle and insidious of such racist commercials."

Numerous protests called for banning the Bandito from the air, but 4 years later, in 1971, the campaign was still running. William Raspberry, a *Washington Post* columnist, devoted two columns to ethnic stereotypes in commercials in general and to the Frito Bandito in particular:

> The point is that ethnic stereotypes, bad enough no matter whom they depict, are intolerable when they pick on people who are daily victims of American racism.

> And if the point had escaped those who created the Frito Bandito ads, the complaints from Mexican Americans have removed whatever innocence there may have been.

Respondents to Raspberry's column wondered why the protesting Mexican groups couldn't take a joke. After all, the Frito Bandito was a cute and harmless character. Raspberry devoted a second column to the issue of ethnic jokes:

> The mistake is too often made that ethnic jokes are essentially innocent because they amount to nothing more than commentaries on ethnic idiosyncrasies. . . .

> . . . When you show that you believe the stereotype to the degree that you make it tough for a man to get a decent job or home or education, don't expect him to laugh at your jokes based on the stereotype.

The Frito Bandito advertising campaign was discontinued in September 1971 in response to criticism from Mexican American groups. Frito-Lay noted, however, that in surveys done by outside professional research organizations in five major cities with heavy Mexican American populations, the Frito Bandito was liked by more than 90 percent of the Mexican American respondents. The company does not plan to use the Bandito character in future ads.

Use of a stereotype in a major advertising campaign. (Bill Raspberry, Washington Post Writers Group.)

bitter charges of gross stereotyping at network leaders. The National Association for the Advancement of Colored People (NAACP) insisted that the show be taken off the air and gave compelling reasons:

It tends to strengthen the conclusion among uninformed and prejudiced people that Negroes are inferior, lazy, dumb and dishonest.

Every character in this one and only TV show with an all-Negro cast is either a clown or a crook.

Negro doctors are shown as quacks and thieves.

Negro lawyers are shown as slippery cowards, ignorant of their profession and without ethics.

Negro women are shown as cackling, screaming shrews, in big-mouth close-ups, using street slang, just short of vulgarity.

All Negroes are shown as dodging work of any kind.

Millions of white Americans see this Amos 'n' Andy picture and think the entire race is the same.[27]

Blacks in Other Programming

Blacks also appeared in early television variety shows and in situation comedies, mostly in roles of servitude such as handymen, maids, and gardeners. Television networks remained adamant about maintaining the goodwill of predominantly white audiences. They would not offer programs that might appear offensive to them lest the loss of white audiences result in reduced advertising income. In those years, even advertisers feared negative audience reaction in the marketplace by having their products associated with a black face.

Freeman Gosden, *left*, starred as "Amos," and Charles Correll as "Andy" in the most popular radio series of the 1930s. But the application of black sterotypes to the various roles cast hardly made "Amos 'n' Andy" the delight of American blacks. (Culver Pictures, Inc.)

Portrayals of American Indians were similarly carved from the mold of stereotypes firmly implanted in the public mind. A "friendly" Indian, a rarity indeed, was a subservient, poker-faced being in the image of Tonto, the Lone Ranger's sidekick (played by the late Jay Silverheels, a bona fide American Indian) who, in spite of his association with whites, remained stone-faced and communicated mainly by grunting. Much of this form of stereotyping was an extension of the old movie westerns rerun on television, complete with footage of war parties on the attack and shootouts with the cavalry (populated, in turn, by large numbers of whiskey-guzzling Irish brawlers). Indian groups objected strenuously to these characterizations. On behalf of its Indian population, the state of Oklahoma passed a resolution denouncing the use of gross stereotypes in the mass media. The Association on American Indian Affairs (AAIA) offered recommendations aimed at improving the accuracy of such portrayals:

> Accurate portrayal . . . requires that the American Indian be presented as a brave defender of his homeland and of a way of life as good and free and reverent as the life dreamed of by the immigrants who swarmed to these shores.[28]

Asian-Americans have also suffered from the stereotype gap. They have traditionally been portrayed in the media as laundrymen, houseboys, cooks, waiters, servants, and karate experts, always cunning, inscrutable, and given to quoting the luminaries of Oriental philosophy, especially Confucius.* Asian-American women have traditionally been portrayed in the media as either "docile, submissive, and sexless" or as "exotic, sexy, and diabolical."[29] (The latter classification was most notable as the glamorous, slinky Dragon Lady introduced to the comic strip, "Terry and the Pirates" by Milton Caniff during World War II.)

Since racial minorities in the United States are almost always poor, it is appropriate to place the two categories together momentarily in an effort to trace how and why they "use" the mass media along with the effects media might have on them. For example, a Nielsen survey covering an eight-week period in 1974, found that television is viewed in nonwhite households an average of 52.1 hours per week, 16 percent more than in white households.[30]

Sociologist Neil P. Hurley provides keen insight into why this is so.[31] Hurley points out that for the poor, radio and television sets are absolute essentials because the rural and urban poor are captive audiences. "The cascade of flickering images enriched by melody, laughter, humor and dramatic sounds is a necessity for the marginal peoples; it is not a luxury."

*Cruel stereotyping certainly contributed to popular support for moving thousands of Japanese-Americans from their homes in California to inland internment camps following the attack on Pearl Harbor in 1941. Many of them were American citizens who had never seen Japan. They were the only ethnic group in the nation treated in such fashion even though the United States was also at war with Germany and Italy.

The poor make what appear to be irrational purchases—irrational for the poor—of one or more television sets—*color television sets.* Why? "Because with the twist of a dial, a shabby hovel or rat-infested slum apartment can be magically transformed into a sports arena, a playhouse, a movie theater, a shopping center, a newsroom, a game parlor—in short, into an escape hatch that takes a viewer into the boundless world of vicarious experiences previously foreclosed to the poor."

Effects of Television on Minorities

Evidence supports the claim that watching television tends to alter the attitudes and behavior of the poor. In a controlled experiment with Mexican villagers who were provided free television sets, fundamental family habits underwent remarkable changes. Families visited less frequently, paid less attention to radio and the movies than before, stayed up later in the evening, but conversed less frequently. In addition, male adults became more interested in news, public affairs, and sports broadcasts than before. Women devoted daytime hours to watching soap operas, movie reruns, situation comedies, and talk shows. Young women changed their hairstyles and modes of dress. Boys underwent career preference changes on the basis of shows that featured police officers, lawyers, doctors and space scientists.

The report of the Civil Rights Commission shows that most of the nonwhite characters portrayed in television dramas were males.[32] Among nonwhites, blacks appeared on the tube more than any other minority. Those of Spanish origin appeared only rarely. Most nonwhite women characters had no identifiable occupation and nonwhite men and women given token roles in television series and movies acted in stereotyped fashion.

Males Always "In Control"

The social structure presented by television dramas reveals a condition in which males are in control of their own lives and the lives of others. Regardless of race, males were portrayed as older, more independent, more frequently cast in serious roles, and holding more prestigious occupations than female characters did. Females were younger and played comic roles more frequently than men. Those characters who worked were portrayed in stereotyped and sometimes subservient occupations.

The study found that female "weakness" is the counterpart of masculine "control." This is found in an exaggerated way in portrayals of nonwhite females most of whom are in their twenties, unemployed, and the group most likely to be the victims of violence. The frequent portrayal of black females as prostitutes reflects their place in the violent world of television programming. In the world of television, males held more impressive jobs than females but white males held more impressive jobs than nonwhite males. The same held for white and nonwhite females.

Improvements for Nonwhite Performers

Even so, matters improved for nonwhite performers over the time span studied by the commission. Over the survey period, the proportion of nonwhite characters almost doubled from 6.6 to 12.5 percent. Most of the increase was made by minority males. Over the same time span, the proportion of white male characters decreased from 68.2 to 64.6 percent and the proportion of white female characters went down from 25.1 to 22.9 percent. Hence, during the period studied, white males dominated television dramatic programs even though the proportion of nonwhites, especially males, increased. White females lost ground.

Obviously the development of minority-oriented series featuring all-minority casts, most of them black, has improved the employment picture on television for some minorities. These changes have also substantially reduced the traditional stereotyped portrayals in favor of more real-life portrayals. The major drawback to minority programming as it has developed is that too few characters serve as constructive hero-heroine images for young minorities to emulate. There are no black Marcus Welbys, black Mary Tyler Moores, or black corporate giants, or space scientists, or cancer researchers, or judges. Yet there was "Roots"—and it gripped the nation.

Problems Remain

Table 4.10 Race, Sex, and Occupation of Nonwhite Major Characters in Network Dramatic Programs from 1973 Prime-Time Television Sample

Males		Females	
Blacks			
		Occupation Unknown	
Doctor			
Teacher			
Comedy Writer			
Art Gallery Manager			
Junkyard Owner			
Associate Junkyard Owner			
Police Detective (2)			
Policeman			
Corporal, U.S. Army			
Private, U.S. Army			
Unemployed Veteran			
Wagon Master			
Itinerant Con-Man			
Pimp			
Number and Percent	15 (75.0%)	Number and Percent	1 (100.0%)
Asian Americans			
Priest			
Mob Leader			
Number and Percent	2 (10.0%)	Number and Percent	0 (0.0%)
People of Spanish Origin			
Auto Parts Salvager			
Ex-con/ex-acrobat			
Number and Percent	2 (10.0%)	Number and Percent	0 (0.0%)
Native Americans			
Ranch Foreman			
Number and Percent	1 (5.0%)	Number and Percent	0 (0.0%)
Total Males	20 (100.0%)	**Total Females**	1 (100.0%)

SOURCE: U.S. Civil Rights Commission Report.

Unfortunately the improvements gained by minorities in the television industry do not apply to the mass circulation print media. Even with the advances
made through the Civil Rights Movement of the 1950s and 1960s, affirmative
action programs, and integration in public schools and housing, blacks must
still rely in the main on black newspapers for news of the black community.
Even in metropolitan areas having large black populations, the major newspapers offer little positive information of and about blacks although crime and
other negative aspects get some attention.

Stereotypical representations of blacks frequently come to the surface in
the print media. For one thing, the Civil Rights Movement, as a movement,
seems to have slowed down at least in terms of the goals originally established
and *how* they were pursued in earlier times. "The black movement at the
street level has virtually disappeared," one observer notes. "The movement,
in general, has turned to politics."

Table 4.11   Minority Hiring on U.S. Newspapers

Newspaper or Chain	Number of Journalists	Minority Journalists	Percent Minority
Albuquerque Journal	70	3	4.3%
Akron Beacon Journal	106	12	11.3
Arizona Star	75	9	12.0
Atlanta Constitution	110	9	8.2
Atlanta Journal	156	5	3.2
Arkansas Gazette	80	2	2.5
Austin American Statesman	100	7	7.0
Baltimore News American	110	16	14.5
Boston Globe	330	16	4.8
Charlotte News	69	5	7.2
Charlotte Observer	120	7	5.8
Chicago Sun Times	266	28	10.5
Chicago Tribune	430	19	4.4
Corpus Christi Caller and *Times*	80	8	10.0
Dayton Daily News	80	8	10.0
Dayton Journal Herald	65	8	12.3
Des Moines Register and *Tribune*	199	10	5.0
Detroit Free Press	155	10	6.4
El Paso Herald-Post	32	5	15.6
El Paso Times	65	23	35.4
Gannett Newspapers	2715	147	5.4
Harte-Hanks Southwest Group	90	3	3.3
Houston Post	125	6	4.8
Jackson Daily News	40	3	7.5
Knight-Ridder Newspapers*	4762	287	6.0
Linsay-Schaub Newspapers	234	4	1.7
Los Angeles Herald-Examiner	135	12	8.9
Los Angeles Times	572	28	4.9
Memphis Commercial Appeal	120	5	4.2
Miami Herald †	320	51	15.9
Miami News	75	4	5.3
Minneapolis Tribune	135	5	3.7

Examples of positive kinds of news involving blacks span a variety of programs sponsored by the Black Muslims including drug rehabilitation programs for blacks and buying and renovating housing for blacks. Muslims confined to a state prison cleaned and painted their cells, organized a banquet, and collected $1,500 for prisoners. News of this type is plentiful within the black community but it is not being reported other than in the black press. Dr. Napoleon Vaughn, a Philadelphia psychologist, indicated that various obstacles stand in the way. One is that "lots of people don't know how to handle the information once they get it." Whites are not listening and blacks are not talking, he said. Another problem is the overall attitude toward stories dealing with black activities.

"Crime stories yes, others no or maybe," said Claude Lewis, a black reporter for the *Philadelphia Bulletin*. Lewis complains that racial coverage in the established press is unfair in that the mass media do not apply the same

Black Reporters and the Established Press

Newspaper or Chain	Number of Journalists	Minority Journalists	Percent Minority
Minneapolis Star	119	4	3:4
Newsday	319	18	5.6
New York Times	670	40	6.0
Oakland Press (Mich.)	63	9	14.3
Ottaway Newspapers	492	5	1.0
Palm Beach Times and Post	125	5	4.0
Philadelphia Bulletin	274	14	5.1
Philadelphia Inquirer	250	17	6.8
Port Arthur News	36	3	8.3
Portland Oregonian	167	4	2.4
Raleigh News & Observer	75	3	4.0
Rochester Democrat & Chronicle and Times-Union	216	11	5.1
St. Louis Post Dispatch	180	20	11.1
San Angelo Times (Tex.)	52	4	7.6
San Diego Union	140	7	5.0
San Francisco Examiner	200	23	11.5
Springfield Union and Daily News (Mass.)	160	2	1.2
Springfield Sun and News (Ohio)	40	1	2.5
Trenton Times	93	4	4.3
Tucson Daily Citizen	75	3	4.0
United Press International	857	52	6.0
Waco Tribune-Herald	50	1	2.0
Wall Street Journal	220	12	5.4
Washington Post	353	35	9.9
Washington Star	186	10	5.4

SOURCE: Reprinted from the *Columbia Journalism Review,* March/April 1979.

NOTE: These statistics cover professional news employees—editors, copy-desk personnel, reporters, and photographers—at 186 daily newspapers and United Press International. (The Associated Press declined to make figures available.) They are based on interviews with newspaper-group executives, newspaper editors, and reporters conducted by the author, with the assistance of Jim Dawson.

*Includes some managerial and professional personnel outside the news departments.

†Includes 30 Hispanic employees of a special Spanish-language section.

Claude Lewis (The *Bulletin,* Philadelphia, Pa.).

criteria to stories of black news events that they apply to white, especially when the black stories are positive. Even though black reporters have found increased employment opportunities with "establishment" newspapers, their roles as "professionals" are sometimes difficult to define. Claude Lewis is a case-in-point: He was told by an editor that if he remained with the *Bulletin,* he could become the paper's Ralph Bunche. "Being black is a full-time job," he said. "You're always involved in that battle and it is a battle. Because the media need black reporters doesn't mean they should make every black reporter a black specialist. The world is so much larger than race . . . Nobody ever thinks a black will be interested in other things."[33]

Other Stereotypes

Other stereotypes that occasionally surface in the media include the absent-minded professor—a squat, unkempt type with gravy stains on his vest, a wild look in his eye, and the inability to remember if he is coming or going; the brittle schoolmarm or librarian—tall, thin, staring demandingly through pince-nez glasses clamped to her nose, an emotionless shrew dedicated to torturing her students; the myopic honor student—in a perpetual daze and given to profound utterances and polysyllabic words, the target of barbs from the "in" crowd; the grandmothers—fat and jolly; the grandfathers—lean and crammed with wisdom; the clergyman—hands clasped devoutly over his navel, repeating eternally, "Yes my son!" to males in trouble and "Yes my child!" to females in trouble. Stereotypes have served the mass media through their history, educating generations to categorize human beings by putting each where he or she "belongs" because it is easy to do. It is, except that it doesn't work that way. It never really did.

Summary

The mass media of the United States are unique in the world for various compelling reasons. For one, they cover a vast assortment of events and personalities on local, state, regional, national, and international levels. Their findings go to more than 200 million people spread out over a land mass roughly 3,000 miles wide and 2,000 miles north to south. Freedom of the press is guaranteed by the Constitution although the media serve as the adversary of government. The media are also a giant business enterprise, the only one having such protection. They offer all manner of editorial viewpoints, liberal to conservative. Most publications are general in orientation but many serve special interests, racial, religious, linguistic, and others.

In the American system, the people are concerned with issues and problems that affect them most. And while people know much about their media, the media are on less certain footing about the people they serve.

Media consumers are selective in what they take from their newspapers and newscasts. And with such large audiences depending on them, media tend to offer a little for everyone. The result is neglect in some informational areas. Hence, many consumers are concerned that they are not getting what they need in essential news categories. Younger, better educated, and more involved generations have entered the consumer market since the end of World War II, and these people have become critical of some aspects of press performance because it does not serve them adequately.

Within the mainstream of media audiences are special interest groups. A sizeable number of them are the victims of stereotyping by the mass media especially in entertainment content. That is because stereotypes are ready-made and easily identifiable to audiences. Stereotypes frequently reflected in the media include the elderly, women, and minorities, particularly impoverished, poorly educated minorities. The United States Civil Rights Commission has painstakingly documented the cruelties of stereotyping in the American media system. Minorities are also neglected by the mass media both in entertainment roles and in coverage of minority news.

The mass media's major concern as with any business, is to serve its public. It does so by respecting them, enlightening them, and guiding them to be functioning citizens in a democratic society. Anything less appears to be a departure from what the First Amendment promises.

Notes

1. Joe D. Smith, Jr., "A Free Press Is Up To You," *Family Weekly,* April 24, 1977, p. 4.
2. "Journalism's Failure to Explain the Public's Right to Know," The *Quill,* January 1978, p. 18.
3. Emmet K. Smelser, "Illegitimate Issue! Who Are We To Say?" The *Quill,* January 1978, p. 4.
4. Ken Gjemre, Letter to the Editor, *Washington Journalism Review,* January/February 1978, p. 4.
5. "Ten Best Censored Stories of 1976," *Intellect,* November 1977, p. 187.
6. Alan Barth, "Freedom of the Press—Like Big Watchdog," The *State Journal,* Lansing, Michigan, September 11, 1977, p. 1–E.
7. Louis Harris, The Harris Survey, New York: Chicago Tribune-New York News Syndicate, January 12, 1978.
8. Eric Sevareid, "Commentaries: Media Power," Symposium, *Society,* November 1977, p. 10.
9. With permission. From *Webster's New World Dictionary,* Second College Edition. Copyright © 1980 by William Collins Publishers, Inc.
10. John Hulteng, *The Messenger's Motives* (Englewood Cliffs, N.J.: Prentice Hall, 1976), p. 132.
11. Barbara Isenberg, "TV Ignores Faithful Companion—The Elderly," The *State Journal,* Lansing, Michigan, August 12, 1977, p. 3–C.
12. Janet Staiher, "TV's Slant on Elderly Hit," The *State Journal* (Associated Press), Lansing, Michigan, September 9, 1977, p. 3–A.
13. Barbara Isenberg, "TV Ignores Faithful Companion—The Elderly," p. 3–C.
14. Terry Ann Knopf, "Does TV Oppress Senior Citizens?" *Detroit Free Press,* January 29, 1978, p. 8–B.

15. Janet Staiher, "TV's Slant on Elderly Hit," p. 3–A.
16. This and the following information on "Why Do Elderly Complain?" and "Positive Images of the Elderly" from Terry Ann Knopf, "Does TV Oppress Senior Citizens?" p. 8–B.
17. Marvin Stone, "TV's Drivel—and Worse," *U.S. News and World Report,* November 21, 1977, p. 108.
18. Roy Hemming, "No Ray of Sunshine," *Retirement Living* (Now *50 PLUS Magazine*) March 1976, p. 62.
19. Ann Frank, "Views of the Elderly," The *Quill,* May 1977, p. 11.
20. "Public TV Focuses on Older Americans," *Aging,* September/October 1977, p. 8.
21. "AoA-Funded TV Series Wins 2 Academy Awards," *Aging,* August 1977, p. 19; "TV Entertainment Leaders Discuss Image of Elderly," *Aging,* August 1977, p. 18.
22. Jack Wintz, OFM, "Women: Struggling for Equality in a Sexist World," *St. Anthony Messenger,* September 1975, p. 20.
23. Dan G. Drew and Susan H. Miller, "Sex Stereotyping and Reporting," *Journalism Quarterly,* Spring 1977, p. 142.
24. Published by permission of Transaction, Inc. from *Society,* Vol. 14, No. 1, 1976. Copyright © 1976 by Transaction, Inc.
25. Information on the USCRC report and "Sexism and Advertising" from *Window Dressing on the Set: Women and Minorities in Television.* A Report of the United States Civil Rights Commission. Washington, D.C., 1977, pp. 11–13.
26. John B. Sisk, "Sexual Stereotypes," Reprinted from *Commentary,* October 1977, p. 58, by permission, All Rights Reserved.
27. "Window Dressing on the Set," p. 4.
28. "Window Dressing on the Set," p. 6.
29. "Window Dressing on the Set," p. 7.
30. "Nielson Newscast: TV Usage Greater Among Non-whites," in *Readings in Mass Communication,* Michael C. Emery and Ted Curtis Smythe, eds. (Dubuque, Iowa: Wm. C. Brown Company Publishers, 1977), 3d ed., p. 269.
31. Information on "Broadcasting Vital to the Poor" and "Effects of Television on Minorities" from Neil P. Hurley, "The 'Drop-Ins': Mass Media and the Poor," *America,* November 26, 1977, p. 377. Reprinted with permission of America Press, Inc., © 1977, All Rights Reserved.
32. "Window Dressing on the Set," p. 40.
33. Patricia McBroom, "Race Issue: Now You See It, Now You Don't," Supplement to the *Columbia Journalism Review,* September/October 1973, p. 29.

For Further Reading

"AoA-Funded TV Series Wins 2 Academy Awards." *Aging,* August 1977, p. 19.

Drew, Dan G., and Miller, Susan H. "Sex Stereotyping and Reporting." *Journalism Quarterly,* Spring 1977, p. 142.

Frank, Ann. "Views of the Elderly." The *Quill,* May 1977, p. 11.

Hurley, Neil P. "The 'Drop-Ins': Mass Media and the Poor." *America,* November 26, 1977, p. 377.

"Journalism's Failure to Explain the Public's Right to Know." The *Quill,* January 1978, p. 18.

"Public TV Focuses on Older Americans." *Aging,* September/October 1977, p. 8.

Sevareid, Eric. "Commentaries: Media Power." *Society,* November 1977, pp. 10–25.

Sisk, John B. "Sexual Stereotypes." *Commentary,* October 1977, p. 58.

Stone, Marvin. "TV's Drivel—and Worse." *U.S. News and World Report,* November 21, 1977, p. 108.

"Ten Best Censored Stories of 1976." *Intellect,* November 1977, p. 187.

Tuchman, Gaye. "Mass Media Values." *Society,* November/December 1976, p. 51.

"TV Entertainment Leaders Discuss Image of Elderly." *Aging,* August 1977, p. 18.

United States Civil Rights Commission. *Window Dressing on the Set: Women and Minorities in Television.* Washington, D.C., 1977.

Wintz, Jack OFM. "Women: Struggling for Equality in a Sexist World." *St. Anthony Messenger,* September 1975, p. 20.

News in Pictures

Mass Media and Government 5
The Executive Branch

Upon completing this chapter you should be able to—

explain the nature of "privacy" and "secrecy" in government and how they affect news gathering

discuss the basic issues and problems of press coverage of the executive branch of government

understand the implications of certain forms of government public relations as they impact on the First Amendment and the democratic society generally

gain insights into how some government agencies "use" the news media, the FBI and CIA in particular

Chapter Objectives

Privacy in Government   Tends to limit access to public information. (p. 143)

Conflict of Interest   In this chapter, it refers to reporters becoming personal friends with the public officials they cover, with the possibility that the friendship will take precedence over the reporter's obligation to evaluate professional performance. (p. 146)

Key Terms

An evil magistrate, entrusted with a power to punish words, is armed with a weapon the most destructive and terrible. Under the pretense of pruning off the exuberant branches, he frequently destroys the tree.

James Alexander, 1737,
Colonial New York

Political Power and the First Amendment

George Bernard Shaw observed: "Power does not corrupt men: Fools, however, if they get into a position of power, corrupt power." In America, it is the responsibility of the press to sit in judgment over the greatest collective power on the globe, the government of the United States, and to alert the people to abuses of that power. Only then can citizens right wrongs and call abusers to account. That is the balance put together by the nation's founders and it has survived 200 years of turmoil.

Yet, as the *Boston Globe* editorialized, "the public's right to be informed by a free press under the protection of the First Amendment is under the strongest attack in our nation's history."[1] Involved here, the editorial goes on, is "the well-being of the people, their ability to make a decent living, to speak freely and knowledgeably, to be able to tell whether they are treated fairly or are cheated, and if the latter is the case, to do something to change it. All this is basic in a democracy."

People's Rights under Attack

Part of the blame, the *Globe* says, lies with the news media. Frequently they could have been more fair and accurate, less sensational, and more willing to admit that they have faults. Some are trying, "but what is needed is a workable ethical standard." Still, the editorial goes on, "a free press does not mean necessarily a press that is all good. It means a press in which the good has a fighting chance to correct the bad." At the same time, pressures from government inhibit freedom and, thus, keep essential truths from the people. Without truth there can be no solutions to the problems of government.

The most stormy confrontation in which the American press ever finds itself is in its adversary relationship with the power and authority of government— national, state, and local. The very fact that government officials are elected, or appointed by the elected, establishes predictable barriers that rise between them and the news media. The press must get news of government to the

The Adversary Relationship

people as the First Amendment provides. But government officials fear that the news might place them in a negative light before their constituents, in whom the basis of their power lies.

Former presidential press secretary Jerry terHorst wrote:

> A truly free press does not have an obligation to support government policy; indeed, it has an obligation to refrain from support. Otherwise, it is only a propaganda arm of government. . . . The press need not be hostile, but it must remain an adversary—willing to test, investigate and challenge governmental decisions.[2]

The Press and Watergate

The public disclosures of the Watergate crimes brought the adversary relationship between press and government to a massive collision. The verbal fallout appears to have brushed all public officials throughout the nation. Aware that attaining and maintaining power depends on the whims of voters, some officials demanded instant reform while others became the targets of reform. A handful were given short-term prison sentences and the matter seemed to be over. But the rumbles of discontent are still felt, mostly in the press.

Watergate "Backlash"

One Michigan newspaper commented that the Watergate "backlash" "is not a frenzied thing as some suggest. It is rather a unified demand from an electorate that was profoundly shocked by the Watergate disaster—a demand that such corruption and power abuse will no longer be tolerated at any level of government."[3] Perhaps so, but many people didn't seem to care beyond wondering about the deleted expletives on the Nixon tapes or the identities of the White House "plumbers." Many even complained when their daytime television programs were preempted by live coverage of the Ervin Committee hearings into the scandal. Unless the press can somehow convince citizens to take an interest in the actions of their officials, the power of government is likely to continue eroding the provisions of the Bill of Rights, the First Amendment in particular.

The Need to Arouse the Public

In recent years, the nation has borne witness to the arrests of 12,000 antiwar protesters in the nation's capital in spite of the constitutional "right of the people to peaceably assemble, and to petition the government for a redress of grievances." More than 40,000 days of illegal wiretapping and bugging were accomplished by government during a two-year period without court approval. Examples abound!

Increasing Secrecy in Government Business

In another sector, journalist Jack Landau, executive director of the Reporters Committee for Freedom of the Press, warns that officials on all levels of government are increasingly making public records secret under the guise of "privacy."[4] They include records of convictions, criminal indictments, foreign and domestic policy making, and multibillion-dollar programs in health, welfare, education, and defense, all supported by public funds.

"Secrecy in government is where we are headed," Landau wrote. "The public wants privacy. People are sick of their health records, insurance records, their credit ratings and other private matters being made readily available to all seekers." People are being duped, he went on, into believing that the personal privacy concept supports secrecy in government as well. He cited the many bills pending before Congress and state legislatures that, in one way or another, limit access to public information. For example, the new Federal Privacy Act prohibits government from revealing any personal information dealing with recipients of government grants extending from welfare recipients all the way to million-dollar research grants. Again, these programs are supported by public monies. Yet the press, in the name of the people, is not permitted to know who is funded and why.

The Federal Privacy Act

Columnist Sydney J. Harris observed: "The only remedy for the ills of democracy is more democracy, but when the ills get acute enough, we usually reverse the process and revert to some form of despotism. Fascism is simply democracy's failure of nerve."[5]

It is necessary, then, to explore how the different branches and structures of government function and how they report on their actions to the American people.

Reprinted by permission of the Chicago Tribune-New York News Syndicate, Inc.

V. M. Newton, of the *Tampa Morning Tribune,* commented on the adversary role between press and government in this manner:

The Politician and the Press

The politician seeks to lull the people with pleasantries of government. The journalist seeks the cold, hard facts of government. Sometimes these don't always jibe, whereupon the politician reaches for the nearest microphone and assures the people that the journalist is the worst sort of skunk.[6]

Max Frankel, former Washington bureau chief for the *New York Times,* suggests that, in general, the press draws a reasonably accurate portrait of the strengths and weaknesses of the presidency. "But if the underlying truths are obscured, one must begin by noting not the power for occasional deception in the White House but the *habit of regular* deception." He adds that a president who chose to tell the truth could "very rapidly turn the wolves of the press into lambs."[7]

President Carter and the Press

James Reston, of the *New York Times,* poses significant questions about President Carter's relations with the news media.[8] Are the president's policies wrong or does the president merely present them inadequately, as some in the media suggest? Does the press fail to appreciate the complexities of the problems that face the president each day? Big business blames him for inflation; the unions blame him for high unemployment. The farmers turn sour because of low prices for farm goods while consumers complain because prices are too high. Blacks criticize the president because his efforts and expenditures on behalf of the cities are too meager, while the middle class complain because he is taxing them into poverty. The press hears the gripes and, because gripes are newsworthy, prints them or reads them over the air. But the stories contain little about the failure of Congress to cope with the problems of the nation. The president may suggest but Congress must act. The news media, Reston says, appear unable to understand how the system works.

An example of the gap that seems to separate the news media and President Carter is reflected in his speech on current issues and problems before the American Society of Newspaper Editors in 1978. At no point during the address did his audience applaud. Yet frequent applause is a form of courtesy at these annual proceedings. Two questions beg responses: How well do the media understand Jimmy Carter *the man*? How comfortable is Jimmy Carter with the press?

The President as Media Consumer

While the press is an adversary of government it is also vital to the workings of government. Presidents are avid consumers of media information. They must keep up with the temper of the nation. President Carter employs a staff of five persons who read 100 newspapers each day and some fifty magazines per week, and they monitor the three television networks and the wire services

on a daily basis. They then condense all that into news "summaries," which *News Summaries*
the president reads each weekday evening. Copies of the summaries also go
to 175 White House staffers the following morning. In addition to that voluminous bundle of information, President Carter reads the *New York Times*
and the *Washington Post* every morning and, when he can work them in, the
Wall Street Journal and the Atlanta papers as well.[9]

If a president is personally affronted by something he reads—an attack *Forms of
Presidential Response*
against him personally or his policies—there is little he can do to vent his
wrath. In Richard Nixon's White House years, an offending journalist's name
might be added to the official "enemies list," which, in time, became a kind
of "honor roll" among members of the press. When President Kennedy found
something uncomplimentary about himself in the pages of the *New York
Herald-Tribune,* he promptly cancelled his subscription and let the world
know about it. When Bert Lance, President Carter's former budget director,
ran afoul of Congress over questionable banking practices, he lashed out at
the press for careless, erroneous, and biased coverage of the affair. More
significantly (for a former top aide to the executive branch), Lance warned *A Warning
to the Press*
the media that continued negative treatment of public officials could well lead
to censorship of the press. "There are more muckrakers around these days
than muckmakers," he said.[10] Since Lance issued his veiled threats of censorship, new clouds have gathered over his head. One involves charges of
illegal arrangements for bank loans to himself and relatives.[11] He was recently
indicted for questionable banking practices. Thus, Mr. Lance has reason to
embrace press censorship.

Reprinted by permission of the Chicago Tribune-New York News Syndicate, Inc.

New Foundations

Reprinted by permission of the Chicago Tribune-New York News Syndicate, Inc.

Executive "No-Shows" In another sector of the executive branch, Jimmy Carter, shortly after entering the White House, found federal managers who had not been seen in years earning up to $50,000 annually. One administrator commented, "We found $50,000 welfare cases." And when President Carter's new staff tried to institute dismissal procedures against the no-shows, they found that it required 30 percent of their work time to do the paperwork, only to have cases dismissed due to minor errors. Another Carter appointee could not account for a $50,000-a-year member of his staff. When he looked into it he was told that the person spent most of his time giving speeches around the country and firing him would be too much trouble.[12] There is much bona fide grist for the mills of journalism without stooping to the gutter sludge of witch-hunts, as some charge the press with doing.

Reporter and Executive "Temptations" Reporting the actions and policy making of government can be fraught with perils. Reporters who labor close to the seats of political power are open to various temptations. It's the nature of the work. They are placed in close contact with public officials about whom they write for the public pleasure. They cannot help but develop personal ties with some of them. It's a heady experience for a reporter to have a Cabinet member invite him to the club for a round of golf or to have dinner at the White House. Sometimes these relationships bring rewards in the form of "inside" information, a timely tip, a tempting "news leak." At other times, the association becomes an artful form of intimidation when the journalist is exposed to the seamier side of power. By holding back what he may know about a powerful figure, he keeps the figure indebted to him.

The Dark
Side of Power

Ithiel de Sola Pool, press observer and professor of political science at the Massachusetts Institute of Technology, sums up the relationship in this manner: "It is a gentle and often unconscious blackmail that keeps the reporter's channels open for more information to come and, at the same time, tames the reporter from going the last mile in his exposés." These close associations may also draw him to the center of the political orbit to the point where "he becomes part of the system and comes to feel more stake in supporting the system than in exposing abuses." The late Walter Lippmann, who spent many years reporting on the Washington scene, urged journalists to keep an "air space" between themselves and public officials—not a wall or a fence—but an "air space" in order to keep their integrity intact.[13]

At the same time, the honest journalist—and most are honest—is constantly aware of and bothered by the temptations that abound in Washington and other governmental centers. His job is a contradiction: he must get close enough to political figures to draw from them information that the public must have, but not so close as to have relationships improperly influence his work. "To do his job he must develop confidential relations with sources and protect those sources, but his job is also to strip the veil of privacy from everyone else's business."[14] Political reporting is essential to the workings of democracy; it can also be a terribly trying vocation.

The Nub
of the Problem

The press conference has long been a tradition in Washington journalism. As a means of bringing the executive and the news media together, it extends, in one form or another, far back into American history. Its structure, its effectiveness, the frequency of the meetings, and what does and does not get done depends largely on how the executive branch views the press. That, in turn, depends directly on the problems to be aired and the willingness of government to provide all available details. How successfully the press conference serves the interests of both sides also depends on the personality of the chief executive.

Presidential Press Conferences
Basic Ingredients

In the early years of Franklin Roosevelt's presidency, press coverage of the executive branch tended to reflect the passivity of those depressed times. FDR handled the media with ease. He "scorned and ridiculed his questioners," James Reston wrote. "He once pinned a Nazi Iron Cross on John O'Donnell of the *New York News* during the Second World War, and ordered Robert Post of the *New York Times* to put on a dunce cap and stand in the corner." He probably would have greater difficulty handling the press of today. President Harry Truman took a good many bumps and bruises from the press in

Past Experiences

his White House years and it seems to have had its effect. "Asking President Truman a question was like pitching batting practice to the Yankees," Reston added. "He decapitated you and then grinned."[15] But Truman seems to have appreciated the value of the press in the democratic order. "There's a lot wrong with the newspapers and the radio and television and all of that," he said years later. "But in the long run, like Jefferson said, about newspapers, that is, we'd be worse off without them."[16] Dwight Eisenhower was "amiably incomprehensible," Reston recalls, while John Kennedy charmed the press with his ready wit and intellectual skills.

*Press Conferences
with LBJ*

Lyndon Johnson held press conferences only when he felt like it. When he did, it was in his own office away from the cameras and with no advance notice. He usually scheduled them on weekends when only a few reporters were on duty.

Nixon Hostile to Press

Richard Nixon was uncomfortable with the press, distrusted it, and was hostile to it. Reporters sensed it and responded in kind. At one conference as the reporters leaped to their feet and called for recognition, President Nixon nodded to CBS correspondent Dan Rather and asked, "Are you running for something?" And Rather fired back, "No, sir, Mr. President, are you?" Even so, President Nixon utilized television to get his messages directly to the people more than any other president.[17]

**Shortcomings
of the System**

The main shortcoming of presidential press conferences is that the president controls them rather than the news media. The president can hold a press conference or not hold one. He can hold one in the morning, at high noon, or in the middle of the night as he sees fit. Once the press has assembled and the chief executive appears before them, he is not required to answer any of their questions. Or he may give partial answers to questions. The president also determines which reporters will be recognized. That means he may ignore those whom he considers offensive or uncooperative. This lack of formal struc-

*Comparison:
The British System*

ture contrasts sharply with the British system in which the prime minister is legally answerable to Parliament. Thus, he must submit to the scrutiny of frequent question and answer periods in the House of Commons. House members control these sessions, not the prime minister, and they are covered carefully and responsibly by the British press for public consumption.

Other Problems

Another problem with presidential press conferences is that increasingly, they are not scheduled on a regular or frequent basis. When they are scheduled, they are often tied to major announcements which the president wishes to make, not to news of the executive branch generally. President Franklin D. Roosevelt held two press conferences per week; the frequency alone was valuable in terms of permitting journalists to get to know the president on a reasonably intimate basis. That intimacy of frequent contact appears to be on the way out. Some White House reporters have suggested alternatives to the traditional press conference. One option having considerable merit is to hold frequent conferences, each dealing with a single overall topic—the national economy, public health matters, education, or defense. Another is for the news media to use its influence with the people to demand that more question and answer sessions be held in which meaningful issues and policies would be aired.[18]

Lester Kinsolving, of Panax Newspapers and editor of *Washington Weekly*, sees other problems with the conference system. He bemoans the use of exclusive interviews between members of the executive branch and selected reporters. He also criticizes the practice of reserving front seats and ready recognition by the president for "highly paid reporters who represent Big Business in Media."[19]

Richard Nixon attacking the press. (Ralph Crane, *Life* Magazine © 1969 Time Inc.)

President Carter at one of his press conferences. (Bill Fitz-Patrick, The White House.)

Daily Press Briefings

Daily White House briefings are in even greater difficulty. They are usually held by the presidential press secretary to inform the media about general business and events scheduled for the day.

Ann Compton, White House correspondent for ABC news, indicates that White House press briefings have become a shambles, characterized by good-natured banter and chitchat between reporters and White House personnel. She takes issue with the change of scheduling briefings from 11:30 A.M. to midafternoon, which is inconvenient for media people. "Where do we turn?" she asks. "Not to the semi-monthly presidential news conferences. There are deficiencies there, too."[20]

Public Relations and the Executive Branch

The executive branch has also developed an elaborate system of reaching the American people beyond dealing directly with the news media: government public relations. The system has grown significantly in output, cost, and impact in recent years and it guarantees the projection of only positive images of government officials, their policies, and practices.

The United States Government spends over $65 million per year in salaries for public relations services and as much as $200 million per year for advertising. It also spends as much as $500 million each year turning out motion pictures that deal with government matters. This vast output, *American Film* magazine noted, makes Paramount and MGM studios look like "cottage industries." The total annual expenditure for promoting government to the American people now approaches $1 billion.

Some examples:[21] White House aide Hamilton Jordan got into difficulty at a Washington singles bar when he reportedly spat a mouthful of sizzle at a young woman he had unsuccessfully accosted there. The gossip mongers picked up the story and it spread rapidly. In order to shore up Jordan's image, the White House composed and distributed widely a thirty-three-page report defending Jordan's behavior. Compared to President Carter's fifteen-page State of the Union address, the Jordan document became a major informational vehicle despite its content. Mr. Jordan has since given executive branch public relations people additional work to do to shore up his public image.

Hamilton Jordan and the Singles Bar

Some agencies of the executive branch offer free telephone services for broadcasters who may call in and tape government "news" for their listeners. The "news" includes general information, tapes of speeches given by public officials, visuals as well as audio and statistical materials designed to make a program or policy look good. This gimmickry is popular among low-budget stations that have inadequate reportorial staffs. It helps fill gaps and voids that otherwise might hang heavy as dead air. But even some big money stations go along with it. The practice raises serious ethical questions for journalists. According to Raymond Coffee, of the *Chicago Tribune,* "the question becomes, should the taxpayers be footing the bill for radio stations all over the country to be calling Washington and getting 'news' recordings selected and edited by government officials?"

Free Telephone Services for Media

Much of the public information output by the executive branch is useful, at times even important to the American people, such as that related to public health matters, social improvement programs, and so forth. Still, its primary purpose is "the selling of the government, to retail, package and promote government policies, programs and personalities, and to withhold information when it is believed to be against the administration's interest." Funding of government public relations has been banned since 1913. But the ban is conveniently sidetracked by government agencies that simply roll these expenditures into their total budgets.[22] Some journalists have supported these activities by willingly accepting informational handouts and releases and feeding them directly into the media. Unfortunately, much of the general population does not know the difference and accepts these publicity puffs as bona fide news.

The Main Thrust of Executive Public Relations

A Frequent Result

The Agencies of the Executive Branch

The far-flung bureaucracy spawned by the executive branch, the proliferation of official agencies and bureaus, makes *total* press coverage of this vital branch virtually impossible. Guided by the legislative branch and overseen by the courts, the agencies are within the jurisdiction of the executive branch whether on national, state, or local levels. The news media have traditionally concentrated their forces in those agencies that regularly produce hard news having

J. Edgar Hoover.

broad interest for media consumers. In attempting to serve that interest, other bureaucracies are frequently neglected.[23] Yet, the lesser arms of government bear examination via the media's First Amendment mandate as much as the major news-producing agencies do. Enormous amounts of money are allocated to and spent by these agencies each year. Their staffs are large and what they do—and do not do—is of significance to the American people. This situation has significant impact on First Amendment guarantees.

Two bureaus in particular hold substantial power to deal directly with American citizens and yet rarely do they deal openly with the press in an informational way. Both have been steeped in controversy in recent years in terms of their overall authority and operations and, more importantly, in their official dealings with and attitudes toward the press. They are the Federal Bureau of Investigation (FBI) and the Central Intelligence Agency (CIA).

The Press and the FBI
Duties of the FBI

The Federal Bureau of Investigation is an arm of the United States Department of Justice, under the overall leadership of the attorney general, who is also a cabinet member and the nation's chief legal officer. As a fact-gathering agency of government, the FBI is responsible for enforcing all federal *criminal* laws except those covered by other agencies. That is, the FBI deals with criminals who have violated certain federal laws. Ongoing investigations into the activities of the bureau in recent years indicate that it has strayed dangerously from the carefully defined limits of authority originally granted to it. The excesses of the bureau, supported by its long-time director, the late J. Edgar Hoover, have affected the press in two important ways. One has to do with the official FBI view of the press as a militant foe; the other with the press as a means of achieving bureau ends.

The FBI and the Press

It is commonly known that during Hoover's lengthy tenure as director, the bureau collected information about and opened files on many journalists whom it considered to be critics or enemies of the FBI.[24] It is also evident that the FBI gathered assorted data on specific newspapers that had been critical of Hoover or of bureau practices. The files included the results of criminal record checks on media executives and reporters. The *Charleston* (W. Va.) *Gazette* is a case-in-point. After determining that the bureau had compiled a file on the *Gazette*, the paper's management asked to examine its content under the new Freedom of Information Act, which requires government agencies to permit those whom it has investigated to have access to findings. A year later the *Gazette* file arrived. It provided interesting reading.

Case of the Charleston Gazette

The file had been opened when *Gazette* editorials began praising the bureau. Then, when the paper began to question the government's witch-hunt tactics aimed at uncovering Communists in the 1950s, the bureau's mood toward the *Gazette* took a sharp turn. The file revealed that an assortment of messages had arrived at the Washington headquarters of the FBI which, despite being marked "Urgent," contained nothing more "criminal" than *Gazette* editorials that were critical of the bureau or of Hoover. Other information was based on reports by special agents who had visited the *Gazette* offices to speak with editors who seemed friendly toward the bureau. Still other documents had been sent in by persons who warned that the paper was leftist. To the latter, Hoover had sent thank-you notes along with personal copies of his anti-Communist statements.

In another case, Nina Totenberg, an attorney and legal counsel for the *National Observer,* once wrote a lengthy profile of J. Edgar Hoover and the questionable tactics he employed as bureau director. Apparently Hoover became angered over the profile and on several occasions tried to get Totenberg fired. The fact that he wrote more than one letter about her to the *Observer's* editor strongly suggests that the FBI had opened a file on her as well.[25]

Case of the National Observer

At one point late in the existence of the Nixon administration, White House leaders decided that CBS newsman Daniel Schorr had become too critical of administration policies. In short order, the FBI launched a full-blown investigation into Schorr's private life. His friends, associates, and neighbors were questioned at length. When some of them asked why the investigation had been undertaken, the agents replied that Schorr was being considered for appointment to a position of trust in the government. "Job or no job," Schorr later told a Senate committee, "the launching of such an investigation without consent demonstrates an insensitivity to personal right. An FBI investigation is not a neutral matter. It is an impact on one's life, on relations with employers, neighbors, friends."[26]

Investigation of Daniel Schorr

There are other cases too numerous for inclusion here. But the pattern is clear. If a journalist or a newspaper were to support the FBI, regardless of its tactics, it would apparently result in a small show of appreciation. Criticize its methods and one would be investigated.

In the 1960s, Jacque Srouji was a thirty-two-year-old general assignments reporter for the *Nashville* (Tenn.) *Banner.*[27] Whatever personal reasons prompted her, she sought to combine her journalistic activities with assisting the FBI on a part-time basis without compensation. At the time, her reporting responsibilities centered on coverage of civil rights and antiwar groups in Tennessee. The FBI also had an interest in these groups so Srouji began to serve two masters. She even travelled on assignment to Berkeley, California, and to New York City and on at least one occasion the bureau reimbursed the *Banner* for her travel expenses.

Journalists as Bureau Informants

Then, on a trip to Northern Michigan to cover a rally of the Students for a Democratic Society (SDS), a radical antiwar group, she wrote nothing for her newspaper. But, posing as a reporter, she filed a fifty-five-page report with the FBI about her observations. After about eighteen months with the *Banner,* she left journalism but continued to provide the FBI with reports on militant groups in Nashville, especially black students at Tennessee State University.

The Fifty-five-page Report

Throughout these activities, her husband knew nothing of her private arrangement with the bureau. In fact, the agents had used the husband's ignorance of this association as a lever to keep her involved.

A Book on
Nuclear Power
Eventually Srouji began preparing a book on nuclear energy, a project in which the FBI became "intensely interested." In pursuing that interest, they gave her access to secret FBI records and files and put her in touch with top bureau executives. Her efforts resulted in various stories that found their way into the pages of the *Tennessean,* the other Nashville paper. This is an amazing story of a practicing journalist who worked as an FBI informant to the point of gaining access to classified bureau information, some of which she got published.

Why the FBI Recruits
Journalists as Agents
What prompted the Federal Bureau of Investigation to turn to journalists to achieve certain investigative goals? The answer is hazy at best: one reason is that law enforcement organizations tend to lack contact with political dissenters who are not "criminals" in the accepted FBI sense of the word. But reporters routinely gain admittance to inner circles of dissidents who wish to publicize their views and goals. So posing agents as newspeople, or hiring newspeople to play cloak and dagger roles, appears to the FBI to be an acceptable tactic for investigating suspects.

The practice has also created considerable hostility between legitimate reporters and meaningful news sources. In the late 1960s and early 70s, as antiwar forces accelerated their efforts, a number of police officers and federal agents posing as journalists were uncovered by the radicals. Suspicion of all reporters quickly developed and journalists were physically assaulted and barred from meetings to which they had been previously admitted. As a result, the American people lost direct contact with a major, ongoing news activity.

Suspicion of
All Reporters

El Tiempo
In 1967, bureau agents recruited Louis Salzberg, a photographer for *El Tiempo,* a Spanish language newspaper, as a paid informer.[28] Salzberg eventually worked his way into the radical community in New York City and opened his own studio to funnel photographs to the radical press. In time Salzberg became friendly with several of the Chicago Seven, who eventually went on trial for antiwar activities, and appeared as a witness against them. There he admitted that the FBI had been paying him $600 a month to spy on dissenters.

KFMB-TV
Another witness against the Chicago Seven was Carl Gilman, a TV reporter-cameraman for station KFMB in San Diego. Gilman admitted that for the previous two years as an FBI informant, he had been paid between $7,000 and $8,000 plus an additional $2,000 for expenses.

Other Cases
Reporters for the *Boston Globe* and *Washington Post* covered a draft-card burning outside the United States Supreme Court building in June, 1968. In the course of talking with demonstrators they recognized men they knew to be FBI agents posing as journalists and using television cameras and tape recorders to interview the demonstrators.

In 1971, *Los Angeles Times* reporter Jack Nelson was covering a meeting held by Congressman William Anderson to discuss the prosecution of the Berrigan brothers, radical Catholic priests active in the antiwar movement. Nelson suddenly recognized another "reporter" as a special agent of the FBI. When questioned, the man denied any association with the bureau but fled when asked to identify himself. He drove away in a waiting car. *Life* magazine traced the license number and determined that the car was owned by the FBI.

There are numerous other cases portraying similar circumstances of agents acting as journalists to gather evidence against citizens not engaged in criminal activities.

J. Edgar Hoover denied that the bureau recruited informants and it is true that Salzberg and Gilman initiated their contacts with the FBI. But, as the task force of the Twentieth Century Fund determined, that is hardly the point. That concerned group protested that when journalists are paid "for providing information to the FBI or any other law enforcement agency, the result is an infiltration—and sullying—of the (journalism) profession. The Task Force concludes that the practice is damaging to press independence and is wrong."

Hoover Denials

The Press and the CIA

The Central Intelligence Agency (CIA) was organized on the order of President Harry Truman after World War II.[29] Its purpose was to bring all intelligence reports from the many agencies of the executive branch into a single organization. In that manner, the president would have to read only one report at any given time rather than many. In Truman's personal view, the CIA was to be engaged in gathering intelligence, i.e., *information,* related to developments in foreign nations, which might be significant to the security of the United States. "Now as nearly as I can make out," the former president commented years later, "those fellows in the CIA don't just report on wars and the like, they go out and make their own, and there's nobody to keep track of what they're up to. They spend billions of dollars on stirring up trouble so they'll *have* something to report on. . . . It's become a government all its own and all secret. They don't have to account to anybody."

Purpose of the CIA: Harry Truman

General George C. Marshall, then Secretary of State, had misgivings about the establishment of the CIA from the start. He informed President Truman that intelligence matters should be handled by the State Department where they rightly belong. "The powers of the proposed agency (CIA) seem almost unlimited and need clarification," he said.

The CIA has come under strong criticism in recent years, much of it aimed at those covert operations that appear to violate the basic tenets on which the nation was founded. To repeat President Truman's concern, "They don't have to account to anybody."

CIA Under Criticism

One aspect of CIA activity is of particular concern to the American press. CIA is an agency of the executive branch of government; the press is the watchdog of government. A clear division separates the functions of gover-

The CIA and the Press

nance and the press. And, as we have seen, the First Amendment protects this separation. Yet for years the CIA has been recruiting journalists to aid and abet their operations.

400 U.S. Journalists
Helped CIA

Carl Bernstein estimates that more than 400 American journalists carried out secret assignments for the CIA over a twenty-five-year period.[30] Bernstein, who with Bob Woodward blew the lid off the Watergate story, said that American journalists have been used "to help recruit and handle foreigners as agents, to acquire and evaluate information and to plant false information with officials of foreign governments."

Bernstein also reported that high-level executives of the print and broadcast media appointed CIA agents having no journalism training or experience to positions on their news staffs as "covers" for their real activities. These news executives also ordered their staffs to provide the CIA with information. Such cooperative efforts extended from the early 1950s to the early 1970s. In Bernstein's words:

> Some of these journalists' relationships with the agency were tacit; some were explicit. There was cooperation, accommodation, and overlap. Journalists provided a full range of clandestine services—from simple intelligence-gathering to serving as go-betweens with spies in Communist countries. Reporters shared their notebooks with the CIA. Editors shared their staffs. . . .

THE MUSES

Pat Oliphant, © 1978 The *Washington Star*, Reprinted with permission, Los Angeles Times Syndicate.

The late James S. Copley, owner and publisher of Copley Press and the Copley News Service, volunteered his service as an intelligence unit of the CIA. Reports indicate that, at one point, at least twenty-three Copley employees worked for the CIA, though Copley executives have denied it. Arthur Hays Sulzberger, late publisher of the *New York Times,* permitted "about ten" CIA agents to pose as employees of his newspaper.[31]

Other Cases of CIA-Press Cooperation

In a copyrighted story for the *Los Angeles Times,* Robert Scheer reported that the Columbia Broadcasting System (CBS) and the CIA collaborated in several areas of interest during the 1950s and 1960s. It became standard procedure for CIA agents to monitor reports of CBS correspondents in the field without their knowledge as the reports were transmitted to the United States. Sig Michelson, then news president for CBS, admitted that foreign correspondent Austin Goodrich, assigned by the network to its Stockholm bureau, had in fact "been placed there by the CIA and was working for them." Current CBS news president Richard Salant told Scheer that the practice was "unhealthy for journalists to do and I had it stopped." He also indicated that the practice should be viewed in terms of their times. "It was considered normal then."[32]

Some Americans tend to view press and CIA (or FBI) alliances as a form of patriotic endeavor, a vehicle by which the citizen-reporter may aid his country against potential foreign enemies. The major problem with that position is that it constitutes a gross conflict of interest on the part of the news media. The watchdog ceases watching and becomes part of the system, a system that bears watching as the First Amendment requires. For the press to fulfill its Constitutional mandate it must be *separate* from government, not a working part of it. As the late Walter Lippmann recommended, there needs to be an "air space" between the two. One cannot be part of the other.

The Gist of the Problem

That the press-CIA link is a contradiction in the democratic order is reflected in the growing concern of journalists themselves. During congressional hearings into relations between the CIA and the news media, three editors testified that the United States cannot argue that other governments subvert the role of the press if it is prepared to do the same thing.[33] Eugene Patterson, president of the American Society of Newspaper Editors (ASNE), asked Congress to enforce strict policy in the matter, even to the point of limiting CIA funding.

The Modern Picture

Admiral Stansfield Turner, CIA director, agreed that the agency's new policy would prohibit CIA agents from having direct relationships with American journalists "in the interest of and out of respect for the separate responsibilities and status of the United States press as a free and independent institution." Nor may CIA employees utilize "the name or facilities" of any American news organization as a cover. But the new policy does not exclude dealing with the media of foreign nations whose services the CIA would continue to buy. In addition, it does not exclude accepting free-lance American

New CIA Policy

journalists for paid intelligence work or nonjournalists who work for news organizations. The CIA would also continue to welcome translation services from American journalists and their presence at CIA training sessions. The new policy would also permit unpaid voluntary relations between the agency and American journalists who have intelligence to offer.

The Press View   Most journalists who testified before the congressional committee took the position that it was not the function of the journalist to seek out information for the government. Herman Nickel, former correspondent for *Time* magazine, addressed the issue forcefully: "A reporter who moonlights for the CIA or any other intelligence service because of the lure of money prostitutes himself. . . . Our patriotic duty is to keep our independence."

The *Detroit Free Press* editorialized on the CIA's new policy:

> It can contribute to the subversion of a free press abroad. And indirectly, it can poison the news Americans receive through international news channels. If the CIA plants a false story in a British or French news agency, for instance, that story may very well appear in American media. News knows no national boundaries. . . . Admiral Turner owes it to us to go further and clearly remove the CIA from covert efforts to warp or falsify the news.[34]

Summary   In this chapter we have explored the immense power of the executive branch of government, and the difficulties involved in the relationship between the mass media and that branch. Journalists and government officials recognize certain strengths and weaknesses in each other, depending on the particular issues or problems under scrutiny. Sometimes the relationship is congenial, at other times it is not. Government's need to present a positive image to the people often requires circumventing the news media in favor of public relations campaigns designed to project positive images of government. Finally, we have seen how particular agencies of the executive branch have manipulated the news media to their own ends, a maneuver that has reflected negatively on the press itself.

Notes   1.   "The People's Need to Know—1; A Bill of Complaint," Courtesy of the *Boston Globe*, January 21, 1973, p. 6–A.
2.   As quoted in Susan Heilmann Miller, "Reporters and Congressmen," *Journalism Monographs* (Lexington, Ky.: Association for Education in Journalism, 1978), p. 1.
3.   " 'Backlash' Here to Stay," The *State Journal*, Lansing, Michigan, April 3, 1978, p. 4–A.
4.   Jack Landau, "Secrecy Is the Trend," The *Quill*, May 1977, p. 27.
5.   Sydney J. Harris, "History Is Important, Progress Is Perilous," *Detroit Free Press*, March 2, 1978, p. 19–A.
6.   William L. Rivers and Michael J. Nyhan, eds., *Aspen Notebook on Government and the Media* (New York: Praeger Publishers, 1973), p. 13.

7. Rivers and Nyhan, *Aspen Notebook,* p. 23.
8. Information on "President Carter and the Press" from James Reston, "Editors are Keeping the Pressure on Carter," *Detroit Free Press* (*New York Times* Service), April 13, 1978, p. 11–A.
9. Jean Callahan, "Claudie Townsend, Associate White House Press Secretary," *Washington Journalism Review,* January/February 1978, p. 36.
10. "Hurt by Press, Lance Warns of Censorship," *Detroit Free Press,* April 13, 1978, p. 1–C; "Lance Warns Press Censorship Possible," The *State Journal,* Lansing, Michigan, April 13, 1978, p. 3–A.
11. "Bert Lance Accused of Covering Up Questionable Loans," The *State Journal* (Associated Press), Lansing, Michigan, April 27, 1978, p. 3–A.
12. "Absent Officials: No Work, Full Pay," *Detroit Free Press,* May 5, 1978, p. 4–A.
13. Rivers and Nyhan, *Aspen Notebook,* p. 14; "Behind the Lines," Public Broadcasting Service. Videotape No. 501, School of Journalism files, Michigan State University, East Lansing, Michigan.
14. Rivers and Nyhan, *Aspen Notebook,* p. 14.
15. James Reston, "The Press, the President and Foreign Policy." *Mass Media and Communication.* Charles S. Steinberg, ed. (New York: Hastings House, 1972), pp. 413–14.
16. Merle Miller, *Plain Speaking: An Oral Biography of Harry S. Truman,* Copyright © 1973, 1974 by Merle Miller, Reprinted with permission of the Berkeley Publishing Corporation, p. 376.
17. Dan Rather, *The Camera Never Blinks* (New York: Morrow, 1977), p. 18; James Reston, "The Press, the President and Foreign Policy," pp. 413–14.
18. Rivers and Nyhan, *Aspen Notebook,* pp. 34–41.
19. Lester Kinsolving, "Beyond the Fringe," *Washington Journalism Review,* April/May 1978, p. 62.
20. Ann Compton, "It's a Three-Ring Circus at The White House," *Washington Journalism Review,* January/February 1978, p. 44.
21. Information on Hamilton Jordan and "Free Telephone Services for Media" from Raymond Coffee, "What's Government Promoting for All That Money?" *Detroit Free Press* (from the *Chicago Tribune*), April 27, 1978, p. 11–A.
22. Dom Bonafede, "Uncle Sam: The Flimflam Man?" *Washington Journalism Review,* April/May 1978, p. 65.
23. George S. Hage, Everett E. Dennis, Arnold H. Ismach, Stephen Hartgen, *New Strategies for Public Affairs Reporting* (Englewood Cliffs, N.J.: Prentice-Hall, Inc., 1976), pp. 176–79.
24. "Uncovering More Undercover Work," The *Quill,* January 1977, p. 6.
25. "J. Edgar Hoover Gets Revenge," The *Quill,* February 1978, p. 2.
26. David Wise, "The President and the Press," *Readings in Mass Communication,* Michael C. Emery and Ted Curtis Smyth, eds. (Dubuque, Iowa: Wm. C. Brown Company Publishers, 1977), 3d ed., p. 361.
27. Information on Jacque Srouji from Sanford J. Ungar, "Among the Piranhas: A Journalist and the FBI," *Columbia Journalism Review,* September/October 1976, pp. 19–26.
28. Information on this and other cases of FBI involvement with news reporting from *Press Freedoms Under Pressure: Report of the Twentieth Century Fund Task Force on the Government and the Press,* pp. 87–88, pp. 29–34, Background paper by Fred P. Graham. © 1972 by the Twentieth Century Fund, Inc., New York.
29. Information on Truman and the formation of the CIA from Miller, *Plain Speaking,* p. 420.
30. Information on Carl Bernstein from "400 Newsmen Worked for CIA?" The *State Journal* (Associated Press), Lansing, Michigan, September 12, 1977, p. 3–A; Warren K. Agee, "Bernstein—Will: The Newsman as American Citizen," The *Quill,* November 1977, p. 33.
31. "CIA Limits Spying on the Media," The *News Media and the Law,* The Reporters Committee for Freedom of the Press, April 1978, p. 38.
32. "Sights Set on CIA Ban and CBS Tells of Old Ties," The *Quill,* June 1977, p. 10.
33. Information on the CIA and congressional hearings from "Editors Warn against Any CIA Use of Press," The *State Journal* (Associated Press), Lansing, Michigan, January 6, 1978, p. 5–A.
34. Editorial, "Journalists and the CIA," *Detroit Free Press,* December 20, 1977, p. 6–A.

For Further Reading

Bonafed, Dom. "Uncle Sam: The Flimflam Man?" *Washington Journalism Review*, April/May 1978, p. 65.

Callahan, Jean. "Claudia Townsend, Associate White House Press Secretary." *Washington Journalism Review*, January/February 1978, p. 36.

"CIA Limits Spying on the Media." *The News Media and the Law*, The Reporters Committee for Freedom of the Press, April 1978, p. 38.

Compton, Ann. "It's A Three Ring Circus At the White House." *Washington Journalism Review*, January/February 1978, p. 44.

Freedoms Under Pressure: Report of the Twentieth Century Fund Task Force on the Government and the Press. New York, 1972.

"J. Edgar Hoover Gets Revenge." The *Quill*, February 1978, p. 2.

Landau, Jack. "Secrecy Is the Trend." The *Quill*, May 1977, p. 27.

Rather, Dan. *The Camera Never Blinks*. New York: Morrow, 1977.

"Sights Set on CIA Ban and CBS Tells of Old Ties." The *Quill*, June 1977, p. 10.

"Uncovering More Undercover Work." The *Quill*, January 1977, p. 6.

Ungar, Stanford J. "Among the Piranhas: A Journalist and the F.B.I." *Columbia Journalism Review*, September/October 1976, pp. 19–26.

News in Pictures

Mass Media and Government 6
The Legislative Branch

Upon completing this chapter you should know—

how laws become laws

how the news media cover the legislative branch and the nature of the problems and issues involved

how congressional public relations information appears in the mass media as "news"

the basic issues and problems of press coverage of state and local legislative bodies

Chapter Objectives

Veto Invoked by the chief executive of government (president, governor, mayor, etc.) when he or she opposes a bill approved earlier by the legislative body. (p. 165)

Lobbyists Representatives of nongovernment bodies (labor, private industry, social groups, etc.) who try to influence legislation to their clients' interests. (p. 166)

Marathon Sessions As the official legislative session nears its end, bills still not acted upon are passed (or killed) with little discussion or debate but are as binding as other laws. (p. 166)

News Leak In this chapter, a leak occurs when elected officials "tip off" news people of confidential government information to achieve certain advantages. (p. 167)

Key Terms

There is no liberty in this country which is held more dear than that of the press . . . for if it is destroyed, what else to boast of is gone in an instant. Arbitrary ministers (and none but such) are enemies to this liberty, because it has ever been a check upon their tyranny.

Samuel Adams, *The Boston
Gazette*, June 10, 1765

The Legislative Process

The basic purpose of the legislative branch of government, whether the national Congress, state legislature, or city or town council, is to create laws that benefit the people. Regardless of the size or structure of the legislative body, the lawmaking process is essentially the same among all.

Ideas are developed in the mind of a legislator, which he might discuss with other legislators and/or private citizens or groups. If an idea seems promising, he forms it into a *bill*, which is then introduced to the whole legislative body. As a rule, the bill is then sent to an appropriate legislative committee for analysis and discussion. The committee may change part or all of the bill, or kill it, or pass it as is. The committee might also decide that the bill is of sufficient importance to hold public hearings to collect additional viewpoints. If the committee finally approves the bill, it then goes to the entire legislative body, which may further alter it, kill it, or pass it into law. If the latter happens, the legislation then goes to the chief executive officer—president, governor, or mayor—who may approve it or "veto" it. If vetoed, the legislative body may accept the veto or vote to override it, which means that the bill will become law even without the approval of the executive officer.

Bills thus become laws, and laws affect each citizen directly whether on the national, state, or local level. Laws are created in many forms and for many reasons. Mainly, they are devised to cope with social, educational, medical, or judicial problems or combinations of problems. Social legislation alone requires enormous expenditures of public monies to support medical care for the elderly, care for homeless children, welfare recipients, public housing programs, and so forth. The possibilities are virtually endless.

Since the primary function of a democratic government is to serve the people, the First Amendment requires that the people be kept informed about the kinds of laws the government wishes to enact in their name. And since governmental programs are financed from tax monies paid by citizens, citizens

**The Press and
the Legislative
Process**

are entitled to know about the programs as they develop through hearings and debates, and later when they become laws. If that system is to work, the news media will need to cover legislative activities more thoroughly than in the past, and report their findings to the people in complete and understandable terms. That is precisely what the Founding Fathers had in mind when they "legislated" the First Amendment to the United States Constitution.

Problems of Press Coverage

Regardless of how dedicated the press may be, it faces almost insurmountable problems in covering the legislative branch, especially in states where the governmental process is confusing at best.[1] A relatively small number of trained reporters are expected to oversee a vast amount of legislators and legislative activity. Some legislatures have taken on large research staffs to aid lawmakers in identifying problem areas and creating bills to deal with them. The result has been the creation of hundreds, even thousands, of pieces of legislation in a single annual session that might not otherwise have been developed. Even the most dedicated reporters have difficulty understanding the complexities of these bills much less explaining them to the public.

Frequently the process is further muddied by the activities of paid "lobbyists" and other special interest groups who apply pressures to legislators to get certain legislation passed or not passed, depending on how it fits the designs of the special interests they represent. Conditions become even more bizarre for both officials and reporters when the regular legislative session nears its

Marathon Sessions

end. At that point, "marathon sessions" take over and many bills pass in the final hours with little or no discussion or debate. Yet they are as binding as the laws that have been put together with great and loving care.

To observe the legislative process at work and the press's involvement in it, it is essential to separate the national Congress from the state and municipal legislatures and examine the mechanisms that make each work or not work.

The Congress of the United States

How Well Press and Legislatures Work Together

In her study of how well members of Congress and the press work together, Susan Heilmann Miller found considerably more cooperation than opposition between the two groups.[2] She determined that members of Congress and their aides have a mutual assistance relationship with reporters by the very nature of their collective activities. In the period analyzed, she found that "reporters assisted officials by what they wrote—whether they chose to or not. And reporters were largely dependent on officials and their staffs for the information on which those stories were based." Miller also found that reporters sometimes bring significant subject matter to the attention of legislators, including new information or names of persons who could testify in congressional investigations. Coverage of such investigations by media could increase the chances of reform by "feeding public demand for Congressional action."

One strategy employed to move committees of Congress to hold hearings on important matters is for concerned legislators or their aides to "leak" information to the press. The press presents the information to the people and the committee is thus "forced" to hold hearings on the issue or problem. One congressional aide commented: "I speak to my boss through the newspapers. I'm saying, 'This is a big issue. You ought to spend some time on it.' " Another said: "Of course I try to get publicity for the senator. That gives him an incentive to continue our investigation."

Information "Leaks"

At the same time, Miller found, the "close working relationship" between the press and members of Congress often results from each functioning *apart* from the other, as contradictory as that might sound. Some journalists even resist helping public officials enhance their public images. They feel it is not their function to do so. Yet one reporter commented on how fruitless it would be to put out a newspaper and not include stories that tended to enhance the images of public officials. Those officials also serve as major sources of news and, therefore, they "actively cultivate publicity" about themselves whether reporters like it or not. So the relationships that exist between members of the press and members of Congress take many forms.

Reporters and Public Imagery

George Galloway, a legislative specialist for the Library of Congress, observed that contact between members of Congress and the press is "close, constant, and as a rule mutually advantageous." House and Senate members seek favorable publicity for themselves and their programs.[3] With current public disenchantment with Congress as high as it is, members have developed profound concern about their public images and how to improve them. A recent national survey by the Louis Harris organization reflected that Americans hold negative views of the actions of Congress by a whopping 63 to 28 percent.[4]

The Press as Congressional Image Maker

Press coverage of Congress is handled primarily by the wire services, Associated Press (AP) and United Press International (UPI), plus the Washington bureaus of major newspapers, news magazines, and broadcast networks. In addition, various news syndicates offer news and feature services to smaller media outlets that cannot support bureaus or correspondents of their own. The bureaus tend to give special coverage to the activities of those officials whose home bases lie within their circulation areas, providing readers with local impact of congressional action or inaction as the case may be.[5]

Who Actually Covers the Congress?

Both Houses of Congress also have impressive "galleries" for the electronic media, radio mostly, and now the American people have regular live television coverage of congressional debates.

Obviously, Congress enjoys excellent media coverage of its major activities. But so "voluminous is the daily output of the legislative mills that only the highlights of the most noteworthy developments are reported." In addition, Galloway reports, it is not uncommon in Washington for newspeople, "in their

Extensive Media Coverage of U.S. Congress

restless search for copy, to create controversy where none exists." Little "news" comes from harmonious associations between reporters and public officials.[6]

The Public's Right to Know

As we have seen, in the interest of the public's right to know, it is essential that both media and their audiences seriously consider the public's right to know *what*? How *much*? What kinds of things? Certainly the public is not entitled to know the details of troop movements, their numbers, and their destinations during a time of war. The legislative arm of the national government has seen fit to pass laws that permit secrecy in those circumstances and *in the public interest*. The Atomic Secrets Act, for example, prohibits the publication of information that deals with atomic weaponry geared for the defense of the country.

Secrecy and the Legislative Branch

The news media rarely debate the logic of excluding such information from public consumption.[7] But beyond those basic concerns, it is certain that government regularly restricts information that the news media and the public have a right to know but cannot get. Legislators are extremely sensitive to voter power in their home states or districts. Some home areas are highly and critically involved in the actions of their elected officials. Others are abjectly passive and profess little or no interest in what their representatives do or fail to do. Hence, officials may sometimes consider it the better part of wisdom to hold back from the media certain kinds of information, especially when it is personally uncomplimentary to them. In that fashion, much information not related to national defense, atomic secrets, or other sensitive areas is quietly tucked away. Yet, it is very much in the public interest for voters to have *all* information on their elected representatives to insure that they are being represented competently on all levels of activity, professional and personal. Evidence strongly indicates that good news about a member of Congress reaches the home base with greater frequency than bad news.

The Folks Back Home

The Right to Information

One important aspect of our political system is that the Constitution guarantees the right of citizens to a press that is free of government controls. But, according to some, the First Amendment does not guarantee anyone the *right to information*, the press included. Under the provisions of the First Amendment, no publication or broadcast station has enjoyed the right to compel government to release specific information. So the public's right to know remains one of the grayest of all areas in the press-government arena.

Charged as they are with formulating new laws on behalf of society, Congress and some state legislatures have recently become active in creating laws that would make public business truly public as a rule and not as an exception.

The Freedom of Information Act (FOI), passed in 1966 and amended in 1974, permits the news media to report on governmental activities as recorded in official public records. In 1976, the Congress passed the Government in the Sunshine Act, which stipulates that meetings of federal agencies must be open to the public and must be announced in advance. Where such legislation has been passed on federal and state levels, it has helped bring a balance of "secrecy within a framework of openness."

The Freedom of Information Act

If reporters are to wail about government's lack of cooperation with the news media, they must also recognize that part of the problem lies with them. Morton Mintz, of the *Washington Post*, poses some significant questions about the failure of the press to cover important congressional business when it has the opportunity to do so.[8] "How much of it is owed to reporters? To editors? To a possible miscalculation of resources? To a system that eludes internal audit by either reporters or editors?" In response, Mintz offers a selection of major news stories growing out of congressional investigations and hearings that were all but ignored by the news media. Some examples follow.

The Other Side of the Coin

Dr. Helen Taussig, a pediatric cardiologist and discoverer of the Blue Baby operation, went to Germany to investigate the high incidence of births of armless and legless infants. It became a major story in Europe. But the American news media, which are represented in Europe, hardly took notice. Later, Dr. Taussig told the House Antitrust Subcommittee that the cause of the deformities was a tranquilizer called thalidomide. *Much later*, the American press reported that a drug firm had released 2.5 million thalidomide tablets to American physicians on a supposed experimental basis.

The Thalidomide Story

Congress adopted without notable dissent a joint resolution for the establishment of a National Commission on Product Safety. The resolution declared that "the American consumer has a right to be protected against unreasonable risk of bodily harm from products purchased on the open market for the use of himself and his family." This was important legislation, but the press appeared to be busy elsewhere. The new commission then launched a study that found that 30,000 Americans are killed each year, 110,000 are permanently disabled, and 20 million are otherwise injured from use of consumer products. For more than two and one-half years the commission held hearings in Washington and elsewhere to gather evidence. One of the hearings dealt with possible hazards from the use of sliding glass doors made of cheap glass that shatters easily. The commission learned that 100,000 children had been injured, some fatally, by colliding with the doors which, in some cases, they did not know were there. A Washington police officer testified that his son was badly cut after walking into such a door. "I took my hand and I put his nose back where it belonged," the father said. The story received scant media attention.

The National Commission on Product Safety

the roll call . . .

Michigan Senate

WETLANDS: The Michigan Senate passed, 25–8, and sent to the House legislation protecting environmentally valuable wetlands areas. Supporters argued that the bill was necessary to protect wetlands from increased commercial encroachment. Opponents said it would restrict economic growth throughout the state and would hamper mining operations in the Upper Peninsula. The first vote shown below is on an amendment proposed by Sen. Joseph S. Mack, D-Ironwood, that was defeated 11–23. It would have exempted the mining industry from the wetlands bill's provisions. The second is on the bill itself. Here is the vote on the Mack amendment. A yes vote is a vote in favor of weakening the bill.

Democrats
☒ Yeas ■ Nays ☐ Not Voting

☐ Brown	☒ Guastello	☒ Irwin	■ O'Brien
■ Corbin	■ G. Hart	■ Kammer	■ Pierce
■ DiNello	☒ J. Hart	☒ Kelly	■ Plaweckl
■ DeSana	☒ J. Hertel	☒ Mack	■ Ross
■ Faust	☐ Holmes	☒ Miller	■ H. Scott
■ Faxon	☐ Huffman	☒ Monsma	☒ J. Vaughn

Republicans
☒ Yeas ■ Nays ☐ Not Voting

■ Allen	☐ DeMaso	■ Geake	☒ J. Welborn
■ Arthurhultz	☒ Engler	☒ Mowat	☒ R. D. Young
☒ Bishop	☒ Fredricks	☒ Sederburg	
☒ DeGrow	☒ Gast	☒ VanderLaan	

Here is the vote on the main wetlands bill. Sen. John Welborn, R-Kalamazoo, was present for the final vote on the bill but abstained from voting because he owns property that may be classified as a wetland and felt he might have a conflict of interest. A yes vote is a vote for the bill.

Democrats
☒ Yeas ■ Nays ☐ Not Voting

☐ Brown	☒ Guastello	■ Irwin	☒ O'Brien
☒ Corbin	☒ G. Hart	☒ Kammer	☒ Pierce
☒ DiNello	☒ J. Hart	☒ Kelly	☒ Plaweckl
☒ DeSana	☒ J. Hertel	■ Mack	☒ Ross
☒ Faust	☐ Holmes	☒ Miller	☒ H. Scott
☒ Faxon	☐ Huffman	☒ Monsma	☒ J. Vaughn

Republicans
☒ Yeas ■ Nays ☐ Not Voting

☒ Allen	☐ DeMaso	☒ Geake	☐ J. Welborn
☒ Arthurhultz	☒ Engler	■ Mowat	■ R. D. Young
■ Bishop	■ Fredricks	☒ Sederburg	
■ DeGrow	☒ Gast	☒ VanderLaan	

U.S. Senate

STANDBY GAS RATIONING AUTHORITY: After two modifications, by a 58–39 vote, the Senate approved President Carter's request for standby gasoline rationing authority in times of acute shortage. The proposal was subsequently killed in the House. Under the plan, the president would have authority to allot gasoline to each state based on its previous record of consumption. If a shortage occurred, the president would send a rationing proposal to Congress along with his reasons for restricting gasoline consumption. Congress would then have the right to veto the proposal. Rationing would be done by means of coupons allotted to each registered vehicle within a state.

Democrats
☒ Yeas ■ Nays ☐ Not Voting *Paired

☒ Riegle	☒ Levin

U.S. House

STANDBY GAS RATIONING AUTHORITY: By a 159–246 vote, the House rejected President Carter's request for standby authority to ration gasoline in times of acute shortage. The Senate had approved the Carter plan the previous day, but the House action killed the proposal. Supporters said the plan was necessary to cope with shortages should there be a cutoff of oil imports from the Middle East. They added that the plan would insure that all areas of the country would be treated on an equal basis should shortages occur, rather than having the problem concentrated in areas more dependent upon imported oil. Opponents of the plan said all areas of the nation would not be treated fairly under the Carter plan, noting provisions in the plan that would raise statewide gasoline allocations for predominantly rural and western states. Some opponents questioned whether the Energy Department could be trusted to administer the plan effectively or fairly.

Democrats
☒ Yeas ■ Nays ☐ Not Voting *Paired

■ Albosta	■ Carr	☒ Dingell	☒ Nedzi
☒ Blanchard	☒ Conyers*	☒ Ford	☒ Traxler
☒ Bonior	☒ Diggs	☒ Kildee	☒ Wolpe
☒ Brodhead			

Republicans
☒ Yeas ■ Nays ☐ Not Voting *Paired

■ Broomfield	■ Pursell	■ Stockman	■ VanderJagt
■ Davis	■ Sawyer		

The *Detroit Free Press* reports regularly on its editorial page how state and congressional representatives vote on bills. (*Detroit Free Press.*)

At another point, the Internal Revenue Service (IRS) levied assessments against large American oil companies after they had posted illegally high prices for crude oil from the Persian Gulf. Thus, the companies inflated the already sizeable benefits that they reaped from oil depletion allowances. The IRS secretly settled the matter with the companies for about fifty cents on the dollar. The media passed up this story, too.

The IRS and the Oil Companies

The General Accounting Office released a report that stated that 40 percent of food manufacturing and processing plants in the United States are to some degree filthy. The report, said Mintz, "was distributed like confetti" and was brought up during at least two other congressional hearings. Again, the media failed to show interest.

Food Processing

Examples abound. In some cases, because of the overloaded schedules of reporters and editors and the crush of daily deadlines, meaningful stories are passed up. But, Mintz indicates, the standard excuses hold little water. One reason is that the media prefer covering the executive branch to the legislative and end up "over-covering the one and under-covering the other partly because it's easier." Another is that some reporters are lazy or prefer to cover "glamorous" assignments. A third is the "ego" problem. That sets in when, after a reporter invests considerable time and effort in developing a story from a congressional hearing, its value becomes inflated over another hearing that could be a lot more important.

Some Reasons Why

Covering Executive vs. Legislative

Public libraries in the United States routinely gather various government documents for general readership as well as to provide various forms of "evidence" related to discussions and debates of government in action. One of the primary sources of such evidence is the *Congressional Record*, which supposedly contains verbatim accounts of legislative activity in the Congress. Unfortunately, it is not always dependable even within government circles. In 1873 the *Record* became the official "record" of House and Senate deliberations. It was to be a permanent record that might be explored immediately or by future generations interested in the workings of the democratic process.

The Congressional Record

It was a good idea, but the *Record* has not always been what it was intended to be. In fact, many reporters feel that its value is limited and that it has been the record of what individual members of Congress *want it to be*. Practice has permitted members to insert speeches and other matter that were never delivered and to later alter for the public's eye what had been entered during actual debate or discussion. Worse, there has been no way by which the reader could detect one form of content from the other. Therefore, in terms of accuracy, the *Record* has been a questionable instrument of government, especially for the press and interested citizens who do not regularly attend actual sessions of the Congress.

A Good Idea Gone Bad in Practice

Under new rules, a speech inserted in the *Congressional Record* but not actually delivered as part of an official proceeding must be preceded by a "bullet" symbol to distinguish it from content literally presented in formal sessions. It would appear that, at last, the problem of inaccuracy has been solved. But the new rules contained a loophole. The catch is that if a member of Congress formally delivers the first portion of his "nonspeech"—even a single sentence—the bullet symbol is eliminated. In brief, the voters will still not know how the material actually got into the *Record*—by legitimate presentation in the chamber, or later when it serves no purpose beyond stoking the official's ego and impressing the folks back home. As one editorialist noted, "We can see it now. Senator X rushes breathlessly into the chamber and says, 'I am here today to talk about the energy crisis.' Then he departs for a luncheon engagement and leaves the speech for the printers."[9]

Thomas Griffiths, a former editor of *Life* magazine, characterized the *Record*'s content as a collection of "windy indulgences that fill column after column."[10] To the extent that that comment reflects the real value of the *Congressional Record*, and to a great extent it does, the people are the losers. An accurate record of congressional business made available to citizens via libraries and personal subscriptions might improve the machinery of government. It might also make elected officials truly responsive to the needs of the nation generally and, in particular, to those they represent.

The "Little Legislatures"

Many congressional observers evince growing concern about increasing secrecy in governmental deliberations. Secrecy has become the rule rather than the exception when legislatures debate the strengths and shortcomings of bills placed before them. When the nation was smaller and less complicated and government was more personally accessible, citizens could learn from attending meetings of their legislature, state or national, how the lawmaking process worked. In most cases, this is no longer possible. The reason is that so many bills are debated by legislative *committees* behind closed doors. What takes place before the entire membership is usually only "the formal and final confirmation of decisions really made in the closed sessions of committees."

Legislative "Secrecy"—It's Nothing New

J. Russell Wiggins, former editor of the *Washington Post*, points out that the practice of secrecy in legislative matters began in earnest shortly after the opening of the twentieth century. It has increased in spite of passage of the LaFollette-Monroney Congressional Reorganization Act of 1946, which states: "All hearings are required to be open to the public except where executive sessions for marking up bills, or for voting or where the committee by a majority vote orders a secret executive session in the interest of national security."[11]

A second law dealing with congressional reform and requiring more open meetings was passed in 1970.[12] Yet, according to *Congressional Quarterly*, "Congressional committees conducted 40 percent of their hearings behind closed doors in 1972," the year *after* the Legislative Reorganization Act of 1970 took effect. And when meetings are "private," it means that the news media are excluded along with private citizens.

The House of Representatives of the Congress bars the public from committee meetings more frequently than the Senate does. In 1971 and 1972, 79 percent of all House committee meetings were closed to the public, a year after passage of the Reorganization Act requiring open meetings. (The vitally important House Appropriations Committee was not included in the *Quarterly*'s survey of meetings during those years.) According to these annual surveys, of a total of 2,640 House committees that met in 1953, 893 (35 percent) were held in private. In 1972, of 4,073 meetings, 1,648 (40 percent) kept the public and the press out. Because of their political strength, the committees have become known as "little legislatures."

Barring the Public and Press

When one examines the enormously powerful and influential committees that do business on Capitol Hill each year, much of it beyond public scrutiny, one begins to comprehend what legislative secrecy is all about. In 1971 during the Ninety-second Congress, the House Appropriations Committee met 455 times, 36 of the meetings in open session. But 419 meetings were closed—92 percent of the total. The same percentage held for 1972. The House Armed Services Committee met 188 times in 1971 of which 78 meetings (41 percent) were closed. In 1972, of 152 meetings held, 74 (49 percent) were closed to the public and press. In 1971, the House Administration Committee met 56 times and closed 47 of those to the public (or 84 percent). The following year the same committee met 51 times and closed its doors 45 times for an 88 percent figure. It is also important to note that the House Committee on Standards of Conduct (of House members) met 14 times in 1971 and closed 13 of those meetings (93 percent). In 1972, that Committee met 11 times and closed all of them.

The Extent of Legislative Secrecy

It should also be noted that some committees of the House scored impressively with open meetings. The House Committee on Education and Labor closed a mere 3 percent of its meetings in 1971 and closed none in 1972. The Post Office and Civil Service Committee closed only 3 percent of its meetings in 1971 and 1972. But committees such as these obviously do not have the impact that others have.

In view of the wishes of the Founding Fathers to have the public participate in the democratic order at all levels, secret legislative actions would appear to be a massive violation of their intentions. True, most Americans cannot

Secrecy and the People

travel to Washington, D.C. to participate directly in the business of government. The Founders recognized that and, under the First Amendment, assigned the news media to do the job in the name of the people. When the press is also barred from the essential legislative processes, it is government by secrecy. Again the people lose.

Congressional Imagery

The more frequently a public official appears in the news media of his home area, the more firmly established he becomes, for better or worse, in the minds of voters of that area. Therefore, it is basic to his interests to curry favor with those media. As one means of doing that, every member of Congress—all 435 of them—maintains a personal press staff headed by a former newsperson. He or she is familiar with accepted writing and editing styles of newspapers and broadcast outlets, their deadlines, and news values. Equally important, the press staff sees to it that the media have to exert themselves as little as possible to publish a solid story on the official or project it over the air.[13]

The News Media as Propaganda Vehicles

According to media analyst Ben Bagdikian, the news media, accidentally or on purpose, have made themselves vehicles of propaganda between members of Congress and the American people.[14] And that development "has contributed to the growing impotence and insensitivity of the Legislative Branch of the federal government while the Judicial and the Executive have become overpowering."

The House of Representatives of the Congress should be the most sensitive of the three branches to the needs and wishes of the people, since its members must stand for reelection every two years. Presumably then, they need to expose their records to the voters with considerable frequency. Yet, a recent congressional election featured 330* incumbents asking their districts to return them to Washington. Only 10 were defeated. As Bagdikian notes, "the renewal of the House on the basis of performance and changes in public desires is not working." A major reason why it is not working, he says, is that most of the news media are not analyzing congressional performances. More importantly, the media are accepting political propaganda from elected officials and feeding it to the people as *news*.

Low Turnover a Problem

Roots of the Problem

As previously mentioned, each member of Congress has on his payroll at least one former journalist (Senator Lowell Weicker, R-Conn., has four) who knows how to put a news story together so that it will project a positive image of the boss, and how and where to place it in the media. (Suffice it to say that information uncomplimentary to a public official is not considered acceptable fare to be funnelled to the folks back home.)

*The remaining incumbents had retired, died, or had lost in primaries held earlier.

Why the courts are running America

By RICHARD REEVES

CINCINNATI—The sign of the decline of American politics is in the window of Batsake's Cleaners on Walnut Street. It's a poster showing a blank-faced young man holding a telephone. Under his picture are two words: "Luke Listens."

"Luke" is Charles Luken, a Democratic candidate for the City Council. He doesn't have to identify himself further because he is the son of Congressman Thomas Luken. Voters, presumably, have a vague idea of who he is because the family name gets some recognition.

The poster reminded me of something said by Wilson Wyatt, the former mayor of Louisville and Adlai Stevenson's campaign manager in the 1956 presidential election. "The sure sign of the decline of politicians," Wyatt told me last winter, "is those slogans that say 'So-and-so Cares' or 'So-and-so Listens.' That's an absolutely meaningless phrase unless it means that so-and-so doesn't intend to do anything in office."

Usually, in fact, so-and-so doesn't intend to do anything. Making decisions, doing something, is what gets voters mad—if a politician just listens and cares, no one will notice him and he might get re-elected forever. So who governs America? Part of the answer to that question was two blocks up Walnut Street, in Room 822 of the United States Courthouse. A three-judge panel of the 6th Circuit U.S. Court of Appeals—Anthony Celebrezze, Bailey Brown and Cornelia Kennedy—was ordering the state of Ohio to revise its welfare procedures because of a lawsuit brought by four Franklin County residents. "Go back and tell the Legislature," Judge Celebrezze said, "to hire more hearing officers."

COURTS RULE because elected politicians—the "Lukes" of America—refuse to take stands or actions that might make anybody mad. They just listen and care—like cocker spaniels.

On that day, Oct. 17, Cincinnati newspapers were reporting the latest developments on a state court order to city officials to renovate or close the city's old jail, which was originally built to house Civil War prisoners. And, the federal government was threatening Ohio with court action because state officials have not been able to come up with an effective environmental protection law. Chicago, at the same time, was being threatened with court action because that city's officials have been unwilling to approve a school desegregation plan.

"A lot of the cases that come in here are pushed in because local officials, county commissioners for instance, didn't want to take responsibility for a decision," said U.S. Magistrate J. Vincent Aug in his office in the Cincinnati federal

> Courts rule because elected politicians refuse to take stands or actions that might make anybody mad. They just listen and care—like cocker spaniels.

courthouse. "The courts' power is becoming awesome because they're the only place you can find decision-making. Judges may not want to make some of those decisions, but they don't shy away. They know that's what they're here for."

THE "LUKES" do shy away. And the situation is not healthy—not if you believe in democracy. If elected officials won't move, unelected ones have to move in or take over. In some cases the courts have already taken over—schools in Boston and prisons in Alabama are examples—and that may soon happen with the crumbling old jail in Cincinnati.

Rule by judiciary has become so common, in fact, that J. Skelly Wright, the chief judge of the U.S. Court of Appeals in Washington, has said publicly that judges "must restrain themselves . . . be more hesitant about filling the void, when, in our judgment, the elected branches of government have acted and failed." But it's becoming harder and harder to hesitate while "Luke" does nothing but listen."

A member of Congress "blows his horn." (Illustration by David Seavey, *Washington Journalism Review.*)

With so few American media having their own Washington bureaus or correspondents, most depend on other sources of information on and about Congress: 72 percent of the nation's newspapers, 96 percent of television stations, and 99 percent of radio stations have no direct informational ties with Washington, D.C. The approximately 1,400 American correspondents in the capital cover only the major stories, which means that most members of Congress are ignored by the media. Thus, the political public relations release becomes a most fruitful informational instrument between the elected official and the voters back home. It is also a highly questionable vehicle in terms of the "balance" of information the voters get from it and on which they must base decisions at the polls. In the main the releases are, in Bagdikian's words, notorious distortions of truth.

Congress's Public-Image Factory

To assist representatives in maintaining positive public images with their voters, Congress offers, at the taxpayers' expense, a $500,000 facility where they may make their own films and audio and video tapes designed to make them look good, at a fraction of the cost charged by commercial businesses. The facility has sixteen trained people to handle technical and other matters. The House offers two video studios with color cameras, one used for filming, the other for video taping. The facility also has four radio recording studios plus impressive processing and duplicating equipment.

The tapes or films are sent back to the representative's district, where broadcast stations put them on the air sometimes under a "From Our Man In Washington" kind of heading, but frequently as part of regular newscasts. Either way, they typically appear to viewers as news, not as personal promotion gimmicks, which is what most are. Sometimes the official is shown in an "interview" setting with one of his aides posing as a reporter. The aide asks rehearsed questions to which the official responds in what appears to be his professional role. The practice of showing these tapes *as news* openly violates regulations of the Federal Communications Commission. They go mostly to stations in medium- and small-size cities, which means the majority of the nation's 705 commercial television and 6,800 radio stations. With little media competition available on the local level in those markets, the propaganda impact is significant.

The House facility (the Senate has its own) offers various standard "sets," which a representative may choose to impress the folks back home. He may choose a library setting, which has impressive-looking books on the shelves. Or he may select a blue curtain backdrop or even a "carefully contrived photograph" of the Capitol dome as if it stood outside the office window. (In fact, no member of Congress has such a view.) In one recent year, 353 of the 435 House members utilized the studio, most of them on a weekly basis.

"Sets" in the House

With such up-to-date image-building technology on hand, and at such low cost, it is little wonder that so few members of Congress are defeated at election time. A Congressman from a Western state admitted in a New York speech, "A challenger needs $25,000 just to get even with me."

As Bagdikian wrote:

> It is not farfetched to say that this dearth of firsthand Washington correspondence contributes to the failure of Congress to renew itself as the social environment changes—the incumbents have too strong a tax-subsidized propaganda machine and the news media are too tolerant of it for the voters to get the sort of balanced input they need to make informed decisions.

In effect, closer coverage by the news media of the professional and personal doings of members of Congress would create *needed* periodic changes in the membership. New blood! That was the original idea!

Bagdikian indicates that those officeholders from districts whose press has correspondents in Washington are at a disadvantage over those who do not. Newspapers that can afford to support a reporter or a bureau in the nation's capital tend to keep close tabs on the personal and professional performances of their senators and representatives. Their observations are revealed to voters at home via the media. Reelection of incumbent members of Congress from those districts is considerably lower than for those whose media are not represented in Washington.

Balanced Coverage: The Vital Connection

James Reston, of the *New York Times*, points up the differences in relationships between the press and the executive branch and the press and the legislative branch.[15] Members of the executive branch, in general, tend to view the reporter with suspicion, the source of trouble. Even if an official should reveal nothing "the mere fact that he is known to have seen the reporter may lead his superiors to blame him for something the reporter prints several days later." Thus, the official must be wary.

Differences between Press Coverage of the Executive and Legislative

The view of the press by the Congress is an entirely different matter. Representatives tend to view the news media as vital to the growth of their political careers, getting reelected being the most important part of it. And since reporters need information, a workable arrangement helpful to both is formed. "They exchange information in a discreet way, and sometimes in ways that are not so discreet."

The executive branch must go to Congress for funding for its programs. To bring that off, it must answer Congress's questions and that means disclosing considerable information that the news media is delighted to pick up. Thus, committee hearings can be significant sources of news.

Reston says:

Influence of the Press on Congressional Conduct

The influence of reporters on the conduct of individual members of the House and Senate, particularly the House, is much greater than is generally realized. For example, if reporters tend to play up the spectacular charges or statements of extremists on Capitol Hill and to play down or ignore the careful, analytical speeches of the more moderate and responsible members—as, unfortunately, they do most of the time—this inevitably has its influence on many other members, particularly new members. The latter are trying to establish themselves. They are eager to say things that will get into the news and be read back home before the next election. Accordingly, if the moderate and the serious statements are ignored by the reporters and the spectacular trivialities are emphasized, the new Congressman often draws the obvious conclusion and begins spouting nonsense to attract attention. This is one influence of a popular press that merits more attention than it gets.

Congressional Investigations

"Media Events" and the Congress

One of the most formidable personal publicity vehicles for members of Congress is the House or Senate investigating committee. Douglass Cater, director of the Aspen Program on Communications and Society, has observed this form of "media event" and how it personally benefits committee members to a greater extent than it solves problems.[16] The tactic of the investigating committee, in Cater's terms, is "geared to the production of headlines on a daily and even twice daily basis. It is able to create the news story which lingers week after week on the front pages to form an indelible impression on the public mind. No institution of the Executive Branch is capable of such sustained and well-manipulated publicity."

Press Is Essential to Investigations

The press is so important to any congressional investigating committee that reporters are given special seats up where the action is. Close to the witness table crouch the press photographers prepared to "shoot" witnesses in the unfolding drama. Elsewhere the blinding lights of television and motion picture crews create constant heat, confusion, and general physical and psychological discomfort for witnesses.

As Cater notes, major committee investigations are rarely "investigations" in the commonly accepted sense of the term. "They are planned deliberately to move from a preconceived idea to a predetermined conclusion." The investigative activity has taken place before the hearing begins. What remains is the "staging of an arresting spectacle" that will attract the attention of the public. The committee need not compose a statement of purpose; it may proceed on the most shallow procedural rules and its leadership is not subject to review by a higher authority. It can, as Cater says, "stage the kind of spectacle that will produce news and attract public attention." It might even create political heroes of minor actors in the drama, as politically motivated members of Congress are thrust into the limelight and saluted by their parties as newcomers on the move.

The Staging of the Spectacular

During the Watergate-filled summer of 1973 when the Ervin Committee went after the Nixon administration, committee members took their lumps from frustrated soap opera and quiz show fans whose favorite entertainment had been preempted by the upper body of the Congress. But many other citizens sat captivated through the lengthy hearings. Some were even moved emotionally by the cast of characters.[17] Senator Edward Gurney's telephones came alive with inquiries about his public and personal life. Women wanted to know if he was "unattached and available." Requests for him to speak to groups and organizations doubled. Newfound fans urged him to run for national office.

The Drama of Watergate

Instant Celebrities

Reprinted by permission of the Chicago Tribune-New York News Syndicate, Inc.

Reprinted by permission of the Chicago Tribune-New York News Syndicate, Inc.

Others did the same for Senators Howard Baker, Daniel Inouye, and Herman Talmadge. Committee Chairman Sam Ervin, seventy-seven, received a proposal of marriage from a woman in Dallas. Requests for him to make speeches doubled in number over the previous year, some carrying offers as high as $5,000 per appearance. Senator Talmadge turned down $10,000 and a free trip to Acapulco to address a group there. Senator Baker, then a relatively new face to television viewers, received approximately 100 love letters including one from a sixty-nine-year-old woman who wrote, "I could vote for you for President all day, and all night too!" A poll of Atlanta beauty shops determined that Hawaii Senator Inouye was "the sexiest man on the Watergate Committee." Talmadge came in second and Baker third. Even low-key New Mexico Senator Joseph Montoya, who "interrogated" Watergate witnesses from questions composed in advance by his staff, signed an agreement with a speaker's bureau.

Granted, the Senate investigation into Watergate was a mountain among ant hills compared to typical congressional investigations. But it reveals dramatically the impact the news media have, particularly television, when public officials bask in the glare of major media events. To the sorrow of many Americans, Senator Joseph McCarthy learned that lesson well in the 1950s.

Congress and Koreagate

Another major congressional "event" turned up under the media label Koreagate.[18] It involved a Korean national named Tongsun Park, a world rice manipulator who allegedly paid off various members of Congress in exchange for their help in channeling American foreign rice purchases through him.

Mass Media and Government: The Legislative Branch

' HI, FELLAS! "GOOD TIME TONGSUN" IS BACK IN TOWN! '

Reprinted by permission of the Chicago Tribune-New York News Syndicate, Inc.

The news media covered it as a major political event as it was. Many Washington officials started running scared. The news media rushed to the scene to record the unfolding drama.

The Senate Ethics Committee indicated its concern that the late Senator John McClellan (D-Ark.) violated the law by failing to report a $1,000 contribution from Park in 1972. Park also testified that he made financial contributions to Senator Birch Bayh (D-Ind.) and gave between $5,000 and $10,000 to the late Senator Hubert Humphrey's presidential campaign.

Park also testified that he gave between $16,000 and $21,000 in contributions to eight members of the United States Senate. Park, who made a practice of throwing lavish parties for members of Congress, also admitted making $850,000 in contributions to thirty members of the House.

Four other present or former senators admitted that Park had given them contributions. The late Senator Joseph Montoya accepted $3,000 from Park; Senator Spark Matsunage (D-Hawaii) took $1,500; Senator Harry F. Byrd (I-Va.) and former Senator Stuart Symington (D-Mo.) accepted $500 each.

Four Confess to Accepting Funds

Former Representative Otto Passman (D-La.), seventy-seven, was ordered to trial for his part in the influence-buying scheme. He was charged with "conspiracy to defraud the United States, bribery and accepting an illegal gratuity." He was also charged with having accepted approximately $213,000 from Park in exchange for helping him get American rice accounts. Eventually the Committee formally charged four current and two former members of Congress with taking cash from Park. It also exonerated nine others.

So the issues and problems that exist between the news media and the United States Congress are many and complex. Whatever they are and whatever measures are devised to cope with them, these issues have impact on the people who vote for individuals who, in turn, make decisions in their name. If the system is to continue to work, and it is badly battered now, the public needs to be informed by an informed press. There is no other way. Watergate and Koreagate are two awesome examples of the need for press vigilance in matters of public concern.

State and Local Government

By way of comparison, the United States government has roughly the same number of employees it had at the end of World War II although the federal budget is almost ten times higher now than then. Probably the single most important reason behind this phenomenon is the size and cost of state government, which the federal bureaucracy helps to support.

Growth of State Governments over Federal

While the per capita federal employment has grown only 1.9 percent in the last twenty years, employment has increased 182 percent in state government. At the same time, the budget for federal government has bounded from $3.6 billion to $42.2 billion, most of it to support programs in public health, education, and welfare that have been created in the states nationwide. In the same period, membership of the American Federation of State, County, and Municipal Employees leaped in numbers from 77,000 in 1947 to about 750,000 at present. As *Washington Monthly* magazine commented: "To the extent that we've had a big government boom in the past two or three decades, it has been on the state, not the federal level."[19]

Press Coverage of State Legislatures: The Problems

As impressive as all that is, news coverage of state legislatures is a far cry from the media attention given the national Congress. And yet, in a collective sense, the states are where American government is biggest, most powerful, and most expensive in terms of tax dollars. Understaffed media coverage of state government business is part of the problem. Veteran legislative reporters Ralph Whitehead, Jr. and Howard M. Ziff note that the Associated Press (AP) assigns one person to cover the Alaska legislature. That includes coverage of the governor, all the agencies of government, the courts, the activities of 11,000 state employees, the State Senate and House and their eighteen committees. By comparison, AP's bureau in Sacramento, California has a staff of seven to cover the same form of governmental structure that is covered by one person in Alaska. Even so, since the problems to be covered in California are compounded by a larger and more complex legislature, greater expenditures for more programs, and more and greater problems statewide, covering legislative matters in California might not be that far ahead of AP's Alaskan effort, if at all. Charles Davis, then executive secretary of the National Conference of State Legislatures, commented: "Most newspapers have an abysmal understanding of what a state legislature really is."[20]

A case in point:[21] West Virginia's annual operating budget is now about $1.6 billion a year—$700 million in federal funds—or three times what it was ten years ago. To nobody's surprise, since the state is a poverty pocket, the major legislative programs developed in West Virginia have been in health, education, and welfare. Seven years ago, the state welfare department employed 1,937 persons. It now employs 3,385. The state's colleges and universities had 7,904 persons on the payroll seven years ago but have since grown to 9,827. Other state departments also report impressive increases in numbers of employees.

"No News" in West Virginia

Increasing State Payrolls

Creating new jobs is a significant part of seeking federally funded programs in the states. That is because putting people to work, especially in economically depressed states like West Virginia, assists the economy, the unemployed, and makes public officials look good, and at no cost to the state. The system sometimes creates problems regarding what all these employees *must do* to earn the readily available salaries.

Creating New Jobs

Journalists assigned to the West Virginia statehouse agree that, in the main, government employees have few demands on their energies, a view supported by the state's director of employment security. She told the *Charleston Daily Mail* that since she took over in 1977, she has found about seventy-five employees of her agency "who have done no work, can't define what their job is, or are physically or mentally unqualified to hold their jobs." She also stated that one suburban branch office was labeled "the country club" and that another office in Charleston is equipped with a bar.

In spite of such excesses, media coverage of state legislators is badly lacking. In a study of all fifty legislatures, observer John Burns wrote, "The media generally do not value state government news very highly. . . . Such news usually ranks a poor third behind national and local news."

Poor Media Coverage

For broadcasters, it is easier to cover the executive than the legislative branch of state government for the same reason that it is easier to cover the president of the United States than the Congress. The governor "can present a single face, a single voice." Broadcast journalists "tend to rely on cloakroom interviews of legislators" and no more. The detail work of state legislatures is thus left to the print media.

Broadcast Coverage of State Legislatures

The fact that legislative seats have a heavy turnover in each election year— 35 percent—means that an impressive number of legislators do not "stay around long enough to develop expertise of their own." That, added to a high turnover among legislative reporters, complicates journalistic coverage even further. The only group that remains reasonably fixed are the lobbyists who, because of lengthy experiences around state government, give the new people in the legislature and the press a helping hand.[22] The question of who should be educating whom in such an environment offers interesting responses.

All the attendant problems notwithstanding, the state legislatures have charged ahead of the Congress in realistically coming to grips with the problems and issues that face them, from ethical and regulatory legislation to energy and urban issues.[23] They have also surged forward in modernizing the lawmaking process. Perry Duryea, Republican minority leader of the New York Assembly, said: "When I first came to Albany 17 years ago, we had one secretary for every nine assemblymen, and only leaders had offices. Now everyone has his own office and staff. We've moved out of the dark ages." James Manderino, majority leader of the Pennsylvania House, recalled that ten years ago the 107 members of his party had to share three telephone booths and a secretarial pool of fifteen. And increased legislative activities require increased media coverage, but it has not worked out that way.

Legislatures are also meeting more frequently than ever before, with Texas being the only large state that meets only every other year. "Without those annual sessions," Speaker Dale Cochran of the Iowa House said, "a void is created that is ultimately filled by Congress, and that means federal involvement in issues better handled by the states."

What should be especially meaningful to the news media has been the relaxation of rules of access to legislatures for the press and public since Florida passed the first "sunshine law" in 1967. The law, in effect, opens official records of legislative proceedings to the public. Since then thirty-seven other states have passed similar laws. In addition, forty-four states now permit regular telecasts of legislative activity from the chambers on a regular basis. Most states also require that lobbyists register and periodically report on their spending, making them less free to wheel and deal behind the scenes as they once were. Even with those dramatic changes, however, the news media still tend to give primary attention to other news. William Pound, director of state services for the National Conference of State Legislatures, says: "The press continues to focus more on scandals and trivia than it does on legislative issues." And that attitude badly abuses the First Amendment charge to the press.

Just as the Congress of the United States ultimately bowed to pressures and permitted television coverage of its proceedings, employment of technology to assist news gathering in state and local government is on the increase. In Wisconsin, Attorney General Bronson LaFollette ruled that the legislature may not keep reporters from using tape recorders during public sessions of governmental bodies. LaFollette based his decision on Wisconsin's open meeting law, which says: "The public is entitled to the fullest and most complete information regarding the affairs of government as is compatible with the conduct of governmental business." In Illinois, Associate Circuit Judge Thomas Vinson ruled that electronic equipment may not be excluded from public meetings of the Joliet Fire and Police Commission. In a suit brought by WMAQ-TV in Chicago, Judge Vinson based his decision on a new amendment to the state's Public Meeting Act, which guarantees to broadcast stations the same rights of coverage granted to print media.[24]

Where press involvement in state legislatures has been active, it has made life for some of the members uncomfortable, sometimes insufferable. According to one legislative observer, the job of state legislator might be going begging, even though in most states it pays well, offers a cushy expense account, paid vacations, and a fair amount of prestige.

Impact of Media Coverage on Legislators

Financial recompense for legislators in the United States varies widely with basic two-year salaries and expense allowances extending from a low of $600 for Rhode Island lawmakers to a high of $61,599 in California. Alaska pays its legislators $43,500, Illinois $46,192 to House members and $45,904 to state senators. Michigan legislators receive $46,500, Ohio $35,000, and so on down the line.[25]

Yet in a recent campaign year in Michigan, more than 100 seats in the House and nearly 40 in the Senate were up for reelection. But few stood up to challenge those in office. The reasons seemed to be "a blend of apathy, general disillusionment with politics and the rigors of holding office." The House Republican leader indicated that the legislative arm of government has been coming under increased public evaluation, primarily through the media, which seems strong enough to scare people away from politics. "It's just more of a hassle to hold public office," he said. "The job isn't that attractive to many people."[26]

Part of the problem could be the company one sometimes must keep while serving the public, wheeling and dealing aside. In 1978 in the Pennsylvania legislature, House Speaker Herbert Fineman was indicted for allegedly accepting payoffs in exchange for aiding students to gain admittance to graduate schools in the state. Fineman was found innocent of those charges but was convicted of obstruction of justice. Harold Cianfrani, chairman of the Senate Appropriation Committee, pleaded guilty to charges of tax evasion, mail fraud, racketeering, and obstruction of justice.[27]

Political Corruption a Problem

The media coverage of criminal activities among officeholders, which is certainly justified under the First Amendment, has made many citizens wary of becoming part of a system in which the corruption of some might taint all. A few cases in point: an editorial in the *Detroit Free Press* indicated that five members of the Michigan legislature were responsible for a spate of negative publicity raining down on the whole body. In one year, one member was convicted of embezzlement and drummed out of the legislature by his colleagues (though promising to run again in the next election). A second was charged with padding his state expense account; a third with accepting $5,000 from a lobbyist-promoter of dog racing in the state. Two more were arrested for drunk driving, one of whom spent the night in jail. This was followed by a public statement by the State Council on Alcohol Problems contending that eleven members of the legislature are alcoholics. Other legislators have been cited for *soliciting* campaign contributions from known lobbyists which, at least in the public mind, is certain to favor special interests and not voters.[28]

*Innocents
Suffer as Well*

The negative publicity generated by these and other cases puts worry lines on the brows of many legislators who fear that the political fallout will land on those who have done no wrong. They worry that voters will lump everyone together, the good and the bad, and make reelection difficult for all. That prospect is especially gloomy in light of drooping public attitudes towards legislators in general, including members of Congress, who have been in trouble with the people for some time. Public esteem of the legislative unit is lower now than at any time in recent memory.[29]

The Media and Local Government

The issues and problems associated with press coverage of city and town governments are similar to those of the states and the nation, but on a smaller scale.[30] Large cities function almost on the scale of states in terms of their multimillion-dollar budgets and vast numbers of major programs supported by them. In recent years, officials of metropolitan cities have come together to plead with the federal government for even more financial support. Obviously, metropolitan communities require more programs than nonmetropolitan areas do, especially in such critical areas as welfare, crime control, public transportation, and education. The primary difference is population.

*Functions of
Local Government*

But the *basic functions* of local government are the same in all: to provide essential services to the citizens—streets, sewage, refuse disposal, police and fire protection, and other services not provided by higher levels of government. As one authoritative source states: "The central problem of municipal government is to provide the necessary and desirable services at the lowest cost."

The City Council

The legislative arm of local government is the city council or board of aldermen or board of selectmen—various names and formats are used. For simplicity's sake, we will refer to it here as the *council*. Essentially, it is an elected legislative body that develops programs and budgets to support municipal programs in the same sense that state legislatures and the Congress support their programs.

As we have seen, local *news*, in general, is the bread and butter of local news media; local *government*, as such, is rarely at the top of the priority list. What happens in city hall is essential to the process of government, but too frequently local news media do not give it the attention it merits, even though *all* government is the people's business. School board or council meetings may be covered routinely, but many editors view the latest doings in the assessor's office as a bore certain to be passed over by readers. By comparison, a ruptured watermain that floods the downtown business district gets major attention because it's a "people" story that directly affects local citizens, is highly visible, and will probably cause inconveniences to most. Yet the boring routine of local government might well conceal as much corruption and political highhandedness as are found on higher levels of government, perhaps more so. In many instances, local officials are happy to be ignored by the media (except at election time). Some even display open hostility to the local press on the rare occasions when it does burrow to the roots of city hall activities, especially those not discussed or debated in public meetings. Some dedicated editors who bothered to look have uncovered evidence of crimes and political excesses and have taken considerable heat from the centers of power because of it.

City Hall Is "Small News"

Boredom Conceals Corruption

In Jackson, Mississippi, Bill Minor, owner of the weekly *Capital Reporter*, was subjected to all manner of financial pressure and personal violence as he took on "corrupt politicians, racketeers and Ku Klux Klansmen" in the community.[31] In issue after issue, "he flung his findings into the faces of the city fathers." The city stopped giving him paid public notices, which he had been publishing regularly in his paper, the income from which he needed to remain solvent. Then local advertising generally fell off despite a steady increase in circulation. Then a rock was thrown through his office window. The rock throwing was repeated several weeks later, followed by a break-in in which his printing machinery was vandalized. After that came the smashing of vending machines around town that offered his paper for sale. Finally, a flaming cross was placed against the *Capital Reporter* building, which was saved from total destruction when an off-duty fireman knocked it to the ground.

The Jackson Case

The windows are boarded up but Bill Minor keeps publishing his newspaper. As columnist Jack Anderson commented: "Thomas Jefferson had men like Bill Minor in mind when he declared that if he had to choose between a government without newspapers and newspapers without a government, he would take his morning paper."

The *Dewitt County Observer* is a scrappy weekly newspaper in Clinton, Illinois, population 16,000.[32] It has a reputation for watching the workings of local government and making editorial noises when it finds something out of kilter. The paper is owned by a husband and wife team, Charles and Virginia

The Dewitt Case

Russell, with Virginia as editor. At one point the paper ran a story on possible conflicts of interest involving city officials and local banking of public monies. The paper also called for the resignation of the mayor. The mayor refused to resign but the city government did agree to seek bids for banking services.

On another occasion, the paper charged that a state official was meddling in local affairs. The official resigned. "We try to tell the truth with regard to whose toes we step on," Virginia Russell said.

Power to Close
a Newspaper

Then Charlene Hettinger, a reporter for the paper, got word that improprieties existed in the county sheriff's office. She and reporter Edith Brady began looking into it. The word got out. Sheriff Long reportedly reacted to the news by promising to "get" the reporters and the paper as well. "I have the power to close that paper," a witness quoted the sheriff as saying. Long denied it.

Russell backed off to protect her reporters, but a state official who had learned of the paper's investigation and the sheriff's opposition to it approached the *Chicago Daily News* and asked for assistance. Larry Green and Rob Warden went to lend a hand. The result was an exposé published by both the *Observer* and the *Daily News* that charged Long with "misuse of funds, nepotism, violence and gross noncompliance with the law." The exposé also charged that inmates in Long's jail had been "beaten, maced and sexually assaulted" and that Long had forced employees to "kick back two percent of their pay into what might be a political fund." A full investigation by county, state, and federal agencies is under way.

A Newspaper
in Hawaii

A few years ago, Jack Stephens and James Franklin decided to launch a daily newspaper on the Island of Maui, Hawaii. Local officials were cold to the idea. Before the first issue could be published, police presented the two with a letter from the county attorney, which threatened them with legal action if they published testimony presented during a *public hearing* of the County Civil Service Commission over the dismissal of a police officer. The police also presented copies of the letter to the paper's printer and "virtually all other Maui printers and publishers." Because of the county attorney's action, no local printer would accept their business and they had to go to Honolulu to publish their newspaper. Stephens and Franklin brought suit against the Maui County mayor, the county attorney, three policemen, the former chairman of the police commission, and an employee of the police department. After four and one-half years, the case was settled in favor of the newspaper with a $51,000 award.[33]

The Newburg
City Council

Two reporters from the *Middletown* (N.Y.) *Times Herald-Record* arrived at the Newburg City Council to cover deliberations on urban renewal of the waterfront area. Council members ordered the reporters to leave because, they said, the law required open meetings only when a formal vote was to take place. The newspaper brought suit on the grounds that the council order violated New York's open meeting law. The Orange County Supreme Court supported the council, indicating that that body had the right to close "work sessions." The paper appealed to the appellate division of the state supreme court, which overturned the original decision. The latter verdict drew on the wording of the state legislature when the law was passed: "It is essential to the maintenance of a democratic society that the public business be performed in an open and public manner." The court added: "We believe the legislature intended to include more than the mere formal act of voting or the informal execution of an official document. Every step of the decision-making process, including the decision itself, is a necessary preliminary to formal action."[34]

So some community-oriented papers do try.

The Role of the Weeklies

Everett T. Rattray, a veteran weekly newspaper editor, wrote that the responsibility of the community newspaper is to "print the news and raise hell," and that some newspapers perform that way.[35] "Yet," he added, "it is also true that a good many more, big and little, do not." And the First Amendment is weakened when they don't.

The basic responsibility of weeklies, Rattray believes, is to keep an eye on the doings of local government, since the dailies usually take care of state, national, and international news primarily. That means city council matters, the school board, budgets, spending, and all the rest. In one locale, Rattray says, the village board of trustees decides to create a municipal parking lot but the village ladies improvement society wants to keep some trees to shade the proposed lot. The village attorney calls it "meddling." The paper reports that and hell is raised.

"Small potatoes?" Rattray asks. "Of course, but it is big news to people who are close to their small local government, and important news if it opens a public peephole into wrongdoing or poor judgment."

The Failure of Some Weeklies

Unfortunately, many small dailies and weeklies keep a closer eye to personal financial gain than to informing readers and improving community life. They skirt issues and avoid chancey stories that might offend advertisers. They run editorials—when they run them at all—on watered down topics like the need for safety helmets for little leaguers or the quality of local scenery. Or they run "canned editorials" purchased from national syndicates, which rarely relate to any local issues or problems. This kind of editorial fare, which Rattray calls "panting boosterism," tends to reinforce readers' ideas of "how good they are" and that human failings do not exist in their midst. Rattray indicates that editorials that interpret local events with intelligent and honest commentary are few and far between in community-oriented newspapers. "Newspapers are newspapers," he wrote, "and their responsibility is to print the news and raise hell. Most of them, weekly and daily, are not performing their functions very well."

Summary   This chapter assesses the enormity of the problems involved in efforts of the news media to cover and report on the legislative branches of government on all levels. The number of reporters needed to cover the Congress and most state legislatures is prohibitive because of the large numbers of public officials involved and the huge volume of public business that they generate. In many cases where the availability of reporters is not a problem, in local municipalities especially, the press typically restricts certain kinds of government news as unimportant. Additionally, many legislators take advantage of reporter shortages by using tax-supported media centers to offer their one-sided presentations as "news" to the media back home. In the United States, government is *public* business and government officials are really *public* officials. If the mandate of the First Amendment is to be met, if the public is to be kept informed, they need to know what their legislators are doing. To bring that about, the news media are required to improve their performances in the public interest.

Notes

1. Information on the "Problems of Press Coverage" from George S. Hage, Everett E. Dennis, Arnold H. Ismach, and Stephen Hartgen, *New Strategies for Public Affairs Reporting* (Englewood Cliffs, N.J.: Prentice-Hall, 1976), p. 210.

2. Susan Heilmann Miller, "Reporters and Congressmen: Living in Symbioses," *Journalism Monographs* (Lexington, Ky.: Association for Education in Journalism, 1978), pp. 3–4.

3. George B. Galloway, *The Legislative Process in Congress* (New York: Crowell, 1953), p. 220.

4. Louis Harris, "Congress Given 'Poor' Rating," The *State Journal*, Lansing, Michigan, Feb. 6, 1978, p. 4–A.

5. Galloway, *The Legislative Process*, p. 221.

6. Galloway, *The Legislative Process*, p. 224.

7. Information on legislative secrecy and the right to information from Charlene J. Brown, Trevor Brown, and William L. Rivers, *The Media and the People* (New York: Holt, Rinehart and Winston, 1978), pp. 218–21.

8. Information on Mintz, including examples of the press' failure to cover congressional business, from Mortin Mintz, "Professionalism in the Newsroom," *Nieman Reports*, December 1972/March 1973, pp. 5–13.

9. Editorial, "Nothing New Under 'Dome'," The *State Journal*, Lansing, Michigan, April 3, 1978, p. 4–A.

10. Thomas Griffiths, "A Few Frank Words About Bias," *Ethics and the Press*, John C. Merrill and Ralph D. Barney, eds. (New York: Hastings House, 1975), p. 213.

11. J. Russell Wiggins, "Emigration of Power to the Little Legislatures," *Congress and the News Media*, Robert O. Blanchard, ed. (New York: Hastings House, 1974), p. 59.

12. Information on open and closed congressional meetings from *Congressional Quarterly Report* as in Blanchard, *Congress and the News Media*, pp. 61–66.

13. John L. Hulteng, *The Messenger's Motives* (Englewood Cliffs, N.J.: Prentice-Hall, 1976), pp. 152–55.

14. Information on congressional propaganda from Ben Bagdikian, "Congress and the Media: Partners in Propaganda," Blanchard, ed., *Congress and the News Media*, p. 388.

15. Information on the press and the legislative and executive branches from James Reston, *The Artillery of the Press* (New York: Harper and Row, 1967), pp. 72–73.

16. Information on congressional media events from Douglass Cater, "The Congressional Hearing as Publicity Vehicle," Blanchard, *Congress and the News Media*, p. 346.

17. Information on Watergate's "Instant Celebrities" from Jeannette Smyth, "TV Lights, Invitations, Kisses and Phone Calls," Blanchard, ed., *Congress and the News Media*, p. 367.

18. Information on Koreagate from "Conflicting Testimony Cited on Korean Bribes . . . Passmann Hearings Continue," The *State Journal* (Associated Press), Lansing, Michigan, June 20, 1978, p. 3–A.

19. "The *Real* Big Government is in the States," *Washington Monthly*, April 1978, p. 23.

20. Ralph Whitehead, Jr. and Howard M. Ziff, "Statehouse Coverage: Lobbyists Outlast Journalists," *Columbia Journalism Review*, January/February 1974, p. 11.

21. The West Virginia case from James A. Haught, "A Report from West Virginia," *Washington Monthly*, April 1978, p. 28.

22. Whitehead and Ziff, "Statehouse Coverage," p.12.

23. Information on state legislatures from "State Governments Take on New Vigor," *U.S. News and World Report*, March 20, 1978, p. 39.

24. "Broadcasters Gain in Wisconsin and Illinois," The *Quill*, March 1978, p. 8.

25. "What Your State Pays Its Legislatures," *U.S. News and World Report*, March 20, 1978, p. 43.

26. Rob Wilson, "Legislator: It's a Job Few Want," The *State Journal* (Associated Press), Lansing, Michigan, June 11, 1978, p. 1–B.

27. "In Pennsylvania: Plenty of Trouble and Few Signs of Change," *U.S. News and World Report*, March 20, 1978, p. 40.

28. Editorial, "Lansinggate: More Than Five Legislators Should Be in Trouble," *Detroit Free Press*, April 18, 1978, p. 6–A; "11 Legislators Alcoholics?" The *State Journal* (Associated Press), Lansing, Michigan, April 19, 1978, p. 7–B.

29. Malcolm Johnson, "Lawmakers Wince Under Welter of Bad Publicity," The *State Journal* (Associated Press), Lansing, Michigan, April 17, 1978, p. 1–B.

30. Information on city and town governments from Chilton R. Bush, *Newswriting and Reporting Public Affairs* (New York: Chilton Books, 1970), pp. 479–89.

31. Information on Bill Minor from Jack Anderson, "Newspaper Editor Pressured Financially," The *State Journal*, Lansing, Michigan, May 26, 1978, p. 4–A.

32. Information on this case from Larry Green and Rob Warden, "When a Small-Town Sheriff Says, 'I Am the Law'," The *Quill*, January 1977, p. 7.

33. "The Press Collects," The *Quill*, January 1977, p. 8.

34. "Appeals Court Generous on Open Meetings," The *Quill*, March 1978, p. 9.

35. Information on the role of the weeklies from Everett T. Rattray, "The Weekly Newspaper's Responsibility to Print the News and Raise Hell," *The Responsibility of the Press*, Gerald Gross, ed. (New York: Fleet Publishing Corp., 1966), p. 102.

"Appeals Court Generous On Open Meetings." The *Quill*, March 1978, p. 9.

"Broadcasters Gain in Wisconsin and Illinois." The *Quill*, March 1978, p. 8.

Green, Larry, and Warden, Rob. "When a Small-Town Sheriff Says, 'I am the Law'." The *Quill*, January 1977, p. 7.

"In Pennsylvania: Plenty of Trouble and Few Signs of Change." *U.S. News and World Report*, March 20, 1978, p. 40.

Miller, Susan Heilmann. "Reporters and Congressmen: Living in Symbioses." *Journalism Monographs*. Lexington, Ky.: Association for Education in Journalism, 1978.

Reston, James. *The Artillery of the Press*. New York: Harper and Row, 1967.

"State Governments Take on New Vigor." *U.S. News and World Report*, March 20, 1978, p. 39.

"The Press Collects." The *Quill*, January 1977, p. 8.

"The *Real* Big Government Is in the States." *Washington Monthly*, April 1978, p. 23.

For Further Reading

News in Pictures

Mass Media and Government 7
The Judicial Branch

Upon completing this chapter you should—

be able to identify the bases of confrontation between the news media and the courts

understand how judges become judges and the nature of criticisms of judicial performances

be familiar with landmark cases in the news media-judiciary confrontation along with appropriate legal terms

Free Press vs. Fair Trial   The term used to reflect the frequent constitutional clashes between the press and the judiciary over those basic rights that come into conflict. (p. 195)

Judiciary   Refers to courts, judges, or court decisions. (p. 195)

Contempt of Court   Open disrespect or willful disobedience of a court of law, grand jury, or legislative body. (p. 199)

Gag Order   A judicial order issued to limit or prohibit entirely media access to police and court information in a criminal case. (p. 205)

The Warren Commission Report   This report criticized the conduct of the news media in its coverage of the assassination of President Kennedy and associated events and asked the American Bar Association to make recommendations for the future. (p. 205)

The Reardon Report   Based on the Warren Commission findings, it made recommendations to court officers to limit information to the news media related to arrests of suspects and pending trials. (p. 205)

Sequestered Jury   A jury removed from exposure to all media during the course of a trial. (p. 209)

Subpoena   A legal order to appear in court or before a grand jury or legislative body for the purpose of giving evidence. (p. 212)

Forced Disclosure   An order to a media representative who has gained information of interest to a court, grand jury, or legislative body to testify about that information or release notes and/or other evidence under threat of fine or imprisonment or both. (p. 212)

Shield Law   A law in some states that protects journalists from forced disclosure. (p. 217)

Search and Seizure   In the news media sense, the act of law enforcement agents entering, without advance warning, the offices of news media to examine and, if desirable, to seize information gained by reporters that may be related to a criminal activity even if the reporters are not suspects: police must first gain a search warrant from a judge. (p. 221)

The liberty of the press is a great bulwark of the liberty of the people: it is, therefore, the incumbent duty of those who are constituted the guardians of the people's rights, to defend and maintain it.

Massachusetts legislature,
January 1768

Bases of Confrontation

The basic issues in the free press vs. fair trial controversy are based first on how each of the two forces interprets its rights, functions, and responsibilities in the democratic order. Secondly, they are based on how each views the rights, functions, and responsibilities of the other.

The press recognizes the judiciary as one of the three branches of government along with the executive and the legislative. Therefore, the courts are public property as are their proceedings. As such, officers of the court are answerable to the people through the press just as those in the other branches are answerable. Without media coverage, courts would function in secret. And in the American system, secret trials are as repugnant as the total secrecy that typically surrounds governments by dictatorship. While members of the American judiciary would embrace that view in principle, many of those members have come to view the press as a disrupter of legal order and a threat to the fair trial provisions of the Sixth Amendment. Many basic issues are tied to that view, but especially irksome to the courts is the matter of pretrial publicity, which they feel might improperly influence an entire community from which a jury must be selected, thus making a fair trial unlikely or impossible. Thus the stage is set for conflict between the two.

In the actual function of this frequently heated relationship, the press has been steadily losing ground. While some judges experiment with televised trial proceedings, many others bar photographers and representatives of the broadcast news media from court sessions even though the age-old arguments for keeping them out no longer apply (large, cumbersome equipment disrupting courtroom order, flashing bulbs distracting jurors, etc., are no longer problems). The presiding judge is the unquestioned leader in court. He or she rules in every facet of the trial or hearing and cannot be overruled by anyone throughout the duration of the trial. Once the trial has ended and a verdict reached, only a higher court may change that verdict. Therefore, a presiding judge makes personal decisions that determine whether full, limited, or no press participation will be permitted.

The Courts as Government

The Press as Disrupter of Legal Order

Pretrial Publicity

The Judge: The Unchallenged Ruler

According to CBS Legal Correspondent Fred Graham, "we see too many journalistic decisions being made for legal reasons, not journalistic reasons." Graham, who is also an attorney, points to pressures applied to the news media by the courts in the form of gag orders, subpoenas, contempt citations, efforts to force reporters to disclose their sources of information, increased incidents of closed trials, and application of the Privacy Act. He urged journalists to become aware of the legal obstacles they must face and to resist self-censorship if it is just a means to avoid legal action.[1]

Those who favor controlling press coverage of trials argue that the Constitution does not protect the public's right to know, that, in fact, the right to know has been restricted at times as special circumstances have required, e.g., in time of war, regarding information on atomic secrets, and so forth.[2] They also caution the press that the Sixth Amendment guarantee of a public trial protects the person on trial and not the "rights" of the public. So, the reasoning goes, press coverage of a trial has little or no public significance because the trial is the defendant's business and nobody else's.

On the other side, the press claims its First Amendment "rights" as watchdog of government, which it exercises in the public interest. That means that, for the public benefit, the press must cover and evaluate the professional conduct of all officers of the court, as public officials, to insure that those accused of crimes receive speedy, fair, and impartial hearings at the hands of competent judges, prosecutors, and defense attorneys.

While the judiciary may be coequal with the other two branches of government, the executive and legislative, it is rarely covered as thoroughly by the press. Indeed, it has traditionally received almost a hands-off treatment for reasons beyond its control. If members of the other two branches make questionable decisions in their official public roles, reporters corner them and demand explanations. But rarely do judges have to defend their decisions before the press. "Few reporters ever get a comment from an appellate judge explaining or elaborating on a decision, unless the judge is seeking publicity for a coming election," one critic writes.

Much of the decision making of the judiciary takes place behind closed doors. This is especially true of courts of appeal where the details of a case are debated before a decision is announced. In the end, the public learns of the decision but nothing, or nearly nothing, of *how* the decision was reached. At the same time, when members of the executive or legislative branches go into closed sessions to privately debate a pending action, the press justifiably howls about government secrecy.

Many court decisions have had major impact on American citizens in general—decisions dealing with pornography, civil rights, aid to nonpublic schools, youthful offenders, and so forth. But the judges handing down such critical decisions feel no obligation to go before the press and explain the bases of their decisions. However, the president of the United States, who devises new strategy for coping with a saber-rattling potentate in the Middle East, is expected to explain the whys and hows of the new strategy.

Newsroom searches rapped by official

WASHINGTON (AP)—A decision allowing police searches of newsrooms was the most serious of recent Supreme Court rulings that were unfavorable to the press, a reporters' organization says.

Jack Landau, executive director of the Reporters Committee for Freedom of the Press, spoke about the high court's rulings on press freedom during the court term that ends today.

"YOU CAN'T talk about the current term without reserving a special place for Zurcher," Landau said of the newspaper search decision. "It's just so awful for the concept of a free press . . . stripping away the last line of defense which is keeping police out of the newsroom."

In the "Zurcher" decision, a divided court said newsrooms are subject to police searches for criminal evidence even if neither the paper nor its staff is involved in the crime.

The decision is not limited to newsrooms, however. The justices said there is nothing unconstitutional with so-called "third-party"

searches—that police may obtain search warrants for the premises of persons not suspected of a crime, but believed to have evidence that may be useful in criminal investigation.

SOME MEMBERS of Congress are trying to write legislation designed to prevent abuses resulting from the decision.

"From Zurcher on down, we took our lumps," Landau said.

In a series of decisions, the court refused to make it easier to gather information.

IT RULED last week that the news media and public have no constitutional right to learn what's happening inside government institutions such as prisons and mental hospitals.

Executive directives or legislative actions must first provide a right to know, the court said.

In another case, the court refused to review a judicial order in South Carolina that barred all participants in the criminal trial of a state senator from talking to reporters.

Associated Press.

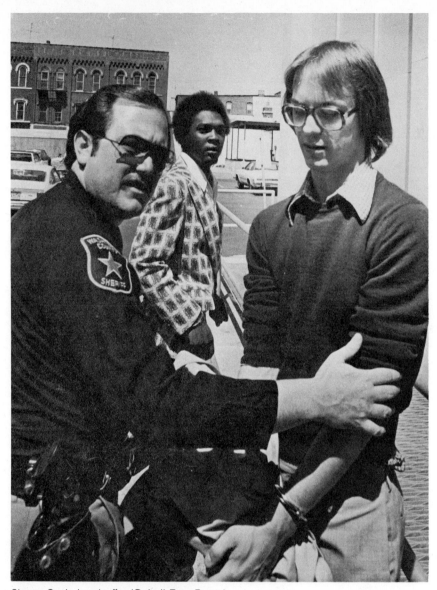

Steven Orr in handcuffs. (*Detroit Free Press.*)

*Court Secrecy
Compared with Nixon
Tape Controversy*

As Detroit journalist Bert Falbaum indicates, the argument that secrecy in court matters must be honored to protect open discussion is the same logic applied by President Richard Nixon when he resisted surrender of the White House tapes. In the end, the Supreme Court ruled that Nixon had to release the tapes "in light of our historic commitment to the rule of law." Yet a Norfolk, Virginia newspaper was fined by the court for publishing the name of a judge being investigated for judicial misconduct.[3]

As stated previously, the authority of the presiding judge in the courtroom is total as shown by actual cases. A judge cited a University of Michigan coed for contempt of court and had her placed in handcuffs for almost two hours because she refused to reveal how she had voted in a mayoral election in Ann Arbor. A second woman also refused to reveal how she had voted but was not cited for contempt, although the same judge warned that she could be so cited if she remained uncooperative.[4] Yet privacy in the voting booth is a cherished constitutional privilege.

Examples of Judicial Authority

On another occasion, *Detroit Free Press* reporter Steve Orr, twenty-three, was covering a divorce action in Washtenaw County Court, presided over by Judge Henry T. Conlin. The husband in the action gave Orr a copy of a report prepared by the county friend of the court, which dealt with the placement of the couple's child. Returning the child to the wife was not recommended. The attorney for the wife decided that Orr should not have access to the report because it was confidential. A *Free Press* attorney disagreed on the grounds that the copy had been given to Orr by one of the parties in the case. Nonetheless, Judge Conlin ordered the reporter to surrender the document or go to jail. Orr refused and was arrested and jailed for contempt of court. While in custody, he copied the information from the report. Three hours later he was returned to court in handcuffs and surrendered the report to the judge.[5]

The obvious point is that the judge is the supreme authority in the courtroom, which is as it must be if the court is to function responsibly. But the system has created many excesses in judicial authority for the simple reason that some judges are not as responsible as they are authoritarian, as we shall see. And the Founding Fathers did not make an exception of the judiciary when it authored the First Amendment.

Responsibility vs. Authoritarianism

How Judges Become Judges

Again, the news media's interest in covering the judiciary as one of the three branches of government is based on the view that judges are public officials in the same way that governors, senators, and city councilors are. The denominator common to all, for better or worse, is their humanity. Human beings have shortcomings; they make mistakes, have personal biases, have bad days as well as good. The Watergate and Koreagate cases reflect this profoundly. Judges, prosecutors, and defense attorneys are also human beings.

Admittedly, the overwhelming majority of bar members are likely to be persons of high purpose, well trained, and serious about the vital roles they play in society. But others are weak, morally bankrupt, blatantly self-serving, ignorant, and even incompetent. In some states, judges are appointed to the bench by the governor and, again, some of them provide outstanding services to the people. Frequently, others are former officeholders who swap favors with political leaders and "retire" to the bench, where many become dispensers of hollow justice. In other states many elected judges manage to avoid the smoke-filled dens and the political wheeling and dealing that is part of public life. Unfortunately, many do not and their outlandish play for political support denigrates the office that they hold or hope to hold. Equally unfortunate is that the biggest vote-getter is not always the best candidate, especially for as sensitive a post as the bench. Minorities and other disadvantaged persons are frequently abused by a judge's tilted view of what justice is and how it is to be dispensed. If only a few judges in each state perform in that manner, it is up to others, the press mainly, to report their conduct to the people who will, it is hoped, reject them and return judicial proceedings to proper form.

Public Access to Court Proceedings

Jack Landau, executive director of the Reporters Committee for Freedom of the Press, said that the courts should be the most accessible of all agencies of government. "Justice is not a private affair," he said. "Judges are public officials and like other politicians, they can be intelligent or dumb, honest or corrupt. They have no more right to decide what the public should know than have other branches of government."[6]

In those states where judges must be elected to office, most of their campaign funding comes from attorneys who handle cases in their courtrooms. Even if a judge tries hard to ignore an attorney's financial contributions, or lack of them, the parties to a case justifiably wonder if he *can* ignore them. "Sometimes, too, the effort seems not to have been made."[7]

Judicial Election Procedures in Michigan

In 1977, the Michigan legislature passed into law a bill that gives special advantages to incumbent judges running for reelection over those running for the first time or running for unfilled seats. Under the new law, the names of current circuit court judges will be listed in a special place on the ballot apart from the names of other candidates for the bench. In effect, the new candidates will run against each other rather than against the incumbents. A year later, an effort was made to repeal the law, and five circuit court judges "lobbied unabashedly" in favor of keeping the law as written. According to one of the five, repealing the law would "throw judges back into the election process," which would mean they would have to actively campaign for votes. "Judges panic when they get opposition," the judge told a House committee, "and they go out and campaign just like you do." That means, in his terms, "they're not up to 100 percent [in court] when they're running election parties at night." One who opposes the new law complained that it prohibits legitimate challenges to those already in office. "Though an incumbent judge is rarely defeated," he said, "it is good to make them go out into the community every six years and run on their records."[8]

A bill now before the Michigan legislature would require candidates for the state supreme court to gain nomination by the public, in primaries, rather than at state political conventions as is the current practice. It is part of a plan to remove selection of justices from the realm of party politics and "harmful political influences."[9] Other states appear to be moving in the same direction. But still the problems basic to the election of judges remain.

Judges under Fire

News media evaluations of the performances of judges seem to be increasing in number and depth. In early 1978, the *Washington Star* published an incisive report on the competence of area judges. At about the same time in New York City, The *Village Voice* did the same thing in a story headlined, "10 Worst Judges." The *Detroit Free Press* published the results of a painstaking survey of judicial competence and incompetence in Recorder's Court.[10] In the latter survey, practicing attorneys—defense counsels and prosecutors—were asked to rate the best judges on the bench in terms of professional performance and abilities. They were also asked to rank them in terms of "the quality of their knowledge of the law, their judicial temperament, their work habits and their courtesy from the bench." Of the eighty-nine attorneys who participated, sixty-six named judges who had "significant problems" as judges. Comments entered by those who named the worst judges included a broad pattern of complaints. One judge came across as " 'Insecure, despotic' . . . 'explosive temper' . . . 'very volatile';" another " 'Indecisive, inconsistent' . . . 'can't make up her mind' . . . 'immature, unable to make a decision'."

Four of the attorneys surveyed said that one judge "did crossword puzzles while presiding over trials." Thirteen of fourteen lawyers commented that another judge "told jokes in court during serious felony trials." One prosecutor noted that the latter judge "makes jokes throughout the trial to cover up his inadequacies as a judge. Jurors laughingly release felons back on the streets," he said.

Thirteen lawyers called yet another judge "lazy." Nicknamed "Half-A-Day," this judge wasted considerable time to "bumble through miscellaneous matters and lengthy breaks."

While high marks went to other judges in the survey, it is clear that defendants in Recorder's Court face a mixed bag of justice depending on which jurist presides over their trials.

Elsewhere, a Judicial Tenure Commission filed fourteen charges against a municipal court judge, most of them related to cases in which he had presided. The charges included violations of defendant's rights to have attorneys appointed to them, trial by jury, reasonable bond, and rights of appeal. The commission accused the judge of abusing his power to cite individuals for contempt of court and "harassing defendants, and trying to draw guilty pleas by threats and promises of leniency." The commission also named five drinking

The Press Evaluates the Bench

Lawyers Rate the Judges

Findings of the Judicial Tenure Commission

establishments in which the judge was frequently seen intoxicated. On one occasion, the complaint continued, he had to be driven home by a police officer, and on another he "solicited a bar patron for an immoral act."[11]

Judicial Action in Georgia

In Georgia, Cobb County Superior Court Judge Howell Ravan took exception to a story written about him in the *Marietta Daily Journal*. He responded to the "lies" in the story by barring *Journal* reporters from his courtroom and offices. The story stated that Ravan had been involved in an attempt to remove the county's public safety director. Judge Ravan said the charge was false and ordered bailiffs to keep the reporters out. Journal reporter Otis Brumby said that the story was accurate and was based on information from at least six sources.[12]

Investigating Judges in Virginia

In Virginia it is a crime to report that a judge is under investigation before the review panel decides to file a formal complaint before the state supreme court. Early in 1978, the state high court upheld the conviction of a Norfolk newspaper on such a violation. More recently, Richmond Newspapers, Inc. was fined $2,000 for doing the same thing. The company's *Times Dispatch* and *News Leader* have filed a suit in federal court declaring that the state law is unconstitutional. The Norfolk paper is appealing to the United States Supreme Court.[13]

The Supreme Court justices. (Supreme Court Historical Society.)

Despite the angered protests of three of its members, the United States Supreme Court ruled in March 1978 that judges are virtually immune from prosecution for improper rulings from the bench even when made maliciously. The five-to-three decision was based on an Indiana case in which a fifteen-year-old "somewhat retarded" girl was sterilized without her knowledge but with the approval of Judge Harold Stump of DeKalb County.[14] The girl's mother and her attorney received Judge Stump's approval without his first appointing an attorney to represent the girl. No hearing was held nor was the arrangement entered in the court record. The girl was told that she was to have her appendix removed. When she eventually married and could not become pregnant, she learned that she had been permanently sterilized. The United States Circuit Court of Appeals ruled that Judge Stump's order was not a judicial act "because of his failure to comply with elementary principles" of constitutional law.

The United States Supreme Court disagreed. The majority opinion by Justice Byron White indicated that Judge Stump possessed the authority to issue the order, which means that it cannot be challenged. Joining White in the majority vote were Chief Justice Warren Burger, Justices Harry Blackmun, William Rehnquist, and John Paul Stevens. The minority opinion, written by Justice Potter Stewart and supported by Justices Thurgood Marshall and Lewis Powell, Jr., called Stump's action "lawless conduct." Reading his opinion from the bench to underscore its importance, Justice Stewart said, "A judge isn't free, like a loose cannon, to inflict indiscriminate damage whenever he announces that he is acting in his judicial capacity." The opinion went on:

> A judge's approval of a mother's opinion to lock her daughter in the attic would hardly be a judicial act simply because the mother had submitted her petition to a judge in his official capacity.

The American Civil Liberties Union also condemned the action: "The Supreme Court has ruled that judges can violate citizens' constitutional rights and get away with it."[15]

The Case of Peter Reilly

What might be called a classic confrontation between the press and the judiciary also serves as a monument to the stubborn dedication of local journalism.[16] On September 23, 1973, eighteen-year-old Peter Reilly, a "naive and insecure" boy, arrived home from a church meeting and found his unmarried mother murdered on the floor of their home in Falls Village, Connecticut. He telephoned for help and within minutes an ambulance and state police cruiser arrived. Officers checked the body, the premises, and interrogated the stunned, trembling boy. There was no evidence—no blood, no sign whatever—of Peter's involvement in the killing. In fact, witnesses corroborated his story of his whereabouts prior to his arrival home.

Yet within a day's time and after twelve hours of exhausting questioning, Peter Reilly confessed to the murder. He was arrested and jailed for five months before his case went to court. Then the state's attorney tried to bar the press from pretrial hearings. At the trial's end, Peter was convicted of manslaughter and sentenced to prison for six to sixteen years. Donald S. Connery, who wrote a book about the case, said that local people knew Peter to be a gentle youngster who had enjoyed a tender relationship with his mother despite her reputation as a town character. The personal knowledge of some about his activities on the night of the murder "gave them good common-sense reasons to question the circumstantial case the state had developed," Connery said.

Reilly Convicted

The Community Responds

The story spread quickly. Celebrities like playwrights Arthur Miller and Mike Nichols, novelist William Styron, and others who resided in affluent communities nearby took a personal interest. They recruited a new defense attorney and a private investigator, both of whom served without pay. A year later they presented new evidence at a hearing for a new trial. The investigation also received a major boost from the dedicated efforts of Joseph O'Brien, a veteran reporter for the *Hartford Courant,* and Roger Cohn, of the *Torrington Register*. O'Brien found that Barbara Gibbons, Peter's mother, had been slain by one or more persons in the act of robbing her: missing were a new wallet and about $100 from a check cashed the same day. Cohn traced the exact time that Peter had telephoned for help on the evening of the crime. His arrival home was found to be fifteen minutes later than the time the prosecutor had given the jury. There could not have been enough time for him to have done all he was accused of doing. A new trial was ordered.

A Local Hero

Even with the notable efforts of O'Brien and Cohn, Connery indicates that, had it not been for the persistent reporting of the small town *Lakeville Journal*, all might have been lost. The paper, with 6,000 paid circulation, is owned and edited by Robert H. Estabrook, who spent twenty-five years on the editorial staff of the *Washington Post*. Connery writes: "The *Journal* coupled solid reporting in its news section with fair, but stinging commentary in its editorial pages. . . . Its relentless coverage was felt far beyond the paper's circulation area." Estabrook and his *Journal* won several impressive awards for their persistence.

Peter Reilly eventually regained his freedom. He also fired off a $2 million lawsuit against the commissioner of the Connecticut State Police and the former chief of detectives.

The very fact that officers of the court are human beings subject to the same shortcomings, potential or acute, as everyone else, strongly indicates that their personal and professional actions should be witnessed, evaluated, and reported to the people as the First Amendment requires. It is obvious that the most direct and efficient mechanism for doing that is the medium recognized by the Founding Fathers—a press free of the pressures and restrictions of government.

The Need for Media Presence in Court

One point of major confrontation between the press and the courts is in the area of judicial "gags" placed on reporters for the purpose of reducing or eliminating information dealing with a trial. Fred Graham, an attorney and legal reporter for CBS News, refers to the label "fair trial—free press" as "the lawyers' tidy term for the chaotic relationship that has developed between the news media and a judicial system that is groping for a partial exemption from free journalistic scrutiny."[17]

Gag Orders
A First Amendment Issue

The problems in this particular press-government arena began in earnest with the 1964 publication of the Warren Commission report on the assassination of President John Kennedy. Among other matters, the commission criticized the way the news media had conducted themselves in their attempts to cover all aspects of the drama. The modern mass media are vastly different from the press of earlier times, especially in terms of the electronic media, which have revolutionized the gathering and presentation of "live" news events. The fact that accused assassin Lee Harvey Oswald was shot to death on *live television* before millions of viewers is a meaningful, if ghastly, measure of how the technology of the mass media has developed in recent times. To what extent media coverage might have impaired Oswald's right to a fair trial (or the rights of Jack Ruby, who killed Oswald) is debatable, since neither case went to trial. Nonetheless, critical questions have been raised because of those awesome events. They probe deeply and profoundly into the right of a free people to be informed and the right of a defendant to a fair trial. The Warren Commission said of this:

The Warren Commission Report

Critical Questions

> The experience in Dallas during November 22–24 [1963] is a dramatic affirmation of the need for steps to bring about a proper balance between the right of the public to be kept informed and the right of the individual to a fair and impartial trial.[18]

The Warren report recommended to the American Bar Association (ABA) that it establish a special commission to explore the issues and recommend guidelines to control pretrial publicity at its source—that is, with police and officers of the court. In 1968 that special commission submitted its report to

Reardon: A Significant Recommendation

Gags and Closed Hearings

By Paul Magnusson
Free Press Staff Writer

CHICO, Calif.—In hunting terms it is known as a "clean kill." The .30 caliber bullet entered the shoulder from the rear, broke the bone in the upper left arm and burrowed through the heart. Jimmy Lee Campbell, a 22-year-old deaf and mentally retarded black man, dropped to the railroad tracks and died almost instantly.

When his body was discovered the following morning by an almond rancher in a driving rainstorm, Campbell's death appeared to be a random hunting accident. Police knew of no one who might have wanted the simple man dead.

As police quickly learned through informants, Campbell had indeed been the victim of hunters, but the shooting had been no accident. Campbell was one of five blacks who had been stalked by three white hunters who, unable to find deer to shoot, had gone looking for "dark meat," as they gleefully put it.

THE JANUARY 1979 crime followed by less than two weeks the implementation of a California ballot initiative that allows the death penalty for racially motivated killings. The arrest of the three white hunters took only 11 hours and the statements they gave to police clearly implicated them in the killings.

Yet, it was not until this month that the reason for the shooting became known, after a county judge lifted a year-old gag order. And by that time, all three had been allowed to plead guilty in return for lesser sentences. One of the three, a woman, will have her case reviewed this month by a county judge who may legally grant her probation.

Among the ironies of the case is the response of the NAACP, which has argued in federal courts for decades to have the death penalty outlawed. The civil rights organization is supporting Campbell's mother in her demands for the San Quentin gas chamber for the murderers of her son.

And an organization of black attorneys in Sacramento, while generally opposing the death penalty, has been critical of the plea bargaining that saved the lives of the three killers. The group will ask the trial judge to impose the harshest sentence possible.

At the urging of the California speaker of the House, who also claims to oppose the death penalty, the state's attorney general has begun his own investigation into the plea bargaining arrangement.

NONE OF THIS has left law enforcement in Butte County happy. Unaccustomed to public scrutiny—judges there close virtually all major preliminary hearings and frequently issue gag orders—officials are on the defensive. . . .

the ABA. Called the Reardon report, in the name of its chairman, it urged that limitations be placed on information made available to the news media by prosecutors, defense attorneys, police, and other court officers. Under the recommendations, key participants in a pending case would be forbidden, under penalty of fine or imprisonment, to discuss "alleged confessions, prior records, potential witnesses, potential pleas and other comments as to guilt or innocence of the accused." In actual practice, application of the ABA guidelines have gone much further.[19]

Harold R. Medina, senior judge of the United States Court of Appeals, has urged attorneys to steer clear of the ABA guidelines.[20] Long a defender of press rights, Medina told a seminar on communications law that if any judge tries to implement the guidelines, "the most fatal thing you can do is go in there and participate." In the matter of gag orders, Judge Medina has also warned the news media to "fight like tigers every inch of the way" against the guidelines.

*Judge Medina
Opposes the
Guidelines*

Since the framers of the Constitution did not give priority to one amendment over another, it is proper to assume that they are all equal: the First Amendment, which guarantees a press free of government interference is coequal with the Sixth Amendment, which guarantees a fair trial. But since adoption of the ABA guidelines, the First and Sixth Amendments have co-existed in a state of turmoil. The issuance of gag orders by the courts against the press, almost unknown until the recent past, are at the center of the controversy.

*Equality of
Constitutional
Amendments*

Fred Graham undertook an informal survey of the application of judicial gag orders since ABA adoption of the Reardon report.[21] He could find none prior to 1966. But in 1966 two such orders were issued. He found four in 1967; fifteen in 1968, five in 1969; nine in 1970; thirteen in 1971; ten in 1972; twenty-two in 1973, and at least twenty in 1974, the end of the survey period. Gag orders have obviously become a favored instrument of the courts to hold the free press at bay.

*Increases in
Applications of Gag
Orders*

The increasing employment of gag orders against the news media clearly pits one constitutional guarantee against another. That questionable arrangement is further advanced by a new court weapon known as the Dickinson rule, which came out of a case in Baton Rouge, Louisiana, in 1972. In that case, a presiding judge ordered the press not to publish the details of a *public hearing,* and then convicted two reporters for contempt after they wrote stories about it. An appeals court ruled that the judge's order was unconstitutional but *upheld* the conviction on the grounds that the reporters should have done as they were told and *then* appealed the order. As Graham points out, "It was the first time in the history of this country that newsmen had been held for contempt for reporting a public hearing in the face of an admittedly

The Dickinson Rule

unconstitutional order." Then the United States Supreme Court refused to review the case, which left all judges free to apply the Dickinson rule to gag the press whenever it pleased them to do so.

How to dress for credibility in the courtroom

Dear Mr. Molloy: I am an attorney and have been working before juries for years. My standard outfit has been a blue or gray pinstripe suit, a white shirt, and a bright paisley tie with a matching handkerchief worn in the breast pocket.

My partner has been insisting for years that my tie and handkerchief combinations make me look like a gigolo. He finally persuaded me to throw out the handkerchief completely and to replace my lively ties with dull substitutes.

I may be misreading the juries' reactions, but I feel that since I have made the change I have cut down on my ability to communicate.

I'd like your comments. Do bright handkerchiefs help?

M.B., Baltimore

Dear M.B.: In your case the handkerchiefs may have helped.

You are probably reading the juries correctly. You may be turning them off in your new, more conservative outfit.

Dark gray and blue pinstripe suits worn with white shirts and conservative ties tell the jurors two things: that you are a member of an elite group and that you may be an expert.

Obviously, if your message to a jury is, "I am your friend, so listen to me," you are now giving off contradictory verbal and non-verbal messages. The jurors' friends do not dress in pinstripe suits.

When you wore flashy ties and gaudy pocket handkerchiefs, you lowered the socio-economic level of the entire outfit, which must have had a positive effect on your ability to communicate.

Unfortunately, you also sent out a negative message. By wearing a strange combination of clothing, you communicated the impression that you are somewhat erratic and unreliable and cut into your credibility.

Being a friend of the jury and being a highly credible attorney are not mutually exclusive messages. You can have the best of both worlds.

Replace those blue and gray pinstripe suits with traditional businessmen's plaids. The best color combinations are dark blue dominant with light blue; blue dominant with gray; blue dominant with beige; and blue dominant with dark gray.

These suits will work best when worn with white shirts and solid navy blue or maroon ties. When you want to be very authoritative, wear a navy blue suit, a white shirt and a small pattern maroon tie.

If damaging media coverage of a crime does occur to the point that a defendant's protection under the Sixth Amendment is in jeopardy, the presiding judge possesses specific powers to deal with it. The judge may order a change of venue, which means moving the trial to another part of the state where media coverage was minimal or nonexistent. He might elect to postpone the trial and thus allow for a cooling-off period. He might also sequester the jury. In that case, jurors are isolated from media coverage throughout the trial period by restricting their access to the news media and by keeping them together for meals and in hotel rooms overnight under the watchful eyes of court officers.

Court Means of Coping with Media Coverage

The Sheppard case was a landmark of the free press-fair trial controversy.[22] In July 1954, Dr. Samuel Sheppard was arrested for the murder of his pregnant wife in a suburb of Cleveland. In one of the most flagrant abuses of press coverage of a murder case in this century, the newspapers of Cleveland went to extremes to produce a torrent of sensationalism for the explicit purpose of selling more newspapers. Sheppard was convicted and served nearly ten years in prison.

The Sheppard Case

'Before we start, do you want a nice, quick, quiet trial—or do you want the damn media?'

© 1979, James Stevenson.

At that point his attorney asked for a review of the case by the United States Supreme Court, indicating that the inflammatory publicity had violated his rights. The high court agreed, ordered him released and a new trial held. In the lengthy majority decision written by Justice Tom C. Clark, the court took issue not with the excesses of the press but with the judge for failing to utilize the powers available to him to protect Sheppard's rights. From the beginning of the investigation, the decision said, public officials made irresponsible public statements to the news media, many of which were inflammatory and harmful to Sheppard. "From the outset officials focused suspicion on Sheppard," Justice Clark wrote. Front row seats were reserved, by the judge, for media representatives.

Inflammatory Comments by Court Officials

The trial began, he went on, "two weeks before the November general election at which the chief prosecutor was a candidate for municipal judge and the presiding judge, Judge Blythin, was a candidate to succeed himself." The jury was not sequestered, and returned to the community after daily sessions to bathe in media sensationalism. Nor was change of venue sought to protect the rights of the accused, nor a cooling-off period ordered to permit media coverage to die down before bringing the case to trial. "The fact that many of the prejudicial news items can be traced to the prosecution, as well as the defense, aggravates the judge's failure to take any action," the majority decision said. Only rarely is it in the power of the press to be overtly irresponsible in a court proceeding without the willing cooperation of officers of the court. On press coverage of trials, Justice Clark wrote:

Personal Political Ambitions

Justice Clarke on the Sheppard Case

> The principle that justice cannot survive behind walls of silence has long been reflected in the "Anglo-American distrust for secret trials . . . ." A responsible press has always been regarded as the handmaiden of effective judicial administration, especially in the criminal field. Its function in this regard is documented by an impressive record of service over several centuries. The press does not simply publish information about trials but guards against the miscarriage of justice by subjecting the police, prosecutors, and judicial processes to extensive public scrutiny and criticism.

At no time did the Supreme Court decision in the Sheppard case recommend the use of gag orders or other such "controls" in press coverage of court proceedings.

More Judicial Gag Orders

Press Barred from Court in South Carolina

In more recent times, three Columbia, South Carolina, reporters were removed from a pretrial hearing of a state senator charged with fraud and misappropriation of funds associated with a federal housing project. Chief United States District Judge J. Robert Martin, Jr. imposed a gag order that prohibited witnesses, lawyers, and other officers of the court from "talking or mingling" with newspeople. The order also prohibited reporters from gaining access to lists of jurors and from photographing or hand-sketching the jurors. The local chapter of the Society of Professional Journalists, Sigma Delta Chi, filed a suit against the order arguing that it was constitutionally vague and had a "chilling effect" on press coverage of the trial. A three-judge panel of the Fourth Circuit United States Court of Appeals dismissed the suit on the grounds that it was based on improper legal steps. "We realize the questions concerning the press deserve timely consideration," the verdict read, "yet no reason is shown why that might not otherwise be attained than disruption of a criminal trial." The United States Supreme Court refused to review a second appeal presented by South Carolina journalists.[23]

Judge John Shearer, of the Southwest Florida Circuit Court, asked reporters to leave a hearing in the case of a man charged with the murder of a nine-year-old. The local news media resisted the order and threatened to challenge Shearer's action. The judge then reversed his decision.[24]

A Judge Reverses His Order

One of the most notable examples of the gag issue occurred in Nebraska several years ago. A man was arrested in the rape slayings of a Lincoln County family, including children. County Judge Ronald Ruff held a preliminary hearing to determine whether there was due cause to hold the suspect, Erwin Charles Simants, for trial. At that point, Judge Ruff issued an order prohibiting the news media from reporting details of the hearing. Local media appealed. District Court Judge Hugh Stuart threw out Ruff's order but imposed one of his own, which was less sweeping than the original gag, but a gag nonetheless. The case eventually went to the United States Supreme Court, which overturned Stuart's gag order because, as in the Sheppard case, the judge had not exhausted the powers available to him before ordering the gag. But the Supreme Court also indicated that gag orders might be required in the future under extraordinary circumstances, but only after the trial judge had invoked all other measures at his disposal.[25]

The Nebraska Gag Rule Case

In spite of the Supreme Court's decision in the Nebraska case, restrictions on press coverage of trials continue to harass the news media. In New Jersey, a judge threatened to jail any reporter who talked with members of the jury *following* the murder trial of boxer Hurricane Carter. Judges in California continued gag orders, or applied new orders, in three criminal cases including the Alphabet Bomber case.[26]

Other Gag Cases

In Iowa, a member of a motorcycle gang was murdered and in the subsequent trial, the presiding judge tried to prevent publication of the names of jurors selected to serve. The judge feared that they might be subjected to violence by other gang members. The gag order was challenged by the Des Moines Register and Tribune Company and other news organizations. The Iowa Supreme Court overturned the gag order and invoked legal principles similar to those applied by the United States Supreme Court in the Nebraska case.[27]

The conflict between press and courts over gag orders goes on and is likely to remain a thorny issue for years to come. In response to these tactics, some journalism executives have begun to take action on their own. In Pennsylvania, editors have formed the First Amendment Coalition in response to increased judicial and other government restraints against the press. Gene Roberts, executive editor of the *Philadelphia Inquirer,* said "We believe [the situation] has reached emergency proportions, both in geographic breadth and the scope of the issues." Ed Miller, executive editor of the *Allentown Call-Chronicle,* called it "open warfare." Particular targets of the coalition are the secret pretrial hearings of W. A. "Tony" Boyle, former president of the United Mine Workers charged with the murder of Joseph Yablonski, a union opponent; court restrictions of the news media in Blair and Montgomery counties; and banning photographers from courthouses. The group is also devising plans to provide legal services to newspeople and to develop and publish materials dealing with the First Amendment.[28]

Other Media-Court
Clashes

The press and the courts collide in ways other than the issuance of gag orders. In recent years there has been a noticeable increase in court efforts to force newspeople, under threat of fine or imprisonment, to reveal the sources of their information, to surrender to public officials their personal notes, film, or television tapes of news events, and to accept unannounced police search and seizure raids on the private offices and files of the news media.

Subpoena and Contempt Power

Court Demands on Private Information

In its monumental study, the task force of the Twentieth Century Fund determined that the number of subpoenas issued by courts and grand juries to force newspeople to reveal their confidential sources of information "has mushroomed since 1969 and spread to state and local law enforcement agencies."[29] It now appears that the once-standard practice of police negotiating with news media for access to such information has been abandoned. The increased activity in this area began when certain government agencies decided to investigate radicals and radical groups who openly opposed American involvement in the Vietnam War. The agencies had little or no knowledge of what the radicals had done or might do. But they knew that the news media had been covering the activities of the groups for some time. Soon the United States Department of Justice began issuing subpoenas to journalists, which required surrender of "notes, tapes, film, photographs, financial records and personal testimony from representatives of newspapers, news magazines and the broadcast media." The fact that the news media are clearly not an investigative arm of government but function to provide the American people with needed information *about* government has not deterred law enforcement agents. The following are *some* cases in point.

Early in 1970, federal officials subpoenaed tapes and outtakes (news film not used on the air) of a CBS news show on the Black Panther party. The following day a second subpoena demanded surrender of all correspondence, memoranda, notes, and telephone calls related to the program, which covered an eighteen-month period leading up to the broadcast.

Federal agents subpoenaed unedited and unpublished photographs belonging to *Time, Life,* and *Newsweek* magazines, which related to the Weathermen, an extremist faction of the Students for a Democratic Society, then being investigated by a grand jury for radical activities.

New York Times reporter Earl Caldwell, a black who covered the Black Panther party in the San Francisco Bay area, was subpoenaed to appear before a federal grand jury "with notes and tape recordings of his interviews with party officers and spokespersons during the preceding year." Caldwell refused to honor the subpoena on the grounds that his very appearance before the grand jury would destroy the bond of trust he had created with the Panthers and thus shut off a source of valuable information to the public.

Earl Caldwell (*New York Times* Pictures).

Louisville Courier-Journal reporter Paul M. Branzburg received subpoenas from two county grand juries because of articles he had written on the manufacture of hashish and how the marijuana trade in the area functioned. The stories were based on information from confidential sources. Branzburg claimed First Amendment protection and refused to appear.

Paul Pappas worked as a reporter-cameraman for WTET-TV in New Bedford, Mass. At one point he managed to gain the confidence of a Black Panther group there who, expecting a police raid on their headquarters, invited him to spend the night. Pappas agreed to report on police tactics should the raid take place but to do nothing if a raid failed to materialize. The police did not arrive so Pappas wrote nothing. Yet he was subpoenaed to testify about the Panthers before a grand jury. He refused and was cited for contempt.

As the task force reported, numerous incidents similar to these took place in which subpoena power was applied to force disclosures of confidential press sources.

The Branzburg Decision
The Media's Constitutional Defense

Caldwell, Branzburg, and Pappas carried their appeals to the United States Supreme Court. In the end, all three lost in spite of the array of liberal constitutionalists who filed briefs on their behalf. The briefs argued that when a newsperson gains information from confidential sources and is then subpoenaed to testify about those sources and reveal their identities, the sources "are terrified of disclosure and consequently shut up." Worse yet, "the resulting loss of confidence spreads rapidly and widely to other newsmen, thus critically impairing the news gathering capacities of the media and impoverishing the fund of public information and understanding."[30]

In his dissenting opinion, Justice William O. Douglas wrote:

Justice Douglas Dissents

The intrusion of government into this domain is symptomatic of the disease of this society. As the years pass the power of government becomes more and more pervasive. It is a power to suffocate both people and causes. Those in power, whatever their politics, want only to perpetuate it. Now that the fences of the law and the tradition that has protected the press are broken down the people are the victims. The First Amendment, as I read it, was designed precisely to prevent that tragedy.[31]

Other Cases
A Broadcaster in Wichita

Joe Pennington, an investigative reporter for station KAKE-TV in Wichita, was sentenced to sixty days in jail for contempt for refusing to divulge the source of a *rumor* he learned about but never used. The rumor related to the trial-in-progress of Mrs. Milda Sandstrom for the murder of her husband. The unnamed source told Pennington that Mr. Sandstrom had had an argument with an individual who later became a state's witness against Mrs. Sandstrom. When he could not verify the rumor, Pennington decided not to use it on the air. But in the *process* of trying to verify it, he had checked with the defendant's attorney, who then subpoenaed him and demanded that he name the source of the rumor. Pennington refused on the grounds that it would violate his right to keep his sources confidential. Pennington appealed the sentence "because of my personal and professional dedication to what I believe are the rights and responsibilities of a free press." His appeal is pending.[32]

Four Newsmen in Fresno

In California, four newsmen were jailed by a judge for refusing to reveal the identity of a news source. They were cited for contempt as a lever to force them to disclose the source of a grand jury transcript that they had read. According to George Gruner, managing editor of the *Fresno Bee* and one of the group, the judge ultimately recognized that their resolve could not be shaken and that "the confidentiality of a news source isn't just something the four of us made up." Even so, the judge termed their stubbornness an "act of fanaticism." Gruner cited the warning of former United States Supreme Court Justice William O. Douglas that the First Amendment is a weather vane indicating stormy times for journalists: "Get your cold weather gear," Gruner said, "the storm is upon us."[33]

The Myron Farber Case

In a major controversy of recent times, a reporter for the *New York Times* went to jail for refusing to surrender his personal notes and documents related to a murder trial in New Jersey.[34] On January 7 and 8, 1976, the *Times* carried by-line stories by investigative reporter Myron A. Farber related to the mysterious deaths of patients at Riverdell Hospital in Oradell, New Jersey, ten years earlier. The stories resulted in the indictment of Dr. Mario E. Jascalevich, who was charged with poisoning five patients.

Farber Named as Witness

At the outset of the trial in early 1978, Farber was barred from the courtroom by official order when the defense counsel indicated that he would be called as a witness. Farber and the *Times* appealed, but a New Jersey superior court ruled that "if a newspaper reporter assumes the duties of an investigator, he must also assume the responsibilities of an investigator and be treated equally under the law. . . . It is this Court's opinion that the rights of the press under the First Amendment can never exceed the rights of a defendant to a fair and impartial trial."

Farber's Notes Subpoenaed

Thus on May 19, trial judge William J. Arnold issued an order allowing the defense to subpoena all notes and documents in Farber's possession and others held by the *Times*. On June 30, Judge Arnold informed Farber and the *Times* that he wished to examine the materials in private. Both refused. Citing press protections under the New Jersey shield law and the First Amendment, they presented repeated legal and jurisdictional challenges to the order. Finally the court convicted both Farber and the *Times* of contempt. The paper, which would be strikebound most of the summer and fall, was fined $100,000 plus $5,000 a day until it decided to obey the order. Farber received a $1,000 fine and a six-month jail sentence for criminal contempt, which was to begin *after he surrendered* the contested materials, although he was to be jailed in the meantime.

Times *Fined*

Myron Farber in the Bergen County jail. (Wide World Photos.)

Farber Jailed   Appeals to the United States Supreme Court went unheeded and Farber eventually went to the Bergen County jail. Then Judge Arnold introduced a new element into the controversy. He ordered two book publishers, Doubleday and Warner Communications, to surrender all materials related to a book manuscript authored by Farber, which dealt with the Jascalevich case. Immediately the confrontation moved out of the area of confidentiality of a reporter's sources, which had been the issue thus far. The fact that Farber had made formal plans to publish a book on the case appeared to be the clincher.

On August 18, the *New York Times* surrendered its files on the Jascalevich case. Ten days later, Judge Theodore W. Trautwein of the New Jersey Superior Court "rewarded" the paper for its cooperation by accusing its management of having "sanitized" (or cleaned up) its files before turning them over. The judge also ruled that the paper must continue paying its $5,000 per day fine.

Finally at the end of August, matters took another turn after Farber had spent twenty-seven days in jail and the *Times* had spent $130,000 in fines. The state supreme court agreed to look into the dispute. On September 21, it ordered Farber back to jail. The order was held up until the United States Supreme Court could rule. And on October 6 that body ordered Farber back to jail if he continued to be uncooperative. On October 12, Farber was returned to the Bergen County lockup.

Farber Returned to Jail

Ultimately the court found Dr. Jascalevich innocent. Farber was released and the *New York Times,* still crippled by the strike, stared at a staggering $285,000 in fines plus more in attorneys fees levied against it.

About Farber's Book

The fact that Myron Farber had contracted with two publishers for a book on the Jascalevich case before the trial began was seized upon by some court officials as a sign of bad faith. He was criticized, even by some journalists, for presenting himself as a defender of the First Amendment at the same time he was planning to earn money from it. As one judge said, "This is a sorry spectacle of a reporter standing on First Amendment principles, standing in sackcloth and ashes, when in fact he is standing at the altar of greed." The judge also charged that Farber thus had a personal stake in the conviction of Dr. Jascalevich.

In balance, Myron Farber is not the first reporter to turn a major news story into a book and for profit. Woodward and Bernstein became wealthy as a result of their Watergate efforts. Jimmy Breslin has done the same many times as have countless others. Most significant to the Farber case is the issue of forced disclosure of a reporter's private property. That was the nub of the Farber case, not the morality of creating a media spinoff that might or might not provide him with additional income.

The *Columbia Journalism Review* commented on Farber's troubles in New Jersey. After reviewing the issues, it said editorially:

> However, one thing is certain: subpoenas ordering the surrender of reporters' notes to judges, once a rarity, have increased many fold and will continue to increase with this tacit encouragement, to the point where reporters may start to wonder whether it wouldn't be practicable to submit their notes before they write the story.

Shield Laws

Prior to the time when courts and grand juries began going after reporters' notebooks, video tapes, outtakes, and other forms of privately gathered information, some states passed "shield laws" designed to protect reporters and editors from forced disclosure of sources. By 1975, twenty-six states had adopted shield laws. Most of them protect journalists from having to reveal the *information* as well as the identity of the sources and the notes taken. By and large, existing shield laws, passed at a time when press-bar relationships were more cooperative than at present, are totally inadequate to meet the

Most Shield Laws Protect Sources and Information

demands of out-and-out confrontation between the two sides. For example, in the cases of Earl Caldwell and Paul Pappas, the names of the sources were known to police and officers of the court, but the information was not. So they attempted to pry the information from reporters—personal notes, film, out-takes, tape recordings, and so forth. There have also been efforts to force newspeople to testify as witnesses in court cases and grand jury investigations because of what they might have observed in their news-gathering activities. Hence, existing shield laws do not meet the demands of current press-court relations.[35]

Some Forms of
Confidentiality Are
Protected by Tradition

The so-called Branzburg Decision, in which the United States Supreme Court ruled on the Caldwell, Branzburg, and Pappas cases, determined that newspersons do not have the "privilege" of withholding from grand juries either confidential information gathered in the performance of their duties or the names of confidential sources. Fred Graham and Jack Landau point out that hundreds of thousands of Americans enjoy the privilege of not being forced to testify in criminal cases either about information made known to them or about identities of those who volunteer information. These include vast numbers of physicians, lawyers, and clergy* who "counsel" on a confidential basis with patients, clients, or penitents. They function in the security of knowing that what is revealed to them will not be forced from them. Graham and Landau favor a *national* shield law to protect journalists in every state from forced disclosure of information and/or identities of sources. Other journalists oppose such a move since, to be effective, it would have to be passed by Congress and, the reasoning goes, Congress has no business or authority to legislate anything dealing with a free press.[36]

A National Shield Law
May Not Be Workable

Controversy
in California

A proposal to include the state's shield law in the state's constitution is being considered in California. If approved, it would prohibit judges from jailing newspeople who refuse to divulge the sources of their information. In several recent cases, the courts ruled that existing shield laws do not protect a reporter's privilege, that honoring such a privilege would interfere constitutionally with the authority of the courts to control their proceedings. Those in favor of including the shield law in the state constitution fear that defeat of the proposal might reinforce the court's interest in applying contempt powers to the mass media.[37]

New Jersey's shield law has been expanded to include broadcast news as well as print. The change stemmed from an incident in which a reporter for WHWH in Princeton was ordered to surrender to the county prosecutor radio tapes he had developed while looking into the activities of the Ku Klux Klan in New Jersey.[38] But since the New Jersey shield law proved totally ineffective in the Myron Farber case, its continued value is open to serious question.

---

*Clergy have not formally been recognized as a "privileged" group because the courts have never heard a case involving clergy-penitent confidence.

It has become dramatically evident that the news media are losing their struggle to protect the identities of confidential news sources, along with the information coming from such sources. As we have seen, a large number of states do not have shield laws, and most of those that do provide poor protection at best. If sources of information fear retribution at the hands of police departments, grand juries, or courts, it is certain that a great deal of information vital to the public interest will be lost. Seemingly, the excesses that the Constitution expressly prohibits by acts of Congress or other legislative bodies are being enacted by law enforcement agencies and the courts on an individual, case by case basis.

Is the Press Unable to Protect Its Sources?

The End Result

The Underground Press

As confrontations between the courts and the news media have heightened in intensity and frequency, so have confrontations between the news media and law enforcement agencies. The alliance of police and the courts is a natural one since, in function, one is the extension of the other. Both are public agencies, both play powerful roles in society, and both appear to be increasingly hostile to the news media. The task force of the Twentieth Century Fund reported that some newspapers have seemingly been set apart from the mainstream newspapers and given "special attention" by police.[39] The protection of the First Amendment does not distinguish between metropolitan daily newspapers and country weekly newspapers. Nor does it distinguish between the labor press and the foreign language press or other kinds or levels of journalistic activity. It states only that Congress shall pass no laws abridging freedom of the press. Presumably that means all of the press and not merely particular *kinds* of press.

Freedom for All the Press

In the late 1960s and early 1970s, a new hybrid of antiestablishment publications developed in the United States, most of them newspapers. These were founded and staffed mostly by political and social dissidents who were, typically, anti–Vietnam War and pro–civil rights advocates who found no outlet for their views in the established media. In that sense, the new papers were "underground" papers and were commonly referred to as such. Their profits were borderline, the papers being sold in the streets by dedicated vendors with no real "controlled" circulation as the commercial newspapers have. In its study, the task force found that these publications have had "little or none of the protective political power of the established press." They have frequently been the targets of assorted police actions although they are local in character and lack the persuasive power among mass audiences that the established papers enjoy. That seems to have mattered little. Some instances follow.

The Underground Press Defined

Courts expanding their power by default, law official says

By Carey English
Free Press Staff Writer

U.S. Solicitor General Wade McCree said in Detroit Monday that the American people will be the big losers if the courts are forced to continue filling roles that rightfully belong to the executive and legislative branches of government.

McCree, who spoke to the Economic Club of Detroit, said at a press conference that the courts have increasingly undertaken untraditional tasks "because of a default on the part of the other branches of government" and not because they are power-hungry.

"Judges are running school districts, they're running hospital systems, they're running penal institutions, they're running mental hospitals and they usually do that because the legislature or the executive that's supposed to respond to grievances in these areas frequently avoids these very sensitive political issues," he said.

But McCree, a former federal appeals court judge from Detroit who is the Justice Department's third highest official, suggested that the trend needs to be reversed.

"There's nothing in the training of a judge that equips him to do this kind of thing," he said. "And yet, around the country, one sees these phenomena and I think we're going to continue to see it unless the other two branches of government take charge in areas where they're expected to. I think the public will suffer as a consequence."

McCREE SAID THE COURTS should no longer be regarded "as the final arbiter of all problems."

Detroit Free Press.

Cases in Point

In 1969, the publisher of the *Los Angeles Free Press* was fined $1,000 and given three years probation for having published a list of state narcotics agents gained by questionable means.

Police in Dallas, Texas, conducted an "obscenity" raid against an underground paper in October 1968. They carried off two tons of material belonging to the establishment. Yet they failed to obtain an obscenity conviction that would stand the test in a federal court.

Buffalo, New York, police put the Black Panther newspaper out of business by announcing that it would arrest anyone selling the publication on the streets.

The office of the *San Diego Street Journal* was raided by police without a warrant in the fall of 1969, its vendors "handcuffed, searched and jailed for loitering and obstructing the sidewalk."

Of these developments the task force wrote: "There has been a double standard of treatment, one for the underground and one for the established press—a double standard that is inconsistent with the First Amendment's guarantee for all the press." The established newspapers remained silent about the plight of the alternative papers, yet they now find themselves embroiled in police activities that are similar in method and purpose.

A Double Standard

Dan Rios, a photographer for the *Escondido Times-Advocate* in California, was arrested while taking pictures of an overturned oil truck on a city street. He was charged with making it difficult for the area to be cleared and with resisting a police officer in the performance of his duty. After the arrest, Rios was not permitted to remove his camera from around his neck or to lock his van, which contained valuable photographic equipment. Nor would police lock the van for him. He was held for two hours before police permitted him to make a telephone call and seven hours before he was released. About one month later, Rios went to trial and was acquitted of all charges.[40]

A Newspaper Photographer

Police obviously feel that private citizens and organizations should cooperate in official investigations of criminal activities, or suspected criminal activities, and many do for the betterment of all. But efforts to force those who have constitutional protection to do so is another matter. In these cases, the organization is the press, which investigates on its own in the public interest as the First Amendment requires. Police departments are the law enforcement agents of government. They also investigate and apply their findings to the judicial process. The two are necessary but separate functions. And when a constitutionally mandated organization can be forced by a government agency, under threat of fines or imprisonment, to reveal the fruits of their private investigations, the battle is joined. That is the issue. It is a highly charged issue with "right" seeming to serve both sides at the same time. The clashes are increasing in number and intensity and have moved into a new arena referred to in legal parlance as "search and seizure."

The Police-Press Confrontation

In Providence, Rhode Island, WJAR-TV showed a news clip that contained details of a teacher's strike held earlier that day. The clip included an incident in which a former union president allegedly assaulted an unemployed teacher who crossed a picket line at a school in Coventry. Several days later, Coventry police appeared at the station and asked to view the tape as part of their overall investigation. The station's policy permits interested persons to view tapes. The police officers viewed the footage and asked that a third party be permitted to see it later in the day. Again the station complied. At no time did the police indicate that they intended to take the tape with them. Had they done so, said Steve Caminus, news director, he would have refused to

Search and Seizure and Newsrooms
WJAR-TV and the Teacher's Strike

surrender it. Yet the following day, Coventry and Providence police returned to the television station without notice, but with a search warrant. Attached to the warrant was a written statement indicating that the tape was on the premises and contained evidence related to the commission of a crime. The police seized the tape.[41]

Houseboats in Sausalito

In Sausalito, California, houseboat owners demonstrated against the construction of a marina which, they claimed, would eventually drive them out of the area. Sheriff's deputies were routinely assigned to the scene and clashes broke out between them and the demonstrators. Thirteen persons were arrested. The incident received major coverage by local news media. About ten days after the incident, police officers, armed with search warrants, conducted surprise raids on the newsrooms of four San Francisco area television stations and demanded the surrender of film and video tapes related to the violence. Two of the stations released only those portions of the footage that had been shown on the air. The station manager of a third television outlet refused to surrender any footage and ordered the police off the premises. The fourth station complied with the demands of the warrant. Local media condemned the court and police action, branding it "repugnant" and comparable to "Nazi Germany at its height."[42]

The Student Newspaper

One of the most far-reaching cases related to police search-and-seizure activities developed in Palo Alto, California. Local police, armed with a search warrant, entered and searched the offices of the Stanford University student newspaper. They sought photographs taken by staff members during a sit-in at Stanford Hospital three days before. The officers found nothing useful. But the students took the matter to court, which ruled that issuance of the warrant was illegal. Later, a federal appeals court upheld the decision. On that oc-

Court of Appeals and the First Amendment

casion, the Nineteenth United States Court of Appeals ruled that third parties not suspected of a crime have greater protection under the law than criminal suspects do. This is especially true, the court stated, in cases involving the press when First Amendment interests are at stake. The appeals court also held that the Fourth Amendment's allowance for reasonable search and seizure required that evidence held by a noncriminal must be taken by *subpoena* rather than by seizure. The court emphasized that that procedure is particularly appropriate in the Stanford case since it involves press freedom as protected by the First Amendment.[43]

The United States Department of Justice then filed a friend-of-the-court brief with the United States Supreme Court, which had agreed to consider the Stanford case. The brief indicated that the First Amendment does not provide special protection against surprise raids by police who are seeking confidential or other information in the files of news media offices. United States Solicitor General Wade H. McCree, Jr. informed the high court that the Justice Department opposed the verdicts of the lower courts in the Stanford case "as applied to searches of the press." He further indicated that it must be the responsibility of each magistrate to use his own discretion in determining if a surprise raid violates the First Amendment rights of the news media. The National Association of District Attorneys and seventeen state attorneys general also filed briefs requesting reversal of the lower courts' rulings.[44]

Supreme Court Decision on Search and Seizure

On May 31, 1978, the United States Supreme Court ruled five votes to three that police may launch surprise search-and-seizure raids against newspaper offices and those of other news media provided they obtain warrants beforehand.[45] Justice Byron White, who wrote the majority opinion for the Court, declared that—the decisions of the two lower courts notwithstanding—the Fourth Amendment offers no special protection to newspapers:

> We decline to reinterpret the [Fourth] Amendment to impose a general constitutional barrier against warrants to search newspaper premises, to require resort to subpoenas as a general rule or to demand prior notice and hearing in connection with the issuance of search warrants.

White, joined in the majority decision by Chief Justice Warren Burger, Justices Harry Blackmun, Lewis Powell, and William Rehnquist, indicated that the need of police to gather evidence before it disappears outweighs the right of privacy and threats against the press.

Justices Potter Stewart and Thurgood Marshall, who dissented, called the ruling "self-evident that police searches of newspaper offices burden the freedom of the press." Justice John Paul Stevens also dissented.

© 1978 Don Wright, Distributed by New York Times Special Features.

Considering the relative ease with which judges issue warrants to police officers, newspeople generally are dismayed by the ruling. Ernie Schultz, an Oklahoma broadcaster and president of the Radio-Television News Directors Association, predicted: "In many cities and towns, it could become open season on journalists." Mike Maloney, managing editor of the *Santa Ana Register* in California, said that the decision "leaves us, the newspapers, with no pre-search way of resisting the warrant. . . . It really opens up the door to newspaper offices." Keith Fuller, president and general manager of the Associated Press, indicated his disappointment: "My main concern is that this could open the door to harassment in situations where local authorities are irritated over news coverage." Ben Bradlee, executive editor of the *Washington Post,* said that the Pentagon Papers never would have been revealed to the public had the ruling been in force at that time. "The police would have entered newspaper officers and seized them before newspapers could bring the facts to the people," he said. "If this decision were in force during Watergate, it requires no stretch of the imagination to see police in these offices on a regular basis on a fishing expedition." Anthony Day is editorial page editor of the *Los Angeles Times* and chairman of the Freedom of Information Committee of the American Society of Newspaper Editors. To him the high court ruling is ominous: "The decision is so broadly written that in effect it makes a newspaper the potential arm of the prosecution. I don't think that Byron White and his colleagues in the majority understand what kind of animal they have let loose here."

Until this historic and much-debated decision, police had the right to request those who possessed "evidence" to surrender it voluntarily. If the individual refused to do so, police could request a court order *requiring* the individual to surrender the evidence or face the wrath of the court. As one editorial writer observed, the Supreme Court decision "affects not only newspapers, television and radio and magazines, but all other citizens as well."

Justice John Paul Stevens emphasized that the decision affects numerous "law-abiding citizens—doctors, lawyers, merchants, customers, bystanders—(who) may have documents in their possession that relate to an ongoing criminal investigation. The consequences of subjecting this large category of persons to unannounced police searches are extremely serious."[46]

Syndicated columnist Jack Anderson is of like mind. Of the decision he wrote: "These are dangerous steps toward putting the press under the control of government and blotting out all sources of information that compete with the official version."[47]

In response to the Supreme Court decision, James Reston, of the *New York Times,* addressed an open letter to Justice White. He stated that "I have no doubt that most people would agree that we deserve no privileges denied to businessmen or even gamblers, but I have a few nonlegal questions." He then asked which employee of an offending newspaper would be called the "culprit" in a press-police standoff. The publisher? The editor who assigns the story?

The reporter who is only carrying out an assignment? "In short, Mr. Justice, who goes to jail under this Supreme Court judgment?" Reston also raised the likelihood of the Nixon administration covering up the Watergate scandal by ordering the files of the *Washington Post* to be seized. "They tried to do it anyway," he added. If the police can gain entry to newspaper files with the blessings of the Supreme Court, he went on, then anyone who has information critical of government will hesitate to release it. Reston continued:

> If the press is told by the Supreme Court that it is subject under government court orders to turn over its notes and files, it will have to do so, but the most important thing is that its sources of information, fearing exposure, will dry up, and this, Mr. Justice White, will change both the press and the courts beyond anything that you expected.[48]

Several years ago, two young men from Rochester, New York, aged sixteen and twenty-one years, were arrested in relation to the death of a Rochester area police officer. News reports indicated that both suspects had made incriminating statements to the police, and their attorneys requested that the judge at their pretrial hearings hold proceedings in private.[49] Judge Daniel DePasquale then ordered all spectators to leave the courtroom. The action was taken, in DePasquale's terms, to minimize potentially harmful publicity and thus ensure a fair trial for the suspects.

Closed Pretrial Hearings

The Gannett media group, headquartered in Rochester, objected to the closed proceedings and appealed the judge's order. Then an appeals court upheld DePasquale's order on the grounds that pretrial publicity would likely hamper the selection of fair-minded citizens who would sit in judgment of the accused. Gannett pressed its case to the United States Supreme Court, arguing that open pretrial hearings serve the rights of all citizens as well as defendants.

Gannett Responds

Among other groups, the Reporters Committee for Freedom of the Press supported Gannett's position, indicating that nine out of ten criminal cases never come to trial but are settled one way or another in pretrial hearings. And that could have potentially dangerous results both for defendants and the community.

Reporters Committee

In July 1979, the United States Supreme Court ruled that, in fairness to the rights of defendants, courtrooms may be closed to avoid pretrial prejudicial publicity. The eighty-five-page majority decision indicated that the right to a fair trial belongs to the defendant, not to the public. And that, according to one constitutional lawyer, ignores "a judicial tradition dating back 150 years, giving strong support to the assertion (that) the press and public do have a right in."

The High Court Rules

Four of the justices disagreed with the verdict and produced a dissenting opinion. Though allowing for closing courts to the news media under certain rare circumstances, the four emphasized that those circumstances must be

Four Justices Dissent

News officials unhappy with court ruling

WASHINGTON (AP)—The vast majority of criminal cases could be closed to the public now that the Supreme Court has decided judges can hold pretrial criminal proceedings in private, news officials unhappy with the ruling contend.

The 5–4 ruling Monday upheld the right of a New York State judge who barred the news media and the public from a 1976 pretrial hearing in the case of two men accused of killing a former police officer.

The decision was immediately criticized by representatives of news organizations, who argued it meant "judicial censorship" and was "dangerous."

SINCE 90 PERCENT of criminal indictments are resolved in pretrial hearings, the press officials argued, the Supreme Court was opening the way to keep reporters and the public from most criminal cases.

"Nine out of 10 criminal cases are disposed of in pretrial proceedings," noted Charles Bailey, editor of the Minneapolis Tribune and chairman of the Freedom of Information Committee of the American Society of Newspaper Editors.

"Defendants offer to plead guilty to certain charges if they are assured of certain kinds of sentences. Bargains are struck. Some charges are dropped, others reduced.

"NOW JUDGES can close all of those proceedings, which are the heart of the criminal justice system, if they want to do so. We think that is dangerous," he said.

In the decision, Justice Potter Stewart said, "The Constitution nowhere mentions any right of access to a criminal trial on the part of the public." Rather, he said, the right belongs to the accused.

He said judges have broad discretion to prevent prejudicial publicity from being made public. And he said closing pretrial hearings is "often one of the most effective methods" that a trial judge can use to try to make sure "the fairness of a trial will not be jeopardized by the dissemination of such information throughout the community before the trial has ever begun."

THE NEW YORK case was brought by the Gannett Co., a major newspaper group with headquarters and two newspapers in Rochester. The State Journal is a member of the Gannett group.

On Nov. 4, 1976, Seneca County Judge Daniel DePasquale granted a defense request, with the prosecution agreeing, to exclude all spectators from the courtroom during a pretrial hearing to examine the admissability of confessions given by two suspects in the former officer's death.

Hearings on suppression of evidence traditionally have been open to the public.

DISSENTING WITH the majority, Justice Harry A. Blackmun said the court had established a rule "that if the defense and the prosecution merely agree to have the public excluded from the suppression hearing, and the trial judge does not resist . . . closure shall take place."

He said the result is "the important interests of the public and the press in open judicial proceedings are rejected and cast aside as of little value or significance."

OTHER CRITICISM:

—Allen H. Neuharth, chairman and president of Gannett, said the opinion "is another chilling demonstration that the majority of the Burger court is determined to unmake the Constitution."

—Jack C. Landau, who heads the Reporters' Committee for Freedom of the Press, said the court had approved "judicial censorship of the rankest kind."

—Jerry W. Friedheim, vice president and general manager of the American Newspaper Publishers Association, said the ruling "appears to substitute censorship for common sense and . . . may encourage some judges to conduct judicial proceedings in secrecy.

"This opinion is especially baffling when the court's own narrow majority states that a trial judge may close judicial proceedings even when this is 'not strictly and inescapably necessary.' Such reverse reasoning, championing non-necessity, is completely inconsistent with the protection of the American people's First Amendment liberties."

narrowly defined, that unfavorable publicity in such cases would have to be so biased as to cause irreparable harm to the right of the defendant to a fair trial.

Then, after a year of upheaval within and without the judiciary, the debate reached a historic climax.[50] On July 2, 1980, the Supreme Court disavowed its 1979 decision. More importantly, for the first time in history, the Court, in its seven to one vote, now recognizes the First Amendment right of "access to information." Chief Justice Burger's written decision states that, though not expressed literally in the Constitution, the public right of access to the courts is clearly guaranteed by those clauses that protect freedom of speech, press, and public assembly. It is further supported by the Ninth Amendment's guarantees to "the people" of "certain rights" not formally stated elsewhere.

The Court Corrects Itself

In his concurring opinion, Justice Brennan wrote: "The First Amendment embodies more than a commitment to free expression and communication interchange for their own sakes. It has a structural role to play in securing and fostering our republican system of self-government."

In short, the Supreme Court now believes that the people have the right to know about the business of government. It is likely that the spirit of this decision will eventually come to include all government business.

The relationship between the news media and the court system in America is unique among all other press-government relationships. This is a relationship that is undergoing radical changes from past practices, changes which place two vital social institutions in head-to-head conflict. On the one hand, the news media attempt to fulfill their First Amendment obligations by gathering needed information from many sources and reporting their findings to the American people. On the other, officers of the court seek to fulfill Sixth Amendment guarantees by probing antisocial activities, uncovering criminal suspects, and holding fair trials. Both work in the public interest. Both function on their abilities to gather, process, and apply information. Public information generated by the courts may be cut off from the public. Increasingly, information gathered by the news media that the courts cannot gather on their own is being forced out of journalists by application of court orders and threats of fine or imprisonment. Workable solutions to the conflicts have not yet been found. And without workable solutions, the conflicts must certainly increase.

Summary

Notes

1. Sheldon Peterson, "More News Decisions Are in the Courts' Hands," The *Quill*, February 1978, p. 5.
2. Information on "The Court's and the Public's Right to Know" and "The Press View" from Mary M. Connors, "Prejudicial Publicity: An Assessment," *Journalism Monographs* (Lexington, Ky.: Association for Education in Journalism, 1975). p. 8.

3. Bert Falbaum, "The Secret Branch of Government," *Columbia Journalism Review,* January/February 1978, p. 14.

4. Gregg Krupa, "Coed Defies Judge in Election Lawsuit," *Detroit Free Press,* October 5, 1977, p. 3–A.

5. Ken Fireman, "Free Press Reporter Jailed in Court Dispute," *Detroit Free Press,* May 4, 1978, p. 11–A.

6. Jack Landau, "Secrecy Is the Trend," The *Quill,* May 1977, p. 27.

7. Editorial, "Influence: Pilot Plan to Cut Role of Big Money in Judicial Elections," *Detroit Free Press,* March 27, 1978, p. 6–A.

8. Gene Weingarten, "Judges Lobby to Blunt Election Challenges," *Detroit Free Press,* April 19, 1978, p. 3–A.

9. "Justices Nominated at Primary Under Bill Before House," The *State Journal* (Associated Press), Lansing, Michigan, April 19, 1978, p. 8–B.

10. Information on judicial competence and incompetence from "From Boyle to Poindexter, How They Rate," *Detroit Free Press,* April 9, 1978, p. 2–C.

11. "Judge Faces 14 Revised Charges," The *State Journal* (Associated Press), Lansing, Michigan, May 25, 1978, p. 7–B.

12. "Ga. Judge Bars Press," *Detroit Free Press* (Associated Press), March 17, 1978, p. 14–A.

13. "For Virginia Judges the Rules Are Different," The *Quill,* June 1977, p. 12.

14. Information on the Indiana case from "Court Upholds Immunity for Mistaken Judges," *Detroit Free Press* (Associated Press and United Press International), March 29, 1978, p. 13–A.

15. "Judicial Immunity Upheld," The *State Journal,* Lansing, Michigan, March 29, 1978, p. 5–A.

16. Information on "The Case of Peter Reilly" from Donald S. Connery, "The Press and Peter Reilly," The *Quill,* April 1978, p. 25.

17. Fred P. Graham, " 'Gag' Orders Leave a Quagmire," *Mass Media and the Supreme Court,* Kenneth S. Devol, ed. (New York: Hastings House, 1976), p. 291.

18. Fred P. Graham, "Responsibility of News Media: The Warren Commission," *Mass Media and the Supreme Court,* Kenneth S. Devol, ed. (New York: Hastings House, 1976), p. 317.

19. Fred P. Graham, "Trial by Newspaper," *Mass Media and the Supreme Court,* Kenneth S. Devol, ed. (New York: Hastings House, 1976), p. 267.

20. Information on Medina and "Equality of Constitutional Amendments" from "Medina Warns Again," The *Quill,* January 1977, p. 9.

21. Information on the Graham survey from Fred P. Graham, " 'Gag' Orders Leave a Quagmire," p. 291.

22. Information on the Sheppard case from *Sheppard* v. *Maxwell, Mass Media and the Supreme Court,* Devol, p. 274.

23. Robert M. Hitt, "Gag Upheld," The *Quill,* February 1977, p. 31.

24. "Change of Mind," The *Quill,* January 1977, p. 8.

25. Ted Curtis Smythe, "Court Control of 'News' After Nebraska," *Readings in Mass Communication,* Michael C. Emery and Ted Curtis Smythe, eds. (Dubuque, Iowa: Wm. C. Brown Company Publishers, 1977), 3d ed., p. 154.

26. "Journalism's Failure to Explain the Public's Right to Know," The *Quill,* January 28, 1978, p. 18.

27. Rules for Gags," The *Quill,* January 1977, p. 8.

28. " 'Open Warfare' in Pennsylvania," The *Quill,* November 1977, p. 10.

29. Information on the task force, including "Some Actual Cases" from *Press Freedoms Under Pressure: Report of the Twentieth Century Fund Task Force on the Government and the Press* (New York: The Twentieth Century Fund, 1972), pp. 61–85.

30. Charlene J. Brown, Trevor R. Brown, and William L. Rivers, *The Media and the People* (New York: Holt, Rinehart and Winston, 1978), p. 224.

31. *Branzburg* v. *Hayes,* 408 U.S. 665 (1972).

32. "Reporter Protects Source of Rumor He Didn't Use," The *Quill,* January 1978, p. 8.

33. Barbara Biewer, " 'The Storm Is Upon Us,' " The *Quill,* January 1977, p. 24.

34. Details of the case from "The Press and the Courts: Is News Gathering Shielded by the First Amendment?" *Columbia Journalism Review,* November/December 1978. p. 43, p. 20; "The Supreme Court Declines," *Columbia Journalism Review,* January/February 1979, p. 25.

35. *Press Freedoms Under Pressure,* p. 65.

36. Fred P. Graham and Jack C. Landau, "The Federal Shield Law We Need," *Readings in Mass Communication,* Michael C. Emery and Ted Curtis Smythe, eds. (Dubuque, Iowa: Wm. C. Brown Company Publishers, 1977), 3d ed., p. 139.
37. "Does Shield Law Belong in State's Constitution?" (*Los Angeles Times*) The *Quill,* February 1978, p. 9.
38. "Shield Law Now Includes Broadcasters," The *Quill,* November 1977, p. 34.
39. Details of the task force report from *Press Freedoms Under Pressure,* pp. 34–36.
40. Jim Julian, "Letter to a Sheriff," The *Quill,* January 1977, p. 24.
41. "Police Raid Providence TV Station," *The News Media and the Law,* Reporters Committee for Freedom of the Press, December 1977, p. 4.
42. "Police Raid TV Stations for Film Out-Takes," *The News Media and the Law,* The Reporters Committee for Freedom of the Press, April 1978, p. 14.
43. "That Stanford Case," The *Quill,* March 1977, p. 6.
44. "Newsroom Raids Supported," *The News Media and the Law,* The Reporters Committee for Freedom of the Press, April 1978, p. 14.
45. Information on the Supreme Court decision and press reactions from Aaron Epstein, "Court OKs Searches of Newspaper Offices," *Detroit Free Press,* June 1, 1978, p. 1–B; "Open Season on Newsmen Next?" The *State Journal* (Associated Press), Lansing, Michigan, June 1, 1978, p. 9–A.
46. Editorial, "Court Decision Dangerous," The *State Journal,* Lansing, Michigan, June 6, 1978, p. 6–A.
47. Jack Anderson, "Supreme Court Stifles Free Press," *Detroit Free Press* (New York Times Service), June 11, 1978, p. 3–C.
48. James Reston, "A Decision That Will Change the Press," *Detroit Free Press* (New York Times Service), June 5, 1978, p. 15–A.
49. Information on closed pretrial hearings from Richard Carelli, The *State Journal* (Associated Press), Lansing, Michigan, November 7, 1978, p. 7–A; Carol Morello, The *State Journal,* Lansing, Michigan, July 8, 1979, p. 1–A.
50. "Public Access to Trials Is Upheld," *New York Times,* July 3, 1980, p. 1.

Biewer, Barbara. "The Storm Is Upon Us." The *Quill,* January 1977, p. 24.
"Change of Mind." The *Quill,* January 1977, p. 8.
Connery, Donald S. "The Press and Peter Reilly." The *Quill,* April 1978, p. 25.
Connors, Mary M. "Prejudicial Publicity: An Assessment." *Journalism Monographs.* Lexington, Ky.: Association for Education in Journalism, 1975.
"Does Shield Law Belong in State's Constitution?" The *Quill,* February 1978, p. 9.
Falbaum, Bert. "The Secret Branch of Government." *Columbia Journalism Review,* January/ February 1978, p. 14.
"For Virginia Judges the Rules Are Different." The *Quill,* June 1977, p. 12.
Hitt, Robert M. "Gag Upheld." The *Quill,* February 1977, p. 31.
"Journalism's Failure to Explain the Public's Right to Know." The *Quill,* January 28, p. 18.
Julian, Jim. "Letter to a Sheriff." The *Quill,* January 1977, p. 24.
Landau, Jack. "Secrecy Is the Trend." The *Quill,* May 1977, p. 27.
"Newsroom Raids Supported." *The News Media and the Law,* The Reporters Committee for Freedom of the Press, April 1978, p. 14.
" 'Open Warfare' in Pennsylvania." The *Quill,* November 1977, p. 10.
Peterson, Sheldon. "More News Decisions Are in the Courts' Hands." The *Quill,* February 1978, p. 5.
"Police Raid Providence TV Station." *The News Media and the Law,* The Reporters Committee for Freedom of the Press, December 1977, p. 4.
"Police Raid TV Stations for Film Out-Takes." *The News Media and the Law,* The Reporters Committee for Freedom of the Press, April 1978, p. 14.
"Reporter Protects Source of Rumor He Didn't Use." The *Quill,* January 1978, p. 8.
"Rules for Gags." The *Quill,* January 1977, p. 8.
"That Stanford Case." The *Quill,* March 1977, p. 6.
"The Press and the Courts: Is News Gathering Shielded By the First Amendment?" *Columbia Journalism Review,* November/December 1978, p. 43.
"The Supreme Court Declines." *Columbia Journalism Review,* January/February 1979, p. 25.

For Further Reading

News in Pictures

Mass Media Controls
Sex and the Mass Media

8

Upon completing this chapter you should—

be able to explain the constitutional questions involved in the ongoing debate over the use of sexually oriented content in the mass media

know the details of appropriate First Amendment cases as interpreted by the courts, including the United States Supreme Court, and media reactions for and against them

know how and for what purposes sex-oriented themes are applied to advertising

know thoroughly the recommendations of the Presidential Commission on Obscenity and Pornography

Chapter Objectives

Obscenity   Lewdness; offensive sexual portrayals or activities; indecent: personal views differ as does the "right" of persons to circulate obscene materials under First Amendment protection. (p. 233)

Prurient Interests   Obsessive interest in sexually explicit materials by an individual or group. (p. 234)

Local Community Standards   The most recent Supreme Court measure of what is legally obscene and what is not. No national standards exist as such. Thus, different parts of the country may have different, but legally-binding, interpretations. (p. 235)

Obscene vs. Indecent   Materials judged "obscene" cater to prurient interests; "indecency" under the United States Criminal Code is a form of "public nuisance." (p. 255)

Key Terms

However little some may think of common newspapers, to a wise man they appear the Ark of God for the safety of the people.

Pennsylvania Gazette,
January 7, 1768

The Issues Defined

With increasing ardor, Americans continue to debate whether or not sex-oriented content in the mass media should be accepted with great rejoicing, only tolerated, or banned altogether. Over the years, sexual portrayals in the mass media have spanned the spectrum from the soap opera dasher nuzzling his truelove (both gasping suggestively) to the publication of sexually explicit centerfolds and films in living color. It is probably the most difficult of all media issues to resolve, if, indeed, resolution is possible. For one thing, the individual citizen's notion of what is obscene and what is not is a profoundly personal and deep-rooted phenomenon. Just as one's view of the mass media is based on many personal variables, one's view of public nudity and sexual portrayals in the mass media are the sum of many or all his experiences as a person. This view is based on an individual's feelings about himself and his place in the changing world. It is based on the state of the individual's emotional and physical condition and the freedom to face what nature offers.

Each Person His or Her Own Judge

"Obscenity" in the mass media is a major "controls" issue because, as content, it is the most visible. Thus, it is debated more than any other form. The activities of various social, political, and religious groups to cope with obscenity demonstrate that considerable effort is expended to place "controls" on it. Other efforts seek to loosen or negate existing controls. Hence, confusion reigns.

The constitutional questions involved in the obscenity issue are weighted with complications. Do sexually explicit magazines, books, newspapers, advertisements, and films come under the protection of the First Amendment? Should sex-oriented vehicles in our media be allowed complete freedom to function and circulate? Would such freedom likely bring about a serious erosion of our social fiber? And, most importantly, do Americans, as members of a free society, have the individual, personal right to select what they wish to read

Constitutional Questions

or view in a publication or film without having to defend themselves in a court of law? If Americans do not have that individual right, who is to decide what is acceptable for each person (which means *all* persons) and on what basis will that referee base these judgments? These are serious and profound questions. They reflect a continuing controversy that affects every American.

Obscenity Defined

Webster's dictionary defines "obscene" as: "1. offensive to one's feelings, or to prevailing notions, of modesty or decency; lewd. 2. disgusting; repulsive."[1] The definition appears to say that obscenity, like beauty, is in the eye of the beholder. In responding to obscenity, the observer brings many attitudes and experiences to bear in making a judgment. Again, it is a thoroughly personal response. Hence, one may wonder if the word can ever be meaningfully "defined."

Major Obscenity Cases
Roth v. United States

The first modern test of the legality of obscenity laws came in 1957 with the landmark case of *Roth* v. *United States*.[2] Roth operated a business in New York City that produced a variety of sex-oriented books, photographs, and magazines. He advertised his wares via circulars and similar vehicles, which he designed and distributed through the United States mails. Eventually he was arrested and charged with violating the federal obscenity law. A jury for the District Court for the Southern District of New York convicted him on four counts of a twenty-six-count indictment charging him with mailing obscene circulars and advertisements. A court of appeals upheld the conviction, which then went to the United States Supreme Court for review.

At stake in the Roth case, according to Justice William Brennan, who wrote the Court's opinion, was the constitutionality of obscenity laws. In this case, the Court ruled that the federal and California obscenity laws were indeed constitutionally sound and that obscene matter does not enjoy First Amendment protection. At the same time, and this is significant, the Court did *not* rule that all obscenity is *illegal*.

A "Test" for Obscenity

Among other essential principles of law, Justice Brennan attempted to provide a yardstick for measuring obscene matter. He defind the measure as "whether to the average person, applying contemporary community standards, the dominant theme of the material taken as a whole appeals to prurient interests." If it does it is obscene.

Rulings Since Roth

In the years immediately following the Roth case, considerable judicial progress was made in dealing realistically with obscenity cases involving adults. The Supreme Court ruled that a bookstore owner could not be expected to have knowledge of the contents of every book in his stock. Hence, police could not enter a store and arrest the proprietor on an obscenity charge if he was not aware that a publication was obscene. The Court also insisted that acts of search and seizure in obscenity cases had to insure the legal rights of those involved. In 1966, the Court further liberalized its position on obscenity by requiring that a suspected obscene work be "utterly" without redeeming social value. Yet another decision permitted state and local legislative bodies to enact laws that would prohibit children from buying questionable sex-oriented materials even though adults were free to make such purchases. In its final case on obscenity, the liberal Warren Court ruled that adults could read obscene materials in the privacy of their own homes.

President Nixon's appointment of Warren Burger as Chief Justice of the United States Supreme Court brought changes in the Court's position on the issue. In a series of decisions, the Court tended to encourage obscenity prosecutions on state and local levels. One way was to indicate to those courts that the high court would not intervene in their decisions. In short, if a local court were to convict a defendant on an obscenity charge, the Supreme Court would not voice concern.

Obscenity and the Burger Court

In *Miller* v. *California*, an obscenity case tried in 1973, Chief Justice Burger altered Justice Brennan's earlier "test" for obscenity and, in effect, turned such cases back to the states for judgment.[3] Burger's updated "test" reads as follows:

Miller v. California: A New "Test"

> The basic guidelines for the trier of fact must be: (a) whether "the average person, applying contemporary community standards," would find that the work, taken as a whole, appeals to the prurient interest, (b) whether the work depicts or describes, in a patently offensive way, sexual conduct specifically defined by the applicable state law, and (c) whether the work, taken as a whole, lacks serious literary, artistic, political, or scientific value.

Chief Justice Burger then offered the states "a few plain examples" of what would constitute obscenity as applied to point (b) of the test:

Chief Justice Burger's Examples of Obscenity

> (a) Patently offensive representations or descriptions of ultimate sex acts, normal or perverted, actual or simulated.
> (b) Patently offensive representations or descriptions of masturbation, excretory functions, and lewd exhibition of the genitals.

In addition, the decision went on, sex and nudity "may not be exploited without limit" in motion pictures or still photographs or drawings shown in public "any more than live nudity can be exhibited or sold without limit in such public places."

The Miller decision also endorsed the principle of "local option" by which individual communities may determine what is obscene according to local norms rather than by any broad national yardstick. The chief justice wrote: "It is neither realistic nor constitutionally sound to read the First Amendment

"Local Community Standards" As Criteria

as requiring that the people of Maine or Mississippi accept public depiction of conduct found tolerable in Las Vegas or New York City." The result has been a flurry of new obscenity cases in which defendants have been tried and convicted by local courts even though they neither hold employment in nor reside in those communities. Their publications or films have merely circulated there.

Sex and the Print Media

The Goldstein Trial

As one authoritative source commented: "the Miller decision is an invitation to prosecutors in conservative communities to play censor for the nation." A case in point: Al Goldstein, publisher of *Screw* and *Smut*, sex-oriented tabloid newspapers, mailed fifteen copies of *Screw* from New York City to Kansas at the request of Kansas postal authorities, who then returned them unopened. But because the copies had entered the state, Goldstein was tried and found guilty of violating Kansas obscenity laws. His trial was held in Wichita based on its "community standards." At the outset of the trial, the prosecutor commented, "If they mail to all 50 states, and they make profits in all 50 states, then they should be tried in any of the 50 states, not just New York."[4]

Larry Flynt and *Hustler*

Larry Flynt at the time of his trial. (© The *Cincinnati Enquirer*, 1978.)

The most publicized obscenity case of recent times was the trial and conviction of Larry Flynt, founder and publisher of *Hustler* magazine.[5] It had come to the point where even liberal constitutionalists agreed that *Hustler* had achieved what its founder had set out to prove, "that barnyard humor has a market appeal." Employing "illustrations of genital and gynecological oddities, articles about dismemberment and cartoons on bestiality," *Hustler* wended its way through the marketplace. It quickly shocked many Americans by then accustomed to the comparatively sedate likes of *Playboy, Penthouse,* and *Playgirl*. Among the shocked were nine jurors of the Common Pleas Court in Hamilton, Ohio. Under the Supreme Court's "community standards" ruling, the jury determined that *Hustler* was indeed obscene and its owner guilty of pandering obscene materials in their community. As in the less publicized (because *Screw* was less known) Goldstein trial, the jurors were instructed to vote to convict if they found that the publication appealed to the prurient interest in sex, portrayed sexual conduct in a patently offensive way and, taken as a whole, did not have serious literary, artistic, or scientific value. The jurors were also instructed to consider themselves "average persons, applying contemporary community standards" to the case. Flynt was convicted of "pandering obscenity," which carries a $1,000 fine and six months in prison.

He was also convicted of violating a new Ohio law, "organized crime," a felony that carries an additional seven to twenty-five years in prison and a fine of $10,000.

Flynt's View

With his conviction under appeal, Flynt went to a Toledo radio station to present his grievances on the air. Among other things, he said that the court was requiring him to compromise rights held by all Americans. "Our First Amendment gets its vitality and meaning from the unrestricted right of free choice by each individual, and there is no way that any man can compromise these principles and retain his dignity." In Flynt's terms, upholding his conviction would cause "publishers and producers around the country to shelve a lot of creative ideas and thoughts merely because they may violate the most conservative community standard."

Flynt's Supporters

Many in and out of publishing sped to Flynt's defense though few wished to support him as a person. As the *Quill,* a magazine for journalists, put it, "Holding their noses and donning rubber gloves," they stood up for Flynt's right to publish. Bob Greene, a columnist for the *Chicago Sun-Times,* referred to Flynt as a "scum" and a "degenerate." He also said: "The government should not be empowered to imprison American citizens for printing what they choose. If a Larry Flynt has to be driven off the newsstands, let him be driven off by the public and not by prosecutors and judges." Arthur Kretchmer, editor of *Playboy,* commented: "I don't have delicate sensibilities, but *Hustler* has succeeded more than once in shocking them. Flynt's magazine is as shamelessly vulgar as its reputation suggests. It is not merely sexually explicit, it is perverse; the magazine thrives on gross, racist and scatological humor. Its overt aim is to shock one and all." But Kretchmer denounced Flynt's conviction on First Amendment grounds. Journalist Robert Yoakum brands both *Hustler* and *Screw* pornographic. And he agrees that there appears to be "new confidence by prosecutors" that higher courts are prepared to uphold obscenity convictions. The difference in the Goldstein, Flynt, and other recent cases, he said, is that convictions are being handed down by court jurisdictions in which the defendants neither work nor live.

Illustration by Kenneth Stark, from the June 1977 issue of the *Quill,* published by the Society of Professional Journalists, Sigma Delta Chi.

Newspaper editorials also responded, reflecting the breadth of the debate. A few examples follow. The *Washington Post* labeled *Hustler* as "the most vulgar of the new breed of slick sex magazines." It was quick to add, however, that "government ought not to be in the business of telling adults what they can read or see, even if other adults find the books, magazines, and movies offensive." *Newsday* wrote that to suppress *Hustler* "would be a step along the road to the book bonfire." The *New York Times* commented: "There is little virtue in leaping to the defense of admirable publications. The test of our commitment to a free society lies in the courage to defend the disreputable or the vulgar in the service of a higher goal."

LARRY FLYNT: AMERICAN DISSIDENT

Dissident writers and artists in the Soviet Union and other nations are being vilified and imprisoned, and President Jimmy Carter has stated his deep concern. In the wake of recent events, we urge the president to take a closer look at the restrictions of freedom of expression in America itself.

In Cincinnati, Ohio, publisher Larry Flynt was convicted of using *Hustler* magazine to pander obscenity and of engaging in organized crime. Ohio law states that engaging in organized crime is five or more persons conspiring to commit a crime. Mr. Flynt was accused of working with members of his staff to produce *Hustler*—a charge such as this could easily be leveled at any publisher in the country. This clearly amounts to government harassment of a dissident publication.

As a result, Flynt was immediately sentenced to 7 to 25 years in prison and was fined a total of $11,000. Bond was originally refused, pending appeal—an obvious infringement of his rights.

We the undersigned wish to protest the infringement of Mr. Flynt's rights under the First Amendment because it is a threat to the rights of all Americans. We cannot, under any circumstances, approve of government censorship. Further, we urge President Carter and all our fellow citizens to strengthen their commitment to protecting every American's right to freedom of expression.

Woody Allen	John Dean	Gerald Green	Arthur Kretchmer	Eric Norden	Peter Stone
Michael Arlen	Joan Didion	Dan Greenburg	Jonathan Z. Larsen	Eleanor Perry	Gay Talese
Joe Armstrong	Digby Diehl	David Halberstam	Nat Lehrman	Gerard Piel	Nan Talese
Chuck Ashman	Larry DuBois	Pete Hamill	John Leonard	Nicholas Pileggi	Gore Vidal
Noel Behn	John G. Dunne	Joe Hanson	Jay Levin	Dotson Rader	Nicholas Von Hoffman
Arthur Bell	Daniel Ellsberg	Hugh Hefner	Thomas H. Lipscomb	Rex Reed	Irving Wallace
Ronnie Bennett	Stanley Fleishman	Joseph Heller	Marshall Lumsden	Richard Rhodes	George T. Wren
Warren Bonson	Bruce Jay Friedman	Tony Hendra	J. Anthony Lukas	Harold Robbins	Jann Wenner
Malcolm Braly	Judge Charles Galbreath	Warren Hinckle	Peter Maas	Ned Rorem	Clark Whelton
Barbara Cady	Brendan Gill	George A. Hirsch	Norman Mailer	Richard Rosenzweig	Bruce Williamson
Vincent Canby	Allen Ginsberg	A. E. Hotchner	Bill Manville	Barnes Rosser	Emanuel L. Wolf
Robert Christgau	Ralph Ginzburg	Peter Kleinman	Milt Machlin	Mike Royko	Robert Yoakum
Ramsey Clark	Herb Gold	Arthur Knight	Rudy Maxa	Mike Salisbury	Sol Yurick
Harry Crews	Al Goldstein	Michael Kramer	Frederic Morton	Robert Sherrill	Mark Zussman
Judith Crist	Jim Goode	Paul Krassner	Philip Nobile	Geoffrey Stokes	

Sponsored by
AMERICANS FOR A FREE PRESS
40 West Gay Street • Columbus, Ohio 43215

Advertisement placed in the *New York Times* by Flynt supporters.

Not all newspaper commentary supported Flynt's position, however (although most newspapers clearly did). The *Chicago Tribune* wrote: "Freedom of the press is not the issue here. Nearly twenty years ago the United States Supreme Court ruled in the Roth case that obscenity, like incitement to rebellion, is beyond the protection of the First Amendment." The *Worcester* (Mass.) *Telegram* stated: "The conviction of Larry Flynt on obscenity charges has produced much radical-chic hand wringing, along with some serious concern about government censorship. We're inclined to think the concern is overdone." The *Wall Street Journal* attacked "the powerful elite in this society that denies the majority's right to censor even the most blatantly offensive sexual publication."

Ninety libertarians affixed their names to a full-page advertisement in the *New York Times* that supported Flynt on constitutional grounds. Then one of the signers, *Harper's* editor Lewis H. Lapham, had second thoughts and removed his name from the list. Lapham took exception to Flynt's self-portrayal as martyr to a lofty cause. He characterized the *Hustler* publisher as a nihilist whose "impulse slouches backward in time between barbarism, magic and death." Lapham had decided that he could not defend the First Amendment rights of a person who "achieved his effects with the subliminal suggestions of cannibalism, homosexuality, sadism, narcissism and homicide." Lapham concluded:

> In the latter years of the eighteenth century people like Jefferson associated the oppression of the human spirit with the coercions of priests and kings. It was against this tyranny that they raised up the idea of the freedom of the press. I find it ironic that their would-be successors have no better use for their liberty than to substitute for the old antagonists the coercions of Mr. Flynt.[6]

Sex in the Funnies

Though decidedly not in the same league with *Screw* and *Hustler,* sexual suggestiveness has even invaded newspaper comic strips via the antics of "Lolly," "Brandy," "Beetle Bailey's" Miss Buxley, "Andy Capp" and his barroom belles, and the suggestive bedroom capers of "Brenda Starr." The same holds for the superwomen who drape the pages of comic books, some of whom have also crept into newspaper comic sections. Charles Abar, a West Coast comic book distributor, says of this: "There are very few flat-chested women super heroes around. Most are still sex objects and wear sexy costumes. There's no question about it, comics are geared to the men buyers."[7]

So the controversy continues and Americans go on debating it, some viewing toleration of sexually explicit publications on newsstands and in bookstores as a cancer on the hide of society. Others see it as the birthright of a free

One artist's version of Larry Flynt's arrival as a "born again" Christian. (Illustration by Pete Wagner, from the January 1978 issue of the *Quill*, published by the Society of Professional Journalists, Sigma Delta Chi.)

people to select from whatever the market wishes to offer. Estimates show that sex-oriented magazines currently enjoy a total circulation of about 22 million per year. In addition, the prosecutor during Flynt's trial indicated that approximately 15 or 16 million Americans attend X-rated film showings each year. Though the figures appear unimpressive in a nation of more than 210 million citizens, many Americans evince alarm.[8]

For what it's worth, American readers may well be turning to fare other than the nudie trade. The *Columbia Journalism Review* reports that the trend towards "splashy, ever-more-explicit treatment of sexual subjects" appears to be ebbing. The exceptions are the "skin" magazines like *Playboy* and *Penthouse,* which usually have more to offer than mere flesh.[9]

Sex and Television

Considerable evidence based on current television programming trends indicates that "sexploitation" on the television tube is on the increase.[10] "The networks are helping to create the appetite," a writer who labors for all three networks recently admitted. "They don't say 'bring us a sexy project,' but there is an atmosphere created in which a certain something is in," said Lynn Roth, director of comedy development for 20th Century Fox Television. "It's not sex. It's more titillation."

TV Sex Portrayals Increasing

Examples include "Three's Company," and "Charlie's Angels." Also included are a variety of movies and pilots being prepared for television. The titles alone reflect the direction of the content: "Roller Girls," "Scandal Halls," "The Cheerleaders," "California Coed," "Legs," "The Beach Girls," and so on.

A writer for 20th Century Fox said: "This is supposed to be a time of women's projects on TV, but somehow all these women are good-looking, well-endowed and running toward the camera."

Tom Cherones, producer of "Roller Girls," a thirty-minute situation comedy currently being cast, says that large breasts are not a requirement in considering women performers for these roles, "but it helps." In the show, a bevy of beauties share a living area, locker room, and front office with the leering, grabby owner-coach of the roller team.

"Criteria" for Casting

Many of the new shows reflect the stereotypical lifestyle of Southern California complete with young women in bikinis. NBC producer Bruce Johnson says: "This is not 'Charlie's Angels.' Our men and women are very young and going to college. They are not sexpots. The idea [behind the beach motif] was not to have to create an unnatural setting in order to get attractive bodies into some form of undress."

Sam Strangiss, president of Ten-Four Productions, says: "Right now I'd say that's the dominant trend. The average producer is not doing sex. He's taking what the networks want, the girls with the good bodies and the looks and putting them in good, solid, honest stories." One of Ten-Four's developing projects for CBS is "Girl's Town." It portrays girls aged seven to eighteen struggling with a variety of tribulations such as "running away, having illegitimate babies and teenage prostitution."

One new face, former model Chris DeLisle, was delighted to be cast in one of the developing shows but worried about the low-cut dresses she had to wear. In one gown, she commented, "you could see all the way to Toledo."

"Laugh-In" producer George Schlatter said, "I think the reason they're doing all these shows is not because there's an audience waiting to see them, but because the producers and executives are having such a good time casting them."

"Three's Company"

According to Paul Klein, NBC's chief programmer, a sexy comedy such as ABC's "Three's Company" could not have succeeded just a few years ago because "girls wore bras then." He added: "I think the show has been enhanced because the girls jiggle." Edwin Vane, vice president of ABC programming stated: " 'Three's Company' passes all our standards and practices criteria . . . we think it's handled within the bounds of good taste." CBS's B. Donald Grant agrees: "The watchword is good taste," he said. "Almost anything can be done on TV if it's done in good taste." A "M*A*S*H" episode on CBS starred busty Adrienne Barbeau. The episode, as one television critic commented wryly, "had no redeeming social value other than to feature the lovely actress in a T-shirt."[11]

" I SEE THE PTA LIKES ONE OF OUR TUESDAY NIGHT SHOWS IN THE NEW SEASON ...CANCEL IT!"
Reprinted by permission of the Chicago Tribune-New York News Syndicate, Inc.

A controversy of national significance erupted over an episode of the now-defunct television series "James at 15."[12] In the episode, James was about to turn sixteen, and to celebrate the occasion he presented his virginity to a sixteen-year-old Swedish girl.

"James at 15"

Word circulated prior to the actual telecast of the controversial story line and concerned citizens made their feelings known to their local NBC affiliated stations. One station, WWJ-TV in Detroit, received complaints from viewers and parent groups who objected, generally, to portrayals of teenage sex on prime-time television. The station then arranged with the network to have a private, advance preview of the show for local concerned persons.

A Citizen Panel

The scene in question depicted young James alone with his sixteen-year-old girlfriend, an exchange student, while a stereo in the background purred the lilting pop tune, "I Love You Just the Way You Are." James kisses the girl with the obvious implication that sexual intercourse would follow. In the next scene, James is portrayed glad-handing his friends at school, laughing, joking, and basking in the delight of his recent adventure. For a time after that, James and the girl agonize over the possibility of her being pregnant. Their fears are eventually dispelled and she returns to Sweden.

A Disputed Scene

The show's writer resigned after higher-ups deleted from the script an indirect reference to birth control. In fact, the show ran with no references at all to the prudence of taking precautions.

One woman previewer commented: "If they think this is sex education then they have warped minds. Nothing is sacred anymore. Why don't they have a program showing the happiness and rewards of waiting until marriage?" Another said: "I can't stand here and not say I was shocked. I'm terribly upset [that] we would let the West Coast writers, whose morality is lower than ours . . . pull down our morality to where theirs is."

Panelists Comment

A second controversial scene proved equally jolting to most of the previewers. At that point, James' Uncle Chester gives him a key to a birthday gift that he, and the audience, think is a car. In fact, it is the key to a hotel room which, among other furnishings, houses a glamorous prostitute and a bottle of brandy. "My Lord, that blew the whole thing," responded one previewer, a nun who administers a home for unmarried mothers.

When the station's general manager indicated that the show would be televised as planned, most of the previewers objected. When he labeled the story "bland," the nun chuckled: "As opposed to what?"

But not all the previewers were hostile. One man, who is director of family counselling services for the county courts, remarked: "For anyone to say 'This is terrible,' they better start talking to their kids. It's real when you see the vast number of children who become pregnant at 15 and 16."

William S. Rubens, a vice president and researcher at NBC, stated that, in his opinion, there is no sex on television.[13] "However, I've heard from people who watch the same programs I do who think they're saturated with sex."

Rubens draws a broad line between "sex" and "violence" on television in that the two words have typically been used together when applied to programming. Violence, he said, is clearly undesirable, especially if and when it causes people to act violently. There is a consensus in society to support that. But, he goes on, there is no such general agreement about sex on television. "Some people feel that sex is a legitimate topic for television to handle. Others feel that showing or discussing anything sexual on TV is in bad taste—or 'filthy.' But the opinions of both groups are based on moral value judgments." He adds that scientific research into the effects of televised sex on the behavioral patterns of youth have reflected no substantive association between the two.

"If 'sex on TV' means 'showing people having sex,' " the findings are clear: "There isn't any sex on TV. TV shows couples kissing and embracing, sex is discussed in a restrained manner, and there is innuendo—but never actual sex." Rubens adds that, because of these restraints, television portrayals of sex are the most conservative of all the mass media. "Every variation of sexual activity has been shown in recent theatrical movies and has been described in recent books, and not far behind are *Playboy, Penthouse,* and *Hustler,* which rank among the nation's best-selling magazines."

If there is no actual sex on television, what are television "sex critics" complaining about?

Several years ago a *TV Guide* survey found that 58 percent of viewers felt that there is too much emphasis on sex in television programming. But Rubens challenges those findings. Most of the complaints about sex on the tube, he says, are about pretty girls in bikinis, jokes and innuendos in comedies and on talk shows, and dramas treating such topics as rape. "All these things are seen as 'filth' and 'permissiveness' on TV, which is perceived as endangering the 'moral fiber of this country.' "

Rubens goes on to say that television is lagging behind society in accepting and coping with the realities of the sexual revolution. His primary concern is "the implied censorship" issue raised by the ability of small pressure groups to influence what is seen by the American public. "The pressure of these interest groups can exert a chilling effect which in a subtler and more insidious manner produces the same consequences as formal, explicit censorship."

According to many highly vocal critics, however, that portion of sex that *is* portrayed on television is offensive in its own right even if it does not "go all the way." Bettelou Peterson, television critic for the *Detroit Free Press,* wrote of her concerns: "Death, disaster and sex, actual or implied, are the surest way for a network programmer to guarantee a big audience."[14]

To the apparent delight of some male fans, sex has even invaded that bastion of masculinity, the vast world of televised sports. Comely cheerleaders exhorting loyal grandstanders to root for alma mater are as old as the game of football. Yet the institution has come a long way in recent years. There is a new look among professional football's cheerleaders as reflected in the scanty, revealing costumes of the Dallas Cowboys' cheerleader squad. Virtually all the pro teams have them now, each seemingly trying to "outstrip" the competition. (The braless bouncings of the Miami Dolphins squad are one of the newest and most daring.) College cheerleaders are sedate by comparison. To compensate for that on behalf of television audiences, the probing eye of the camera searches the college stands to pick out and highlight the comely face, which is frequently attached to a voluptuous body. The camera lingers as the announcer and "colorman" swap innuendoes.

During the telecast of the 1979 Hula Bowl game, the camera saw fit to zero in on and follow the moves of a young woman in a tight dress as she minced her way up a lengthy flight of stadium steps, hips swaying provocatively. This went on *while the ball was in play on the field*. Many viewers have lodged complaints and some professional team owners have tried to cover things up a bit. Some males even complain that all the flesh detracts from the game itself.

The professional-amateur sports presentations that pit professional athletes against movie and television performers also offer sexy starlets in skimpy attire for fun and games with the pros.

All this is good fun and certainly causes no harm to anyone. But that the television networks recognize the allure of sex as a highly marketable product is certain. Some individuals and groups would like to see it stopped, thus, they seek to apply certain "controls" on the television industry. Pressures have been brought to bear on local stations, but collaring three powerful corporate networks is another matter.

The Television Code of the National Association of Broadcasters states succinctly: "Profanity, obscenity, smut and vulgarity are forbidden, even when likely to be understood only by a part of the audience. From time to time, words which have been acceptable, acquire undesirable meanings, and telecasters should be alert to eliminate such words."[15] Though well intentioned, as all such codes are, this statement reflects two problems of media controls. First, the code requires that each decision maker in the industry define profanity, obscenity, smut, and vulgarity on his or her own terms. And since each person does so according to personal standards, not everyone required to make such judgments would necessarily agree on their definitions. Secondly, the code suffers from the same ailment found in all such codes: it calls for voluntary, not compulsory, compliance.

With it all, NBC's William Rubens advances a strong point. Television has maintained a relatively low profile in the sex-oriented aspects of its programming. In terms of both photographic imagery and application of language to portrayals, television remains far behind in sexual explicitness compared to other media including, as we shall see, its first cousin—radio.

Sex in Advertising

Media Dependence on Advertising

As developed in chapter 4, advertising is the economic spinal column of the American mass media.* It guarantees the independence of the media from government control by making them financially solvent. To depict the extent of media's dependence on advertising, a few particulars are in order. For one thing, newspapers and magazines earn only a fraction of their total income from subscription and newsstand sales. The remainder comes from selling space to businesses, industries, groups, and individual citizens. Broadcasting is even more dependent: it receives its *total* income from advertising.

Impact of Advertising on Media and Public

It has been estimated that readers of *Life* magazine over the years paid an average of only twelve cents per issue for a publication that cost forty-one cents to produce. Advertising took up the slack and brought in sizable profits as well. So advertising's contributions to keep the mass media solvent have been impressive. For example, in a recent year, American newspapers, collectively, took in almost $10 billion from advertisers. More than $8 billion of this figure came from local as compared to national advertisers. Magazines earned over $1.7 billion. Advertisers poured almost $7 billion into television, national and local, and nearly one-half billion into radio. Add to that weekly advertising "shoppers," billboard advertising, advertising in theaters, professional and trade publications, and other media and one gains an appreciation of how vital advertising is to the communications industry and to the American economy itself.[16] In addition, the public relies heavily on advertising to determine what goods and services are for sale or rent, where, and at what cost. Thus, along with supporting the media, advertising is an enormously powerful, influential, and pervasive force in its own right.

Examples of Sex-Oriented Advertising

The issue of sex in advertising goes back a long way, at least to the turn of the century when boys gaped goggle-eyed at women's lingerie ads in the catalogues of mail order houses. This has been true even though most advertising is not in the "business" of sex, as such.

*Advertising and the mass media, generally, will be treated in chapter 12.

Sexual roles and portrayals in advertisements cover a broad span from the antics of sexy singer Connie Stevens plugging hammers and pipe wrenches for Ace Hardware to the selling of X-rated films and other sex-oriented items. The latter category includes assorted bust developers, sensuous underclothing and bedwear, massage parlors, and topless (and bottomless) bars. In the late 1960s, some underground newspapers added a new twist to their classified ads sections. This came in the form of notices geared to matching love-starved individuals in heterosexual and homosexual associations and in the recruiting of individuals and groups of "swingers" locally and across the country. Many sex-oriented magazines still offer such advertising along with assorted sex gimmicks, stimulants, and aids.

Much sexual content in advertising is inoffensive. But much of it remains objectionable to some readers and viewers. The most visible and controversial realm of sex-oriented advertising deals with X-rated films and the refusal of certain media to accept their advertising. In Los Angeles, for example, the Adult Film Association attempted to advertise its motion pictures in the pages of the *Los Angeles Times*. The paper refused to accept the account and Adult Film sued. The superior court dismissed the suit, indicating that the *Times* was under no legal requirement to accept such advertising. Other newspapers have also adopted policies outlawing or limiting advertisements for X-rated movie theaters. The trend appears to be growing. In the early 1970s, the *Boston Herald-Traveler* announced its ban on such advertising to the apparently rousing approval of its readers as registered in letters to the editor. The *Detroit News* also banned such advertising. The *New York Times* continues to accept porno ads but limits the size of each and will not print photographic materials if a film is considered pornographic. Other publications have done the same. These kinds of restrictions have come at a time when sexually explicit films, books, magazines, topless waitresses, or whatever have increased in numbers and availability.

Advertising X-Rated Films

Kenneth MacDonald, editor of the *Des Moines Register* and the *Des Moines Tribune* for twenty-three years, points out that public pressures against nudie-type advertising are responsible for the changes in what some newspapers consider to be unacceptable advertising. Readers who earlier might have frowned on a seminude photograph in a motion picture advertisement now take exception to what they *know the film depicts*. As MacDonald says, they are aiming "not at the copy of the ad but at the business which placed it." In short, the courts and legislative bodies were not coping with pornography and other forms of obscenity, so offended persons put pressures on their newspapers to frustrate the porno industries. MacDonald reasons: "X-rated films and massage parlors are indecent; to avoid promoting indecency, newspapers should ban any advertising of them." In his terms, the issue is not merely "condoning or condemning 'indefensible products,' " but what

Refusing Advertising as a Form of Control

constitutes obscenity and what does not. Who is to say? The issue is strikingly similar to the issue of a publication accepting or rejecting questionable editorial content. MacDonald sees this as a real community problem. In his view, since constitutional bodies have not ruled X-rated movies illegal, the newspaper has the obligation to accept such advertising in the interest of providing all facets of community activity to all citizens:

> A newspaper has a responsibility for all of the copy that appears in both its news and advertising columns and should decline copy it considers libelous, inaccurate, misleading, or offensive. But passing judgment on copy is quite different from passing judgment on the product or service advertised *if* the product or service may be legally offered for sale to the general public.[17]

Challenges to Sex-Oriented Advertising

MacDonald has his detractors. C. Randall Heuston asks if MacDonald means that "whatever is legal is necessarily morally acceptable or that a newspaper should never use words against it?" For example, he writes that organized crime remains largely beyond the grasp of law and yet newspapers show much concern about Mafia activities. "Would MacDonald reason that the same newspapers should knowingly do business with gangsters simply because they haven't yet been convicted of anything?" Heuston then makes the connection between organized crime and the porno industry. In fact, he suggests that a case could be made for media slashing the income of organized crime by refusing to carry porno advertising.[18]

Whether or not one accepts the view supported by MacDonald's argument will depend on one's view of the obscenity debate in general. That's why it has been a media issue for so long and will continue to be as long as there is more than one interpretation of media "responsibility" under the First Amendment. Advertising is a vital part of the picture because, as with other facets of business, it is essential to the promotion of sex-oriented goods and services.

Sex in Academe

The sexual revolution has invaded all aspects of society. This includes the nation's schools and colleges. On college campuses, the revolution has created notable changes unthinkable a generation ago. They include acceptance of coed dormitories, elimination of nighttime curfews on student socializing, increased usage by young men and women of language forms traditionally associated with social misfits, more widespread frankness in sexual matters, greater acceptance of sexual intimacy, and the presentation in campus buildings of sexually explicit motion pictures.

After angered resistance by some adults in and out of academic life, the showing of X-rated films has become an accepted medium of entertainment on many campuses. In Michigan, Attorney General Frank Kelley ruled that a college board of trustees may not ban an X-rated film on campus simply because it carries an X-rating. At the same time, he ruled that a board of trustees may ban a film if they consider it to be obscene. The difference between the two categories is that ratings are assigned to films by the motion picture industry, which do not follow court definitions of obscenity. Thus, they may be restricted. It is the college board's responsibility "to decide which films are obscene and whether to ban them," Kelley said. Kelley also indicated that a college board may "regulate" the institution, provided that constitutional rights of students are protected. He pointed to the United States Supreme Court decision of 1973, which ruled that obscene matter, so determined, is not protected by the First Amendment.[19]

Evidence indicates that the actions of boards of trustees against the showing of sex-oriented films are rare. As changes in student attitudes towards sexual matters have liberalized and become more visible in the nation's colleges and universities, the legal "action" has moved to the secondary level.

In Fairfax County, Virginia, seventeen-year-old Lauren Boyd sued her high **The Case of** school principal and the board of education for violating her First Amendment **the *Farm News*** rights.[20] Ms. Boyd, editor of the *Farm News*, the official newspaper at Hayfield High School, had been competently providing her readers with news of school dances, athletic events, and other basics of high school life. Then came the journalistic uproar that spread the name of Lauren Boyd, the *Farm News*, and Hayfield High School throughout the country. The news media picked it up—the *Washington Post*, newspapers in Florida and Nevada, and television stations in Rhode Island and California.

The uproar perched nervously on a survey Boyd had taken on the birth control practices, or lack of such, among sexually active students at the high school. With the aid of Gina Gambino, assistant editor, she found that only ten out of thirty-four of those surveyed utilized birth control protection while having sexual intercourse. In an article written for the school paper, Boyd explained that, according to her findings, lack of information on contraception was the cause of students' failure to protect themselves from pregnancy. And that, she deemed, was due to the failure of fearful parents to inform their offspring of sexual realities. A local official from Planned Parenthood agreed on the need of young people to have information on contraception.

Doris Torrice, principal of Hayfield High School, read the manuscript and promptly censored it. She reasoned that it "might be offensive to members of the community" and that "it interferes with a school program, namely the sex education program" (from which the subject of birth control is excluded).

Boyd and Gambino appealed to the superintendent of schools, who turned the squabble over to an advisory board. That body, in turn, supported the principal's censorship order. Boyd and Gambino then appealed to the Fairfax County School Board, which upheld the earlier decisions (but only by a six to four vote). Then, with their publishing deadline bearing down on them, the two editors took matters into their own hands. They composed and published a headline for page one. It read: "Sexually Active Students Fail to Use Contraception." Beneath Boyd's by-line was a large blank space. Reaction came almost instantly.

Support for the Farm News

The Issues

Other school papers in Northern Virginia came out in support of the Hayfield editors. Some even printed portions of the survey story, without receiving negative reactions from their communities. The *Washington Star* also lent support by running the complete story. Sides were drawn, one insisting that the anticensorship guarantees of the First Amendment apply to student publications as well as to the commercial press. The other faction challenged that position because the school board provides funding for the paper and thus insures its existence. Therefore, it has the right to delete questionable content from its pages. There were many shades of opinion in between.

The Court Rules

Boyd and Gambino took their case to the federal district court in Alexandria where, four months later, the court ruled in their favor. In an eleven-page decision, Judge Albert Bryan, Jr. wrote that the Hayfield newspaper "was conceived, established and operated as a conduit for student expression on a wide variety of topics. It falls clearly within the parameters of the First Amendment." In the debate over school officials having censorship powers because they provide funding, Judge Bryan said: "Even if we are talking about an official school newspaper, funded by the school, this argument does not apply. Once you give a man a soapbox you can't then tell him what to say. You have the choice initially—you don't have to give him the soapbox if you don't want to."[21]

The Case of the *Communique*

A case similar to the *Farm News* adventure erupted in a suburb of Richmond, Virginia, when the Manchester High School newspaper, the *Communique*, also undertook a survey on the sexual exploits and attitudes of its student body.[22] The editorial staff distributed a thousand questionnaires. When the completed forms came back, county Superintendent of Schools Howard O. Sullins ordered that the results not be published in the *Communique* and that future surveys be cleared by school officials in advance. A member of the paper's staff then filed suit in federal court on the grounds that Sullins' action violated the First Amendment rights of the student staff. The school board decided not to stand the test of court action and "reluctantly" permitted publication of the survey results. The board also reluctantly concluded that such matters fall "within those First Amendment rights which have been extended to high school students by the federal court."

Disagreement came from an unlikely source, unlikely in that the respondent was an editorial writer for the *Richmond Times-Dispatch*. In a thundering editorial, Ed Grimsley questioned why, if other First Amendment rights had always had certain restrictions placed on them, should it be unconscionable to place certain restrictions on freedom of the press.

A Journalist Responds

Does this apply also to freedom of the press? Or is it, of all the constitutional rights, absolute and totally unqualified? Some people seem to think so, but this is an arrogant point of view that we do not share. Freedom of the press—like freedom of speech and the right to keep and bear arms—can be restricted under certain conditions.

Grimsley praised Dr. Sullins' decision to suppress the newspaper, stating that every publication must have authority to decide what should and should not be published. Failing that, Grimsley suggested that officials "put an end to any publication that becomes intolerably objectionable."

Not all of Grimsley's colleagues on the *Times-Dispatch* agreed with his reasoning. Some responded to his editorial with "outright anger" as did other professional journalists.

The National Association of Secondary School Principals took emphatic exception to official rulings in these cases. In a memorandum mailed to its 35,000 members around the country, the association claimed that the guiding principles for school publications are being jeopardized by jurists. That is because court opinions "reflect extraordinarily shallow thinking and a lack of understanding." The memo asked, Is a teenager "clairvoyant" to the point where he may determine on his own what is in good taste for the school and community? "Would he add excerpts from *Hustler* magazine, advertise pornographic literature and publish the language of 'Oh, Calcutta' because he can interpret social values much better than his adults, including his parents?"[23]

NASSP Action

Is there a solution? At this point, nobody seems to know. But several months after the Virginia cases had been decided, the *Quill* published an editorial on the issues dealing with First Amendment judgments by high school students. It said that school administrators in many places are becoming increasingly alarmed about the growing number of student editors who are taking seriously their constitutional right to publish material that some view as questionable. Are teenagers "socially and intellectually mature enough" to

Suggestions from Professionals

take full responsibility for what they publish? The *Quill* suggests that the problem lies with the failure of school administrators to appoint qualified, trained advisors for school publications rather than drawing straws to determine who on the faculty will get stuck with the job. (Unfortunately, that system is widespread.) "If high school principals really want to attack the problem and dispense with much of their hand-wringing, they'll see to it that their student journalists are placed in the hands of proper instructors and advisers—people with solid backgrounds in journalism."[24]

Dismissal of
a Faculty Adviser

But even qualified advisers may encounter censorship problems. Journalism adviser James Engmann, of the Union Grove High School in Wisconsin, was dismissed from the faculty because, administrators said, "he failed adequately to supervise the publications class." It was not the first time that Engmann and school officials had clashed over the school newspaper. But this time it seemed that Engmann had gone too far. Though opposed to the move, he had permitted a vulgarity—"pissed"—to appear as part of a headline run over a letter to the editor. He advised the staff against using the word because it would create turmoil and because it detracted from the letter itself, but he would not prohibit the students from using it. Now unemployed, Engmann pondered the dilemma of a newspaper adviser ordered to play censor. "If he does censor, he is violating his students' First Amendment rights," he said. "If he refuses to censor, he apparently can be disciplined, even to the point of having his teaching contract nonrenewed." Engmann has lodged a $65,000 damage suit against the school system.[25]

A Sex Survey
in New York

In 1978, the United States Supreme Court got into the debate by supporting a lower court ruling endorsing the right of school officials to ban objectionable content. The case originated at New York City's Peter Stuyvesant High School when the editor of the student paper tried to distribute a sex survey questionnaire dealing with premarital sex, masturbation, homosexuality, and associated topics. School administrators banned the survey, indicating that it might cause psychological harm to some of the students questioned. The paper's staff took the case to court, where a federal judge upheld the ban for ninth- and tenth-grade students. But he allowed the survey to go forward with eleventh- and twelfth-grade students. The board of education appealed the decision and a higher court ruled that the total ban was reasonable. The decision said that nobody "had the right to importune others" to answer questions if there is reason to believe that the practice may have harmful consequences to some. The United States Supreme Court agreed with that but without issuing any formal commentary.[26]

It is clear that First Amendment interests have moved away from solely professional persons and publications and into the realm of broad citizen concern and commentary by anyone having access to a communications medium. Presumably, issues of censorship could extend beyond traditional student newspapers to include a school's literary magazine, the yearbook, and the student-operated broadcast station. Colleges and universities have long enjoyed greater freedoms to publish than high schools have. Will the latter group now catch up? With the growing interest on the part of American youth to become involved in the issues and problems of society, it is certain that the matter will not rest.

Sex and Language

A character in Jane Austen's novel *Northanger Abbey* commented on "language" as follows: "The most thorough knowledge of human nature, the happiest delineation of its varieties, the liveliest effusions of wit and humor are conveyed to the world in the best chosen language." The key to the quote is obviously "the best chosen language." For, as with the whole subject of self-expression, what constitutes "best chosen" is up for grabs.

"Dirty Words" in Fiction

The employment of vulgarity in American fiction, along with explicit depiction of sexual acts, has characterized many outstanding novels in this century. And while individuals and groups flailed away at all that filth-between-covers, many of the novels in question eventually earned lofty places in literary history. Even so, employment of four-letter and other gutter-type words were, in those days, pretty much restricted to fiction. They were certainly not standard fare in the communications vehicles we know as the mass media. Times are changing.

"Dirty Words" in Fact

In modern times, the "best chosen" language has come to mean many things. One could hardly portray as reality a jut-jawed top-sergeant exhorting his men to victory in battle by having him shout: "Follow me, please! We shall smite the enemy and achieve victory!" It does not ring true given the circumstances of modern war and human reaction to it. The millions of American veterans of the three wars since Pearl Harbor know better. So do others. Hence, when attempting to portray human beings in a real-life situation, the "best chosen" language must be faithful to the portrayal, or audiences will reject it. In recent times, the employment of vulgarity, including sexual references, has become commonplace in the world of written fact as well as fiction. The practice is also controversial and will likely continue to be, especially as it makes greater inroads into the major media.

The Dayton Case

Charlie Alexander, veteran editor of the *Dayton* (Ohio) *Journal Herald*, made an executive decision to include the terms "fucking," "son of a bitch," and "God damn it" in a page-one story.[27] The decision cost him his job. His decision was based on his desire to accurately portray "how what seems like a stupid killing can happen."

Charles Alexander
(*Journal Herald*).

Public Responses

The incident developed when two federal agents stationed in Dayton got into an argument over their common desire to be transferred. The conversation became highly emotional. They began shouting and then one pulled a gun. The other grabbed it and, in the ensuing scuffle, the gun discharged, killing one of the men. The testimony of the survivor provided the basis of Alexander's story.

It is clear that Charlie Alexander is "not a vulgar sensationalist," as one who knows him put it. In fact, the colleague who offered that testimonial also said that the former editor had long made a habit of checking all questionable language written into stories including the word "hell." Why, then, would an experienced journalist choose to use these particular words on this occasion?

In a subsequent editorial column, Alexander wrote: "What the account of Gibson [the surviving agent] tells us with a vividness that I would hope none of us or our children would forget is that killing in most cases is the final, but not the crucial, act. The crux comes when the common love and respect we ought to have for each other dissolves into hate and we turn the corner from passionate verbal combat or quarreling to mortal combat." Use of the disputed words, Alexander reasoned, depicted how the "corner" had been turned in this case.

Offended readers called to complain: "I don't want to read that word;" "You're contributing to the downfall of society!" "Children might read the word!"

Alexander also has his supporters. Among others, he received a letter of commendation from his Presbyterian Church Session, a statement of support in a nationally syndicated column by Carl Rowen and numerous letters to the editor. One of the letters read, in part : "Before Mr. Alexander's resignation, the *Journal Herald* was a better paper. . . . Its pages contained vital and important news unflinchingly reported."

Another wrote: "It is incomprehensible to me that any reader could have read the Gibson article without understanding the message of intemperate language leading to intemperate behavior."

Since four-letter words are commonly used in casual conversations on street corners, in school corridors, in business meetings, in popular fiction and non-fiction books, in factual and fictional magazine pieces, one might think that inclusion of one in a real-life struggle between two impassioned individuals might pass unnoticed or, in this case, carry emphatic meaning. That was Charlie Alexander's intent. At the same time, the word offends many individuals, and some of them react resoundingly when the word is offered to them vocally or in print. It is an ongoing debate, and both sides are entitled to join in.

Another case: A few years ago a man was driving in New York City with his young son.[28] It was early afternoon and the car radio was on. Suddenly the recorded voice of comedian George Carlin came over the air in what seemed to be a typical comedy routine. With one exception! Carlin's voice was uttering a variety of "indecent" words, seven of which affronted the man in the car.

The man filed a complaint with the Federal Communications Commission, which took no action at the time. But two years later it issued an order that restricted the use of the so-called "seven words" (which relate to female organs, excrement, sexual intercourse, sodomy, and incest), to certain times of the broadcasting day when young children would not be likely to hear them. The station's management appealed, and the Justice Department asked the United States Supreme Court to review the case. The Court agreed to do so.

"Dirty Words" and the Broadcast Media

The FCC classified the words as "indecent" because they did not fulfill the Supreme Court's definition of "obscene." That is they did not appeal "to prurient interests." By defining them as "indecent," the FCC banned them under the Federal Criminal Code "as a form of public nuisance."

The Justice Department recently changed its position on the seven words and asked the Court to strike down the FCC order as unconstitutional. In its brief, the Justice Department indicated that the Criminal Code did not support the FCC's "present attempt to absolutely outlaw certain words on radio, wholly without regard to context, for all or most of the broadcast day."

The Supreme Court reviewed the case anyway. On July 3, 1978, it ruled that the FCC has the right to bar unsavory language from the airwaves.

The Charges Defined

The Supreme Court Ruling

The Federal Communications Commission has also shown concern over what Chairman Dean Burch calls "the stock-in-trade of the sex-oriented radio talk show."[29] He referred to talk shows during which listeners may telephone and participate in discussions related to sex and sexual activity. According to Burch, the shows are "garbage," dealing with such "compelling" public concerns as "the number and frequency of orgasms . . . or a baker's dozen of other turn-ons, turn-offs, and turn-downs."

Eventually, the commission decided to try a test case. It aimed its guns at WGLD-FM in Oak Park, Illinois, a suburb of Chicago. It fined the station $2,000 for airing obscene programming. It also invited the station's management to take the case to court for review. But the station turned the tables by paying the fine. Hence, no test case.

Created in the early seventies, the sexy talk shows—labeled "topless radio," among other things—caught on quickly. It was a simple procedure. The station provided the master of ceremonies, typically, a quick-witted male, and

"Topless Radio"

The FCC Acts

only calls from women were accepted. As one observer wrote, "The degree of explicitness in the exchange between female caller and talk jockey depended to a great extent on the seductiveness of the latter."

The FCC went after WGLD-FM again. This time they fined the station $1,000 per program, the most it could levy under existing regulations. The commission justified its action by noting that radio broadcasting goes out to millions in their homes, cars, yards, and while strolling about with portable radios. It goes out "without regard to age, background, or degree of sophistication." And radio frequently arrives "without warning of its content."

The Opposing View

Many took exception to the commission's action, terming it a form of censorship and, therefore, in violation of the First Amendment. In brief, their reasoning was that the FCC had no authority to "investigate and enforce" criminal law and that the law they were trying to enforce was unconstitutional. The opposition also charged that this act of censorship violated a section of the Communications Act, by which the FCC functions. And finally they complained that the action "violated public interest standards," which govern the FCC's regulation of the broadcast industry. (In fact, the courts have never been overly cooperative about supporting the commission's authority to monitor and evaluate broadcast programming.)

The South Carolina Case

In another case, the FCC ruled that a South Carolina station's content was "obscene, indecent, and profane and in violation of the criminal code." The judge would not rule on the obscenity and the public interest aspects. But he did address himself to the issue of obscenity versus censorship. He said that denying renewal of a license because of obscene, indecent, or profane language did indeed constitute censorship. "But," his decision reads, "if it can be so dominated, then censorship to that extent is not only permissible but required in the public interest. Freedom of speech does not legalize using the public airways to peddle filth."

Sexy Song Lyrics

Sexual content in the lyrics of popular music broadcast over the air, aimed primarily at young people, is yet another gray area for the mass media. Paul Hirsch, a sociologist and observer of developments in the rock scene, writes that, as radio became almost totally pop music-oriented with the explosive growth of television, recording artists gained control over management concerning what songs would be recorded. A noticeable increase in sexually suggestive lyrics has resulted. This has been due to what Hirsch terms "the gradual intrusion of the musician's own values into the songs they record. These values are by no means clearly perceived or shared by the mass of young record buyers."[30]

Several years ago, Nicholas Johnson, former member of the FCC, took exception to a commission ruling that makes broadcast licensees personally answerable for the language of popular music aired by radio stations. Johnson labels the FCC ruling "an unconstitutional action by a Federal agency aimed clearly at controlling the content of speech." Refusal or inability of a licensee to police the content of recordings played over the air can result in the loss of the license. While that particular ruling was aimed at policing song lyrics that tend to encourage drug abuse among American youth, Johnson said that policing the content of pop records played over the air is *policing* regardless of the offense involved.[31]

Johnson Dissents

Sexy words and other vulgarities have become staples in the world of sex-oriented magazines, newspapers, and films. They are stock items designed to attract readers and viewers. Common forms of vulgarity have crept into television and radio as well but not to the degree that they appear in certain print forms. In 1939, Clark Gable shocked movie audiences when he spat out the classic line to heroine Scarlett O'Hara: "Frankly, my dear, I don't give a damn!" Few would shock so easily today. The broadcast media have allowed "hell" and "damn" for some time now. How much beyond that they may go will have to be determined as each case arises.

Solutions: A Standoff

As we have seen, those who favor the "community standards" test of what is obscene and what is not are as adamant as the libertarians. Professor Robert A. Rutland, of the University of Virginia, is one who believes that the Founding Fathers recognized that local community standards were invaluable to the young nation. "I hope we do not have to throw up our hands and say that nobody can say what constitutes public indecency." He indicates that local juries should decide what is offensive to the public eye or mind. If they commit errors of judgment, he goes on, it is the price society must pay for trying to uphold public decency.

The Founding Fathers' View?

> My fear is that our society—which is attempting to become a "no-fault" society that never punishes, never fires, never insists on standards in food, service, clothing, or whatever—is trying to take the easy way out of the pornography problem. I think it is good that communities can draw the line. Our Constitution permits those who don't like that line to move on—it does not give them a legal right to try to erase that line by obstreperous conduct or odious stratagems.[32]

The Board of the Society of Professional Journalists, Sigma Delta Chi, decided to explore the issues of obscenity and pornography in hopes of arriving at constructive conclusions.[33] The board hoped to "establish new standards that

The SPJ/SDX Proposal

would protect unwilling viewers and minors from obscenity yet maintain full First Amendment safeguards." After considerable discussion, the board members formulated a statement urging Congress and the Supreme Court to establish workable standards that would achieve these ends.

An outgrowth of the conviction of Larry Flynt, the meeting found that the Supreme Court decision allowing local communities to establish their own guidelines on obscenity left "a chilling effect on freedom of expression." Members called on the Court and Congress to protect unwilling viewers and minors without restricting First Amendment guarantees. "The Society is unalterably opposed to any restriction on free expression and any prior restraint [censorship] on publication," the statement reads.

Board member Jean Otto said, "If obscenity is in the eye of the beholder, then it follows that each individual should decide what is acceptable. This cannot be done by denying publication or distribution of printed, recorded or filmed material. This consequence of the Court's community-standards ruling could lead and, in effect, has led to the prior restraint prohibited by the First Amendment."

A Plea for Caution

Freedom of Information Chairman Scott Aiken wrote that the community standards rule "creates the opportunity for harrassment of a publisher, broadcaster or film maker." But Aiken also issued a warning to absolutists who would hold rights over responsibilities. He wrote that if the absolutist would not permit anyone to define responsibility, the press might one day find itself facing the authority of another form of absolutist—"that of an authoritarian crushing of the free press and of all the other democratic institutions of our society."

A Movie Star's View

Actress Katherine Hepburn, for generations a motion picture actress of great accomplishment, addressed the issue more directly. She thinks the time has come to censor movies. "We're sitting and looking at filth," she told a television audience on CBS's "60 Minutes." "And the critics, I think, have lost their minds. And how can it be stopped? They say, oh, no censorship. No, no, freedom of the press. To hell with that! They've got to do something. . . . Life is full of censorship. I can't spit in your eye!"[34]

Even so, the absolutists on the Society of Professional Journalists Board stood firmly in opposition to tampering with the First Amendment in any way. Two members complained that each Supreme Court ruling on obscenity "has tended to immerse the issue in murkier water." They agreed that obscenity cases must be decided in terms of definitions—"but whose definitions?. . . The First Amendment says, 'Congress shall make no law. . . .' Let's leave it at that."[35]

In 1970, the Presidential Commission on Obscenity and Pornography published its report.[36] Among a variety of points advanced, the commission determined that much of the problem of obscenity in the United States "stems from the inability or reluctance of people in our society to be open and direct in dealing with sexual matters. . . . Direct and open conversation about sex between parent and child is too rare in our society." This failure, the report continues, leads to an exaggerated emphasis on sex, giving it "a magical, non-natural quality," which "makes it more attractive and fascinating." This failure to be open about sexual matters "clogs legitimate channels for transmitting sexual information and forces people to use clandestine and unreliable sources."

The commission went on to say that interest in sex is normal, healthy, and good, and that the institution of marriage is based on sexual attraction, love, and sexual expression. To succeed they require a healthy base, which requires that society maintain healthy sexual attitudes rooted in sound, factual information.

In support of those interests, the commission recommended that all local, state, and federal laws prohibiting or restricting adult access to sexual materials be repealed. The report indicates that thorough investigation determined that exposure to sexually explicit material does not play a significant role in the development of antisocial behavior. The report emphasizes that such factors as disorganized family life and poor peer relationships relate directly to "harmful sexual behavior or adverse character development." But exposure to sex-oriented matter is not a factor in antisocial development. The point is emphasized in the report that exposure to such matter can affect human behavior, increasing freedom of discussion about sex being one benefit.

In the matter of exposure of nonadults to sexually explicit materials, the commission determined that states should enact legislation to prohibit "the commercial distribution or display for sale of certain sexual materials to young persons." The reasoning here is that scientific evidence on the effects of sex-oriented matter on youthful behavior is not yet as clearly defined as it is for adults. The commission also felt hesitant about exposing children to such materials, even in an experimental setting, and that ruled out the possibility of developing such evidence.

Further defining the legalities of sex-oriented content of the mass media will have to come via actions in the courts. It appears that the issues are stalemated and are likely to remain so for some time. This is especially true in terms of the Supreme Court's determination to keep obscenity decisions based in local communities. Even Justice Brennan, in the Miller decision, abandoned his own "tests" of what constitutes obscenity. He "confessed that the Court had failed to define obscenity with sufficient precision to reconcile its suppression" with constitutional principles. He had also come to recognize that the Supreme Court's efforts to regulate obscenity (except to protect children and unwilling adults) had been a total failure.[37] And there the matter lies.

Notes

1. With permission. From *Webster's New World Dictionary*, Second College Edition, copyright © 1980 by William Collins Publishers, Inc.
2. *Roth* v. *United States*, 354 U.S. 476 (1957).
3. *Miller* v. *California*, 413 U.S. 15 (1973).
4. Charlene J. Brown, Trevor R. Brown, and William L. Rivers, *The Media and the People* (New York: Holt, Rinehart and Winston, 1978), pp. 251–53.
5. Details of the Flynt case from "Out Like Flynt," The *Quill*, March 1977, p. 6; Arthur Kretchmer, "Justice for 'Hustler,'" *Newsweek*, February 28, 1977, p. 13; Robert Yoakum, "The Great Hustler Debate," *Columbia Journalism Review*, May/June 1977, p. 53.
6. "On Larry Flynt and the Control of Conduct," The *Quill*, June 1977, p. 20.
7. Darla Miller, "Boom in the Fortunes of Comic Book Heroines," *Detroit Free Press*, January 4, 1979, p. 1–C.
8. Yoakum, "The Great Hustler Debate," p. 54.
9. "Magazine Trends," *Columbia Journalism Review*, July/August 1978, p. 20.
10. Information on "TV Sex Portrayals Increasing" and "Criteria' for Casting" from Ellen Farley and William K. Knoedelsender, Jr., "Sex on TV Has Barely Begun," *Detroit Free Press*, February 26, 1978, p. 7–C.
11. Bruce Blackwell, "Panel Ponders TV Sex," The *State Journal* (Gannett News Service), Lansing, Michigan, March 4, 1978, p. 4–B.
12. Details of the "James at 15" controversy from Ellen Grzech, "A Furor Over TV's Teenage Sex," *Detroit Free Press*, February 9, 1978, p. 1–A.
13. Rubens's opposing view from William S. Rubens, "Sex on Television, More or Less," *Vital Speeches*, January 1, 1978, p. 171.
14. Bettelou Peterson, "Sex and Violence Rule the Ratings," *Detroit Free Press*, January 27, 1977, p. 8–D.
15. "The Television Code of the National Association of Broadcasters," Charles S. Steinberg, ed., *Mass Media and Communication* (New York: Hastings House, 1972), p. 652.
16. Christopher H. Sterling and Timothy R. Haight, *The Mass Media: Aspen Institute Guide to Communication Industry Trends* (New York: Praeger Publishers, 1978), p. 129.
17. Kenneth MacDonald, "Should Newspapers Be Policing Sex?" *Columbia Journalism Review*, May/June 1978, p. 14.
18. C. Randall Heuston, "Sexonomics," *Columbia Journalism Review*, September/October 1978, p. 82.
19. Malcolm Johnson, "X-Rating Doesn't Warrant Ban," The *State Journal* (Associated Press), Lansing, Michigan, April 12, 1978, p. 9–B.
20. Information on the Lauren Boyd case from Stephen J. Cohen, "Sex and the Farm News," The *Quill*, February 1977, p. 26.
21. Stephen J. Cohen, "Update: Students Win," The *Quill*, March 1977, p. 10.
22. Details of the *Communique* from Charles Fair, "Another Sex Poll and a Victory (A Disputed One)," The *Quill*, February 1977, p. 29.
23. "High School Principals: Tragedy Lies Ahead Unless . . .," The *Quill*, June 1977, p. 14.
24. "Editor's Notes: Are They Clairvoyant Enough?" The *Quill*, June 1977, p. 4.
25. "One Word in Print, The Adviser's Jobless," The *Quill*, November 1977, p. 34.
26. "First Amendment Does Not Protect Sex Surveys," The *Quill*, May 1978, p. 12.
27. Information on Charlie Alexander from John McMillan, "That Word," *The Bulletin of the American Society of Newspaper Editors*, May/June 1976, p. 16.

28. Information on the "Seven Words" from "Justice Steps Back from Ban of Seven Words," The *Quill,* May 1978, p. 8.
29. John C. Carlin, "The Rise and Fall of Topless Radio," *Journal of Communication,* Winter 1976, p. 162.
30. Paul M. Hirsch, "The Economics of Rock," The *Nation,* March 9, 1970, p. 32.
31. Nicholas Johnson, "The Censorship of Song Lyrics," in *Readings in Mass Communication,* Michael C. Emery and Ted Curtis Smythe, eds. (Dubuque: Wm. C. Brown Company Publishers, 1977), p. 461.
32. "Those Who Don't Like That Line Can Move On," The *Quill,* November 1977, p. 6.
33. Information on the SPJ/SDX proposal from "Pornography Is a Greasy Subject," The *Quill,* June 1977, p. 39.
34. "60 Minutes," CBS, January 14, 1979.
35. "Pornography Is a Greasy Subject," p. 39.
36. Report of the Commission on Obscenity and Pornography (Washington, D.C.: Government Printing Office, 1970), pp. 265–90.
37. Brown, et al., *The Media and the People,* pp. 252–53.

Carlin, John C. "The Rise and Fall of Topless Radio." *Journal of Communication,* Winter 1976, p. 162.
Cohen, Stephen J. "Sex and the Farm News." The *Quill,* February 1977, p. 26.
Cohen, Stephen J. "Update: Students Win." The *Quill,* March 1977, p. 10.
"Editor's Notes: Are They Clairvoyant Enough?" The *Quill,* June 1977, p. 4.
Fair, Charles. "Another Sex Poll and a Victory (A Disputed One)." The *Quill,* February 1977, p. 29.
"First Amendment Does Not Protect Sex Surveys." The *Quill,* May 1978, p. 12.
Heuston, C. Randall. "Sexonomics." *Columbia Journalism Review,* September/October 1978, p. 82.
"High School Principals; Tragedy Lies Ahead Unless . . . ." The *Quill,* June 1977, p. 14.
Hirsch, Paul M. "The Economics of Rock." The *Nation,* March 9, 1970, p. 32.
"Justice Steps Back from Ban of Seven Words." The *Quill,* May 1978, p. 8.
Kretchmer, Arthur. "Justice for 'Hustler.' " *Newsweek,* February 28, 1977, p. 13.
MacDonald, Kenneth. "Should Newspapers Be Policing Sex?" *Columbia Journalism Review,* May/June 1978, p. 14.
McMillan, John. "That Word." *The Bulletin of the American Society of Newspaper Editors,* May/June 1976, p. 16.
"Magazine Trends." *Columbia Journalism Review,* July/August 1978, p. 20.
Miller v. California, 413 U.S. 15 (1973).
"On Larry Flynt and the Control of Conduct." The *Quill,* June 1977, p. 20.
"One Word in Print, The Adviser's Jobless." The *Quill,* November 1977, p. 34.
"Out Like Flynt." The *Quill,* March 1977, p. 6.
"Pornography Is A Greasy Subject." The *Quill,* June 1977, p. 39.
Report of the Commission on Obscenity and Pornography. Washington, D.C.: Government Printing Office, 1970.
Roth v. United States, 354 U.S. 476 (1957).
Rubens, William S. "Sex on Television, More or Less." *Vital Speeches,* January 1, 1978, p. 171.
"Those Who Don't Like That Line Can Move On." The *Quill,* November 1977, p. 6.
Yoakum, Robert. "The Great Hustler Debate." *Columbia Journalism Review,* May/June 1977, p. 53.

For Further Reading

News in Pictures

Mass Media Controls
Libel and Privacy

9

Upon completing this chapter you should be familiar with—

the elements and issues of libel

media defenses against libel

libel and public figures, including libel via confidential sources and public debate

actual cases provided, including recent court decisions

the four "models" of privacy

privacy and public figures—case studies

criminals and the right of privacy

privacy, rape victims, and juvenile offenders

the position of the news media in privacy matters

Chapter Objectives

Key Terms

Defamation   To attack the good name of one or more persons by libel or slander. (p. 265)

Libel   May be defined in many ways: a workable definition is to defame a person or group in writing or pictorially, directly or indirectly, and thus hold that person or group up to public ridicule or scorn. (p. 265)

Slander   To defame a person or group orally before witnesses. (p. 265)

Civil Libel   An individual or group libeled by another individual or group: most libel cases are civil cases. (p. 266)

Criminal Libel   An individual or group in a libel action against the state: criminal libel actions are rare. (p. 266)

Four Elements of Libel   Defamation, publication, identification, malice. (p. 266)

Principal Defenses against Libel   Truth, conditional privilege, fair comment. (p. 267)

Privacy Refers to the age-old principle that persons are entitled to reasonable privacy: this "right" is implied by the United States Constitution, and to unlawfully "invade" one's privacy may be actionable in court. (p. 279)

Right of Privacy The right of private citizens to be left untouched by the actions of the mass media or other forms of communication. (p. 279)

For Purposes of Trade The profits earned from the entertainment content that a communications medium publishes or airs. "News," as such, is not considered as published "for purposes of trade" since the public must have timely information to function in the democratic order. Hence, news is not actionable in privacy cases. Essentially "entertainment" content is considered a function of trade. (p. 280)

The liberty of the press is the Palladium *of all the civil, political, and religious rights of an Englishman.*

Junius, *Letters* (fl. 1770),
England.

Libel and privacy form a two-headed mass media controls issue of major significance in the modern world. As with the obscenity issue, libel- and privacy-oriented content may clash resoundingly with the public's concept of the "right to know" and the media's concept of the "right to tell." As we have seen in the chapter on obscenity, what is obscene is in the eye of the beholder. As with obscenity, libel or privacy becomes actionable in court only if and when parties decide that it is offensive and not in the public interest. Therefore, a libel or privacy suit seeks to *control,* more or less, certain kinds of information the media may wish to project.

As we shall see, if a medium of communication should fall victim to one or more lawsuits involving major financial penalties, that medium may decide, in the interest of economic survival, to avoid reporting certain kinds of information in the future. Thus, the "control" agent may effect content in a major way. Few would argue in favor of a mass medium's right to destroy reputations for its own sake. But few libel or privacy cases are so clearly defined. Most, at least in the beginning, are in the gray area between right and wrong or between concepts of public good versus media rights and obligations.

The Basic Issue

These are major issues in the American mass media that are not about to go away. It is in the interest of Americans to understand the causes and effects of libel and privacy activity in their society and to determine what it all must mean to the lives they lead, the thoughts they think, and the actions they take.

Libel

As traditionally defined by the courts, to "defame" someone is to attack his or her good name by "libel" or "slander." "Libel" is written or printed defamation of one's good name or character; "slander" is oral or spoken defamation. The difference between the two is in the form of *uttering* the defamation. To "libel" is to defame another via personal letters, pictures, posters, magazines, newspapers, books, and so forth. To "slander" is to defame someone orally in front of witnesses.

The Law of Libel Defined

With the coming of radio and television, the courts had to grapple with a new problem: A defamatory statement made over a broadcast station is "oral" or "spoken," yet it is also "published" by a mass medium of communication. Hence, is it libel or slander? As the broadcast media have developed, the courts generally have adopted the view that if such a statement was actually written before being spoken on the air, as in the case of a television script, it is considered libel. If it was spoken *only,* say in the course of a television talk show, it is slander. Most defamation cases handled by the courts in modern times have dealt with printed defamation—or *libel.*

Broadcasting:
An Exception

Libel is a complicated and frequently confusing realm of the law. Schools of journalism in the United States typically offer one or more courses in mass media law in which all facets of the legal issues and cases are developed as part of the student's stock of professional knowledge. Since entire volumes have been published to support these courses, no effort will be made here to equal their breadth and depth of content. The present effort, then, is to introduce the student to basic mass media legal issues and problems dealing with libel and privacy.

Most Libel Cases
Are Civil

Most libel cases are "civil" cases. That means that they are lawsuits between private individuals—the injured party who brings the suit and the mass medium charged with defamation. "Criminal" libel cases are rare. They involve actions between a private party (or parties) and the state. Thus, they are tried in criminal courts because a "crime" has been committed against the state. The presentation that follows will be limited to civil cases in which the mass media are increasingly involved.

The Four
Elements of Libel

The four basic elements, or parts, of civil libel are defamation, publication, identification, and malice.[1] All four elements must be present for libel to take place. Because of the importance of each element to the case of libel, it is essential to understand all four.

Defamation

1. **Defamation** is any published statement that tends to make an individual the subject of scorn or ridicule and that damages his reputation and causes him to be shunned. For example, it might affect his ability to earn a living and otherwise pursue a normal life. A defamatory communication need not be stated outright but may also be made by suggestion, innuendo, or implication.

Publication

2. **Publication** means any form of written or pictorial communication, usually a print medium, that projects defamatory matter to one or more persons who are able to understand the meaning and apply it to the person identified in the publication. Publication is not limited only to the community in which

the statement is published. It also extends to all places where the medium circulates. If more than one medium publishes the statement, each one may be open to a libel suit if the injured party wishes to bring action.

3. **Identification** is the act of identifying the person defamed. Actually naming the person is the most common and convincing form of identification. However, it can also be done without including the formal name. A description or other identifying measure will suffice if others understand who the party identified really is. Identifying the wrong person, even by mistake, does not change the matter of identification nor the degree of defamation. That's why journalists attempt to provide complete identification of persons in the news.

Identification

4. **Malice** If a defamatory statement in a libel suit is proved to have been made maliciously, i.e., for the purpose of ridiculing someone before his peers, the court might offer the injured party additional damages. For some time, libel rulings involving public figures required that injured parties actually *prove* that a possibly libelous statement was made maliciously before the verdict was awarded. The United States Supreme Court recently changed that as we shall see.

Malice

Under certain circumstances, the news media may publish defamatory statements about persons and be protected against libel suits. That is, in some cases, the media have certain built-in "protections" against libel actions. Three principal media "defenses" are truth, conditional privilege, and fair comment.

Media Defenses against Libel

1. **Truth** In most states, truth is a solid defense in libel cases. If the reporter can prove that the offensive statement is *true*, the court considers that a sufficient defense of and by itself. In states not recognizing truth as a complete defense, the medium would also have to prove that the defamation was published with good motives and for justifiable reasons.

Truth as a Defense

2. **Conditional Privilege** Members of Congress and other legislative bodies enjoy what is called absolute privilege. This is to ensure that debates and discussions related to the business of government be open to all kinds of exchanges and free from censure of any kind. This is essential to the legislative process. This freedom even extends to making defamatory statements. But anything defamatory spoken by a legislator *outside* those privileged places may be cause for libel action.

Conditional Privilege

Reporters do not enjoy *absolute* privilege. But, since they must report on legislative debates in the interest of keeping all citizens informed, the courts recognize that they must have *reasonable* freedom to quote what elected officials say. Therefore, if a legislator makes a defamatory statement in his official capacity, the reporter may pick it up and publish it without fear, provided that the version is accurate and published without malice.

Fair Comment

3. **Fair Comment** In certain cases, the courts recognize the need for the press to serve the public interest as evaluator or critic of various public developments and activities. Recognized aspects of public life open to such evaluation and criticism include the actions and statements of political candidates or public officials, theatrical performers and performances, artists, authors and their works, and others who willingly and knowingly place themselves and their wares on the public market. Some examples follow.

Case Studies
The Football Coach

A high school football team in Dunkirk, New York, went on a losing streak, and a sportswriter for a local newspaper criticized the coach as being inept and incompetent. The coach sued for libel and lost. The court ruled that when the coach accepted his position, he became part of the "habits and customs of the game. His work and the play of his team were matters of keen public interest." Therefore, the coach was open to the commentaries of media critics "no matter how severe, caustic, or ridiculous" this criticism was.[2]

The Cherry Sisters

A classic case in the fair comment domain is *Cherry Sisters* v. *Des Moines Leader*.[3] The Cherry Sisters, Effie, Jessie, and Addie, were a song and dance group that toured the country with their act. While they played various spots in Iowa, the *Des Moines Leader* reviewed their performance in scathing terms. An excerpt:

> Effie is an old jade of fifty summers, Jessie a frisky filly of forty, and Addie, the flower of the family, a capering monstrosity of thirty-five. Their long, skinny arms, equipped with talons at the extremities, swung mechanically and anon at the suffering audience. The mouths of their rancid features opened like caverns, and sounds like the wailings of damned souls issued therefrom. They pranced around the stage with a motion that suggested a cross between the danse du ventre and fox trot—strange creatures with painted faces and hideous mien. Effie is spavined, Addie is string-halt, and Jessie, the only one who showed her stockings, has legs with calves as classic in their outlines as the curves of a broom handle.

The Cherry Sisters sued the *Leader* for libel. And they *lost*. The court ruled that the newspaper's theater critic, as an evaluator of a public performance, had the right to interpret the act as he saw fit. The judge even added his own evaluation: "If there was ever a case justifying ridicule and sarcasm—aye, even gross exaggeration—it is the one now before us."

Increasing Libel Activity

The privileges traditionally granted the press in the public interest are under major assault by a seeming torrent of lawsuits that will likely weaken the media's ability to function in some traditional capacities. The types and character of lawsuits are gaining in number, and verdicts are increasingly going against the press.

Court rules teacher can sue Elks for libel

SAN FRANCISCO (AP)—The California Supreme Court has let stand a federal appeals court decision that school teachers are not public figures and thereby may file libel suits.

The high court Thursday refused without comment to review an appeal by the national Elks fraternal order, which was sued for libel by a high school social sciences teacher criticized for using a book of radical writings in her classroom.

THE ELKS had asked the court to review an appellate court decision that reinstated a complaint filed in 1972 by Virginia T. Franklin, a teacher at San Rafael High School.

A year earlier, Mrs. Franklin bought copies of the book "Movement Toward a New America" for use in an American government class.

According to the appeals court, the book was a "pistache of underground writings concerning revolution, sex and drugs, vividly illustrated and replete with vulgar language."

THE NATIONAL Elks group was sent clippings and correspondence on the matter by the local lodge's Americanism committee.

The Elks Magazine published an editorial in October 1972 strongly criticizing the book. Court records show it also claimed Mrs. Franklin "had been relieved from teaching the same sort of rot in the Paradise school system" after complaints from parents and the American Legion.

Mrs. Franklin was a temporary teacher in Paradise, Calif., in 1967. The editorial claimed she had been rejected by 62 other schools before being hired at San Rafael.

MRS. FRANKLIN maintained the editorial was erroneous and demanded a retraction. She denied ever being fired at Paradise or being turned down by other schools.

Marin County Superior Court issued a summary judgment in favor of the Elks, saying Mrs. Franklin could not meet requirements for libel actions. The court said she was a public figure and had not shown that the Elks used malice in publishing material she claimed was libelous.

The court of appeals said on Oct. 23, however, Mrs. Franklin was not a public figure and could sue for libel.

Associated Press.

David Shaw, a media critic, looked into the matter and noted the changes. They include more than 500 libel actions against the news media. More to the point, the cost of defense goes up to $100,000 each, sometimes higher, even when the news medium *wins*. George Christie, a Duke University law professor, said: "The law in the area of injury to reputation is on the verge of chaos. Attempts by the [Supreme] Court to eliminate confusion have almost invariably increased it." The result has been a growing hesitance by editors to venture into untested areas that might result in libel actions. All this has come after more than ten years of relative calm in both libel and privacy actions against the news media.[4]

Others challenge the idea that the press is floundering under the assault of libel cases, claiming that the media are winning more than they lose. In fact, there is truth in the claims of both viewpoints. Some actual cases follow.

Libel and Public Figures
New York Times *v.* Sullivan

Generally, the modern press has gained considerable advantage from the courts in its role of commenting on the actions of public figures. The trend began with the *New York Times* v. *Sullivan* case in 1964. On that occasion, the United States Supreme Court ruled that *public officials* could sue and collect in a libel case against the news media *only* if they could prove that the libel was published with media knowledge that "it was false or with reckless disregard of whether it was false or not." Subsequently, the standard was expanded to include *public figures,* which went far beyond public officials as such.[5] Then it came to mean any citizen who might become embroiled in "an issue of public or general concern."[6]

Professor Alfred Hill, of the Columbia University Law School, sums up the trend up to that point.

> At the present time media defendants cannot be held for defamation of public officers or public figures except for misconduct that is willful or reckless; and cannot be held liable for defamation of private persons in their private capacities, except upon showing of "fault," which probably is satisfied by proof of negligence.[7]

Edwards *v.* National Audubon Society

Further protection for the press in libel cases involving public figures came in the late 1970s. In *Edwards* v. *National Audubon Society, Inc.,* the United States Court of Appeals for the Second Circuit overruled a lower court decision that had determined that a libel with malice had been committed by the *New York Times.* In an article, the *Times* quoted a National Audubon Society charge that a group of scientists were "paid liars." The appeals court overturned that decision on the grounds that the charges were "newsworthy" regardless of the point that they were also false. The appeals court decision maintained that the *Times* account was fairly presented and thus protected by the First Amendment.

> When a responsible, prominent organization like the National Audubon Society makes serious charges against a public figure, the First Amendment protects the accurate and disinterested reporting of those charges, regardless of the reporter's private views regarding their validity.

The United States Supreme Court agreed.[8]

In New York, Jack Newfield, a reporter for the *Village Voice,* criticized New York Supreme Court Justice Dominic Rinaldi, a public official, commenting, among other things, that the justice was unfit for office and "probably corrupt."[9] Rinaldi sued for libel. (He also sued a New York publisher who had reprinted the criticism in book form.) Rinaldi asked for $5 million in damages on the grounds that Newfield omitted certain facts from an otherwise accurate story.

The New York State Court of Appeals dismissed the suit because, it determined, Rinaldi had not substantiated his charges. He could not prove actual malice on the reporter's part. That is, he could not prove that the offensive statement was false and written with reckless disregard of whether or not it was false.

The appeals court also indicated that the opinions of individuals enjoy constitutional protection. "The expression of opinion, even in the form of perjorative rhetoric, relating to fitness for judicial office or to performance while in judicial office, is safeguarded, no matter how unreasonable, extreme or erroneous those opinions might be."

The United States Supreme Court refused to hear the case.

Another recent libel lawsuit dramatically reflects the court's seeming "sympathy" for the press in actions involving public figures. Former army Lieutenant Colonel Anthony Herbert, a much-decorated hero of both the Korean and Vietnam conflicts, appeared on CBS's "60 Minutes" to present his gripes against the army. (He had claimed that higher-ups had attempted to destroy his career and run him out of the service because of his wartime disclosures of army atrocities against Vietnamese civilians.) After the program, Herbert accused CBS of having libeled him by portraying him as an opportunist and a liar.[10]

Colonel Herbert qualified as a public figure, since he had been in the news and had published a controversial book about his military experiences. But according to measures established in earlier libel cases, he had to *prove* that CBS acted with malice in the comments made about him. His lawyers attempted to question the show's producer about his "beliefs, opinions, intent and conclusions" while putting the segment together. An appeals court rejected that strategy and dismissed Herbert's suit against the network. The appeals court decision stated that unrestricted exploration by a court of law into a journalist's "state of mind" and "mental process" constitutes an "invasion of First Amendment rights." And that would bring "grave implications for the vitality of the editorial process which (courts) have recognized must be guarded zealously."

The Rinaldi Case

Exploring Opinions and Beliefs
Colonel Herbert *v.* CBS

CBS news correspondents, *clockwise from the top*, Dan Rather, Harry Reasoner, Mike Wallace, and Morley Safer. (CBS News Photo.)

Supreme Court Rules on Herbert

But in April 1979, the United States Supreme Court, in a six-to-three decision, ruled that a court of law *could* probe a journalist's state of mind and mental processes in a libel case in order to establish malice. The decision prompted immediate expressions of shocked surprise from within and without the media.

Media Reactions

Commentary from within was immediate and predictable. The decision was part of what columnist Jack Anderson called the "open hostility of the courts to the press," and that Chief Justice Burger was "as antagonistic toward newspeople as Nixon" had been and "whose hate affair with the press now appears to have infected the federal judiciary."

Gannett's Allen H. Neuharth, who is also board chairman of the American Newspaper Publishers Association (ANPA), said that the decision "clearly demonstrates the judiciary's inclination to put itself above the law, even above the constitution."

Even United States Supreme Court Justice Thurgood Marshall spoke out against the decision "in an unusual display of public dissension on the high court bench." Marshall commented in part: "I only hope district and appellate judges will read the decision narrowly."

How much impact the decision will have on current and future cases involving libel of public figures remains to be seen.

Mass Media Controls: Libel and Privacy

'PRETTY SOON WE'LL HAVE THE PRESS TOO SCARED TO CRITICIZE ANYONE――INCLUDING US!'

Up until that decision was handed down, it was evident that the news media were being given an almost free hand in its commentaries about public figures. Why this happened is a question with many answers. Dr. Paul H. Weaver, former political science professor at Harvard and now editor of *Fortune* magazine, saw it as part of the press "backlash," which began in the 1960s. Since then the press, especially the liberal press, has placed itself more and more in the role of adversary to government and its officials. "Increasingly it felt that its proper role was not to cooperate with government but to be independent of it, or even opposed to it." More and more reporters came to view standard and long-accepted restraints on press activity, including the laws of libel, as illegitimate.[11]

A much-disputed aspect of current libel activity reflects the old press-court antagonism—stories based on confidential sources. In an increasing number of libel suits involving stories based on unnamed sources, the press has found rough going. It has become a sufficiently serious threat to the First Amendment concept to give editors and publishers second thoughts about releasing certain kinds of stories to the public. In fact, Mark Collins, publisher of the *Baltimore News-American* saw fit to post a letter on his editorial room bulletin board.[12] Prepared by the paper's attorney, it spelled out certain new procedures for handling stories based on confidential sources:

> Such stories are not to be published unless:
> 1. The sources have given written signed statements which can be used by counsel if litigation develops, or
> 2. Alternate disclosed sources are available to support the publication.

Libel Activity Part of Press "Backlash"

Libel and Confidential Sources
The Press Becomes Hesitant

New Procedures Defined

The problem reflected in the letter is that stories based on confidential sources "are virtually indefensible against libel charges in the courts." Using such sources might also affect the cost of a newspaper's libel insurance even if the paper is in the *right* in a libel action.

Action in Twin Falls   What happened to the *Twin Falls Times-News* in Idaho reflects this hard-line view of the courts. The Sierra Life Insurance Company sued the newspaper upon publication of a series by reporter Bill Lazarus, which made detailed revelations of legally questionable investments by the firm. The series was based mostly on public records, but about a dozen "tipsters" from the company were also involved, informing Lazarus where to find certain revealing documents. The series resulted in the revocation of Sierra's license by the state. In time, company executives learned of the role played by the tipsters and demanded that the *Times-News* identify them. The paper refused. Then the court ordered the paper to name the sources and again they refused. The court ruled that the *Times-News'* refusal to name names prohibited Sierra from proving that the paper acted out of malice. And Sierra had to *prove* malice in order to collect damages in its libel suit against the paper. The *Times-News* held its ground.

As a result, the judge waived away the newspaper's defenses and ordered management to pay a $1.9 million fine. A critical point in these developments is that information from the unidentified sources was *not included* in the articles written by Lazarus. A Washington attorney who is preparing an appeal stated: "If the courts uphold the Sierra Life case in Idaho, there's almost nothing a reporter can do to defend himself . . . even if he is right." This case and others like it are increasing in number and are sending costs of libel insurance for newspapers to all-time highs.

Published Guidelines   Developing guidelines like those posted at the *Baltimore News-American*
a Hazard?   can actually be a handicap for the press. According to one attorney involved, if a publication has established, published rules of procedure and is sued anyway, the one bringing suit may be able to show that the rules were not precisely observed. In that case, "you're in real trouble." As a result, some publications maintain strictly oral guidelines.

Increasing Costs   One insurance group, which handles newspapers of various sizes, increased
of Defense in Libel   premiums for libel insurance from 25 to 50 percent based on the size of each paper involved. The increases are based less on the judgments awarded by the courts than on the huge costs of *defending* a paper from libel actions—even if it wins.

The Examiner *v.*   The largest libel settlement to date came from a suit against the *San*
Synanon   *Francisco Examiner* by Synanon, a drug rehabilitation program. The *Examiner,* a Hearst newspaper, paid a reported $600,000 because a reporter who wrote an exposé about the organization refused to identify his confidential source.

Even so, some within the newspaper industry claim that increases in libel insurance rates have been exaggerated by management. Premiums, they say, amount to about the same paid by other businesses for liability insurance policies. In either case, the real issue is the reporter's ability to right wrongs in the public interest. To do so sometimes requires taking information from knowledgeable sources who fear exposure and for valid reasons.

In another Idaho case, reporter Jay Shelledy, of the *Lewiston Morning Tribune,* observed an arrest incident during which a police undercover agent shot an individual and claimed self-defense. Shelledy wrote a story about it that challenged the agent's recital of the events. He quoted an unnamed "police expert" in disputing the self-defense claim.

Case of the Morning Tribune

The undercover agent then sued Shelledy for libel. In the course of legal proceedings, the court ordered the reporter to identify his "expert" source. Shelledy refused and was ordered to jail for thirty days for contempt. The state supreme court upheld the sentence. It also rejected the claim that the court's action against Shelledy violated the First Amendment. It pointed out that Idaho has no shield law and, therefore, Shelledy had to testify whether he wished to or not. The United States Supreme Court upheld the state high court.

The Reporters Committee for Freedom of the Press issued a warning that "newspapers, at least in Idaho, were now defenseless against anyone filing a libel suit to identify a source."

Jay Shelledy and supporters at the court house.

Jack Cloherty and Bob Owens once worked as investigative reporters for syndicated columnist Jack Anderson.[13] At twenty-six, they decided to go out on their own. Based on their prior experiences as journalists, they managed to sell their own syndicated column to 130 newspapers around the country. Things looked promising. Within a week the team dug up a meaty story that linked a Texas oilman with "daisy-chaining," an illegal, profit-making maneuver of selling oil to various intermediaries before it goes to the ultimate consumers. Cloherty and Owens estimated that the scheme cost consumers some $100 million in overcharges. They based their findings on the files of the Federal Energy Administration. A confidential source within that organization helped them piece their materials together.

Soon after publication of the story the Texas oilman responded with a $10 million libel suit. The case dragged endlessly through the courts. For almost two years Cloherty and Owens paid out "thousands of dollars" in legal fees trying to defend themselves. Then Owens called it quits. The ordeal had been hard on his family. He then joined his father in the insurance business. "I didn't want to take a chance on being sued again," he said. The crucial part was not the $10 million lawsuit. It was the act of *defending* themselves against that suit. The column's clients started to drop away and the 130 newspapers dropped to 100, and then less.

In sum, Cloherty says: "You have to say to yourself, 'Is mentioning this person's name important enough to go to court over? Is it worth $10,000 in lawyers' fees? Being dragged through the courts? You have to pick your spots. And yes, I even feel guilty having second thoughts."

Had Cloherty and Owens had the financial support of a major publication or network, things might have gone differently. But they were free-lancers striking out on their own, and the cost of *defending* what they revealed was their undoing. Cloherty admits: "It's getting to the point that I may have to consider giving up the column and getting a job that pays money. By the time we get to the truth, I'm going to be broke."

The Cloherty-Owens debacle actually involves two media libel problems. The first reflects the pressures brought to bear through libel action to unmask essential, but confidential, sources of information dealing with criminal activities. The second presents the *threat* of libel action as a significant form of *intimidation* in its own right.

Many in and out of the news media feel that the press, generally, has become increasingly vulnerable to lawsuits by those whom it criticizes. Synanon and the Church of Scientology have been especially active in countering media critics with libel suits.[14] In the case of Synanon, it has backed up its antipress campaign with what *Newsweek* calls "harrassment, implied threats and at least one case of outright violence."

In 1976, Synanon reaped the previously mentioned out-of-court libel settlement against the *San Francisco Examiner* in the amount of $600,000. Synanon has also filed a $76.7 million suit against Time Incorporated, a $42 million suit against the American Broadcasting Company (ABC), and is planning a libel action against NBC.

It appears that Synanon has gone even further in an effort to scare media people off. After her special report on Synanon had been aired, NBC producer Patricia Lynch received notes threatening her life. Later, two men believed to be associated with Synanon arrived at the apartment of Fred Silverman, then president of NBC. After publishing information on Synanon, Hedley Donovan, editor in chief of Time Incorporated, was approached by two men from Synanon who warned him, "We are going to ruin your life." Finally in this bizarre scenario, Paul Morantz, a lawyer who successfully engineered a $300,000 lawsuit against Synanon, was bitten by a rattlesnake placed in his mailbox—"allegedly by two Synanon members." Other reporters have also received threats from the organization and have been placed under guard.

Scientology

The Church of Scientology appears a bit more subtle in countering its media critics, but it has notched impressive successes nonetheless. After the *Los Angeles Times* published a series on the church, the Scientologists responded with a $1 million suit. It was not a libel suit, but a charge that the paper had joined with the FBI and the Department of Justice to "violate the church's civil rights." This was done, the Scientologists charged, to poison the atmosphere "before a trial of church officials on charges of scheming to steal government documents."

Case of the Moonies

Some individual authors, along with certain media of mass communications, have been sued and *threatened* with suits for libel by the Unification Church of the Reverend Sun Myung Moon.[15] Author Bruce Nussbaum wrote an article on the church's diplomatic bank, which was published in *American Banker*. The church retaliated with a $10 million libel suit. Though the suit was eventually dismissed, Nussbaum testified to having spent several hundred dollars in attorneys fees, since *American Banker* did not have sufficient libel protection to cover free-lancers. "That shut me up for good," Nussbaum said.

The Unification Church also instituted a $15 million libel suit against author Ted Patrick for his book *Let My Children Go* and E. P. Dutton, its publisher. Three years ago, Reverend Moon himself complained to the Federal Communications Commission that WNBC-TV, New York, had attacked him personally. (The complaint was later dismissed.) After *New York Daily News* reporter John Catter infiltrated the Moon organization, he wrote a series on his experiences and observations. The church then threatened to sue him and the newspaper.

The Unification Church is currently involved in a $4 million libel action against Harper & Row, Publishers and against Dusty Sklar for her book on the Moonies.

Another Texas oilman, Davis Ashton Robinson, took exception to some of the contents of a book about himself and promptly launched a libel suit for $20 million against author Thomas Thompson and Doubleday, his publisher. Among the charges was the claim that the book, "when taken as a whole, falsely implies and insinuates" that Robinson was responsible for his son-in-law's death. An unusual aspect of the case is Robinson's emphasizing "insinuation and innuendo" on the part of the author rather than actual statements, which is typical of libel suits.[16]

Law professor Isidore Silver sees libel as a tempting device by which one may "get back at" critical persons or the mass media themselves. This is true even if the party sued wins, for one is required to spend considerable sums of money even to *win* a lawsuit.[17]

From the opposite corner, some media critics feel that the press only gets what it deserves by exposing itself to the possibility of libel suits. Attorney Jerome Lawrence Merin indicates that freedom "flourishes when it is limited by the boundaries of self-restraint and the rights of others." Hence, he goes on, one does not have the democratic privilege of attacking the reputation of fellow citizens for the sake of doing so. He cautions against abuses of free expression that occur when "the powerful, the unscrupulous, or the careless" choose to defame those whom they oppose. They "shout into silence those with whom they disagree, distort the truth to a guileless population and make an interested citizen cynical and jaded." Thus, unlimited debate becomes the tool of the few. "A person who is afraid to express himself publicly because he may be defamed or ridiculed is as much the victim of suppression as the person who avoids proposing a reform because he fears the secret police."[18]

Libel as Public Debate

In view of mounting libel threats against the news media for attempting to participate in the public debate, Merin's sentiments must also apply *to the news media*. It is basic to the democratic order that one who "expresses himself publicly" must also stand the heat of evaluation and criticism. When threats of libel suits serve to intimidate reporters and the press in general, major evaluators and critics will ultimately be silenced and the public arena will eventually cease to exist. As recognized by the Founding Fathers, without information there is no meaningful debate. The larger news media, those who can most readily afford the expenses of libel actions, have alerted their people to proceed with caution. But the smaller media have increasingly become reluctant to report certain kinds of important stories for fear of lawsuits. *Los Angeles Times* editor William F. Thomas said, "Down the line, everybody is going to start thinking harder about investigating these groups. I don't think you can afford it when you figure out the bills."[19]

Privacy

Libel is not the only form of legal-centered "control" that the press faces in the courts. Invasion of privacy, something of a first cousin to libel, is gaining momentum as well. A report of the Freedom of Information Committee of the Associated Press Managing Editors Association has noted a substantial rise in privacy actions in addition to growing libel problems against the mass media. The report issues timely warnings: "Courts have become increasingly receptive to the plaintiff's [the injured party] point of view in privacy cases. Juries have been willing to compensate plaintiffs for their injuries with large judgments. The trends spell trouble for the press."[20]

Increases in Privacy Suits

To establish the concept of the right of privacy in American life, it is necessary to look, briefly, into the past and explore its roots. Although defining the *right* of privacy of American citizens has proved to be a legal can of worms over the years, there has evolved some agreement on four basic models that constitute legal violations of personal privacy.

Four Models of Privacy

1. Intrusion upon the seclusion or solitude or private affairs of an individual. A media problem in this category might be photographing a person in his or her home and publishing the results without the person's consent.

2. Publicly disclosing in the mass media private facts about an individual that might prove personally embarrassing to him or her. In this category, the courts have typically sided with the right of the press to freely report information.

3. Publishing material that portrays a person in "a false light," that is, in an inaccurate, untruthful, or personally degrading manner. This could develop by publishing photographs, stories, or advertisements that state or imply that the subject endorses a product, service, or some public concept without his or her approval. (Some false light cases lap over into the libel area if, say, the subject is also defamed.)

4. Using a person's likeness or name, without permission, for personal advantage. Many privacy cases have dealt with this aspect, one of which resulted in passage of the first state law related to personal privacy of American citizens.[21] (The case, *Roberson* v. *Rochester Folding Box Co.*, is presented below.) Privacy in law is clearly a child of the twentieth century.

Many years ago, a judge of the Court of Appeals of the State of New York composed a definition of "privacy" that has been widely quoted over the years:

Right of Privacy Defined

> The so-called right of privacy is, as the phrase suggests, founded upon the claim
> that a man has the right to pass through this world, if he wills, without having

his picture published, his business enterprises discussed, his successful experiments written up for the benefit of others, or his eccentricities commented upon whether in hand bills, circulars, catalogues, periodicals or newspapers.[22]

Roberson: A
Landmark Case

The definition came out of the landmark privacy case of *Roberson* v. *Rochester Folding Box Company* in 1902. In that case, young Abigail Roberson of Albany, New York, sued the Rochester Folding Box Company, which, among other items, produced flour sacks. The suit was based on the company procuring a picture of Roberson from a commercial photographer and, without consulting her, transplanting it to 25,000 posters that advertised Franklin Mills Flour. Ms. Roberson was depicted as "The Flour of the Family." The posters were placed in barrooms, stores, warehouses, and other public places. Ms. Roberson sued for invasion of her personal privacy, complaining to the court that she was "greatly humiliated by the scoffs and jeers of persons who recognized her face and picture on this advertisement and her good name had

The Verdict

been attacked." The court dismissed the case because it was not yet a "crime" for one to so invade the privacy of another in that no laws to protect personal privacy had ever been enacted in the United States. Courts do not make laws; only legislative bodies do. Hence, the court could not act in privacy cases.

But Ms. Roberson had gained some supporters, including some representatives of the mass media, who began to agitate for passage of a New York

The First Privacy Law

privacy law to protect innocent citizens from exploitation. In 1903, the New York State Legislature passed the country's first privacy law. It prohibited the use of a person's name or likeness for advertising purposes or other "purposes of trade" without first gaining the person's permission. Other states passed similar laws and still others recognized personal privacy as a right through application of "tradition," or "common law."

For Purposes of Trade

Generally speaking, "for purposes of trade" in this context means that someone stands to make financial or other profit from using the name or likeness of another. Advertisements, as in the Roberson case, are the most obvious example, though there are other forms as well. An advertiser may not procure the name or personal likeness of a private party and make it part of a sales pitch for goods or services without first gaining the permission of the individual named or portrayed.

News Is Safe Ground

The courts have not considered the gathering and publication of news, as such, to be within the confines of trade in the accepted sense of that word. News is news and the public must have it if they are to function in an informed manner as the First Amendment requires. It is also recognized that the news media are entitled to earn income from their wares if they are to remain financially solvent and independent. Where the press sometimes encounters

Is Old News
Good News?

problems is when old news is resurrected and replayed in the form of special features, as, for example, the "What Ever Happened To . . ." fare about people in the news years before. The public may need *news* but, in a strictly

Mass Media Controls: Libel and Privacy

legal sense, they do not *need* old stories replayed anew for the reason that old stories are no longer "news." "News" has an aspect of timeliness or recency. The courts have traditionally viewed the replay of news as being published "for purposes of trade," or more directly, as entertainment content. As such, their main design is to entertain subscribers and, thus, to help sell newspapers or broadcast time, not to keep the public up to date on current events.

Another aspect of privacy developed as a result of agitation by various celebrities. This development was due less to their privacy having been invaded than to the fact that their names and pictures were being used for purposes of trade and they were not being paid for it. For example, in the 1950s, chewing gum manufacturers were distributing millions of baseball cards with their packaged gum that featured photographs of diamond heroes, but without the players' permission. The manufacturers claimed that the athletes were public figures so permission was not needed. The courts disagreed. They determined that the athletes ought to share in the manufacturers' profits, since they helped to sell the gum. Thus, they received the right to prevent others from using their names and likenesses for any purpose other than straight news. Many professional athletes now charge a fee to reporters for featurized interviews and other nonnews presentations. Other professionals, including show business personalities, do not charge in the interest of furthering their careers through the attention received.[23]

Privacy and Public Figures

Baseball Cards

The entire matter of personal privacy in the United States is enmeshed in controversy and confusion. There are many recognized exceptions to one's right to remain private and many court interpretations of what personal privacy really means. The mass media and other segments of society have added to the debates. One of the most hotly debated privacy questions in years has dealt with media coverage of death and dying. Said one critic: "It is not unreasonable to say that one should be allowed to die in peace." Many in such circumstances have "suffered monstrous invasions of privacy."

This preoccupation with the macabre was particularly reflected in the special treatment that the *National Enquirer* accorded the death of singer Elvis Presley. It included a page one photograph of the dead singer in his coffin—in profile. Presley's father commented: "It's just awful and I am heartbroken that anyone would take advantage of a family in this situation." Caroline Kennedy, daughter of the late president, used her name to get into the Presley funeral as a mourner and then "turned the experience into an article for *Rolling Stone*."[24]

Privacy for the Dead and Dying

The Case of Elvis Presley

Two areas of the privacy debate pose particular threats for Americans. One is the Orwellian nightmare of having confidential facts and figures, voluntarily provided by private citizens for various purposes, released to others unknown to them and without consultation. Any American who has attended school, earned a driver's license, been examined by a physician, had a bank account or life insurance policy, or sought employment has created supposedly confidential files on himself or herself. "Details have been filed away or punched into a computer about your family, your health, your money, your skills, your habits, your reputation." These issues have broad implications for our society.

It is clear that the Founding Fathers believed in personal privacy and meant to protect it even though no single constitutional amendment specifies that as such. The Third Amendment prohibits the forced quartering of troops in private homes. The Fourth Amendment prohibits forced arbitrary searches of a citizen's person or home. For that matter, the Bill of Rights in general has been interpreted as meaning that "government would leave you alone unless it had a pretty good reason for interfering. Common law says your neighbors—that is, other citizens and businesses—ought to do likewise." It doesn't always work out that way.[25]

In any case, privacy matters associated with personal, computerized information on citizens is, as a rule, removed from the actions or interests of the mass media. Therefore, at this point it is appropriate to develop insights into those privacy interests the mass media do have.

The right of the individual to be left alone and the right of the press to publish information to support the system sometimes create major upheavals. The clash comes when the media intrude into private lives with probing interviews, by recreating activities from the past, and by dredging up sometimes

minor, but lurid, facts that no longer apply or, in the case of a reformed sinner, might be better left untold. It is true that some citizens might not be entitled to as much personal privacy as others due to their own antisocial actions—known criminals, for example. But the courts have recognized that persons have the right to fall from grace, as it were, and to repent and mend their ways with reasonable assurance that they will be forgiven. While that lofty principle is an extension of the Judeo-Christian tradition, it is also part of the law of privacy.

Numerous court actions have supported the individual's right to reform and have dealt harshly with those who have dug up a reformed person's past solely for purposes of trade. At issue in the press rights versus personal privacy facedown is the question of where one begins abusing the other. This is particularly reflected when many media "messages" seem to be choked with irrelevant and even offensive information. But, as with the obscenity issue, there can be and frequently are vast differences of opinion as to what constitutes irrelevancy and offensiveness. An equally heated question is how much privacy is a person, especially a newsworthy person, entitled to have?

Anthony Harrigan, of the *Charleston News and Courier* in South Carolina, provides meaningful witness to the problem:

An Editor's View

> Readers of news magazines have thrown up before their eyes each week picture stories which show theologians in undershirts heavy with sweat, a bride changing her clothes after the wedding service, the reaction of a pregnant woman to the result of a saliva test used in determining the sex of her unborn child, an exhausted athlete vomiting under the stands after a gruelling race. The moments of life which ought to be private, the property of an individual experiencing whatever is happening to him are recorded on film and transferred to the pages of several millions of copies of magazines.[26]

But gossip-oriented magazines are not the only offenders.

Several years ago, Jacqueline Kennedy Onassis was doggedly pursued by a free-lance photographer who followed her almost everywhere, his camera recording virtually her every move. In one instance, he almost ran over her with his boat while she was swimming. Ms. Onassis took him to court where he claimed protection under the First Amendment. The court did not agree. The decision said in part, "The First Amendment does not allow all conduct designed to gather information about or photographs of a public figure. Mrs. Onassis is a public figure, whose life has included events of great public concern. But it cannot be said that information about her comings and goings, her tastes in ballet . . . bear significantly upon [important] public questions." Another critic commented: "The First Amendment has its costs. Our basic political premise is that freedom of speech and press is worth the disagreeable and even hateful things it necessarily entails. Among them is the care and feeding of our less attractive appetites—our nosiness, our voyeurism, our ghoulishness."[27]

The Free-lance Photographer

Another case reflects the complexities of the problem. Michael Virgil, a body surfer, was one of several subjects in a story published by *Sports Illustrated* magazine.[28] In interviews, Virgil mentioned to the reporter certain bizarre incidents from his youth, including "putting out cigarettes in his mouth and diving off stairs to impress women." While Virgil did not challenge the accuracy of the comments related to him, in checking a prepublication draft of the article, he asked that his name not be included in the final version. He said he hadn't realized that the piece would include other facets of his life beyond surfing. The magazine published his name anyway and Virgil brought suit for invasion of his privacy.

The Body Surfer

The legal question involved was whether the surfer was a "person of public interest" and, therefore, fair game for inclusion in a published article. Federal Judge Gordon Thompson, Jr., had to consider if the "public has a legitimate interest" in the facts presented in the article and whether the publicizing of these facts would prove "highly offensive to a reasonable person, one of ordinary sensibilities." Finally, the judge ruled in favor of the magazine. Thus,

The Court Rules

A Judge's Caution

he expanded the right of reporters to cover the activities of newsworthy persons. Judge Thompson cautioned, however: "This opinion should not be read as in any way endorsing no-holds-barred rummaging by the media through the private lives of persons engaged in activities of public interest." On appeal, the United States Supreme Court refused to hear the case.

Even with many decisions going in favor of the media, there is increasing evidence that the "right to know" in privacy cases is being upstaged by the "right to be left alone." And the battleground is the American court system.

Public Figures May Be Exempt

In recent actions, the United States Supreme Court ruled that socially-prominent Mary Alice Firestone and others in her circumstances are exempt from classification as "public figures" open to press commentary. Similarly, Hugo Zacchini, the "human cannonball," recently won a Supreme Court test when he claimed that an Ohio television station had invaded his privacy when it filmed his act at a county fair and ran it on the evening news. A magazine

Criminal Actions and the Right of Privacy

lost out in another privacy suit after a reporter posed as a patient, and a photographer secretly took pictures to bring to light the doings of an unlicensed physician in California. The verdict was handed down even after the court admitted that the "doctor" was practicing "simple quackery." A federal appeals court ruled in that case that First Amendment privileges extended to the press were not intended to give newspeople license to commit crimes as a means of gathering the news. In a similar case, a television network was fined $250,000 for filming the inside of an elegant restaurant in New York that had been charged with health code violations.[29]

Covering Public Executions
The Texas Case

Several years ago, Tony Garrett, a newsman for KERA-TV, a public television outlet in Dallas, asked that he and other media reporters be permitted to cover the first execution of a criminal in Texas in ten years.[30] He also asked for permission to record the event on film for television viewing. As in other states, newspersons in Texas had served as witnesses to public executions in the past, but the requested filming of such an event would be a radical first. W. J. Estelle, Jr., prison director, rejected the request on the grounds that television would create a "circus atmosphere." He added that the doomed man was a human being and was entitled to his personal privacy in this matter.

A First Amendment Debate

Garrett challenged the decision on First Amendment grounds. He stated that the news media, not public officials, should decide what events should be broadcast. He appealed to a federal court. While critics deluged the station with objections to his petition, Garrett managed to gain the support of the American Civil Liberties Union and at least the moral support of the local chapter of the Society of Professional Journalists, Sigma Delta Chi. The president of the latter group testified in support of the station's request.

Finally United States District Court Judge William Taylor ruled in Garrett's favor. "I'm not passing on the death penalty," he said, "but on the right

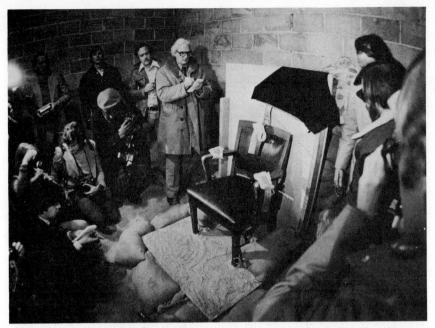

Newsmen and photographers view the chair in which Gary Gilmore sat when facing a firing squad. (UPI).

of the news media to be present. That this act of state could be conducted in secret is inconceivable and unthinkable. And I don't think we can distinguish between the print and the television media. I can't say whether I'd want to view such a report, but the right of the media to do its duty is what's at stake here." By comparison, when Gary Gilmore, another convicted murderer, was executed at his own request in Utah, the court barred all news media.

In a subsequent poll of fourteen Texas television stations, nine said they would not televise pictures of an execution, two were uncertain about it, and three said they would televise them.

Mixed Feelings

In yet another privacy category, many journalists appear to be giving the best of themselves in the interest of fairness, ethics, and common sense. It has to do with the question of omitting the name (and other identifying data) of a youthful offender for a higher purpose, especially if it is a first offense. Some states have laws that prohibit the publication of such information. But many do not. When a journalist omits a name in such a circumstance, it is in the belief that a youngster caught in a criminal act might yet be rehabilitated and become a contributing member of society. To include the name might make that impossible.

Privacy and Juvenile Offenders

Beyond the restrictions imposed by state laws, where they exist, there is broad interpretation and debate over the principles involved. Some media publish all names of juvenile offenders as a legitimate part of the story. Some have a cutoff line at age sixteen, others at eighteen. Still others will include the name of a juvenile wrongdoer only if he or she is implicated in a major crime such as murder or rape.[31]

A grand jury in West Virginia indicted Charleston's two daily newspapers for having published the name of a fourteen-year-old who had been charged with the fatal shooting of a schoolmate. West Virginia law prohibits publication of the name of a juvenile involved in a court proceeding without first receiving permission from the court. The newspapers have challenged the indictment, claiming that the state law is unconstitutional.[32] The United States Supreme Court recently ruled that the name of a youthful offender may be published when tied to a criminal act.

Privacy and Victims of Rape

Similar questions arise in the case of a rape victim, though in much more volatile and emotional terms. That is due primarily to the nature of the crime and the unwarranted stigma typically attached to its victims. The question of publishing the name of a rape victim in a news story is broadly debated with significant meaning at both ends of the yardstick. What is *gained* by identifying the victim? What is *lost* by only partial disclosure? The fact that the focal point of the story—the one raped—is rarely a criminal adds substantially to the controversy.

The View of Women Reporters
According to Washington journalist Susan Seliger, the vast majority of newspaper editors and radio news directors do not reveal the names of rape victims. "But that does not mean they agree on all other aspects of reporting rape." Dorothy Jones, news director of Washington radio station WMAL, said: "Rape is a violent crime and violent crime is news." But she added that WMAL will publish the names of rape victims when the time comes that "men don't look at women who have been raped as something dirty. Then the victim wouldn't be embarrassed."[33]

One Who Would Give Names
Not everyone in the news media agrees. Herman J. Obermayer, publisher of the *Northern Virginia Sun*, is one. He even wrote an editorial in support of publishing the names of rape victims during trial coverage. "I am convinced this custom [of omitting such names] does not serve the cause of justice. Both victim and accused should be identified. Anything else is uneven coverage." Obermayer said that rape victims should receive no special treatment by the press. "Those who argue for rape complainant anonymity say it is cruel and harsh to impose additional pains on innocent crime victims. They are right. But justice is cruel and harsh. A man convicted of rape can go to jail for life."[34] Hence, the names of both parties to the crime should be provided in the interest of justice.

A withering rejoinder came from Katie Sherrod, assistant city editor of the *Fort Worth Star-Telegram*.[35] She pointed out that "the chances of a man being convicted of rape are fairly remote—the conviction rate for this crime is one of the lowest." As for publishing the victim's name, Sherrod said she failed to recognize the logic of including the name of a person accused of a crime with that of revealing the victim's identity. Referring to Obermayer, she said: "He seems to believe that rape victims are guilty until proven innocent while accused rapists are innocent until proven guilty—and even then they were probably favored."

Sherrod added that rape is one of the major unreported crimes in the nation. "How can police hope to persuade women to press charges, or even report the crime, when their names will be published in the local paper for all their neighbors, friends, family, and even other potential rapists to see?"

Wayne Bryan, an Athens, Georgia, radio news director, supports Sherrod's position as most media people appear to. He writes that the policy in his news department prohibits identifying the victim of *any* crime other than for those who lose their lives in the commission of the criminal offense. "We feel that 'who' has lost property or has suffered humiliation or injury is not in the public's right to know. That type of information appeals to that part of human nature that attracts the tabloids at the supermarket check-out counter."

Americans appear to be showing increasing concern over the personal privacy debate. Ron Nessen was formerly a network television correspondent in Washington and presidential press secretary in the Ford administration. He has recently been critical of sensationalism in the news, particularly in privacy areas, and calls for renewed emphasis on meaningful stories. An example of what he terms "tasteless" journalism is the case of a television reporter interviewing a child who had just watched her mother commit suicide. "Why not simply leave people alone rather than exploit them for TV?" he asked. He feels that the news media "should never violate the right of privacy."[36]

Arthur R. Miller, a Harvard University law professor, feels that the press has no legitimate claim to immunity to the rules of privacy and that the citizen's right to privacy requires greater protection against the news media. He cites the United States Supreme Court as the traditional protector of "privacy of personal association, ideology, the home, the marital relationship and the body." Hence, the desire to control the amount and kind of personal information allowed to circulate is a natural extension of the basic right of privacy. Yet, Miller goes on, "The individual is increasingly at the mercy of information brokers who covet, collect and abuse personal information on other people."

An excessively zealous newspaper, television network or radio station poses a significant threat to our right to be let alone. Indeed, disclosures in the public press about one's private life can be more devastating than dissemination of the same information by a credit bureau.[37]

One dedicated privacy advocate has even launched his own publication for concerned citizens. Robert Ellis Smith, an attorney and former newspaper reporter, turns out the monthly *Privacy Journal* from his home in Washington, D.C. His list contains 2,000 subscribers who have personal interests in the privacy debate and in maintaining their own personal privacy.[38]

Summary

The laws of libel and privacy are based in the right of American citizens to pursue reasonable happiness, to enjoy good reputations, and to be safe from the unwarranted glare of publicity, unless one seeks it out in the pursuit of social or antisocial ends.

As with all debates that try to identify *rights* in our society, the issues that create libel and privacy actions are fraught with argumentation and emotion. The court system was devised to protect the personal liberties of the people. The courts also rule on the claims of the press to serve those people. The meeting point between the two is frequently charged with sparks as each declares its virtues and privileges. Of necessity, certain *obligations* are placed on both. Sometimes they are neglected. And when either party steps over the line, the courts must bring all parties together and formulate some form of agreement. The human aspects of the meeting promise only that the challenges will continue for as long as the system holds. These matters will likely not be put to rest—perhaps ever.

Notes

1. Information on the elements of libel from William R. Arthur and Ralph L. Crosman, *The Law of Newspapers* (New York: McGraw Hill, 1940) pp. 35–71.
2. *Hoeppner* v. *Dunkirk Printing Co.*, New York, 1930; 172 N.E. 139; 72 A.L.R.
3. *Cherry* v. *Des Moines Leader*, Iowa, 1901; 114 Iowa 298; 86 N.W. 323; 54 L.R.A. 855; 89 A.S.R. 365.
4. David Shaw, "Court Libel, Privacy Rulings: Media Walk a Narrow, Shifting Line," The *Quill*, December 1977, p. 29.
5. *New York Times* v. *Sullivan*, 376 U.S., 1964, p. 254, pp. 279–80.
6. *Curtis Publishing Co.* v. *Butts*; *Associated Press* v. *Walker*, 388 U.S., 1967, p. 130; *Rosenbloom* v. *Metromedia, Inc.*, 403 U.S., 1971, pp. 29 and 44.
7. As in Max M. Kampelman, "The Power of the Press: A Problem for Our Democracy," *Policy Review*, Fall 1978, p. 14.
8. "High Court Lets Stand Three Press Decisions," The *Quill*, January 1978, p. 9.

9. Information on the Rinaldi case from "Insufficient Evidence from Judge Rinaldi," The *Quill*, September 1977, p. 13.

10. Information on the Herbert case from Jack Anderson, "Hostility Towards Press Linked to Chief Justice?" The *State Journal*, Lansing, Michigan, October 10, 1978, p. 4–A; "First Amendment Defense Sought," The *State Journal*, April 24, 1979; "Court Rulings Criticized," The *State Journal*, May 29, 1979, p. 3–A.

11. Paul H. Weaver, "The New Journalism and the Old," in *Ethics and the Press*, John C. Merrill and Ralph D. Barney, eds. (New York: Hastings House, 1975), pp. 89–107.

12. Information on the *Baltimore News-American*, the *Twin Falls Times-News*, the *San Francisco Examiner*, and the *Lewiston Morning Tribune* from Larry Kramer and Chapin Wright, "Up Against the Wall," *Washington Journalism Review*, September/October 1978, p. 49.

13. Information on Cloherty and Owens from "Cloherty, Owens: Reporters Face $10 Million Libel Suit," *Washington Journalism Review*, September/October 1978, p. 54.

14. Information on these two groups from "Leaning on the Press," *Newsweek*, November 20, 1978, p. 133.

15. Information on the Moonies from "Moon Church Files Libel Suit Against H & R Author," *Publishers Weekly*, May 1, 1978, p. 29.

16. " 'Blood and Money' is Target of $20 Million Suit," *Publishers Weekly*, October 3, 1977, p. 35.

17. Isidore Silver, "A Weapon for the Right," The *Nation*, May 20, 1978, p. 594.

18. Jerome Lawrence Merin, "Libel and the Supreme Court," *William and Mary Law Review*, 11, p. 371.

19. "Leaning on the Press," *Newsweek*, November 20, 1978, p. 133.

20. Warren K. Agee, "The High Cost of Fighting Libel Actions," The *Quill*, December 1977, p. 29.

21. Donald L. Smith, "Privacy: The Right That Failed," in *Mass Media and the Supreme Court*, Kenneth S. Devol, ed. (New York: Hastings House, 1976), p. 261.

22. This definition and further information on the case from *Roberson* v. *Rochester Folding Box Co.*, 1901, 71 N.Y.S. 876; 64 App. Div. 30.

23. Charles Rembar, "Turning *You* Into Movies," *Esquire*, April 1977, p. 75.

24. "Elvis Presley . . .," *Detroit Free Press*, September 1, 1977, p. 16–D.

25. "What Are Your Rights to Privacy?" *Better Homes and Gardens*, September, 1977, p. 36.

26. Anthony Harrigan, "The Surrender of Privacy," *Nieman Reports*, XII, No. 3 (July, 1958), pp. 6–8.

27. "Freedom of the Press," *Senior Scholastic*, January 13, 1976, pp. 6–10; Rembar, "Turning *You* Into Movies," p. 75.

28. Information on the Virgil case from "Publicly Interesting," The *Quill*, February 1977, p. 8.

29. Peter C. Stuart, "Is Nothing Private from the Press," The *Christian Science Monitor*, September 26, 1977, p. 14.

30. Information on the Garrett case from Dave McNeely, "Death Brought to You Live," The *Quill*, February 1977, p. 22.

31. John L. Hulteng, *The Messenger's Motives* (Englewood Cliffs, N.J.: Prentice-Hall, Inc., 1976), p. 66.

32. "Indicted for Publishing Juvenile's Name," The *Quill*, April 1978, p. 11.

33. Susan Seliger, "Twice Invaded," *Washington Journalism Review*, April/May 1978, p. 50.

34. "One Who Will Print Names of Rape Victims," The *Quill*, February 1978, p. 8.

35. Sherrod's comments and those of Wayne Bryan following are from "The Injustice of Printing Names of Rape Victims," The *Quill*, April 1978, p. 4.

36. "Ron Nessen Lambastes Press for Sensationalism," *Boston University Today*, December 1977, p. 12.

37. Arthur R. Miller, "The Press and Privacy," *Current*, July/August 1978, pp. 3–7.

38. Patrick Oster, "A Matter of Privacy: Is 1984 Here Already?" *Detroit Free Press*, February 2, 1978, p. 1–C.

For Further Reading

Agee, Warren K. "The High Cost of Fighting Libel Actions." The *Quill,* December 1977, p. 29.

" 'Blood and Money' Is Target of $20 Million Suit." *Publishers Weekly,* October 3, 1977, p. 35.

Cherry v. Des Moines Leader, Iowa, 1901; 114 Iowa 298; 86 N.W. 323; 54 L.R.A. 855; 89 A.S.R., 365.

"Cloherty, Owens: Reporters Face $10 Million Libel Suit." *Washington Journalism Review,* September/October 1978, p. 54.

"Freedom of the Press." *Senior Scholastic,* January 13, 1976, pp. 6–10.

Harrigan, Anthony. "The Surrender of Privacy." *Nieman Reports,* XII, no. 3 (July 1958), pp. 6–8.

"High Court Lets Stand Three Press Decisions." The *Quill,* January 1978, p. 9.

Hoeppner v. Dunkirk Printing Co. New York, 1930: 172 N.E. 139; 72 A.L.R.

Hulteng, John L. *The Messenger's Motives.* Englewood Cliffs, N.J.: Prentice-Hall, Inc., 1976.

"Indicted for Publishing Juvenile's Name." The *Quill,* April 1978, p. 11.

"Insufficient Evidence from Judge Rinaldi." The *Quill,* September 1977, p. 13.

Kramer, Larry, and Wright, Chapin. "Up Against the Wall." *Washington Journalism Review,* September/October 1978, p. 49.

"Leaning on the Press." *Newsweek,* November 20, 1978, p. 133.

McNeely, Dave. "Death Brought to You Live." The *Quill,* February 1977, p. 22.

Merin, Jerome Lawrence. "Libel and the Supreme Court." *William and Mary Law Review,* II, p. 371.

Miller, Arthur R. "The Press and Privacy." *Current,* July/August 1978, pp. 3–7.

"Moon Church Files Libel Suit Against H & R Author." *Publishers Weekly,* May 1, 1978, p. 29.

"One Who Will Print Names of Rape Victims." The *Quill,* February 1978, p. 8.

"Publicly Interesting." The *Quill,* February 1977, p. 8.

Rembar, Charles. "Turning *You* Into Movies." *Esquire,* April 1977, p. 75.

Seliger, Susan. "Twice Invaded." *Washington Journalism Review,* April/May 1978, p. 50.

Silver, Isidore. "A Weapon for the Right." The *Nation,* May 20, 1978, p. 594.

Stuart, Peter C. "Is Nothing Private from the Press?" *Christian Science Monitor,* September 26, 1977, p. 14.

"The Injustice of Printing Names of Rape Victims." The *Quill,* April 1978, p. 4.

"What Are Your Rights to Privacy?" *Better Homes and Gardens,* September 1977, p. 36.

News in Pictures

Other Controls 10

Upon completing this chapter you should be able to identify—

the issues involved in and cases depicting in-house controls of media content, including the role and function of the ombudsman

big-media controls and the cases for and against

the workings of cross-channel ownership as a control over media content

how various government controls affect the mass media

copyright as a form of control

press councils as control agents

In-house Controls Controls by editorial staff or management that affect what does and does not go into the medium. (p. 295)

Independents Single ownership of a single medium.

Big-media Controls Conglomerates, chains, groups; corporations that have many holdings in one or more media. (p. 304)

Cross-channel Ownership Ownership of print and broadcast media. (p. 309)

Antitrust Government effort to break up corporate ownerships that control all or most activity in a sphere of business or a geographical area in order to increase competition and improve the product. (p. 315)

Government Controls Controls exercised by various government agencies, e.g., FCC, FTC, FDA. (p. 315)

Copyright and Exclusivity Provides exclusive rights of ownership for the creator of a work, e.g., author, composer, painter. (p. 320)

Public Access to Media Basically the issue of forcing media to provide the public with the means of responding, in the pages of a newspaper or magazine or through a broadcast outlet, when they disagree with a medium's position on a public issue. (p. 322)

The Barron Theory Refers to the theory of law professor Jerome A. Barron on forced access to media for citizens who wish to answer back. (p. 323)

The Tornillo Decision   An attempt at forcing access to a newspaper. (p. 324)

Public Access Organizations   Accuracy in Media, Inc. (AIM); Action for Children's Television (ACT). (p. 325)

Press Councils   Usually local citizens' groups who attempt to improve local media performance in order to make media more attuned to community needs. (p. 327)

Should the liberty of the press be once destroyed, farewell the remainder of our invaluable rights and privileges! We may next expect padlocks on our lips, fetters on our legs, and only our hands at liberty to slave for our worse than EGYPTIAN TASKMASTERS, OR—FIGHT OUR WAY TO CONSTITUTIONAL FREEDOM.

Isaiah Thomas, *The Massachusetts Spy*, circa 1770.

The process of selecting news for public consumption is yet another form of content control. As we saw in chapter 3, it is a subtle process that is sometimes suspect, because *elimination* of certain content reduces reader selection in the marketplace of ideas. Media critic Max Kempelman writes that the process makes the news media, television particularly, the nation's critics rather than its informants.[1] "In addition to looking upon himself as a defender of people, the journalist now looks upon himself increasingly as a spokesman for the people."

In-house Controls

During the 1976 presidential primaries, the Democratic party changed the old winner-take-all approach in determining candidate popularity. This time, Democrats became more analytical about the number of votes *each* candidate received as measures of future successes or failures for all of them. But in actual *media* coverage of local state primaries, only the *winner* of a primary received major media exposure. That tended to distort the candidate's real strength in a national sense and as compared to the other candidates. As Kempelman notes, "The result was an exaggerated picture of a candidate's national standing, one that the press with its coverage had helped to create." An example: Candidate Jimmy Carter won 28 percent of the caucus vote in Iowa, hardly an impressive "victory." Yet on the "CBS Evening News," Roger Mudd called him the "clear winner," adding that no amount of "badmouthing" by anyone could reduce the importance of his victory. Yet a Gallup Poll for the same period indicated that Jimmy Carter had only 5 percent popular support nationally. The fact that "CBS Evening News" emphasized one candidate over all the others and gave him a greater boost and more air time removed a great deal of political activity, positioning, and viewpoints from the public arena.

Distorted Election Coverage
Broadcasting

Carter's 28 Percent in Iowa

In the New Hampshire primary that year, Carter won 30 percent of the vote while 60 percent went to one of the four more liberal candidates. Yet Walter Cronkite told a national news audience that Carter had "a commanding head start." Mudd called Carter's win "substantial." NBC labeled Carter "the man to beat."

The Print Media

The print media were not far behind in praising Carter's voter power: *Newsweek* called him the "unqualified winner." Carter's face appeared on *Newsweek*'s cover as well as *Time*'s. Inside these national publications, Carter received 2,630 lines of type while the second-place candidate got 96 lines. All Carter opponents combined received only 300 lines of type. In addition, candidate Carter was covered on television's evening news programs three times as much as his opponents and had four times as much exposure on the front pages of the nation's newspapers.

A week after New Hampshire, Senator Henry Jackson took 23 percent of the vote in the much more meaningful Massachusetts primary. A *New York Times* writer indicated that reporters on the campaign trail did not like Jackson and, therefore, television people dismissed his victories as special cases. The actual vote count in the two primaries was 23,000 for Carter in New Hampshire and 163,000 for Jackson in Massachusetts. Yet Carter's total vote was called "a substantial victory" while Jackson's was called "a strong finish" that "scrambled the race."

Senator Jackson "Victimized"

According to campaign observer Michael J. Robinson, a professor at Catholic University, Jackson appears to have been the candidate most "victimized" by media coverage that year. In six early primaries in which he actively campaigned, he had, collectively, won out over Carter by more than 300,000 votes. Robinson points out that "Carter simply dominated election reporting." Voters were given considerably more information on one candidate than on all others. Yet on that coverage, the electorate was to base their presidential choices, which appears to be apart from the intentions of the First Amendment. Hence, Robinson theorizes that "the key to winning the nomination is merely to be *declared* the winner by the networks in the New Hampshire primary." The same media circumstances have prevailed in other political campaigns.[2]

The Media as Arbiters of Content

The obvious point to be emphasized in these examples is that the news media not only decide, of and by themselves, what the American people receive as news but, sometimes more importantly, what they will *not* receive. As developed in chapter 2, only a fraction of the world's events in any given day are actually *recorded*. An even smaller fraction of these are *reported*. The media themselves must decide what portion of the total is wheat and what is chaff— except that the discarded information isn't *all* chaff to everybody. As reflected in the gatekeeper studies, a number of persons on a newspaper or broadcast news staff have the authority to determine what news content will be reported each day. And gatekeeper studies support the conclusion that much of what is discarded is important to some.

In-house controls over media content are especially apparent in broadcast news. The fact that only a few of the many worthwhile news stories—local, state, national, or international—that develop in any given twenty-four-hour period actually get on the air is an emphatic example. Roger Mudd confessed that he and Walter Cronkite once considered adding a new closing line to the "CBS Evening News": "and for further details, read your newspaper." In an interview dealing with the problem, Mudd said, "We aren't covering all the news. If we think we are, we're kidding ourselves. We are, indeed, a headline service." Mudd also indicated that pictorial drama on television news is sometimes given greater weight than the *importance* of news. "If you have a mine collapse in Pennsylvania, the bodies being carried out, the grieving widows, will have a far greater impact than a reporter talking about the Middle East even though that may be the more important story," he said. "The Evening News goes with the important story but generally not covering it as fully as a story with pictures. It becomes a built-in distortion of the day's events." He added that the importance of television news is in the impact it has on viewers.[3]

At other times differences in the quality or importance of omitted stories are more pronounced.

Charles Thompson's career as a producer for "CBS Evening News" ended abruptly when he continued to dig into a hot energy story after his superiors told him to drop it.[4] After months of investigation, Thompson and another CBS staff member determined that something was amiss in the Georgia Energy Office. Among other items, they found that "While his brother stumped political paths from the Georgia governor's mansion to the White House, Billy Carter kept a two-pump gas station 'alive'—and very profitably—with the help of up to 25,000 gallons of emergency state gasoline a month." The findings were based on records maintained by oil company and Georgia Energy Office records. Thompson put his findings into a story published in the *St. Petersburg* (Fla.) *Times* and later in the *Washington Star*. This happened after CBS officials ordered Thompson to stop investigating his leads on CBS time.

Some of Thompson's associates at CBS say that the story was an indirect and unwarranted attack on the Carter administration and that it bore little relevance to network news. The point was also advanced that the network was not about to go after the White House for the sake of an unimportant story.

Even though communications took place between CBS and the Carter administration about Thompson's findings, some CBS staff members said that

Content Shortages in Broadcasting News

Billy Carter's Gas Station

An Anti-Carter Stance?

the project was getting too complicated for the television news format. Thompson disagreed. He kept digging on his own time and eventually pieced the story together with the help of another reporter. Among other developments, the two found that Billy Carter was one of those who received emergency, or "set-aside," gasoline, calling it "a windfall." In fact, Billy Carter's little gas station in Plains, Georgia, received more gasoline than he would normally have received had he not been Billy Carter. The Department of Energy is now investigating the entire emergency, or "set-aside," program.

Charles Thompson eventually resigned from CBS and became an investigative reporter for ABC news. One of his assignments was the Georgia Energy Office.

Congressmen Who Own Media

In-house control of content also comes in subtle forms. According to one Washington-based reporter, twenty-seven members of the congressional house and thirteen senators own outright or hold stock in communications media amounting in capital to at least $20 million.

Each of nine members of Congress hold outright ownership of a newspaper, television, or radio company. Ten others own majority stock in forty-one newspapers and broadcast media, and twenty-one members of Congress own stock in mass media monopolies.

In terms of in-house influences on media content, Washington-based journalist Tracy Freedman raises a serious question. What happens when a member of Congress owns or controls a piece of media power?

> Are his votes suspect when he sits on the powerful House or Senate Commerce Committees which formulate most media legislation? Moreover, how do we interpret that politician's vote on media bills from which he could gain both financially and politically?

One may also wonder to what extent a politician as owner or major stockholder would manipulate the content of the newspaper or broadcast facility to conceal negative information about himself. This could deprive readers or viewers of the truth, and that is in-house content control at its worst.[5]

Content Controls and the "Doonesbury" Gang

Again, in-house controls of content sometimes take offbeat forms. This includes comic strips and cartoons, particularly those that reflect social or political issues. For years Li'l Abner and the Dogpatch crowd spoofed the manners and morals of public officials and uppercrust society, while Harold Gray's Little Orphan Annie and Daddy Warbucks advanced assorted right wing causes. Pogo ran for the presidency as Mark Trail denounced polluters of the environment (obviously with little permanent impact). The subtle stings of these and other strips upset some readers, who demanded that they be censored or dropped. And when comic strip satirist Gary Trudeau launched "Doonesbury" several years ago, media attempts to control that brand of content reached new highs.

Doonesbury and the Daily News

During the sometimes tacky coverage of the Son of Sam murders by the New York media, Trudeau turned his Doonesbury denizens on the *Daily News* for its part in the hoopla. The *Daily News* also carried "Doonesbury." It countered Trudeau's barbs by refusing to publish that particular sequence of strips, thus depriving their readers of a particular kind of coverage of a major event and issue. In the dropped strips, a would-be slayer, calling himself "Son of Arnold and Mary Leiberman," was portrayed trying to tell his story to the *Daily News.* The paper resumed publication of the strip after the objectionable theme had run its course.[6]

Doonesbury in the Pacific Northwest

In another part of the nation, the *Portland Oregonian,* a leading daily in the Pacific Northwest, held exclusive rights to "Doonesbury" in southwest Washington and most of Oregon.[7] That meant that no other newspaper in that area could carry the strip. That once-happy alliance came to an end when the paper dropped the strip after a readership survey indicated that people were not reading it. The public did not agree. On the first day of cancellation, the paper's switchboard received more than 200 calls of protest. After that, as one witness testified, "the operators stopped counting."

Telephones were also ringing at the New York offices of Universal Press Syndicate (UPS), which handles "Doonesbury." The callers were *Oregonian* competitors who wanted to pick up the strip. In time, the rights to publish "Doonesbury" were awarded to three other dailies and UPS began offering it to still others in that region as well.

A Senate Campaign

One of the most controversial segments involving Doonesbury's lovable leftists was a stinging spoof of newly-elected Republican United States Senator John Warner of Virginia, better known as the husband of actress Elizabeth Taylor.[8] Trudeau's parody developed when the original Republican candidate, who had defeated Warner for the party nomination, was killed while campaigning. With equal suddenness, Warner became the nominee. Trudeau took up his pen.

The strip in question has Dick, the husband of a fictitious congresswoman, telling his wife that he will not go across town "just to meet the wife of some dim dilettante who managed to buy, marry and luck his way into the U.S. Senate."

The follow-up strip portrays Dick asking, ". . . Remember when the Party's original nominee died in that accident? The Warner's were so stricken with sympathy that they offered to take on the campaign debt and to set up a trust fund for the family. Guess who was then tapped the next day?"

A third strip carries a commentary by Dick about Senator Warner's actress-wife: "A tad overweight, but with violet eyes to die for." He adds that he had seen the quote on a bumper sticker.

DOONESBURY

by Garry Trudeau

BUT, DEAREST! IT'S THE VERY FIRST PARTY FOR ELIZABETH TAYLOR AND HER CONSORT!

I'M SORRY, LACEY, YOU'LL JUST HAVE TO GO BY YOURSELF..

I'VE GOT BETTER THINGS TO DO THAN GO ALL THE WAY ACROSS TOWN JUST TO MEET THE WIFE OF SOME DIM DILETTANTE WHO MANAGED TO BUY, MARRY AND LUCK HIS WAY INTO THE U.S. SENATE!

BUT, SWEETEST! I HAVE TO GO! THEY'RE REPUBLICANS!

WELL, I DON'T SEE HOW THAT'S OUR FAULT. THAT'S THE TROUBLE WITH THE G.O.P.— ANYBODY CAN JOIN!

OH, C'MON, DICK, JUST THIS ONCE. THEN WE'LL IGNORE THEM!

WELL, IF YOU MUST. BUT I'M WAITING IN THE CAR.

1-9

DOONESBURY

by Garry Trudeau

NOW, STOP CARRYING ON, DICK! I'M SURE JOHN WARNER GOT TO THE SENATE ON HIS OWN MERITS!

OH, C'MON, LACEY. REMEMBER WHEN THE PARTY'S ORIGINAL NOMINEE DIED IN THAT ACCIDENT?

THE WARNERS WERE SO STRICKEN WITH SYMPATHY THAT THEY OFFERED TO TAKE ON THE CAMPAIGN DEBT AND TO SET UP A TRUST FUND FOR THE FAMILY. GUESS WHO WAS THEN TAPPED THE NEXT DAY?

WELL, THEY DIDN'T HAVE TO OFFER ANYTHING, DICK..

CAN'T YOU JUST HEAR HIM MAKING HIS CASE? "I'LL SHOW YOU MY QUID IF YOU SHOW ME YOUR QUO!"

NOW, DICK, YOU'VE BEEN AROUND POLITICS LONG ENOUGH TO..

TO GROW CYNICAL? NEVER! I'M CONSTANTLY AMAZED!

1-10

DOONESBURY

by Garry Trudeau

LACEY! DEAREST! I'VE BEEN LOOKING ALL OVER FOR YOU!

WE JUST ARRIVED, GAIL. SORRY WE'RE SO LATE!

DON'T BE SILLY! I WAS JUST AFRAID YOU WEREN'T COMING..

WELL, AS YOU KNOW, DEAR, I'M NOT WILD ABOUT FILM PEOPLE. BUT LIZ TAYLOR, WELL..

THRILLING, ISN'T IT? WAIT UNTIL YOU SEE HER! SHE'S..

WE KNOW. "A TAD OVERWEIGHT, BUT WITH VIOLET EYES TO DIE FOR."

WHY, DICK! I THOUGHT YOU JUST GOT HERE!

WE DID. THAT'S FROM ONE OF THEIR BUMPER STICKERS.

1-11

Bill Kling, Warner's press secretary, protested the content of the first two strips as "totally inaccurate." Even more, the twenty-eight Republicans in the Virginia General Assembly voted to censure Trudeau and to "express our outrage and indignation" over the strip's messages.

The contested strips were also published by the *Richmond* (Va.) *Times-Dispatch*. They were accompanied by an editor's note indicating that they might offend some readers but that failure to publish them might be considered censorship.

A Question of Censorship

The "Doonesbury" characters also went after congressional House Speaker Thomas P. "Tip" O'Neill. Two strips, part of a series noting the "Silver Anniversary of the House Ethics Committee's Investigation into the Koreagate Scandals," left Congressman O'Neill "terribly hurt." One strip suggested that the Speaker had accepted a "free interest in a nursing home." The second strip contained a coupon that readers were encouraged to fill out and mail to O'Neill. The coupon was gauged to provide information on those congressmen, O'Neill among them, who supposedly received gifts or money from Tungsun Park, the Korean rice broker.*

Doonesbury and the Speaker

*The House Committee on Standards of Official Conduct has since exonerated Speaker O'Neill of any implication in the Koreagate scandals.

Florence Graves wrote in the *Washington Journalism Review* that O'Neill aide Gary Hymel attempted to pressure Universal Press Syndicate out of running the strips. Universal refused. Then the completed coupons began pouring into Speaker O'Neill's office. The *Los Angeles Times* asked Hymel to comment. He retorted: "Why make another story for you? That's for the funny papers."[9]

How Some Editors Handle Doonesbury

The biting satire by Trudeau and his cast of characters is a two-sided sword for many editors. They may delight in the barbs aimed at the nation's social and political powers, but the barbs sometimes bring strong pressures to silence the strip or render it less offensive. In the latter vein, some editors have transplanted "Doonesbury" from the comics section to the editorial page, which they feel is more appropriate to its content.

The Ombudsman

A fairly recent development in the area of in-house controls over media content is the ombudsman, a kind of complaint department clerk, baseball umpire, marathoner, and public speaker rolled into a three-piece suit from Brooks Brothers. The ombudsman listens to consumers' gripes about content, or the lack of it, and tries to come up with solutions. The job involves checking each issue of a paper with great care to determine how the product can be improved. As a media entity, the ombudsman is the creation of the print media, since broadcasting has its own version in the FCC, as limited as that influence may sometimes be.

Bringing Press and Public Together

The newspaper ombudsman might be characterized as a kind of Goliath positioned arms apart and hands opened flat to keep the public and the press from going at each other. The ombudsman is also in the unlikely position of being employed by the newspaper and serving as its in-house critic in the name of the public, while trying to serve all three. The job appears to be a contradiction both in concept and function, but it is one of the potential solutions to existing credibility problems dealing with mass media content.

Ombudsmanship and the New York Times

A. H. Raskin was assistant editorial page editor of the *New York Times* when he began to consider ways to cope with press credibility problems.[10] In time he envisioned a kind of superofficial who would work for the public good. In the business world, such a person is called an ombudsman. Raskin wrote that a newspaper ombudsman should be "armed with authority to get something done about valid complaints and to propose methods for more effective performance of all the paper's services to the community, particularly the patrol it keeps on the frontiers of thought and action." Among other shortcomings, Raskin detected a smugness and complacency among employees of the news media. "The credibility gap is not a White House exclusive," he said. "It also separates press and people."

While others thought about Raskin's notions, Executive Editor Norman Isaacs, of the *Louisville Courier Journal,* decided to put them to the test. He appointed City Editor John Herchenroeder, a veteran of forty years with the paper, to be the first American newspaper ombudsman. His job included gathering reader's questions, suggestions, and complaints and organizing them into a daily report including how each was followed up by the newspaper. He had access to editors and reporters and even outside sources. Copies of his daily reports went to all editors on the staff and were posted in the newsroom.

The paper also ran full-page advertisements revealing the ombudsman's availability to readers. Public responses in the form of letters and calls began to increase. They totaled 400 the first year, 500 the second, and have since climbed to about 3,000 annually.

The Louisville Experience

The second application of the ombudsman idea to American newspapers came when the *Washington Post* appointed Managing Editor Richard Harwood to the position. His mode of operation differed considerably from that of Herchenroeder in that he was essentially "an internal critic who wrote private memos to executive editor Benjamin C. Bradlee and other high-level editors." The calls from readers, he later said, did not represent a true picture of reader viewpoints. "In my experience the ombudsman was a lightning rod for special-interest groups."

Harwood said that the most valuable aspects of the job were the internal critiques. "I think you get a lot of questions that would not otherwise be raised. . . . The ombudsman perpetually raises your level of consciousness about certain matters such as standards of fairness, attribution, even such things as bad writing and bad heads. He devotes his full time to really reading the paper in a critical way, which nobody else here can do."

The *Post* now has its fourth ombudsman, Charles B. Seib, who writes a weekly column that is syndicated to forty-five other newspapers. He also handles reader complaints. The one exception to Seib as ombudsman is that he is the first "outsider" to get the job—the others were hired from within. Seib went to the *Post* from its crosstown rival, the *Washington Star.* Seib also has a five-year contract that guarantees his salary.

Harwood and the Post

The ombudsman concept is applied in different ways on the various newspapers that have adopted it. But some newspapers have indicated that ombudsmen are unnecessary to the function of the editorial process and that there are more efficient ways to deal with reader complaints. William German, managing editor of the *San Francisco Chronicle,* said: "Why does it necessarily follow that an ombudsman can better solve problems than everybody applying himself to everything?" The *New York Times* seems to agree. A *Times* spokesperson indicated that the paper does not need an ombudsman because editors deal with public complaints and contacts. Theo Lippman, an

The Other View

editorial writer for the *Baltimore Sun,* even believes that in-house critics of journalism performance "have to lie" to some extent because they are part of the operation itself. "If you're tough on underlings, it looks like bullying. If you're tough on overlings, you could get fired. If you're tough on your equals, you could lose friends." But Lippman believes that the modern press "is as important an institution as any it covers" and should be subject "to the same scrutiny the papers now give government." Yet when it comes to evaluation of performance, "it can't really be done by affectionate comrades," he says. "Papers that really want to cover themselves ought to hire it out to freelancers or other qualified critics."[11]

In General
a Lack of Interest

According to a survey done by media researchers at Illinois State University, the concept of the newspaper ombudsman has not increased appreciably over the last ten years. The research team concluded: "Obviously the ombudsman concept has not caught on with the daily newspaper press in the United States." The root of the problem is not that ombudsmen have failed to function well among those papers that have adopted the idea, but that a lack of interest exists on the part of those papers that have not. The latter group might become more enthusiastic were they to familiarize themselves with studies that show that readers support such programs. The Illinois State survey also shows that the "average" ombudsman is fifty-four years old, which implies that important factors in selecting persons for the job are considerable practical experience, training in journalistic skills, and the ability to deal tactfully with sensitive situations. In addition, most ombudsmen have served on the staffs of their newspapers for many years, have had earlier experiences as writers of critical stories, and are involved in professional journalism activities.[12] As for providing the panacea for the ails of the industry, only time can tell to what extent ombudsmanship will serve the future of the mass media.

"Big-Media" Controls

As the United States moves toward the end of the twentieth century, it becomes increasingly obvious that economically powerful media corporations are making themselves known both editorially and in the competitive marketplace. And that may not be a healthy sign in First Amendment terms. Media critic Ben Bagdikian has found that media corporate profits stand at a point 75 percent higher than the profits of other American industries. The *Washington Post* indicates that thirteen of the leading newspaper firms in the United States showed an average of 35.8 percent increase in profits in a single year.

How Big
"Big Media" Are

As another observer notes, the news media in the United States not only provide the principal means of communication and the largest forum for exchanging ideas in the nation, but they also serve as a major force within the business establishment bent on generating huge profits for media owners. "In terms of employment," Max Kampelman says, "the newspaper industry today is America's third largest manufacturer, behind only automobiles and steel."[13]

A First Amendment crisis of major proportions is likely to arise if it is not already upon us. This is not because media corporations are *financially solvent* as they need to be. It is because, increasingly, fewer and fewer media companies are controlling all the media. That means that the kinds of information dispensed and the comparative points of view made available to the public are likely to be affected in a negative way.

Fewer Points of View

The basic issue is the ever-shrinking competitiveness among media owners. Competition is the ingredient that has traditionally kept each communications medium on its editorial toes to insure that its public will be served lest it lose out to its rivals.

Dwindling Competition

The *Washington Post* found that fewer than forty-five American cities currently have two or more competing daily newspapers. And some 1,500 cities have daily newspapers having no competition at all.[14] More and more, noncompetitive papers are, as Kampelman observes, "being swallowed up" by the large chains and groups. If matters continue as they have been going, in twenty years "virtually all daily newspapers in America will be owned by perhaps fewer than two dozen major communication conglomerates."[15]

At the present time, says the *Washington Post,* 72 percent of daily and 80 percent of Sunday newspapers are controlled by companies having two or more dailies.[16]

Former *New York Times* senior editor John B. Oakes was led to comment: "The perception of the press as more interested in private profit than public service is strengthened when it lobbies for special privilege and exemption from, for example, the anti-trust laws."[17]

Private Profit vs. Public Service

Ninety-six percent of the daily newspaper cities in the United States have only one newspaper. That means there is no competition whatever in those cities. As media analyst Donald McDonald wrote, 2,400 daily newspapers served 100 million Americans in 1910. Today 1,775 dailies serve 220 million.[18] Thirty percent of all newspapers in the United States were owned by chains in 1960: 60 percent are chain-owned today.[19] Considering the statistics, then, how well the media "serve" the people becomes an important First Amendment question.

The Need for Competition

Ben Bagdikian reports that newspaper chains are continuing to grow. The twenty-five major chains control 50 percent of all newspaper circulation across the country. But those chains controlled only 38 percent in 1960. As Bagdikian

notes, "never before has so much been under the control of so few." Chains are even buying chains. The conglomerate owned by the late Samuel I. Newhouse, with thirty newspapers, recently bought the eight-paper Booth chain at a cost of $305 million. At the time, it was the largest merger in the history of the newspaper field. And according to the *Washington Post,* the merger of the Gannett chain and Combined Communications Corporation created an even larger arrangement with a $370 million exchange of stock. Gannett, the parent company in that instance, now controls seventy-nine daily and six weekly newspapers, twenty-one television and radio stations, newsprint operations, the Louis Harris survey firm, and a major chunk of the nation's outdoor advertising business.[20] And that is not the entire conglomerate picture.

Kampelman comments: "Today's press is a far cry from the fragile printing presses that the Bill of Rights was designed to safeguard."[21]

The Antitrust Question

Many concerned persons in and out of the media consider that the time has come to seriously ponder applying antitrust measures as a means of containing the corporate giants in the communications industry. This action would involve the huge conglomerates, such as Newhouse and Gannett, who own properties in newspapers, television and radio, and other holdings, depending on the interests of each corporation. The overriding problem of conglomerate ownership of media to the public is that the presentation of different viewpoints in the news, a cornerstone of the First Amendment, is too often curtailed by corporate media power, which controls the content. As fewer owners take control of more media, less variety of information on public issues is likely to circulate. A company "line" is apt to develop on major issues, and this could be projected to the public through all the media controlled by a single conglomerate. As former United States Supreme Court Justice Hugo Black commented, the First Amendment "rests on the assumption that the widest possible dissemination of information from diverse and antagonistic sources is essential to the welfare of the public."[22]

The Panax Case

One of the most notorious examples of conglomerate bullying developed in Michigan a few years ago. It continues to draw bitter comments from incensed persons on both sides. The case involved the editors of two Michigan daily newspapers owned by the Panax Corporation.[23] The Michigan-based company owns eleven dailies and forty-three weeklies in seven states along with other holdings in this country and abroad. Its president is John P. McGoff.

David A. Rood served Panax as editor of the *Escanaba Daily Press* and Robert N. Skuggen as editor of the *Marquette Mining Journal*, both in Michigan. Neither is employed by Panax any longer.

The storm fell when George Bernard, formerly a reporter for the *National Enquirer* and then Panax bureau chief in New York City, filed two stories having potentially "explosive" repercussions. One story was based on an interview with Dr. Peter Bourne, President Carter's special assistant for health issues. From that lengthy interview, Bernard determined that the president of the United States condoned promiscuity for male members of his staff, which was a gross distortion when compared to the actual text of the story. The second story, based on a Bernard interview with a psychologist and the head of a therapy center, said that President Carter was grooming his wife Rosalynn to be his vice-president. Those stories and two others went out to all Panax editors around the country with a memorandum from Panax Vice-President Frank Shepherd. The memorandum read in part:

Two "Explosive" Stories

> Please run the attached stories as soon as possible and credit George Bernard, Panax New York bureau chief—copywritten story.
>   (1) Peter Bourne Release Wednesday. This could be an explosive story . . . run front page if possible. Mail tear sheets to John McGoff a.s.a.p.
>   (2) Rosalynn Carter Release Wednesday. This could be an explosive story . . . run front page if possible. Mail tear sheets to John McGoff a.s.a.p.

The Panax Memo

John P. McGoff (UPI).

Editors Rood and Skuggen received their copies of the story and the memorandum. They found the material "to be laced with innuendoes, unsubstantiated conclusions, quotes out of context and in other ways unacceptable for publication."

Rood Reacts

Rood composed a memorandum of his own and sent it to a superior. "This is advocacy journalism at its worst," he said. "He [Bernard] assumes a position then writes to justify that position. I feel that none of his writing is fit for publication in the *Escanaba Daily Press*. If I am to be editor, with my name on the masthead denoting responsibility for the contents, my decision is not to run the stories." Rood indicated that his judgment was based on his twenty-seven years as a journalist.

Skuggen Resigns

Meanwhile, Robert Skuggen was having misgivings of his own. He decided to ignore the Rosalynn Carter piece and to "drastically rewrite" the promiscuity story and run it as a column at the bottom of the editorial page. But the next day at a meeting at Panax headquarters, he spoke out against both stories. Several days later, he received a written reprimand from President McGoff, accusing him of arrogance at the meeting and dredging up other past examples of poor conduct on Skuggen's part. McGoff's letter was later published in Panax newspapers in what some termed an effort to assassinate the character of the editor. Skuggen then resigned as did his managing editor, his city editor, and three reporters. At about that time Rood was fired. The story then made the rounds and what followed was a hodgepodge of charges, denials, countercharges, and more denials. Panax fired off a public statement defending McGoff's position:

McGoff's Position

John P. McGoff not only has the privilege but the right as principal stockholder, president and chief executive officer of Panax, to distribute whatever news copy he deems appropriate and to demand, if necessary, that such copy be printed.

NNC Responds

The squabble eventually went before the National News Council (NNC). That body decided "not to involve itself with the accuracy, fairness, or responsibility" of the two articles in question. It would also not comment on the firing and resignation of Rood and Skuggen. But the council did address itself to the "relationship of chain ownership to news control." The council determined that McGoff "has highlighted one of the great underlying public fears about newspaper chains—that what the public reads is directed from afar by autocratic ownership." The council found McGoff's policies regressive—a throwback to the crass episodes that marked the journalism of a bygone era" and branded them "a gross disservice to accepted American journalistic standards."

In response, McGoff unleashed a vigorous verbal assault on the NNC led by "An Open Letter," which appeared as a two-page advertisement in The *Quill*, a professional journalism publication. Addressed to "My Fellow Editors and Publishers," the letter denied that Rood and Skuggen were unemployed because of their refusal to run objectionable stories in their papers. McGoff claimed that other Panax editors did not run the stories and were not molested in their jobs. The letter then took the National News Council to task for judging "in unprecedented haste" the actions of the Panax Corporation, "inventing its own definition of what is wrong with group ownership as the premise for its findings." NNC Chairman Norman Isaacs had invited McGoff to appear before the council on his own behalf. The Panax president refused, calling the council a "kangaroo court" and Isaacs a self-styled "public scold."[24]

McGoff on the NNC

As to the quality of the two articles authored by Bernard, The *Quill* found them to be "shoddy journalism on all counts; irresponsibly reported, poorly written, long and boring." Roger Simon, a columnist for the *Chicago Sun-Times* commented: "I have read the first article in its entirety. Rood and Skuggen are being kind. The article is garbage." Neil Munro, of the *Oakland Press* in Michigan, said that "both stories are sensationalistic nonsense." And the *Milwaukee Journal* found that "the Escanaba editor is on firm ground. By today's journalistic standards, the stories were very thin and an insult to the reader's intelligence." The fact that most editors of Panax papers actually published the two stories is a further indictment of big-power journalism over the public's right to have truth. Media scholar John L. Hulteng, of the University of Oregon, commented:

*Media Reactions
to the Two Stories*

> This is a period of ethical reexamination in many walks of American life, particularly including the media of mass communications. Is it unrealistic to hope that a show of determination at the grass roots, seconded by a respected national tribunal, and presumably supported by leading professional voices such as The *Quill*, *Columbia Journalism Review* and *Nieman Reports* might coalesce into a moral force powerful enough to right a blatant wrong and inhibit further abuse of ownership power?[25]

Hulteng's Summation

Cross-Channel Ownership

On March 1, 1977, the United States Court of Appeals in Washington, D.C., struck down a Federal Communications Commission ruling that permitted media companies to own both newspapers and broadcast stations in the same community. (The FCC rule did prohibit formation of such combines in the future.) This form of ownership is called "cross-channel ownership," or "cross-ownership."

The Issues

Some Media Conglomerates

CBS
1976 Fortune 500 rank: 102
1976 Total Sales: $2.23 billion
Principal Operations:
Broadcasting:
owns five TV stations (New York, Los
Angeles, Philadelphia, Chicago, St.
Louis); seven AM radio stations and
seven FM radio stations
Records:
includes labels of Columbia, Epic,
Portrait
Columbia Group:
Record and tapes club;
musical instruments
(e.g., Steinway pianos, Leslie speakers,
Rogers drums, organs);
67 Pacific Stereo retail stores;
Creative Playthings (toys)
Publishing:
Holt, Rinehart and Winston,
Popular Library (mass-market
paperback)
W. B. Saunders—professional
NEISA—Latin American and Spanish
books
Magazines:
Field and Stream
Road and Track
Cycle World
World Tennis
Sea (to be combined with Rudder)
PV4
Popular Gardening Indoors
Astrology Your Daily Horoscope
Astrology Today
Your Prophecy
Psychic World
Popular Crosswords
Popular Word Games
Special Crossword Book of the Month
New Crosswords
Giant Word Games
The National Observer Book of
Crosswords
Popular Sports: Baseball
Popular Sports: Grand Slam
Popular Sports: Kick-Off
Popular Sports: Touchdown
Popular Sports: Basketball
Fawcett Publications:
  Mechanix Illustrated
  Woman's Day
  Rudder

THE NEW YORK TIMES COMPANY
1976 Fortune 500 rank: 394
1976 Total Sales: $451.4 million
Principal Operations:
Newspapers:
New York Times
International Herald Tribune (33.3%)
Six dailies and four weeklies in Florida:
  Gainesville Sun
  Lakeland Ledger
  Ocala Star Banner
  Leesburg Daily Commercial
  Palatka Daily News
  Lake City Reporter

Fernandina Beach News-Leader
Sebring News
Avon Park Sun
Marco Island Eagle
Three dailies in North Carolina:
  Lexington Dispatch
  Hendersonville Times-News
  Wilmington Star-News
Magazines:
Family Circle
Australian Family Circle
Golf Digest
Golf World
Tennis
US
(Sold some eight professional
magazines to Harcourt Brace
Jovanovich in 1976)
Broadcasting:
WREG-TV, Memphis, Tenn.
WQXR-AM/FM, New York City
Books:
Quadrangle/NYT Book Co.
Arno Press, Inc.
Cambridge Book Co.

TIME INC.
1976 Fortune 500 rank: 217
1976 Total Sales: $1.038 billion
Principal Operations:
Publishing:
Time, Fortune, Sports Illustrated,
Money, and People magazines account
for 35% of total revenue
Time-Life Books
Little, Brown
New York Graphic Society (Alva
Museum Replicas)
Minority interests in publishers in
Germany, France, Spain, Mexico, and
Japan
Films and Broadcasting:
Time-Life Films
TV production and distribution,
multimedia, TV books
Home Box Office
Manhattan Cable TV
WOTV—Grand Rapids, Mich.
Newspapers:
Pioneer Press Inc.— 17 weekly
newspapers in suburban Chicago
Selling Areas-Marketing, Inc.
(distributing marketing information)
Printing Developments, Inc. (printing
equipment)
Other:
Forest Products
Temple-Eastex, Inc. (pulp &
paperboard, packaging, building
materials, timberland)
AFCO Industries, Inc. (interior wall
products)
Woodward Inc. (bedroom furniture)
Lumberman's Investment Corporation
Sabine Investment Company

RCA
1976 Fortune 500 rank: 31
1976 Total Sales: $5.32 billion
Principal Operations:
Electronics—Consumer products &
services (25.6% of total sales)

Electronics—Commercial products &
services (12.8% of total sales)
Broadcasting:
NBC: owns one TV station in Chicago,
Los Angeles, Cleveland, New York
City, Washington, D.C., and one AM
and one FM station in Chicago, New
York, San Francisco, Washington, D.C.
(17.8% of total)
Publishing:
Random House (Random House, Alfred
A. Knopf, Pantheon, Ballantine Books,
Vintage Modern Library) (17.6% of
total)
Other:
Banquet Foods, Coronet (carpets);
Oriel Foods (U.K.); Vehicle Renting &
Related Services (e.g., Hertz); Gov't.
Business

GULF & WESTERN
1976 Fortune 500 rank: 57
1976 Total Sales: $3.39 billion
Principal Operations:
Manufacturing (25% of total sales)
Leisure Time:
Paramount Pictures—motion picture
production & distribution, TV exhibition
& series production. Owns: Oxford
Films (distribution of non-theatrical
films).
Magicam, Inc. (rents camera systems),
Future General Corp. (research, special
effects services)
Cinema International (49% interest)—
owns or operates four theaters in
London, one in Amsterdam, two in
Egypt, 17 in Brazil, 10 in other parts of
South America, 19 in South Africa
Famous Players Ltd. (51% interest)—
owns or operates some 300 theaters in
Canada, one in Paris, and owns 50%
of a French company operating 35
theaters in France
Sega Enterprises, Inc.—coin-operated
amusement games
Publishing:
Simon and Schuster—includes Fireside
and Touchstone quality paperbacks;
and mass-market paperbacks from
Pocket Books, Washington Square
Press, Archway (14% of total sales)
Other:
Natural Resources—zinc and cement
(5% of total)
Apparel Products—apparel, hosiery,
shoes
Paper and building products (11% of
total)
Auto replacement parts (8% of total)
Financial services—consumer and
commercial financing, life insurance,
casualty insurance (19% of total)
Consumer and agricultural products—
sugar, Minute Maid (citrus); livestock;
Consolidated Cigar; Schrafft Candy Co.
(14% of total)

TIMES MIRROR COMPANY
1976 Fortune 500 rank: 232
1976 Total Sales: $964.7 million
Principal Operations:

Newspapers:
Los Angeles Times, Newsday, Dallas Times Herald (Tex.), L.A. Times-Washington Post News Service (joint)
Magazine and Book Publishing:
New American Library
Signet, Signet Classics, Mentor, Meridian paperbacks
Abrams art books
Matthew Bender law books
Year Book medical books
C. V. Mosby medical, dental, and nursing books and journals
Outdoor Life
Popular Science
Golf
Ski
The Sporting News
Ski Business
How to
The Sporting Goods Dealer
Television:
KDFW-TV, Dallas, Tex.
KTBC-TV, Austin, Tex.
Owns two newsprint mills, 10 wood products mills and 320,000 acres of timberland
Other:
Information Services
Cable Communications
Directory Printing

THE WASHINGTON POST COMPANY
1976 Fortune 500 rank: 452
1976 Total Sales: $375.7 million
Principal Operations:
Newspapers:
Washington Post, Trenton Times and Sunday Times-Advertiser, International Herald Tribune (30%)
Washington Post Writers Group (syndication and book publishing), L.A. Times-Washington Post News Service (50%)
Magazines:
Newsweek
Books:
Newsweek Books
Broadcasting:
WTOP-TV, Washington, D.C.
WJXT-TV, Jacksonville, Fla.
WPLG-TV, Miami, Fla.
WFSB-TV, Hartford, Conn.
WTOP-AM, Washington, D.C.
Other:
Robinson Terminal Warehouse Corp. (newsprint storage)
Bowater Mersey Paper Co., Ltd. (49%, Canada)

GANNETT
1976 Fortune 500 rank: 426
1976 Total Sales $413.2 million
Principal Operations:
Newspapers:
Pacific Daily News (Agana, Guam)
Sunday News, Enquirer and News (Battle Creek, Mich.)
Bellingham Herald, Sunday Herald (Bellingham, Wash.)

Evening Press, Sun-Bulletin, Sunday Press (Binghamton, N.Y.)
Idaho Statesman (Boise, Idaho)
Courier-News (Bridgewater, N.J.)
Burlington Free Press (Burlington, Vt.)
Courier-Post (Camden, N.J.)
Public Opinion (Chambersburg, Pa.)
"Today" (Cocoa, Fla.)
Commercial News (Danville, Ill.)
Star Gazette, Sunday Telegram (Elmira, N.Y.)
El Paso Times (El Paso, Tex.)
Fort Myers News Press (Fort Myers, Fla.)
News-Messenger (Fremont, Ohio)
Honolulu Star-Bulletin, Star-Bulletin & Advertiser (Honolulu, Hawaii)
Herald Dispatch, Huntington Advertiser, Herald Advertiser (Huntington, W. Va.)
Ithaca Journal (Ithaca, N.Y.)
Journal and Courier (Lafayette, Ind.)
State Journal (Lansing, Mich.)
Marietta Times (Marietta, Ohio)
Chronicle Tribune (Marion, Ind.)
Nashville Banner (Nashville, Tenn.)
Valley News Dispatch (New Kensington-Tarentum, Pa.)
Niagara Gazette (Niagara Falls, N.Y.)
Daily Olympian (Olympia, Wash.)
Pensacola Journal, Pensacola News, Pensacola News-Journal (Pensacola, Fla.)
News-Herald (Port Clinton, Ohio)
Times Herald (Port Huron, Mich.)
Palladium-Item (Richmond, Ind.)
Times Union, Democrat & Chronicle (Rochester, N.Y.)
Morning Star, Register-Republic, Register-Star (Rockford, Ill.)
Capital Journal, Oregon Statesman (Salem, Ore.)
Sun-Telegram (San Bernardino, Calif.)
New Mexican (Santa Fe, N.M.)
Saratogian (Saratoga Springs, N.Y.)
Daily Citizen (Tucson, Ariz.)
Daily Press, Observer Dispatch (Utica, N.Y.)
Daily Times (Mamaroneck, N.Y.)
Daily Argus (Mount Vernon, N.Y.)
Standard-Star (New Rochelle, N.Y.)
Citizen-Register (Ossining, N.Y.)
Daily Item (Port Chester, N.Y.)
Journal-News, Nyack (Rockland, N.Y.)
Daily News (Tarrytown, N.Y.)
Reporter-Dispatch (White Plains, N.Y.)
Herald-Statesman (Yonkers, N.Y.)
Review Press-Reporter (Bronxville, N.Y.)
Suburban Newspaper Group (10 weeklies) (Cherry Hill, N.J.)
Fairpress (Fairfield, Conn.)
Times (Melbourne, Fla.)
Butler County News, North Hills News Record (semi-weekly) Herald (New Kensington, Pa.)
Commercial News (Saratoga Springs, N.Y.)
Taos News (Taos, N.M.)
Star Advocate (Titusville, Fla.)
Broadcasting:
WBRJ (Radio) (Marietta, Ohio)
WHEC-TV (Rochester, N.Y.)

WKFI (Radio) (Wilmington, Ohio)
Other:
Louis Harris & Associates and Louis Harris International

KNIGHT-RIDDER
1976 Fortune 500 rank: 295
1976 Total Sales: $677.5 million
Principal Operations:
Newspapers:
Aberdeen American News
Akron Beacon Journal
Boca Raton News
Boulder Daily Camera
Bradenton Herald
Charlotte Observer
Charlotte News
Columbus Enquirer
Columbus Ledger
Detroit Free Press
Duluth News-Tribune
Duluth Herald
Gary Post-Tribune
Grand Forks Herald
Journal of Commerce
Lexington Herald
Lexington Leader
Long Beach Independent
Long Beach Press-Telegram
Macon Telegraph
Macon News
Miami Herald
Pasadena Star-News
Philadelphia Inquirer
Philadelphia Daily News
St. Paul Pioneer Press
St. Paul Dispatch
San Jose Mercury
San Jose News
Seattle Times
Tallahassee Democrat
Walla Walla Union-Bulletin
Wichita Eagle
Wichita Beacon
Arcadie Tribune (Calif.)
Temple City Times (Calif.)
Monrovia Journal (Calif.)
Duartean (Calif.)
Buena Park News (Calif.)
La Mirada Lamplighter (Calif.)
Huntington Beach Independent (Calif.)
Anaheim-Fullerton Independent (Calif.)
Orange County Evening News (Calif.)
Broward Times (Fla.)
Coral Gables Times and Guide (Fla.)
Florida Keys Keynoter (Fla.)
North Dade Journal (Fla.)
Union Recorder (Ga.)
Other:
Commercial Terminals of Detroit, Inc.
Commodity News Services, Inc. (Kansas City, Mo.)
Knight-Ridder Newspaper Sales, Inc. (New York)
Knight News Services Inc. (Detroit, Mich.)
The Observer Transportation Co. (Charlotte, N.C.)
Portage Newspaper Supply Co. (Akron, Ohio)
Twin Cities Newspaper Services, Inc. (St. Paul, Minn.)

Thus, the court of appeals took exception to the FCC view that existing cross-ownerships should be allowed to continue. The only exceptions would be "those cases where the evidence clearly discloses that a cross-ownership is in the public interest." Otherwise, the court ruled that "the record no more establishes that cross-ownership serves the public interest than injures it." Since then the FCC has grappled with the question of whether cross-owner-ships do, in fact, create less diversity of news made available to the public. That is the nub of the cross-channel debate.

Research Findings William T. Gormley, Jr., a media researcher, decided to take a personal look into the matter.[26] His painstaking labors resulted in at least two major find-ings: (1) cross-ownership of a newspaper and a television station in the same community *does* tend to limit the kinds of news made available to the public; (2) these are particularly noticeable in the smaller cities. Both findings support the view of the United States Court of Appeals.

Gormley's findings indicate that cross-ownership contributes to a sameness in news "by aggravating an already disturbing tendency for reporters to cover stories because other reporters are covering them—the familiar problem of 'pack journalism'." Some specifics uncovered in Gormley's research are in order.

The System in Quincy, Illinois In Quincy, Illinois, the *Herald-Whig* and WGEM-TV, jointly owned, ex-change news tips over the telephone. Early each morning a WGEM reporter calls sheriff's offices and radio stations in outlying areas to check on accidents and incidents of crime. Later in the morning, the *Herald-Whig*'s state editor calls WGEM to inquire about details of these events for the paper's use. One reporter for the newspaper commented: "It is common for WGEM's people and our people to help each other."

The System in Portland, Maine In Portland, Maine, the Guy Gannett chain owns two newspapers and WGAN-TV. Gormley found that both newspapers "were furnishing carbon copies of stories to WGAN before the stories were published" in the news-papers. Carbons of the stories were placed on the desks of the city editors of both papers (which also shared a common newsroom) to be picked up by someone from the television station.

And in Rock Island, Illinois The same practices were observed in Rock Island, Illinois, where the *Argus* exchanged carbons of news stories with its jointly owned station WHBF-TV.

Gormley found many other examples of shared gathering and reporting of news between jointly owned media on the local level.

Research Conclusions Overall, his research shows that cross-ownership "increases the likelihood that a newspaper and a television station will share carbons," and that the "temptation to rely on carbons is strong." It also increases the likelihood that the television station in such a setting will hire a reporter or editor who has worked for the newspaper that owns the television outlet. Thirdly, this joint relationship increases the likelihood that both the newspapers and the television stations "will be located in the same complex of buildings." That, in turn, increases the likelihood of both staffs sharing in the gathering and preparation of news. On the other hand, working as individual media, with separate news staffs, would tend to develop a reasonable level of competition between those media. And that, if nothing else, would increase the variety and diversity of information that goes out to the public. This is reflective of the spirit of the Founding Fathers.

A strident example of applying cross-channel clout on the local level developed in early 1978 in Syracuse, New York.[27] That city and its surrounding communities are served by three newspapers belonging to the Samuel I. Newhouse media conglomerate: the *Post-Standard* (morning), the *Herald-Journal* (evening) and the *Herald-American* (Sunday). Newhouse also owns one of the three commercial television stations in Syracuse, WSYR-TV, as well as WSYR's AM and FM radio outlets. The conglomerate owns, as well, the cable television company, which provides service to 70 percent of the cable subscribers in the suburbs of Syracuse.

Applying Cross-Channel Muscle
A Case of Local Media Control of Information

The only media audience in the vicinity not monopolized by the Newhouse conglomerate (other than the two non-Newhouse radio stations) was cable television service in Syracuse itself—there was no such service. Several years ago, the city government decided to sell bonds to the public for the purpose of financing construction of a cable system that would offer recipients, among other things, a police and fire alarm system for their homes. An advisory committee looked into the matter and reported that the venture would be profitable for the city.

The Issue: Cable TV

From the outset, the Newhouse papers in Syracuse cast a cloud of doom over the project, especially the alarm system aspect of the plan. For without that, the legal basis for selling the bonds would collapse. During the critical few weeks prior to the city council vote, the Newhouse newspapers upgraded their written objections from the editorial page to page one. Headlines included: "Businessman Questions City-Owned Cable System"; "Cable TV Proposal Flounders"; "Cable TV Figures 'Batted About'/Profits in Question"; "Skeptics Raise Key Questions on Cable Issue"; City Cable-Alarm Plan Panned." According to one observer, neutral or favorable headlines "were all but nonexistent, and Newhouse involvement in the cable industry was mentioned only glancingly."

Reports circulated that the publisher of the three Newhouse papers applied pressures on a council vote, which he later termed "a lot of crap." Nonetheless, a key council supporter of the cable plan switched his vote.

Ultimately, the council voted to look into private development of the cable system. But newspaper opposition remained as determined as before. The papers criticized the "public safety" provisions that the system might offer. One of the papers commented: "Members of the Council who reluctantly went along with private development of a cable system could throw a monkey wrench into the plan. It appears the frills—such as fire detectors and burglar alarms—that were part and parcel of the municipal proposal have not been forgotten yet."

Newhouse Fears

One member of the council said that Newhouse interests in the safety aspects of the system were based on personal fears:

> The same people who own the newspapers also own most of the existing cable TV systems in the suburbs surrounding Syracuse. They're afraid that if alarm services are offered to city residents, suburban subscribers may very well demand the same services. That would force NewChannels [the Newhouse cable service] to rebuild its system, and that's not in the Newhouse corporate plan.

Ultimately, a cable company "most acceptable" to local newspapers was given the Syracuse contract.

The Supreme Court Vote

In spite of evidence that cross-channel ownership of media does not always work in the public interest, the United States Supreme Court finally struck down the court of appeals ruling to break up such ownerships. It thus upheld the FCC view that established cross-ownerships in all but sixteen cases may continue to exist. But no new cross-ownerships will be permitted. In the sixteen communities excepted, the Supreme Court ruled that cross-ownership "represented the only newspaper and broadcast outlets for the area."[28] So these cross-ownerships will be broken up.

Concerned Voices

Options to Big Media Ownerships

Congressmen Morris K. Udall of Arizona and Paul Simon of Illinois (former publisher of twelve weekly newspapers) have cosponsored two congressional bills dealing with the press. They seek to amend existing inheritance tax laws to permit family owned newspaper properties to remain in family hands. The inheritance taxes on a family owned newspaper are staggeringly high, so much so that families are frequently forced to sell out to a group or chain just to get out from under. Udall and Simon have also proposed a three-year study of monopolies in basic industries, the mass media being one of them.

NNC Plans

The National News Council (NNC) has also announced a plan to "explore what forms of ownership of the news media best serve the interests of the public in insuring a free flow of information" as provided by the First Amendment. Among the council's concerns are the impact of increasing chain and group ownership of media on press freedom, autonomy of news, editorial decision making, and quality of coverage. The NNC will also inquire into "the accountability of the news media to their readers and listeners, including problems of access and editorial control."[29]

In spite of the concerns uttered by Udall, Simon, and even the National News Council, it appears that governmental clout against further mergers and cross-channel alliances is too weak to work. Toby J. McIntosh, legal-economic correspondent for the Bureau of National Affairs in Washington D.C., writes that as long as media acquire other media beyond the bounds of their own circulation or viewing areas—as opposed to doing so *within* those areas—they will likely remain untouched by government action. He points out that seventy-two newspapers changed owners in 1976 without provoking a single antitrust action by the government. He also points out that government antitrust clout is less dedicated to maintaining a diversity of *ideas* as it is a diversity of *economic monopolies* as such. Antitrust laws were enacted almost a century ago to keep official clamps on the likes of John D. Rockefeller and others of the great oil, railroad, and steel trusts. They were not enacted to protect First Amendment concerns.[30]

Another View

Antitrust Questions

Edwin Diamond is head of the News Study Group at the Massachusetts Institute of Technology. He indicates that part of the problem of big-media ownership is that the media corporations maintain primary responsibility to their stockholders, not to the public. He also says that the right "mix" in ownership is really what is at issue. Some individual family owned properties are poor examples of what a news medium should be. There are also corporate-operated media that genuinely strive to serve the public. It all depends on the nature of the ownership. "Even some monopolies may be good, given the right ownership," he says. "Despite the textbook wisdom, competition doesn't automatically produce quality." In the final analysis, the human element must dictate what the quality of the product will be in light of what the First Amendment promises.[31]

The "Right Mix"

Government Controls of Content

Earlier in this volume some forms of government controls over media content were presented. Those examples deal primarily with the courts and elected officials.* While most of the examples have dealt with indirect controls, other forms relate to the strength of government's hand in influencing content in emphatic and debatable ways. The Federal Communications Commission (FCC) is one of the most involved media controllers.

*See index at the back of the book.

In one case during the 1976 presidential campaign, NBC's "Tomorrow" program saw fit to run a guest interview with Gus Hall, the candidate of the American Communist party. Immediately thereafter, the FCC ordered the network to give "equal opportunity" to the Socialist party candidate. That is, it did not merely chide NBC for not offering time to opponents of Hall's views but ordered the network to bring in the Socialist party candidate—*period*. In another case, in what Irwin Arieff calls "a striking case of dictation of program content," the FCC responded to pressures by environmentalists in Clarksburg, West Virginia, and ordered a radio station to cover strip mining in the area "whether it wanted to or not." At another point, to offset a "rash of equal-time complaints" to the FCC from candidates of minor political parties, ABC network attorneys prohibited any camera shots of then-President Gerald Ford in attendance at baseball's All-Star game.[32]

Such examples may appear extreme to critics of government controls, and some are. They seem to reflect improper intrusions by government on the rights of broadcast journalists to pursue their vocations as print journalists pursue theirs. Yet, in spite of what seem to be occasional "excesses" by the FCC, the issues involved are gray with age and seemingly worn thin from the rigors of debate. To understand the complexity and origin of these issues, it is necessary to look back to the beginnings of commercial broadcasting in the United States, when a swarm of broadcast nightmares brought government controls into being.

Origins of Broadcasting Controls

At the end of World War I, Americans took to radio with considerable delight. As primitive as it was by today's standards, it was revolutionary, it was fun, and it was inexpensive. Yet it barely survived infancy.

Anyone could buy the parts needed to fashion a "crystal set" radio and assemble it without difficulty. At the same time, virtually anyone having the financial resources could get a permit and establish a radio station. The numbers of both skyrocketed in the 1920s to the point, eventually, where radio signals crisscrossed, creating wierd shrieking noises punctuated with crackling static, making the entire experience something akin to electronic madness. Programming, when it could be heard, was dreadful, what with the yowls of would-be yodelers, the strum of banjos, and hucksters promising medical cure-alls and eternal salvation for a fee. The problems developed faster than solutions could be found. Things became so bad by 1927 that sales of radio sets had to be curtailed in the large cities.

The answer to the problem seemed to be in somehow *regulating* the number of broadcast stations allowed to serve each broadcast area.[33] Channels had to be established and maintained, with one station to a channel. But how would all this come about? Who would decide?

Table 10.1 Growth of Radio Stations in U.S., 1921–1977

Year	AM Total	FM Commercial	FM Educational	FM Total	Total Radio Stations	Average Number of Stations: per 5-year Period	Average Number of Stations: per 10,000 Population
1921	5	—	—	—	5		
1922	30	—	—	—	30	—	—
1923	556	—	—	—	556		
1924	530	—	—	—	530		
1925	571	—	—	—	571		
1926	528	—	—	—	528		
1927	681	—	—	—	681	613	.005
1928	677	—	—	—	677		
1929	606	—	—	—	606		
1930	618	—	—	—	618		
1931	612	—	—	—	612		
1932	604	—	—	—	604	603	.004
1933	599	—	—	—	599		
1934	583	—	—	—	583		
1935	585	—	—	—	585		
1936	616	—	—	—	616		
1937	646	—	—	—	646	652	.005
1938	689	—	—	—	689		
1939	722	—	—	—	722		
1940	765	—	—	—	765		
1941	831	18	2	20	851		
1942	887	36	7	43	930	893	.006
1943	910	41	8	49	959		
1944	910	44	8	52	962		
1945	919	46	8	54	973		
1946	948	48	9	57	1005		
1947	1062	140	10	150	1212	1585	.011
1948	1621	458	15	473	2094		
1949	1912	700	27	727	2639		
1950	2086	733	48	781	2867		
1951	2232	676	73	749	2981		
1952	2331	637	85	722	3053	3033	.019
1953	2391	580	98	678	3069		
1954	2521	560	112	672	3193		
1955	2669	552	122	674	3343		
1956	2824	540	123	663	3487		
1957	3008	530	125	655	3663	3684	.022
1958	3196	537	141	678	3874		
1959	3326	578	151	729	4055		
1960	3456	688	162	850	4306		
1961	3547	815	175	990	4537		
1962	3618	960	194	1154	4772	4780	.026
1963	3760	1081	209	1290	5050		
1964	3854	1146	237	1383	5237		
1965	4044	1270	255	1525	5569		
1966	4065	1446	268	1714	5779		
1967	4121	1643	296	1939	6060	6048	.030
1968	4190	1753	326	2079	6269		
1969	4265	1938	362	2300	6565		
1970	4292	2184	413	2597	6889		
1971	4343	2196	472	2668	7011		
1972	4374	2304	511	2815	7189	7206	.035
1973	4395	2411	573	2984	7379		
1974	4407	2502	652	3154	7561		
1975	4432	2636	717	3353	7785		
1976	4463	2767	804	3571	8034		
1977	4497	2837	839	3676	8173	—	—

SOURCES: 1921–1926 data: U.S. Department of Commerce. 1927–1934 data: Federal Radio Commission. 1935–1977 data: Federal Communications Commission, as reprinted in *Stay Tuned*, by Sterling and Kittross (Belmont, Ca.: Wadsworth Publishing Co., 1978), p. 511, which details the secondary sources used for the official data.

In 1912, federal legislation had been passed to prevent one station from creating interference with the signal of another. As a "control" agent, the law became inoperable in the early 1920s. National conferences organized to cope with the problems of broadcasting were held periodically after 1922. Among other things, these bodies urged the adoption of federal regulations limiting the number of broadcast channels. The airwaves really were the property of the American people. Everybody seemed to favor some form of firm control— the public, the radio manufacturers, and even the National Association of Broadcasters, which was founded in 1923.

Radio Act of 1927

The result was passage of the Radio Act in 1927. That created a five-person Federal Radio Commission to find solutions to the problems. The commission set up specific broadcast channels and awarded licenses to broadcasters for three-year periods "in the public interest, convenience or necessity." That was done to provide "fair, efficient, and equitable service" to the nation.

Radio Act of 1934:
Birth of the FCC

The Federal Radio Act of 1934 went even further in policing the broadcast industry "in the public interest." It established the Federal Communications Commission, a special commission under the Congress, which still regulates broadcasting today. It also regulates the telephone and telegraph industries and communications satellites. No censorship of program content is permitted under the First Amendment. However, the FCC is empowered to review program content at the end of the three-year licensing period to determine if each station has, in fact, broadcast in the public interest.

No Censorship
Allowed

Thus, the Federal Radio Act of 1934 remains the regulating force in broadcasting almost fifty years after its inception. Many Americans, especially those within the broadcasting industry, feel that fifty years is too long, that the commission, created when radio was in its infancy, no longer serves the industry as it is today or the American people who depend on it. Many call for a new commission. Others call for loosening government controls and still others for getting government out of broadcasting altogether and letting the industry run itself as other media industries do. Within the public sector, spokespersons argue that if broadcasting content is of such poor quality with controls, what would it be like with *no* controls? And so it has been going.

For those who feel that regulation of broadcasting is no longer necessary, the ghosts of broadcasting's past seem to be with us still.

Current Control
Problems: WOOK

Several years ago, WOOK, an AM radio station in Washington, D.C., took to offering a plentiful diet of religious programs for its large audience.[34] On some Sundays, religious programming added up to as many as thirteen hours. It also added heftily to the income of the station's licensee. The Reverend John W. Dowell liked to read letters over the air during these religious programs. On one occasion he read a letter that told his listeners:

I know that everybody who saw you was blessed last week because the envelopes you gave us . . . had St. Luke 6:39 printed right on it. . . . I read this verse six ways on Tuesday and I thank God that I was able to shout victory Tuesday evening because St. Luke 6:38 brought me out and I know that it was nothing but you and the Good Lord that did it. . . .

As journalist Charles Freund later observed, in Dowell's terms, "St. Luke 6:38 contains a message of undeniable spiritual value (Give and ye shall receive), but its value to Reverend Dowell that Sunday lay in a very different direction; namely in its application to Washington's numbers racket."

The point to Reverend Dowell's homily was clearly understood by at least some of his audience. The previous Tuesday he had written the number 638 on envelopes that he exchanged for donations. He then urged the donors to bet all six combinations of the number. ("Read it six ways. . . .") If they did so they would be "blessed" or, in more concrete terms, come up a winner in the numbers game. The winning number that day was 863. The FCC took a decidedly dim view of these practices and revoked WOOK's license to broadcast.

In another area of public concern, the congressional House Communications Subcommittee listened for six months to a parade of network witnesses relate how they "set up" and telecast major national and international sports events.[35] CBS and NBC representatives admitted to putting on Soviet sports programs just to increase their chances of gaining from the Soviets exclusive coverage of the Summer Olympics in Moscow in 1980. CBS also admitted that four nationally televised "winner-take-all" tennis matches were not winner-take-all as widely advertised. They said they were advertised as such in hopes of attracting larger audiences. "We recognize our wrongdoing," a CBS spokesperson said. And ABC admitted to having made "mistakes" in its United States Boxing Championships telecasts before the series was suspended "amid charges of improprieties." Other questionable tactics were reviewed as well.

Representative Lionel Van Deerlin, chairman of the subcommittee, justified the interest of Congress in sports broadcasting. "The only justification for our getting into it is to ascertain to what extent the networks are becoming part of the events they're covering," he told a press conference. "The larger question is how you can legitimately cover a sports event you have arranged and set up. Where does entertainment leave off and honest reporting of news and sports events begin?"

Substantive reasons might be advanced for maintaining other forms of electronic regulation as well. The FCC recently voted seven to zero to explore what can be done to restrict "junk telephone calls" with an eye to banning them outright.[36] These are calls made to private homes and businesses, which

Controls and Network Behavior

Controls and Junk Telephone Calls

solicit sales or donations of various kinds. The commission indicated that it would seek public assistance to determine if such calls invade personal privacy as opposed to less offensive forms of solicitation, e.g., billboards and direct mail. The commission revealed that it had received over a thousand complaints from the public, mostly letters, that overwhelmingly opposed "automatic dialing machines," which can make hundreds of calls at a time, spewing out sales pitches via recorded messages.

Legislation now pending in the Congress would restrict person-to-person telephone solicitations and the automatic dialing equipment that make the solicitations work. The FCC will also explore other aspects of the problem: whether citizens have the right to inform the telephone company that they do not want unsolicited calls by telephone; whether it would be workable to screen out objectionable calls from those made by charitable organizations, opinion surveys, and the like, which might be in the public interest. The commission will also explore whether it has the legal right to move in these areas given the questions of free speech and right to privacy that are involved.

FCC Charge to Broadcasters

Otherwise, the chairman of the FCC recently warned broadcasters that they must right the wrongs they commit in their communities and must also remain alert to increasingly provide their publics with quality programs.[37] Chairman Charles D. Ferris said that if licensees "mislead the public, they must set the record straight through corrective programming and advertising." He added that licensees are expected to correct their mistakes "on their own initiative" rather than to wait for the commission to assess the damage and inflict the punishment.

In the matter of improving variety and quality in programming, Ferris said that being dedicated to those ends gives the licensee a "reasonable basis for seeking tenure as an individual licensee and as an entire industry." He also warned that "if you are only flipping a network switch or replaying an occasional movie package, then you have not made the case that you are essential to your community—or to the national communications system." He cautioned licensees that commercial broadcasting "can and must represent more than the survival of the tired, the timid and the imitative. And as you increase the options you offer to the public, you will relieve the public's pressure to regulate the content of a limited number of programs."*

Copyright

Who Is Protected?

Copyright is a vital part of mass media law. It deals with yet another realm of "control" over mass media content. Copyright has to do with ownership of a creative "product" of one kind or another. In the main, copyright "owners" are writers of both fact and fiction, artists, composers of music, sculptors,

*For information on possible future regulation practices see chapter 13.

inventors, and playwrights. One may not incorporate into his or her own work the work of another, in whole or in part, without permission and, in most cases, financial consideration. Hence, copyright protects content made available for sale to others.

The United States updated its copyright law in 1976 after almost seventy years of upheaval and confusion as to where one's creative "rights" lay. The new law must undergo future court tests, which may alter its application as actual circumstances require.

The New Law

Copyright law also serves as a form of prior restraint, or censorship. As Professor Don R. Pember notes, "A copyright law does in fact act as censorship since it restricts the right to republish or copy books, articles, photographs, and any such work that is copyrighted."[38] Therefore, restrictions are placed on the ability of others to use certain content, i.e., "copyrighted" content. Before such content may be "printed, broadcast, dramatized, translated, or whatever, the consent of the copyright owner must be obtained. The law grants this individual exclusive monopoly over the use of that material."

Copyright as Censorship

The copyright law gives "exclusive" protection but to *original* works only— literary creations (fact or fiction); musical and dramatic works (including accompanying music); motion pictures and other forms of audiovisual renditions; pantomimes and choreographical creations; pictorial, graphic, and sculptural renditions; and sound recordings.

Exclusivity of Ownership

Copyright is awarded to original works regardless of quality. The law also requires that the "originator" actually expend his creativity to a reasonable degree in order to claim authorship. *Copying* the work of another to an unreasonable degree is reason enough to be refused copyright protection.

The new copyright law provides the author of a creative project exclusive protection for his work throughout his lifetime plus fifty years. The "plus fifty years" allows the author's heirs to enjoy the rewards of the author after his death.

Copyright "Time" Is Extended

Exclusivity does not mean that *nobody* may legally use *any part* of a copyrighted work. The purpose of the original copyright law was to encourage creative productions in the arts and sciences. In defining the new law this sentiment was extended. The law states that "the fair use of a copyrighted work . . . for purposes such as criticism, comment, news reporting, teaching (including multiple copies for classroom use), scholarship or research is not an infringement of copyright."

"Exclusivity" Explained

The rule to be emphasized in dealing with copyrighted material is that one should apply to the originator for permission to use material from that work if the user expects to earn income as a result.

Permission Is Necessary

Public Access as a Control

The debate over the right of American citizens to have ready access to the media has often been heated, even violent, and it has created an ongoing media issue since the First Amendment was instituted. The question basic to the debate is, If the First Amendment to the Constitution allows the mass media special freedoms so that they might inform the people, does it not also, at least by implication, grant to the people the right to answer back to the media, to comment upon how well or poorly the media fulfill their obligations? The reply is not as clear-cut as one might suppose.

For over 200 years, American newspapers have made a practice of considering letters from readers for publication in their pages. Thus, the newspapers have permitted, even encouraged, a form of public access to their pages. For about as long, some of those who wished to "answer back" on public stands taken by their newspapers have complained that this form of "public access" is fraught with peril for the contributor. For one thing, editors generally recognize their right to publish letters to the editor in whole or in part or to not publish them at all. The editor may publish only those letters that support the paper's position in a controversial matter, discarding dissenting letters. In terms of the reading public-at-large, who is to know? Only the contributor and that person's immediate circle knows that a particular letter was composed and sent to the editor. Or, via "selective editing," the editor may include those portions of a letter that *appear* to support his editorial stance and thus render neuter a criticism intended to be shared with others in the community. There is no authority, other than the editor's personal conscience, that can force a newspaper to publish anything it does not wish to publish—nor should there be. Attempts to establish such authority by judicial or legislative pronouncement would clearly violate the First Amendment's provisions. The fact remains, however, that the ability of readers to comment on public policies through their media is subject to the will of media's management.

Reprinted by permission of the Chicago Tribune-New York News Syndicate, Inc.

Beginning in the 1960s, various individuals and groups have sought to change that arrangement. In effect, they have endorsed *forcing* public access on the print media on First Amendment grounds. That is, the public, under force of law, would *require* the news media to provide reasonable time of broadcasters and adequate space in print media to showcase their disagreements with media positions on public issues. The debate has gained in intensity with the growth of media monopolies, which have reduced the *variety* of media opinions made available for public consumption.

The Question of Forced Access

A major drive was undertaken in 1967 when Jerome A. Barron, law professor at George Washington University, wrote an article for the *Harvard Law Review* that supported forced access to the media for readers and viewers of media information. Barron argued that First Amendment guarantees of a press free of government control do not prohibit government from extending to concerned citizens their "right" to reply to the media. Barron claims that the people already have a legal right of reply implied in the First Amendment, and that it does not violate the rights of the media. It remains only for the government to recognize it and force media managers to implement it.

The Barron Theory

The subject of fairness in press coverage and editorializing on public issues has long been the source of debate in the print media.[39] But broadcasting has had a substantially different experience with it. In 1941, the United States Supreme Court ruled that broadcasters could not editorialize (i.e., take sides) in matters of interest to the public. They had to remain neutral and, hence, nobody had need to "answer back." Broadcasters kept trying, however, and in 1949, the FCC permitted them to editorialize *with fairness*. The latter two words are emphatic in the commission's ruling. Since, by act of Congress, the airwaves belong to the public, the public is served "if the airwaves are made accessible to many differing viewpoints." That meant that a station choosing to present one view of a public issue had to then go out "and look for at least one other side" to the issue and provide air time for that view so the public would be served. Thus, the Fairness Doctrine came into being. Though it fell far short of the goals of many public access advocates, it was a beginning.

Forced Access and Broadcasting Media

The Fairness Doctrine

The United States Supreme Court got into the debate again in 1967. In the Red Lion decision, it upheld the constitutionality of the FCC to regulate public access in broadcasting. It also ruled that in the case of a citizen subjected to "personal attack" over the air, either in an editorial or in regular programming, the station must notify the injured party of the attack, provide that person with a script containing the comments made, and offer without charge equal time for a response on the station's facilities. The same conditions apply if a station endorses a political candidate; it must offer station air time to other candidates. The court decision reads in part:

The Red Lion Decision

It is the right of the viewers and listeners, not the right of broadcasters, which is paramount. It is the purpose of the First Amendment to preserve an uninhibited marketplace of ideas in which truth will ultimately prevail, rather than to countenance monopolization of that market, whether it be by the Government itself or a private licensee. . . . It is the right of the public to receive suitable access to social, political, asthetic, moral, and other ideas and experiences which is crucial here.[40]

Thus, it appears that broadcasting has its editorial house in order, that is, in terms of its accessibility to the public *under certain conditions*. And though many broadcasters still resist the notion that they should be treated differently than newspapers on the access issue, the matter rests, if reluctantly, with the FCC blessed by the Supreme Court.

Forced Access and Print Media

Jerome Barron and other supporters of public access feel that the Supreme Court should also extend public access guarantees to the print media. In 1969, the Supreme Court ruled on that issue and laid low the hopes of Barron and other enthusiasts for forced public access to newspapers and magazines.

The Tornillo Decision

Way back in 1913, the state of Florida enacted legislation that made it a misdemeanor for any newspaper to attack the character or public record of a candidate for public office. If a newspaper were to do so, the law read, it must then provide that candidate with appropriate space in the paper, free of charge, to reply. If the newspaper refused, its management would be guilty of a crime under the 1913 law.

In 1972, Floridian Pat Tornillo became a candidate for the state legislature. The *Miami Herald* attacked him on two occasions. The paper charged that Tornillo had failed to file the names of contributors to his campaign as the law requires, that he had organized an illegal strike, and that the Classroom Teachers Association, of which he was president, was actually a powerful special-interest group unconcerned about the public welfare as claimed.

The Herald's Appeal

Under the 1913 law, Tornillo requested space for a reply and the *Herald* rejected the request. Tornillo then sued and the lower court threw the case out on the grounds that the 1913 law was unconstitutional. Jerome Barron, now Tornillo's attorney, then appealed to the Florida Supreme Court, which ruled against the *Herald*. The latter verdict was based on the position that public elections form the basis of democratic order, and that voters are entitled to have all pertinent facts if they are to vote in an informed manner. The *Miami Herald* then appealed to the United States Supreme Court. The newspaper based its case on the claim that the Florida law would "regulate the content of a newspaper in violation of the First Amendment." It also labeled the law "vague," since an editor could not know exactly what words would be in violation, and that the law "fails to distinguish between critical comment which is and is not defamatory."

Chief Justice Burger agreed that the public should have access to the news media, and that freedom is best served via public access to all media. But, he went on, the Florida law "exacts a penalty on the basis of the content of a newspaper." If forced to shape its content on the basis of outside influences, he continued, "editors might well conclude that the safe course is to avoid controversy and that, under the operation of the Florida law, political and electoral coverage would be blunted or reduced." The Court then overturned the verdict of the Florida Supreme Court as being in violation of the First Amendment. Broadcasting, because of its unique controls provisions with the FCC, was not included in the spirit of the Tornillo decision.

The Supreme Court Rules on Tornillo

Public Access Organizations

Public access issues resolved by the courts provide but one measure of interest on the part of some Americans to directly influence the content of their mass media. As presented earlier, various individuals and groups have stepped forward to challenge unacceptable (at least to them) media content such as political posturing, sex-oriented matter, portrayals of violence, keyhole peeping, fluff, and other content forms that they have found distasteful.

In recent years, certain organizations have come together explicitly to influence certain kinds of media content and in meaningful ways, all in the name of the public good. In short, if all Americans are not satisfied with the content of their media and don't know how to strike back, there exist organizations willing to do battle for them. Two major organizations so dedicated are Accuracy in Media, Inc. (AIM) and Action for Children's Television (ACT). There are others, but these two reflect the kinds of concerns formal access groups have and how they have attempted to force media's collective hand. They operate on the assumption that collective force wields considerably more power than individual action.

AIM and ACT

As its name indicates, Accuracy in Media, Inc., is dedicated to improving the *accuracy* of media content. It does this by carefully policing stories and filing formal complaints with news organizations and press councils when inaccuracies and distortions in the news are uncovered.

An actual case: Syndicated columnist Jack Anderson wrote about the International Police Academy, a training school for foreign police run by the United States Department of State. Anderson reported that academy instructors "have developed some chilling views about torture tactics." He indicated that his charges were based on papers prepared and written by five foreign students at the academy. AIM challenged the accuracy of the charges, claiming that the quotes relating to torture had been taken out of context and misrepresented the personal views of the students. AIM asked the National News Council (NNC) to investigate.

AIM vs. Jack Anderson

NNC examined the student papers and determined that Anderson had indeed misrepresented the facts. NNC also discovered that the student papers had been written almost ten years before, a crucial fact not mentioned in the Anderson account. The findings were published in the National News Council Report and the AIM publication.[41]

ACT vs. Children's Commercials

Action for Children's Television (ACT) was formed in 1968 by three women in Newtonville, Massachusetts, in an effort to halt the commercial exploitation of children on television shows geared especially for them.[42] Of particular objection to the three were the overt efforts by the stars of the children's shows to hard sell sponsors' products to the children. Advertising agencies had emphasized the importance of making their product pitches directly at the young viewers. One agency wrote:

> When you sell a woman on a product and she goes to the store and finds your brand isn't in stock, she'll probably forget about it. But when you sell a kid on your product, if he can't get it, he will throw himself on the floor, stamp his feet and cry. You can't get a reaction like that out of an adult.

Late in 1969, ACT petitioned the FCC to establish three rules governing children's television programming: ban commercials from programs geared for children; do not mention products by their brand names; provide fourteen hours of commercial-free children's programs per week as part of the station's public service program requirements.

The response nationally was gratifying as letters of support poured into FCC headquarters. Many newspapers and magazines also lent support. Some children's shows moved voluntarily to stop enticing children to buy their products. It was such a successful access campaign that ACT turned its sights away from commercials and went after other negative influences in the content of children's programs.

RTNDA Fights Back

Even with many notable successes by access groups, not everyone in the mass media is willing to simply knuckle under to their demands. John Salisbury, past president of the powerful Radio Television News Directors Association (RTNDA), warned members that they should begin defending themselves against groups like AIM, along with the "News Watch" section of *TV Guide*, which also evaluates broadcast content.

"Let us not give credence to their carpings by suffering in silence," Salisbury said. "Let us illuminate the ignorance of their accusations by igniting the torches of truth." Then he added: "I would not shut them up, but I would not shut us out from response through the power of our particular medium when the aims of one profession are distorted by the aims of their barbs."[43]

The idea of establishing special media councils to provide community input to local media managers has been around for many years. A product of Europe—Sweden and Great Britain particularly—the idea of a national news council for the United States was advanced in 1947 by the Hutchins Commission. At present about a dozen councils function in various American communities. Free of government ties, their memberships are comprised of public spirited citizens of many callings. Their function is to improve the media of communications in their home areas *in conjunction with* those media and to aid and abet the interests of both.

Typically, press councils meet monthly or several times each year to evaluate the performance of their local media and to advise local newspapers and broadcast outlets how their contents might relate more meaningfully and directly to the community.

The National News Council, mentioned earlier in this chapter, developed as a recommendation of the Hutchins Commission report.[44] The commission recognized the need for a national, nonpartisan body to compare "the accomplishments of the press with the aspirations . . . the people have for it" and to "educate the people as to the aspirations which they ought to have for the press." Though recommended in 1947, the NNC did not come into existence until 1973 with the assistance of the Twentieth Century Fund, which had become concerned about growing media credibility problems on a national scale. As the Hutchins Commission saw it, the council would be "an independent body to which the public can take its complaints about press coverage. It will act as a strong defender of press freedom. It will attempt to make the media accountable to the public and to lessen the tensions between the press and government."

The council's activities would be devoted primarily to the "principal national news magazines, national news syndicates, daily newspapers of nationwide circulation and broadcast networks both commercial and public." Eight of the eighteen members currently serving on the council are from the mass media.

Examples of how the National News Council functions have already been presented via its dealings with the Panax Corporation. As reflected in that heated case, the council has no power of enforcement; it may only make recommendations. For corrective measures to be applied, the NNC must depend on the clout of public opinion. Thus far it has received, as one evaluator wrote, "a heartening amount of cooperation from the media."

Press councils have also been developed to cope with media grievances and problems on more localized levels. California, Oregon, Colorado, and Illinois founded councils in the 1960s, though with only limited success to date. The strongest nonnational councils appear to be Minnesota's and the regional unit covering the New England states. Overall, the press council experience in the United States is still too new to determine its effectiveness, but a bridgehead for the future has been formed.

Summary   Although the National Association of Broadcasters supported controls on their industry in the wild infancy of radio, they do not want them now. It's time they looked to themselves, they say. And while newspapers a generation ago were characterized by green eyeshades and local ownership geared to friends and neighbors, they have steadily surrendered, whatever the reasons, to absentee chain or conglomerate owners far removed from the Village Green. The changes over the years have left many Americans alienated from their information machinery. This is especially so when they can't talk back or when content is bland or irrelevant. *Whatever happened to the good old days when competing papers slugged it out on public issues and the whole community was the better for it?* They're gone.

The process of news selection itself becomes an agent of "control" in that the media discard some news while offering other news. They activate in-house controls by determining what consumers read or view. A strident example is found in media coverage of the election process when "predictions" are advanced by the press on the basis of small samples of public support.

In-house controls over content are especially noticeable in broadcast journalism, which presents daily the smallest fraction of the total amount of information available. These controls are also applied by individual owners of media who project or discard information on the basis of their personal involvement in the news. Political figures who also own media are examples of this form of control. Or, as in the case of the "Doonesbury" strip, the content might be objectionable to media leadership, who then deprive readers of exposure to it. Big-media ownership also exercises forms of controls over content by establishing policies for all members, bearing on the kinds of information found objectionable, and all members are expected to follow orders. Frequently, the result is a reduction in the supply of multiple viewpoints on issues of public concern. The same applies to cross-channel ownership except that the FCC, supported by the courts, has outlawed future ownerships of this kind.

Copyright is yet another form of control in that it limits the availability of information put together by individuals who hope to earn profits from their labors. It is a form of censorship in that it might reduce the availability of certain communications vehicles if the owner refuses permission for further application by others.

Public access to the media is a particularly stormy aspect of media controls. The underlying question in this sphere is, If the Constitution guarantees the news media the right to speak out, does it not also, at least by implication, guarantee the public the right to speak back? The FCC makes allowances for limited public access to broadcasting media under certain, narrow circumstances, but the print media have no such requirement.

Press councils also attempt to influence media content by recommending policy changes and adjustments so that the public will be better served.

Some forms of controls on media content are reasonable and proper. Others are enough to raise hackles on a naked neck. In both cases, spokespersons are prepared to draw up sides and debate. These days it's likely to come out a draw . . . in which nobody really wins.

Notes

1. Information on the primaries from Max M. Kampelman, "The Power of the Press: A Problem of Our Democracy," *Policy Review,* Fall 1978, p. 10.
2. Michael J. Robinson, "TV's Newest Program: The 'Presidential Nominations Game'," *Public Opinion,* May/June 1978, p. 43.
3. Betty Utterback, "Mudd Assesses TV News," The *State Journal,* Lansing, Michigan, April 22, 1978, p. 10–B.
4. Information on Charles Thompson from Peter Behr, "CBS Pulls Producer Off Energy Story," *Washington Journalism Review,* April/May 1978, p. 16.
5. Tracy Freedman, "Strange Bedfellows: Congressmen Who Own Media," *Washington Journalism Review,* September/October 1978, p. 58.
6. "New York News Can't Take 'Doonesbury' Joke," *Detroit Free Press,* September 1, 1977, p. 16–D.
7. Information on the *Oregonian* and its competitors from "Deals: Doonesbury," *Columbia Journalism Review,* November/December 1977, p. 14.
8. Information on the Warner strips from " 'Doonesbury' Satire Censured," The *State Journal,* Lansing, Michigan, (Associated Press), January 11, 1979, p. 4–A.
9. Florence Graves, "Doonesbury Makes News: Tip Is Angry," *Washington Journalism Review,* September/October 1978, p. 19.
10. Information on the *Times, Post,* and *Chronicle* from Michael K. Knepler and Jonathan Peterson, "The Ombudsman's Uneasy Chair," *Columbia Journalism Review,* July/August 1978, p. 54.
11. Theo Lippman, "Why Ombudsmen Lie," *Washington Journalism Review,* January/February 1978, p. 28.
12. "A Closer Look at the Newspaper Ombudsman," The *Quill,* April 1978, p. 7.
13. Kampelman, "The Power of the Press," p. 10.
14. *Washington Post,* July 24, 1977, p. 1–G.
15. Kampelman, "The Power of the Press," p. 20.
16. *Washington Post,* May 9, 1978, p. 10–D.
17. John B. Oakes, "Dwindling Faith in the Press," *New York Times,* May 2, 1978, p. 23–A.
18. Donald McDonald, "The Media's Conflict of Interests," *Center Magazine,* November/December 1976, p. 17.
19. These and the following Bagdikian figures from Ben Bagdikian, "Newspaper Mergers—The Final Phase," *Columbia Journalism Review,* March/April 1977, pp. 18–19.
20. *Washington Post,* May 9, 1978, p. 8–D.
21. Kampelman, "The Power of the Press," p. 12.
22. *Associated Press* v. *United States,* 326 U.S., 1945, pp. 1 and 20.
23. Information on this case from "Statement on John P. McGoff and Panax Corporation Policy: National News Council Report," *Columbia Journalism Review,* September/October 1977, p. 83.

24. "An Open Letter" as printed in The *Quill,* October 1977, pp. 4–5.

25. "What Passes for News at Panax," *Columbia Journalism Review,* September/October 1977, p. 6.

26. Information on Gormley and his findings from William T. Gormley, Jr., "How Cross-Ownership Affects News Gathering," *Columbia Journalism Review,* May/June 1977, p. 38.

27. Information on the Syracuse case from Julius Litman, "Lesson from a Conglomerate," *Columbia Journalism Review,* January/February 1978, p. 16.

28. "Court Reverses Media Groups Breakup Ruling," *Detroit Free Press,* June 13, 1978, p. 7–A.

29. "National News Council Report: Council to Study Ownership Impact on Press," *Columbia Journalism Review,* September/October 1978, p. 87.

30. Toby J. McIntosh, "Whether Government Can't Stop Press Mergers," *Columbia Journalism Review,* May/June 1977, p. 48.

31. Edwin Diamond, "Managers, Monopoly and Money," *Washington Journalism Review,* April/May 1978, p. 36.

32. Irwin Arieff, "Profits or a Free Press: The Effects of Broadcast Regulation," *Washington Journalism Review,* October 1977, p. 40.

33. Information on the Federal Radio Act from Edwin Emery, *The Press and America* (Englewood Cliffs, N.J.: Prentice-Hall, 1972), 3d ed., p. 592.

34. Charles Paul Freud, "WOOK Gets Hook for Making Book," *Washington Journalism Review,* April/May 1978, p. 11.

35. Information on network coverage of sports from Tom Seppy, "House Hearings Show Televised Sports Are *More* Than Meets the Eye," *Washington Journalism Review,* January/February 1978, p. 8.

36. "FCC to Probe Junk Calls for Possible Curb," *Detroit Free Press,* March 16, 1968, p. 11–A.

37. Information on the "FCC Charge to Broadcasters" from "Correct Mistakes, TV and Radio Told," *Detroit Free Press,* April 13, 1978, p. 1–C.

38. Information on the copyright law from Don R. Pember, *Mass Media Law* (Dubuque, Iowa: Wm. C. Brown Company Publishers, 1977), pp. 210–21.

39. Information on "Forced Access and the Broadcasting Media" from Emery, *The Press and America,* p. 610.

40. This quote and the following information on "Forced Access and the Print Media" from *"Red Lion Broadcasting Co.* v. *Federal Communications Commission,"* in *Mass Media and the Supreme Court,* Kenneth S. Devol, ed. (New York: Hastings House, 1976), pp. 324–27, 339–44.

41. "National News Council Statement on Media Ethics," in *Readings in Mass Communication,* Michael C. Emery and Ted Curtis Smythe, eds, (Dubuque, Iowa: Wm. C. Brown Company Publishers, 1977), 3d ed., pp. 85–91.

42. Information on ACT from Douglas Cater and Stephen Strickland, *TV Violence and the Child* (New York: Russell Sage Foundation), pp. 13–15.

43. "Take on the Critics," The *Quill,* January 1977, p. 10.

44. Information on the NNC from *A Free and Responsive Press: The Twentieth Century Fund Task Force Report* for a NATIONAL NEWS COUNCIL (New York: The Twentieth Century Fund, 1973), pp. 3–9; Charlene J. Brown, Trevor R. Brown, and William L. Rivers, *The Media and the People* (New York: Holt, Rinehart and Winston, 1978), p. 202.

A Free and Responsive Press: The Twentieth Century Fund Task Force Report for a NATIONAL NEWS COUNCIL. New York: The Twentieth Century Fund, 1973.

"An Open Letter." The *Quill*, October 1977, pp. 4–5.

Arieff, Irwin. "Profits or a Free Press: The Effects of Broadcast Regulation." *Washington Journalism Review*, October 1977, p. 40.

Bagdikian, Ben. "Newspaper Mergers—The Final Phase." *Columbia Journalism Review*, March/April 1977, p. 18.

Behr, Peter. "CBS Pulls Producer Off Energy Story." *Washington Journalism Review*, April/May 1978, p. 16.

Cater, Douglas, and Strickland, Stephen. *TV Violence and the Child*. New York: Russell Sage Foundation.

"Deals: Doonesbury." *Columbia Journalism Review*, November/December 1977, p. 14.

Diamond, Edwin. "Managers, Monopoly and Money." *Washington Journalism Review*, April/May 1978, p. 36.

Freedman, Tracy. "Strange Bedfellows: Congressmen Who Own Media." *Washington Journalism Review*, September/October 1978, p. 58.

Gormley, William T., Jr. "How Cross-Ownership Affects News Gathering." *Columbia Journalism Review*, May/June 1977, p. 38.

Graves, Florence. "Doonesbury Makes News: Tip Is Angry." *Washington Journalism Review*, September/October 1978, p. 19.

Kampelman, Max M. "The Power of the Press: A Problem of Our Democracy." *Policy Review*, Fall 1978, pp. 7–39.

Knepler, Michael, and Peterson, Jonathan. "The Ombudsman's Uneasy Chair." *Columbia Journalism Review*, July/August 1978, p. 54.

Lippman, Theo. "Why Ombudsmen Lie." *Washington Journalism Review*, January/February 1978, p. 28.

Litman, Julius. "Lessons from a Conglomerate." *Columbia Journalism Review*, January/February 1978, p. 16.

McDonald, Donald. "The Media's Conflict of Interests." *Center Magazine*, November/December 1976, p. 17.

McIntosh, Toby J. "Whether Government Can't Stop Press Mergers." *Columbia Journalism Review*, May/June 1977, p. 48.

"National News Council Report: Council to Study Ownership Impact on Press." *Columbia Journalism Review*, September/October 1978, p. 87.

Robinson, Michael J. "TV's Newest Program: The 'Presidential Nominations Game.'" *Public Opinion*, May/June 1978, p. 43.

Seppy, Tom. "House Hearings Show Televised Sports Are *More* Than Meets the Eye." *Washington Journalism Review*, January/February 1978, p. 8.

"Statement on John P. McGoff and Panax Corporation Policy: National News Council Report." *Columbia Journalism Review*, September/October 1977, p. 83.

"Take On the Critics." The *Quill*, January 1977, p. 10.

"What Passes for News at Panax." *Columbia Journalism Review*, September/October 1977, p. 6.

For Further Reading

News in Pictures

Mass Media Ethics 11

Upon completing this chapter you should know—

how conflicts of interest affect the "image" of the mass media and the ethical performances of media people

specific cases involving "junkets" and "freebies"

why some "contests for journalists" raise ethical questions

the negative aspects of "checkbook" and "confrontation" journalism

the enforcement problems of internal codes of ethics

Chapter Objectives

Conflict of Interest In the sense of this chapter, it refers to favors or gifts extended to journalists by persons or groups hopeful of gaining favorable publicity. (p. 335) In a general sense, it means any behavior that tends to blemish the media's attempts to serve the public interest.

Junkets Expense-free trips for journalists sponsored by private persons or groups hopeful of gaining favorable publicity. (p. 346)

Credibility Believability.

Freebies Free tickets, gifts, meals, etc., from those who hope to obtain special favors from the press. (p. 349)

Contests for Journalists (a) Those sponsored by private organizations hopeful of gaining free favorable publicity vs. (b) those sponsored by journalism groups to honor outstanding journalists. (p. 351)

Checkbook Journalism A communications medium offering money to a person in the news to deal exclusively with that medium. (p. 353)

Confrontation Journalism Doing background research on a newsworthy person, inviting that person to be interviewed, and then hurling accusations at that person. (p. 355)

Key Terms

Be not intimidated . . . by any terror, from publishing with the utmost freedom, whatever may be warranted by the laws of your country; nor suffer yourselves to be wheedled out of your liberty by any pretences of politeness, delicacy, or decency.

John Adams to the editors of
the *Boston Gazette*, circa 1770.

The Role of Ethics in the Mass Media

Like it or not—and some do not—ethical considerations abound in mass media practice. On every level and in virtually every facet of the editorial enterprise, ethics come into direct play. It is difficult to imagine that thoughtful discussion could be had on any subject related to the mass media without ethics being included at least peripherally.

We have already seen this reflected in assorted conflict of interest questions: *Conflicts of Interest* reporters who write speeches for public officials, or editors or reporters who kill worthy stories under pressures from major advertisers. Such tactics create considerable tension and debate, to be sure. But other ethical issues have thus far been left untouched, and they generate even greater media discussion.

Regardless of their ethical posturing in the public eye, when journalists get together to talk shop, chances are excellent that they will raise some significant ethical questions for which they do not have answers, especially in terms of their own personal performances. "They'll concede that it's not as good as it should be. And they'll express concern," as one reporter spoke of it. But will they act? Are they willing to create change on the basis of ethical imperatives?

At recent regional meetings of the Society of Professional Journalists, Sigma **Ethical Behavior** Delta Chi, journalists addressed themselves to their own ethical interests, standards, and performances.[1] One group aired their concerns about the "recklessly aggressive" course being steered by the press since the Watergate days. Another tackled the current debate over the use of unnamed sources in stories "for which it hasn't assessed the consequences." In fact, Robert Clark, then executive editor of the *Louisville Courier-Journal*, raised salient questions over the large number of journalists who base stories on unnamed sources. He said that the practice contributed substantially to public distrust of the news media. "We should describe the sources and give the reasons why they will not be quoted. I want to know what they say is true and I want to know what my paper is printing is true."

CODE OF ETHICS OF THE SOCIETY OF PROFESSIONAL JOURNALISTS— Sigma Delta Chi

The Society of Professional Journalists, Sigma Delta Chi, believes the duty of journalists is to serve the truth.

We believe the agencies of mass communication are carriers of public discussion and information, acting on their Constitutional mandate and freedom to learn and report the facts.

We believe in public enlightenment as the forerunner of justice, and in our Constitutional role to seek the truth as part of the public right to know the truth.

We believe those responsibilities carry obligations that require journalists to perform with intelligence, objectivity, accuracy and fairness.

To these ends, we declare acceptance of the standards of practice here set forth:

Responsibility

The public's right to know of events of public importance and interest is the overriding mission of the mass media. The purpose of distributing news and enlightened opinion is to serve the general welfare. Journalists who use their professional status as representatives of the public for selfish or other unworthy motives violate a high trust.

Freedom of the press

Freedom of the press is to be guarded as an inalienable right of people in a free society. It carries with it the freedom and the responsibility to discuss, question, and challenge actions and utterances of our government and of our public and private institutions. Journalists uphold the right to speak unpopular opinions and the privilege to agree with the majority.

Ethics

Journalists must be free of obligation to any interest other than the public's right to know.
1. Gifts, favors, free travel, special treatment or privileges can compromise the integrity of journalists and their employers. Nothing of value should be accepted.
2. Secondary employment, political involvement, holding public office, and service in community organizations should be avoided if it compromises the integrity of journalists and their employers. Journalists and their employers should conduct their personal lives in a manner which protects them from conflict of interest, real or apparent. Their responsibilities to the public are paramount. That is the nature of their profession.
3. So-called news communications from private sources should not be published or broadcast without substantiation of their claims to news value.
4. Journalists will seek news that serves the public interest, despite the obstacles. They will make constant efforts to assure that the public's business is conducted in public and that public records are open to public inspection.
5. Journalists acknowledge the newsman's ethic of protecting confidential sources of information.

Accuracy and objectivity

Good faith with the public is the foundation of worthy journalism.
1. Truth is our ultimate goal.
2. Objectivity in reporting the news is another goal which serves as the mark of an experienced professional. It is a standard of performance toward which we strive. We honor those who achieve it.
3. There is no excuse for inaccuracies or lack of thoroughness.
4. Newspaper headlines should be fully warranted by the contents of the articles they accompany. Photographs and telecasts should give an accurate picture of an event and not highlight a minor incident out of context.
5. Sound practice makes clear distinction between news reports and expressions of opinion. News reports should be free of opinion or bias and represent all sides of an issue.
6. Partisanship in editorial comment which knowingly departs from the truth violates the spirit of American journalism.
7. Journalists recognize their responsibility for offering informed analysis, comment, and editorial opinion on public events and issues. They accept the obligation to present such material by individuals whose competence, experience, and judgment qualify them for it.
8. Special articles or presentations devoted to advocacy or the writer's own conclusions and interpretations should be labeled as such.

Fair play

Journalists at all times will show respect for the dignity, privacy, rights, and well-being of people encountered in the course of gathering and presenting the news.
1. The news media should not communicate unofficial charges affecting reputation or moral character without giving the accused a chance to reply.
2. The news media must guard against invading a person's right to privacy.
3. The media should not pander to morbid curiosity about the details of vice and crime.
4. It is the duty of news media to make prompt and complete correction of their errors.
5. Journalists should be accountable to the public for their reports and the public should be encouraged to voice its grievances against the media. Open dialogue with our readers, viewers, and listeners should be fostered.

Pledge

Journalists should actively censure and try to prevent violations of these standards, and they should encourage their observance by all newspeople. Adherence to this code of ethics is intended to preserve the bond of mutual trust and respect between American journalists and the American people.

The Associated Press Managing Editor's Association.

At one of the meetings, Barry Lando, of CBS's "60 Minutes," admitted that some of his show's personnel committed both misdemeanors and felonies in developing a particular story. One of his reporters used the name of a deceased person to obtain a social security card, establish credit, and open a checking account for a television segment on developing false identification. In another case, Lando continued, he didn't have the answer to the ethical question of whether having a reporter purchase a pornographic film (to get the goods on the seller) constituted entrapment. Yet entrapment, the act of enticing someone to commit an illegal act that is self-incriminating, is a criminal offense. He also questioned the ethics of a reporter lying just to get a story or not informing persons being interviewed about the nature of the interview or how it would be used. Lando noted that the news media go after the government for spying on citizens but are equally as quick to use bugs, spies, and invasion of privacy for the "higher good" of exposing misconduct or illegal activities. He said that blame for the confusion that frequently exists between press ethics and press performance is due to a lack of working guidelines for the media and the unique circumstances that journalists encounter in their day-to-day activities. He also admitted that a meaningful code of ethics to deal with such issues would be difficult to devise.

Professor John C. Merrill, of the University of Missouri School of Journalism, appears to agree. He termed the Society of Professional Journalists' code of professional performance as "vague and fuzzy." Rather, he said, a code of ethics for professional journalists is a personal entity. "The journalist himself should be an enforcer of his own ethics and the journalist's employer could also enforce the ethical standards which he might consider important."

Clark R. Mollenhoff, Pulitzer Prize winning former Washington Bureau Chief for the *Des Moines Register*, syndicated columnist, and presently professor of journalism and law at Washington and Lee University, offered seven basic rules for journalists, observation of which would insure fair and ethical performances by journalists:

Rule One: Avoid political partisanship.

You will cut off 50 percent of your effectiveness if you investigate only one political party, or even have a special leaning toward investigations of one political party. It will hurt your credibility. There are as many Republican crooks as there are Democratic crooks. And, if you haven't noticed it, there are a large number of bipartisan crooks who have figured how to get a hand in the government treasury regardless of whether Democrats or Republicans are in power.

Rule Two: In seeking facts and answers make a conscientious and determined effort to be equally aggressive whether the public officials involved are men you admire or distrust.

You will do your friend a favor by asking him tough direct questions, because you will be demonstrating that he will be held accountable. It will prod him to be a better public official than he might be if you are too indulgent in excusing him or disregard his errors.

And, it is wise to give those you dislike or distrust the benefit of the doubt as you embark on your investigation. This is your protection against jumping to an unwarranted conclusion that can undermine the soundness of your whole investigation.

Remind yourself constantly that if the case against the public official is really there, it will emerge eventually and his deceptions and falsehoods will weigh doubly against him. This is as true in an investigation of a mayor, a county commissioner, a sheriff, a governor or a congressman as it was in the case of Richard Nixon who told various falsehoods about Watergate.

Leaning overboard to be fair is never harmful to your investigative efforts. It protects you against libel. It makes you more credible.

Above all, common decency and fair play are as basic as due process of law. This is particularly important in those areas of the country, or in those localities, where there is only one newspaper or where there are two or more newspapers under one control.

Rule Three: Know your subject whether it is a problem of city, county, state or federal government, or whether it involves big labor or big business.

In preparing for an important interview do your homework on the facts, the laws, and the individuals involved in your study. (This does not mean that you know only enough to parrot a few wise questions fed by a politically partisan opponent. Nor is it enough to simply read the clipping file, and jot off a quick note or two that may or may not be in context.)

If the subject is important enough for you to seek a serious interview, it is important enough to consult the law, to study the history of the agency, and to have a reasonably full grasp of the background and general motivations of the persons involved.

The rule of knowing your subject cannot be overemphasized. If you are in a highly technical area or are dealing with a complicated fact situation, you may make unintentional mistakes simply because you did not understand what you heard. It is also possible that you will not recognize violations of the law. The poorly informed or half-informed reporter is a sitting duck for a snow job.

Rule Four: Don't exaggerate or distort the facts or the law.

There is enough wrong in our society that you don't have to fabricate or exaggerate anything. This is particularly true of the operations of any of the agencies of the federal government.

If you do a proper job of investigating and follow-through on virtually any federal agency or department, the truth will be more shocking than any fiction you might dream up. Watergate and the investigations that followed dealing with the CIA and the FBI should have driven this point home so it will not be forgotten.

Remember, efforts to sensationalize will discredit your investigation in the long run.

When in doubt, leave it out.

Rule Five: Deal straight across the board with your sources and investigation subjects alike.

Ask straightforward questions that go to the heart of the problem, and do it in a serious manner. Don't use tricks or pretense to get people off guard. Don't use a false name or identity, and particularly do not impersonate a law enforcement official.

If you give someone your word on a confidence, keep your word even if it means personal jeopardy. Above all, don't go around blabbing to your press colleagues the identity of a confidential informant.

If you deal straight with the subjects of your investigation, it is quite likely that they will be your best sources of inside information at some future time if they learn to respect and trust you.

Rule Six: Do not violate the law unless you are prepared to take the consequences.

Any time you violate the law to obtain information you develop a vulnerability that can destroy your credibility as well as the story you are pursuing. It gives the errant public officials an opportunity to get the spotlight off of their corruption and mismanagement, and to focus on the excesses of the press.

If you give the problem sufficient study, there is usually a legal way to obtain information, although it may require more patience than a burglary. Learn how to use the Freedom of Information Act. Know government records. Know information policies and procedures—information is your business.

If you do not know basic information tools you are as lacking in competence as a doctor who does not know basic anatomy or a lawyer who does not understand basic rules of evidence.

Rule Seven: Use direct evidence when writing a story that reflects adversely upon anyone, and give that person an opportunity for a full response to the questions raised.

Direct testimony is often unreliable even when the witness has no personal interest, and chances for error increase geometrically as your source is removed one, two or three steps from the event.

Do not use hearsay, double hearsay or triple hearsay evidence to reflect adversely upon anyone just because some reporters have used such evidence and got by with it. Woodward and Bernstein got by with double and triple hearsay in ''The Final Days'' only because Richard Nixon, as a thoroughly discredited former president, was libel proof.

While the interviewing of second and third hearsay witnesses may be the best or even only avenue open us to what took place, it does not constitute proof of the events or even admissible evidence.

It is not sound investigative journalism to go into print with such information, and this is particularly true when it comes from sources you cannot disclose. No story is worth that risk to your credibility and to your reputation.

If you follow these seven rules you will have been accurate and you will have been fair, and you will not be vulnerable to the inevitable counter attacks.

Nothing I have said here is intended to discourage anyone from aggressive pursuit of the truth that will establish responsibility for corruption and mismanagement. It is simply a warning to test all of the facts and the law, and then proceed with a firm aggressiveness.

The Ethical Dilemma in Practice

The rights and wrongs of ethical journalistic practice provide a cast of many shades. Social "sins" are clearly defined, classified, and categorized, and we have law enforcement agents, courts, and jails to remind potential transgressors that they act at their peril. But one's ethical "sense" is comprised of many human characteristics and ingredients; one's ethical apple is another's worm. That's why the subject of media ethics is so widely and sometimes vehemently debated. Our sense of ethics is based on the many elements that have formed us as persons. We do not always agree as persons; neither do we, as journalists, always agree on what constitutes a high standard or fair play.

Media Ethics as Personal Behavior

Mike Albertson is investigative editor for the *Pensacola Times* in Florida. He characterizes those of his calling in this manner: "We are fact-finders and purveyors of accurate information, watchdogs, checks and balances—and, if the facts warrant it, attack dogs. In most cases, the ends justify our means."[2] He says that stories of FBI and CIA snooping against private citizens have resulted in legislation designed to protect the privacy of American citizens. The problem with that, he says, is that the recent Federal Privacy Act has increased personal privacy for Americans to the point where it interferes with the flow of information that the public at large must have. If a police officer commits wrongdoing and is permitted to resign rather than have his story made public, evidence of his wrongdoing may not be given to another police agency. "Is the Privacy Act unwittingly structured to protect the guilty?"

Albertson also tells of a reporter-colleague who posed as a "nonjournalist" to uncover a phony perfume scheme in Florida. The perpetrator of the scheme called foul play. "That's not fair! You didn't tell me you worked for a newspaper!" Albertson agrees that the method used might have been unethical. But it might have prevented many others from being victimized. "If the ethics of gathering facts are subjected to strict standards of 'fair play', the public will frequently be the loser."

*Ends Do Not
Justify the Means*

Challenging that position is Walter Anderson, former editor and general manager of the *White Plains* (N.Y.) *Report-Dispatch* and now with *Parade* magazine:

> A reporter who pleads that his violation should be overlooked because he was acting for the public good to obtain information is a hypocrite at the pulpit, a living deceit.
>   If the President of the United States is not above generally accepted standards of conduct, by what right do journalists believe they are?
>   None they can justify.[3]

Anderson makes the point that if one breaks the rules to go after an important story, one must take what comes if he or she gets caught. The reporter cannot claim special privileges not accorded other citizens.

He admits that he has violated ethical standards as a reporter and probably will again in order to get the full story. To get to the heart of a meaningful story, he has posed at various times as "gamblers, junkies, johns, pimps and once a minister."

By subterfuge, Anderson uncovered a drug scandal involving police inefficiency and cover-ups related to sales of heroin. His actions brought about the first exposure of the methadone black market. To do this, Anderson "bought quantities of heroin, methadone and other drugs which is breaking the law. Had I been caught and prosecuted it would have been worse than embarrassing." More than fifty heroin pushers were arrested as a result of Anderson's published revelations. Does all that success justify his violating the law? Anderson says it does not.

Ethical problems come in varied sizes and degrees of severity, and many of them directly involve media managers as decision makers.[4] Some newspapers, small dailies with limited staffs particularly, fall headlong into the tired old "canned-editorial" trap by running what appear to be the paper's own editorials and other editorial page matter which, in subtle fashion, advance private causes and interests without informing their readers of the sources. One case presented what seemed to be a series of humorous editorial cartoons. In fact they were carefully couched messages composed by the Mobil Oil Corporation. The cartoons reflected current oil-interest topics such as getting rid of government controls on the oil industry. No source was evident.

In another case, the *New Orleans Times-Picayune* ran an advertisement in *Editor & Publisher* to fill an editorial position on the business-financial desk. Qualifications listed included: experience, good spelling, and a "pro-business philosophy," which suggests little by way of needed balanced coverage.

In still another incident, the *Tampa Tribune* ran a special box on page one announcing a new department of the paper exclusively for the city's large Latino community—"Columna Latina do Tampa"—located on page six. On turning to page six, readers found seven columns of paid advertising in Spanish—no editorial content at all.

Several years ago, ABC-TV took its lumps for using poor judgment in broadcasting an otherwise worthy documentary. The theme of the telecast was malnutrition among children. The sponsor of the show was a manufacturer of baby food products. Conflict of interest?

On the other hand, the news media frequently perform with an admirable degree of ethical responsibility. To its credit, "60 Minutes," the CBS blockbuster, recently televised a detailed exposure of the dry cereal and hair dye industries even though General Foods and Clairol are two major CBS sponsors.

The *Philadelphia Inquirer* switched nightlife and entertainment columnist Bill Curry to other duties after his announcement that he had joined one of his news sources as co-owner of a restaurant-bar business. The paper announced the move in a special story designed to allay public fears of conflict of interest.

Fried chicken king John Y. Brown, owner of the Buffalo Braves professional basketball team, said he would transfer the team to Louisville provided the city's two dailies, the *Times* and the *Courier-Journal*, promised continued support of the team. In spite of wide public acclaim for the switch, Barry Bingham, publisher, publicly rejected the proposal. He could not "guarantee" anything of the sort.

In another incident, the drama critic for NBC's "Today" show commented on his network's made-for-TV special titled, "Charleston" to be aired that evening. The critic gave the show a totally negative review and even urged viewers to watch CBS instead.

Correcting Errors

The human element is omnipresent in the communications media. The human element is also error prone and, in the minds of those who devise quaint sayings, it can be said that an error left uncorrected is an error with a permanent future. Errors left uncorrected also maul media credibility in the public marketplace. The matter of *correcting* errors, then, is of major ethical import to both the media and the people.

Survey on
Correcting Mistakes

The Associated Press Managing Editors Association (APME) sent questionnaires to 104 newspapers asking how they handle errors in news copy.[5] Sixty completed and returned their forms and all said that they "always correct their mistakes." Some editors winced at that. But there appears to be general agreement that American newspapers are becoming increasingly dedicated to not only correcting their errors in fact but to the wisdom of letting the public know that they sometimes make mistakes and want to correct them. Some even urge readers to assist in identifying errors.

Managing editor Joseph Shoquist of the *Milwaukee Journal* says that there has been a "refreshing improvement" in this sector in recent years. "Newspapers historically tended to overlook corrections," he said. "They wouldn't run them unless demanded." Some editors even "had a habit of sneaking in the back door" rather than face reader wrath over inaccuracies.

Illustration by Marcus Hamilton, The *Quill*, published by the Society of Professional Journalists, Sigma Delta Chi.

Paul Poorman, editor of the *Akron Beacon Journal*, agrees. "In the past, newspapers tended to react badly to a suggestion that there had been a mistake." They even made "a big investment in time and effort proving the complainer wrong."

A sampling of how editors react to the question of correcting their editorial mistakes follows. "As quickly as possible," replied Lou Schwartz, managing editor of *Long Island Newsday*. Thomas Jobson, managing editor of the *Asbury Park Press* in New Jersey, responded, "Ungrudgingly." Jerry McElfresh, managing editor of the *Scottsdale* (Ariz.) *Daily Progress*, commented: "We do not go into lengthy apologies or try to go the cute type-gremlins route. And when possible, we try to develop the correction into a story, with quotes from the injured party." Twenty-one APME members reported that they have regular columns to announce corrections, which usually appear in the same place each time for rapid reader identification. Five others indicated that they run corrections on their front pages.

The International Newspaper Promotion Association reported that each of the 77 percent of newspapers in the 100,000-and-up circulation range assign a special place in the paper for editorial corrections. The practice began about ten years ago when the *Louisville Courier-Journal* and *Times* established regular "departments" headed "Beg Your Pardon" and "We Were Wrong." The *New York Times* and the *Wall Street Journal* soon followed suit.

The Fort Meyers (Fla.) *Press-News* runs an established evaluation column called "Check It Out."[6] Its purpose is to evaluate advertising claims. In the course of checking over ad credibility in the paper, writer John Doussard found "an embarrassing discrepancy" in the paper's own promotional advertising. The cost per day delivery price was stated to be fourteen cents when it was actually nineteen cents. The advertisements were corrected and the public informed of the error.

Richard and Polly Keusink, publishers and editors of The *Brookings Harbor Pilot* in Oregon, ran a story exposing the "ripoffs" contained in some of the "business opportunities" ads in their own classified section.

Other strategies devised to cope with error problems include "accuracy questionnaires" that solicit critical evaluations of stories from people in the news and daily "alerts" to readers to inform editors of any errors they spot.

Accuracy Questionnaires

Some Statistical Results

As to the effects of these measures on news-editorial *credibility*, a survey done by the Roper organization showed that 22 percent of the sample taken revealed that newspapers were their most believable source of news, an increase from 20 percent two years before. Television credibility remained at 51 percent.

The Lower case

Sen. Weicker With New Bribe, Camille DiLorenzo Butler
Ann Arbor News 11/7/77

2 Men Accused of Pecans Theft; Sex Charge Filed
(Montgomery) Alabama Journal 11/8/77

Albany Turns To Garbage
(New York) Daily News 10/3/77

Indian Ocean talks
The Plain Dealer 10/5/77

Electrocution Victim Making Comeback Against Long Odds
Kansas City Times 10/15/77

Lie Detector Tests Unreliable, Unconstitutional Hearing Told
The Hartford Courant 11/16/77

Opening ceremonies will be held at noon Tuesday and the dignitaries instead of cutting a ribbon, will cut in half a 10 inch loaf of bread supplied by the Kautman Banking Co. The bread will be given to a home for the needy.
Upstate (N.Y.) Business Journal 10/4/77

Missionary risked dysentery and bigamy in eight day trip to Nigerian villages
The (Gainesville) Times 10/14/77

Time for Football And Meatball Stew
Detroit Free Press 10/19/77

AN ITALIAN SINNER will be served at 5:30 p.m. at the Essex Center United Methodist Church.
Vermonter 10/16/77

Do-it-yourself pregnancy kit to go on sale
The Detroit News 11/17/77

Marion freed after 81-day ordeal
Ottawa Journal 10/28/77

82-day ordeal over
The (Ottawa) Citizen 10/28/77

After 83 days, Marion safe
Ottawa Today 10/28/77

Wives Kill Most Spouses In Chicago
Florida Times-Union 9/8/77

Pancakes to sell for grave flags
University Herald (Seattle) 10/26/77

Montage of editorial goofs. (Reprinted from *Columbia Journalism Review* and excerpts from *Squad Helps Dog Bite Victim* by The Trustees of Columbia University. Copyright © 1965, 1966, 1967, 1968, 1970, 1971, 1972, 1973, 1974, 1975, 1976, 1977, 1978,

The Lower case

Bible Quartet Sings
Saturday Herald and Leader (Lexington, Ky.) 1/28/78

Larry Flynt shot

'Can't wait any longer,' Carter says; Page 3
Chicago Sun-Times 3/7/78

A 14-year-old Ottawa girl told Ottawa police early this morning that while she babysat at a home on Jefferson Street a man tapped on a window then exposed himself to her, city police said today. Police were able to get a partial discription of the man, officers said.
The Daily Times (Ottawa, Ill.) 12/22/78

JOHNNY CASH and his wife, June Carter, one of country music's favorite couples
Fort Myers News-Press 2/19/78

New Missouri U. Chancellor Expects Little Sex
St. Louis Post-Dispatch 2/26/78

He Found God At End of His Rope
Fort Worth Tribune 2/3/78

Shoot kids to halt flu, study says
Orlando Sentinel Star 3/16/78

Police union to seek blinding arbitration
The News (Groton, Conn.) 2/2/78

Solar system expected to be back in operation
Libertyville (Ill.) Herald 3/15/78

About 14 inchs text Pick up standing head
The Seattle Times 3/19/78

Woman Dies in Wreck; Power Cut in Neck Area
The Richmond News Leader 3/13/78

Carcinogens Cause Cancer Says Book
Contra Costa (Calif.) Independent 2/22/78

FOR THE SECOND TIME IN 13 MONTHS, A MAN WHO HAS BEEN SUPPLYING AUTHORITIES WITH INFORMATION ON CIGARETTE SMUGGLING IN PENNSYLVANIA HAS BEEN SLAIN.
Associated Press 3/22/78

Slum-Raising Plan Assailed
The New York Times 2/9/78

ENFIELD — Freshwater Pond Associates could begin construction within 45 days of the 75 housing units planned for the Pond urban renewal area.

Associates' lawyer, Anthony DiFabio Thursday told the Housing Authority that, if local approval is given, "the hovels can go in the ground."
The Daily News (Windsor Locks, Conn.) 3/17/78

One photograph shot at a Capitol social gathering cropped three different ways in three separate editions of the *Washington Star*. In fact, Senator Kennedy was accompanied by Monsignor Francis Lally, a longtime Boston friend. (Walter Oates, The *Washington Star*.)

Although impressive beginnings have been made in correcting errors in the print media, much remains to be done to close the gap between error and accuracy. It is interesting to note the 51 percent believability rate for television news. Whether it is broadcasting policy or not, television news anchorpersons usually correct their errors right on the air, almost as soon as they make them. With a less-than-soaring 22 percent believability rating, newspapers might heed the practices of their electronic cousins.[7]

Junkets and Freebies

Temptations for Journalists

Media food writers and editors are especially vulnerable to the enticements of private enterprise. They are frequently swamped with invitations to take part in a variety of "junkets," such as witnessing baking contests sponsored by producers of flour and other baking products. At other times the invitations are to chicken-baking competitions supported by poultry producers and other allied interests. In return for their presence, the writers are provided with free travel, hotel accommodations, and entertainment. "The hope—often realized—of the public relations people who plan such events is that the writers will return to their media and write or say favorable things about cakes or chickens,"[8] or whatever the sponsor happens to be pushing. And a major ethical problem begins.

Mass Media Ethics

It has been argued by insiders that food, fashion, and travel pages in newspapers would not exist were it not for the advertising offered by private food, fashion, and travel industries. These interests make available, free of charge, news and feature materials on tempting recipes, how to set an attractive table, proper wardrobe matchings for the "Gal-on-the-Go," and where to find fun vacation spots, all at the right price. If the industries are willing to pour all that into the press, why is it so horrendous for editors and writers in these specialties to accept paid trips to observe new developments firsthand? The best answer to the question is an actual case in point. Again, not everybody involved applied the same ethical references.

The Debate Joined

The ITT Case

International Telephone and Telegraph (ITT) built a Florida land development called Palm Coast. It includes beaches, condominiums, recreation areas, and docks for boats. For the grand opening, ITT invited more than sixty newspaper editors and writers from around the country to look the place over—all expenses paid.[9] The visiting journalists were feted to exquisite food, posh living facilities, and entertainment of a high order. What the developers had in mind was that the editors and writers would be so overwhelmed at what they witnessed that they would go home and promote the resort to their readers as the ideal place to go.

One Side of the Coin

The editor of a Dearborn, Michigan, newspaper was one who accepted the plum, and she later enthused about her experiences: "We accepted it. We got there. We had a marvelous time, I was a dinner companion of Richard Boone, which was quite exciting. The whole thing was beautiful."

She then justified her participation:

> Isn't it my duty as editor of a newspaper to let the people who read my newspaper know whether Palm Coast is in fact a good community for them to buy property in? And when there's no money—because a small newspaper does not have enough money to send their editor off to Timbuktu, to Florida in this case—to find out whether Palm Coast is everything they advertise it to be—then the company itself takes a calculated risk in inviting an editor of a weekly newspaper to make that trip to see the product for himself—herself in this case.

The Flip Side

A travel reporter for the *St. Petersburg Times* also went on the Palm Coast junket but her expenses were paid by her newspaper. When the party was over, she went home and wrote about the hazards of junketing. She later commented on her observations:

> This relaxed atmosphere was, of course, abetted by Bloody Marys, which seemed to appear in everybody's hands just automatically. We were having a free lunch, a free weekend, and we were expected to sing for our suppers. . . .
> You could not possibly do the job that needed to be done in that length of time—especially when you had to do so much partying. . . .

One thing that is most interesting that happens as a result of this publicity is that . . . these news stories that emanate from these junkets . . . become public relations vehicles. They become part of sales packets. . . . This kind of thing definitely occurs, and it's, of course, the kind of advertising that is far better than a paid advertisement and is worth probably hundreds of thousands of dollars.

Another participant in that junket observed:

I think the press owes a greater obligation to do a little digging, than to merely appear at a piece of property—sponsored by the owner, who is selling nation-wide—and accepting at face value what is said. I don't know how many of those journalists contacted state agencies. I don't know how many of those journalists contacted people that were living in the area. But their coverage was obviously—if not biased—inaccurate.

Seminar on National Issues

In another freebie extravaganza, thirty-four editors, editorial writers, and other opinion-influencing journalists and their spouses went to a National Issues Seminar in Washington, D.C., all expenses paid. They represented the *New York Daily News*, the *Florida Times Union*, the *Cincinnati Enquirer*, the *Chicago Tribune*, the *New Orleans Times-Picayune*, and the *Omaha World-Herald*. The gala fete was held at L'Enfant Plaza Hotel and was sponsored by the United States Industrial Educational Foundation. The latter is a business-action group whose avowed purpose is "to express the voice of free enterprise from the conservative viewpoint."[10]

Wooing Television Critics

Other news personnel especially susceptible to the lures of freebies and junkets are television writers and critics serving newspapers and magazines. Previewing the upcoming offerings of a new television season is big news to the public. More significantly, it's also a matter of *survival* for television network executives. Hence, network brass invite critics and writers from around the nation to gather in New York, Hollywood, or other attractive places to preview the new programs, to meet the stars, and to relax and play in lavish surroundings with the best in food, drink, and lodging—all expenses paid. The obvious expectation, or at least desire, of the network people is that the journalists will be so taken by the lures of the junket and freebies that they will go home and write enthusiastically about every program and person they have seen. Certainly many writers can and do expose themselves to such temptations without mauling their integrity or tainting their honor. But the *possibility* of them becoming conduits of propaganda between private interests and the reading public is sufficient cause for concern.

In yet another department of the news media, sports writers are routinely given free tickets to athletic events that they cover.[11] Innocent, perhaps, yet the New York Yankees baseball team had a standing practice of presenting the *New York Times* with sixty-five tickets to each home game. Admittedly, one reporter can easily cover one Yankee baseball game, even if the paper wanted to send two or even three. But, one might fairly ask, what was the *Times* supposed to do with sixty-five tickets to a single game? Basketball's New York Knicks sent the *Times* forty-five tickets to each home game. Presumably other New York papers, magazines, and broadcast outlets also received free tickets. The question remains—how many reporters can fit into one press box on a single occasion? Some suggest that the practice was intended to charge up *all* journalists, even nonsports writers, to write favorably about local teams, even if circumstances did not always warrant it. In actual practice, most of the freebie tickets went to family members or friends, local or out of town. The matter became so ludicrous that the *Times* recognized the ethical implications and called a halt. The paper announced that free tickets would be given only to those who actually cover the games.

EDITOR ATTITUDES TOWARD CONFLICTS OF INTEREST

The Associated Press Managing Editors association conducted a survey in 1974 to determine how editors feel about certain kinds of conflicts of interest. A total of 214 editors responded to the 50-question survey. APME found that:

- 59 percent do not accept free airplane tickets from an industry or business to a news event of some significance.
- 47 percent rule out gifts.
- 85 percent of the newspapers never accept ads with a promise that a staffer will write a story in return.
- 89 percent of the respondents said nonadvertisers get the same treatment in the news columns as advertisers.

- 53 percent said their sports editors or other news staffers will not accept a season ticket outside the press box.
- 56 percent of the editors will not permit sports editors or sports writers to write for a pro ball club in the area.
- 46 percent said they do not accept free transportation on road trips for sports writers.
- 42 percent said they allow staffers to moonlight for non-competitors only.
- 76 percent said they do not place restrictions on outside financial interests, such as stock ownership or proprietory interest in financial venture.
- 13 percent of the editors said they have a stated policy on the handling of corrections.

The Associated Press Managing Editors Association.

Official Scorers

Sports writers have also traditionally worked as "official scorers" for home baseball games. They are paid by the home team to so serve. Might that practice tend to influence what such a reporter might write or say about that team, especially if his thoughts are uncomplimentary?

The Matter of Press Passes

In Long Island, New York, a local prosecutor began looking into the practice of individuals using press credentials to gain admittance to places and events. These persons were not employed by the news media, nor were they pretending to be. They had simply been given press passes by journalist friends, which gave them free admission to town beaches, swimming pools, and parks. That led the *Columbia Journalism Review* to comment that old practices die slowly, "that anybody who claims to be a member of the press is entitled to get for nothing what ordinary citizens have to pay for. It puts one in mind of the attitude Bernard Shaw was satirizing when he said, as he passed a beggar outside a theater, 'Press.' "[12]

Serving Proper Ends

As John Hulteng comments, freebies and junkets, whether involving a few baseball tickets or a lavish trip to Rome, represent "an effort to subvert the newsgathering and disseminating media and shape the news to serve the ends of various special interests."[13]

Those opposed to junkets argue that wire and feature services, and state and local governments, happily provide materials on resorts and vacation spots free of charge. Many resorts have promotional staffs of their own with detailed literature available for the asking. All that makes it unnecessary for small-budget publications to give in to the "junket" interests. Secondly, as the argument goes, small newspapers that cannot afford to pay their staffs to attend junkets are typically local in character anyway. They should dedicate their energies to gathering local news and events, not to distant vacation paradises. Nonlocal news should be left to the media service organizations mentioned earlier. Finally, practice tends to show that when journalists accept junkets and freebies, they invariably end up writing favorably about the sponsors' products or services. To many in and out of the news media, that is reason enough to protect one's professional purity. Such developments caused Charles Long, editor of the *Quill*, to muse:

> There's nothing new about the freebie game. It's being played all the time and shows up in hundreds of different places and with varying sets of rules. Freebies— meaning token as well as expensive gifts, tickets to events large and small, junkets to simple and exotic places—have been floating in and about newsroom operations for as long as there has been a way of saying thanks for good publicity.

Contests for Journalists

What might be termed a first cousin to the junket and freebie is the media "contest" in which private interests offer cash and other awards to lure professional journalists to publicize products and services in their newspapers and magazines. Professional media organizations also sponsor competitions for writers that extend all the way from the local press club's award for excellence to the Pulitzer Prize itself. But these are *professional* competitions, judged by professionals, and geared to singling out and rewarding outstanding achievement in the various fields of journalism. Some are for specialists in medical writing, or science, or environmental journalism; others are for investigative reporting and so forth. All are a far cry from the contests sponsored by vested interest groups.

Serving Private Interests

Professional Media Contests

According to *Editor & Publisher*, close to 300 contests for professional journalists are currently offered by business-oriented organizations on national, state, and local levels.[14] Prizes for winning entries go up to several thousand dollars each. In some cases they include expense-paid trips to national conventions. The purpose of these contests is to get the name or product of the sponsor into the mass media via the journalists who compete in the contests. Some sponsors include the National Association of Realtors, the National Bowling Council, the National Helicopter Association of America, and so on. Some are legitimate competitions judged by impartial, or at least nonindustrial, persons. Others are patently self-serving in the interest of advancing the name of a firm or industry and its products. The American Prune Growers Association has an annual contest for the best published stories in newspapers and magazines dealing with prunes. The American Cigar Association, in its fliers to newspapers, coaxes press photographers to "put a cigar in your pictures and you might win $4,000." This is a national contest run each year.

Private Interest Contests

Gary LaBelle is public relations director for the Recreational Vehicle Industry Association. His organization offers journalists three prizes of $1,000 each plus expense-paid trips to the annual National Recreation Vehicle Show in Louisville, Kentucky. This is innocent enough on the surface, but the contest is designed for the avowed purpose of promoting the industry and its products and services in the mass media. LaBelle says that his organization "wouldn't want anyone to lose their objectivity." But he frankly admits (as others deny) that "we hope when people are writing a story about R.V.'s and know about our award that they will go out of their way to do an especially nice story."

A Statement of Purpose

Reprinted by permission of the Chicago Tribune-New York News Syndicate, Inc.

Analyzing Media Contests

The University of Wisconsin's School of Journalism and Mass Communication undertook a study of media contests in general at the request of the Associated Press Managing Editors (APME) Professional Standards Committee.[15] In capsule form, the survey determined that—

1. generally, such contests are held in esteem by newspapers, most of which submit entries and eventually win something;
2. the principal virtue of the contests for individual journalists and newspapers is personal recognition;
3. the negative aspects include the taint of being sponsored by nonmedia groups and individuals and questionable quality of judging entries;
4. although the majority of newspapers have established policies dealing with conflicts of interest generally, there is little regulation of participation in contests;
5. two-thirds of the editors who responded to the survey indicated that they favor the development of ethical guidelines relating to contests.

Some editors added personal comments to the questionnaire. John W. Eure, managing editor on the *Roanoke* (Va.) *World-News*, wrote:

The value, indeed acceptability, of contests varies widely; the chief factor is the sponsorship. We look askance at those sponsored by a commercial firm or trade association and having to do with a product or service of the firm or association, though we do not ban participation outright. We look with more favor on the contests sponsored by professional organizations—the bar or medical societies, though the distinction is by no means clear and easily defended.

As other responding editors did, Eure distinguished sharply between those contests sponsored by strictly business or industrial interests and those sponsored by newspaper societies or other organizations in which the profession itself rewards the work of participants. Winners in the latter category help recruit competent new people to newspapers. They also impress readers of those newspapers that enter and win.

As we saw in the section on junkets and freebies, many journalism contests sponsored by strictly private corporate interests are not offered for the purpose of improving the journalistic product which, in turn, would enhance the information flow to the American people as the First Amendment requires. Unlike the professional competitions that *are* geared to encouraging professional improvement, these are devised to maintain or increase corporate profits. They seek to do so by involving writers, supposedly dedicated to a higher purpose, in promoting strictly private interests. The means of promoting the goods and services of the business community already exist via an especially powerful and readily accessible medium—commercial advertising. It would seem that it hardly needs media contests to supplement all that that vehicle offers.

Not in the Public Interest

Checkbooks and Confrontations

It is in the tradition of the First Amendment for the public to benefit from total media efforts so that, in the end, truth will surface and the people will be the better for it. As with other forms of private enterprise in the United States, this system has worked most effectively in the public interest via competition between representatives of the mass media. "The first with the most" has been a workable formula for some. But surely "everyone with a lot" is desirable if the public is to be served. As we saw in chapter 10, mergers and monopolies in media industries have cut back on the "lot." It is being cut back further, mostly by the swollen treasuries of certain media giants who seem to prefer being the exclusive "owners" of the news rather than to compete for it with others. The ethical reverberations have been loud.

Shortly after Gerald Ford departed the White House, he and former Secretary of State Henry Kissinger signed long-term contracts with NBC news. Kissinger was designated an "adviser-consultant." He would appear on one news special per year. In addition, he would participate in a maximum of eight

Who Owns Whom?

special interviews related to international issues for both the "Today" show and the evening news. For those commitments he was paid $1 million. At the same time, the Ford family agreed to certain exclusive broadcasting arrangements with NBC for a fee in the neighborhood of $1.5 million. Thus, these newsworthy personalities gave the network "exclusive rights" to their services. The name of the game is "checkbook journalism." As a rising media gimmick, its main feature is that it significantly reduces the availability of certain kinds of news and news personalities to all the media and, therefore, to the public.

Edwin Diamond, of the News Study Group at the Massachusetts Institute of Technology, explains the limitations inherent in alliances such as those forged between Kissinger and Ford and NBC:

> The Ford and Kissinger arrangements . . . came with more than the usual strings attached to them. Both men reserved their rights *not* to cover certain subjects, or to perform their services in certain restricted ways. These strings have proved to be nooses around the neck of serious journalism as far as the Ford and Kissinger projects are concerned.

As to actual performance, in the first six months of the "arrangement," the network managed to get one carefully structured program from Gerald Ford, approved in advance, and one out of Kissinger. When broadcast, *Henry Kissinger: On the Record* received the lowest network rating of the entire week. As Diamond comments, the program also offended "scholars and specialists in the field of European studies. It was dull as television and deceitful as contemporary history—in short, a double turn-off."[16]

The Critics Speak   *Columbia Journalism Review* commented: "The special made an impressive platform—or pedestal—for Henry Kissinger. For NBC News, it turned out to be an expensive ninety minutes of prime time, not just in money, but also in compromising its own journalistic standards of candor and fairness."[17]

The presentation, wrote Anthony Lewis in the *New York Times*, "raises much more serious questions about the professional standards of television journalism." The basis of Lewis's concern is that "Mr. Kissinger's statements were not tested by informed questioning" by host David Brinkley, "a talented and particularly skeptical man . . . reduced to echoing Mr. Kissinger's alarmist views on the Communist threat."[18]

The doubts created extend beyond that particular episode. As Lewis comments, "If a television network pays $1 million to a political figure for five years of programs, will it let its reporters ask him real questions? Or will it be inclined to give him a kind of immunity to protect its investment?" Lewis adds: "For a news organization to buy exclusive rights in a former statesman and sell him like sugar-coated cereal is worrying."

On another network front, G. Gordon Liddy, convicted of criminal activities in the Watergate scandals, was paid by CBS for his appearance on a "60 Minutes" segment. Critics rapped the show for engaging in poor journalism practices.

Another Watergate character, H. R. Haldeman, received money for two one-hour appearances on CBS. Donovan Moore, a reporter for Boston's public television station, characterized that as "a comic opera played out in the press with Haldeman as the news whore and the crew at CBS as the horny sailors."

Moore then posed the question: If an individual comes to you and says he can show you where to find Jimmy Hoffa's body, what do you do? In fact, "60 Minutes" took out its corporate wallet, paid the tipster for the exclusive rights to the "find," and "asked questions later." The body was never found.

It is the idea of a single media outlet *purchasing* exclusive rights to significant information and/or personalities that is repugnant to an increasing number of critics. Again, competition between newspaper and/or broadcast media has been an essential part of the news gathering process in the American experience. That has insured that, with a variety of news vehicles at their disposal, the people would likely keep in touch with important developments. And checkbook journalism reduces the availability of that information.

Furthering the "checkbook" approach to news gathering is another ethically questionable gimmick also spawned by the show biz facet of television news. It is politely termed "confrontation journalism." "60 Minutes" is the top network news show on television, drawing 41 percent of the audience in its Sunday evening time slot. Throughout the years its popularity has been based on the high quality of what CBS brass calls investigative reporting. Donovan Moore says it's a good deal more than that.

Confrontation journalism is the ethically questionable practice of "getting the goods" on someone and then setting up a televised interview without revealing that fact to the subject. Then, on camera, the reporter begins hurling accusations at the subject and asking embarrassing questions, virtually "nailing the person to the wall." The practice creates a hero of the reporter and the program content becomes intense. But, as Moore asks, "Is it fair? Well, decide for yourself."

According to Moore, the person "calling the shots" on the executive end of "60 Minutes" makes such decisions routinely. He is Don Hewitt, the show's producer. With thirty years invested in CBS, Hewitt says: "Anyone who submits to an interview on television is fair game for anything . . . within his field of expertise." That serves as an accurate description of confrontation journalism. It is new; it is gaining in popularity especially among television newspeople. It also creates an ethical dilemma in the mass media generally.

Back to the Codes

With growing concern about proper operating principles for the mass media, or the lack of them, some are beginning to seek solutions in media conferences, board meetings, and other problem-solving formats. Among those, concerned practitioners are looking to *codes of conduct*, even though there is really little that is unique about them.

Weaknesses of Codes of Conduct

ASNE's Code

The *Canons of Journalism Ethics* were adopted by the American Society of Newspaper Editors (ASNE) back in 1923. It was a well-intentioned action designed to correct the gross journalistic abuses of the Pulitzers and Hearsts and the whippersnappers of the Jazz Age. But in actual practice, the *Canons* turned out to be more window dressing than hard-rock rules to be honored in the observance.

Other Media Codes

In the years since, a variety of ethical codes have been devised by national journalistic organizations. These include the codes of the Society of Professional Journalists, Sigma Delta Chi, and the Associated Press Managing Editors Association. Still others have been created to cope with ethical problems in certain journalistic specialties, such as the National Conference of Editorial Writers and the Newspaper Food Writers and Editors Association. Additionally, some individual newspapers have set up codes of professional conduct for their own employees. Broadcasting has an industry-wide code overseen by the National Association of Broadcasters. The National Advertising Review Board keeps an eye to the doings of advertising and the Public Relations Society of America has attempted to monitor professional performance in that field. (Even the motion picture industry has its Production Code, though many wonder these days about its actual authority within the industry.) It is clear that the interest in proper media performance is there. But compliance by all members is another matter.

Lack of Enforcement Powers

It has been widely accepted since the ASNE grappled with its *Canons* in the early twenties that any code of journalism conduct that does not include some form of policing is limited in what it may do to keep its house in order. Other professions have codes that carry considerable clout—the legal, medical, and dental sectors being emphatic examples. Because of tightly regulated provisions, those organizations come down hard on members whose professional conduct casts negative vibrations on their fellow members. Attorneys must be formally admitted to the bar, and they may also be disbarred by their peers if their professional conduct requires. That means that their means of livelihood is removed by the profession itself. The same applies to physicians, dentists, and other formally structured societies. That is sufficient to keep most in line. But those societies do not have to grapple with First Amendment guarantees that permit, even encourage, individual practitioners to determine for themselves what responsible conduct is or should be. The difference is significant.

As the ASNE struggled with these considerations more than a half-century ago, Casper Yost, then editor of the *St. Louis Globe-Democrat*, wrote:

> The ethics of journalism must be somehow expressed in definite form, and somehow established as the rule of practice of an influential number of journalists, before we can have professional recognition. Individual standards will always remain individual, and continue to be as varied as individual nature, until the profession of journalism, through collective consideration and action, establishes a code of professional ethics by which all journalistic conduct may be measured.[19]

Seemingly with those sentiments in mind, the management of the daily *Pottstown* (Pa.) *Mercury* recently put together a code of ethics without first entering into collective bargaining with the Newspaper Guild, the union for editorial employees. The Guild complained to the National Labor Relations Board (NLRB), which ruled that management had not violated federal labor laws in so proceeding.[20] But, and this could be essential in enforcing the code, the NLRB did rule that the publisher, Peerless Publications, could not discipline any employee for violating the code without negotiating with the Guild to establish procedures for handling ethical violations.

A Case of High Purpose

The *Mercury*'s code includes a provision to encourage the editorial staff to avoid outside employment or other activities that might compromise the integrity of the paper. It also prohibits accepting "freebies." The NLRB indicated that the new code has been adopted "to protect and enhance the credibility and quality of the newspaper." It was, therefore, legally acceptable. But the clout remains weak as a disciplinary device.

As to whether formal codes actually improve press performance and the quality of journalism itself, a forum held in Boston found wide skepticism among media practitioners.[21]

Back to Basics

Loren Ghiglione, a member of the National News Council and publisher of the *Southbridge* (Mass.) *Evening News*, said that journalists are reluctant to admit that such codes "don't help in many cases."

Timothy Leland, managing editor of the *Boston Sunday Globe*, agrees. He added that, from a strictly selfish viewpoint, newspapers have to maintain a reputation for fairness or lose the respect of their readers. So they don't really need codes.

ASSOCIATED PRESS MANAGING EDITORS CODE OF ETHICS

This code is a model against which newspaper men and women can measure their performance. It is meant to apply to news and editorial staff members, and others who are involved in, or who influence, news coverage and editorial policy. It has been formulated in the belief that newspapers and the people who produce them should adhere to the highest standards of ethical and professional conduct.

Responsibility

A good newspaper is fair, accurate, honest, responsible, independent and decent. Truth is its guiding principle.

It avoids practices that would conflict with the ability to report and present news in a fair and unbiased manner.

The newspaper should serve as a constructive critic of all segments of society. Editorially, it should advocate needed reform or innovations in the public interest. It should expose wrongdoing or misuse of power, public or private.

News sources should be disclosed unless there is clear reason not to do so. When it is necessary to protect the confidentiality of a source the reason should be explained.

The newspaper should background, with the facts, public statements that it knows to be inaccurate or misleading. It should uphold the right of free speech and freedom of the press and should respect the individual's right of privacy.

The public's right to know about matters of importance is paramount, and the newspaper should fight vigorously for public access to news of government through open meetings and open records.

Accuracy

The newspaper should guard against inaccuracies, carelessness, bias or distortion through either emphasis or omission.

It should admit all substantive errors and correct them promptly and prominently.

Integrity

The newspaper should strive for impartial treatment of issues and dispassionate handling of controversial subjects. It should provide a forum for the exchange of comment and criticism, especially when such comment is opposed to editorial positions. Editorials and other expressions of opinion by reporters and editors should be clearly labeled.

The newspaper should report the news without regard for its own interests. It should not give favored news treatment to advertisers or special interest groups. It should report matters regarding itself or its personnel with the same vigor and candor as it would other institutions or individuals.

Concern for community, business or personal interests should not cause a newspaper to distort or misrepresent the facts.

Conflicts of interest

The newspaper and its staff should be free of obligations to news sources and special interests. Even the appearance of obligation or conflict of interest should be avoided.

Newspapers should accept nothing of value from news sources or others outside the profession. Gifts and free or reduced-rate travel, entertainment, products and lodging should not be accepted. Expenses in connection with news reporting should be paid by the newspaper. Special favors and special treatment for members of the press should be avoided.

Involvement in such things as politics, community affairs, demonstrations and social causes that could cause a conflict of interest, or the appearance of such conflict, should be avoided.

Outside employment by news sources is an obvious conflict of interest, and employment by potential news sources also should be avoided.

Financial investments by staff members or other outside business interests that could conflict with the newspaper's ability to report the news or that would create the impression of such conflict should be avoided.

Stories should not be written or edited primarily for the purpose of winning awards and prizes. Blatantly commercial journalism contests, or others that reflect unfavorably on the newspaper or the profession, should be avoided.

No code of ethics can prejudge every situation. Common sense and good judgment are required in applying ethical principles to newspaper realities. Individual newspapers are encouraged to augment these guidelines with locally produced codes that apply more specifically to their own situations.

The Associated Press Managing Editors Association.

Jonathan Moore, head of Harvard University's Institute of Politics in the John F. Kennedy School of Government, says that reporters don't have to follow "arbitrary rules" to function responsibly. However, they should recognize ethical issues as they arise. "Don't be pompous," he urged. "Challenge and cross-examine your own actions." And there the matter lies.

Summary

In this chapter we have seen how professional ethics impact on the editorial process. Although there are common points of agreement on particular media issues, one's ethical sense dictates his actions. That comes from a deeply personal reflection of one's character and general view of what one owes the people under the First Amendment. Some readily do what others would not do, and both might consider that they have upheld their personal codes of conduct.

Similarly, the people have their own sense of what's right and what's wrong. They will borrow from those who tell them and then determine what of that they will keep and what they won't.

Carl Sandburg wrote:

> The storm of propaganda blows away.
> In every air of today the germs float and hover.
> The shock and contact of ideas goes on.
> Planned economy will arrive, stand up,
> and stay a long time—or planned economy will
> take a beating and be smothered.
>> The people have the say-so.
>> Let the argument go on.
>> Let the people listen.
> Tomorrow the people say Yes or No by one question:
>> "What else can be done?"
> In the drive of faiths on the wind today the people know:
> "We have come far and we are going farther yet."
>
> *The People, Yes*[22]

Notes

1. Information on the meetings, including Clark Mollenhoff's rules of performance from "What They Said at the Regionals About Ethics," The *Quill*, June 1978, p. 20.
2. Albertson quotes from Mike Albertson, "Ethics: In Most Cases, the End Justifies Our Means," The *Gannetteer*, July/August 1977, p. 1.
3. This and other Anderson quotes from Walter Anderson, "Lie? Deceive? If You Are Caught, No One Remembers Your Good Intentions," The *Gannetteer*, July/August 1977, p. 5.

4. The following examples in this section from "Darts and Laurels," *Columbia Journalism Review*, September/October 1977, p. 7; September/October 1978, p. 27; September/October 1976, p. 8; January/February 1978, p. 22; November/December 1978, p. 22; September/October 1978, p. 26; March/April 1979, p. 20.
5. Information on handling errors from Jack Williams, "There's Little in Common on Handling of Errors," The *Quill*, January 1978, p. 12.
6. This example and the one following from "Darts and Laurels," *Columbia Journalism Review*, January/February 1979, p. 23; September/October 1978, p. 27.
7. Gay Sands Miller, "To Err Is Human, To Correct Divine, Newspapers Believe," *Wall Street Journal*, October 20, 1977, p. 19.
8. John L. Hulteng, *The News Media: What Makes Them Tick?* (Englewood Cliffs, N.J.: Prentice-Hall, 1979), p. 64.
9. Journalists' comments on this junket from "Journalism Ethics," Public Broadcasting Service, April 25, 1974.
10. "Darts and Laurels," *Columbia Journalism Review*, January/February 1978, p. 21.
11. Information on sports departments from John L. Hulteng, *The Messenger's Motives* (Englewood Cliffs, N.J.: Prentice-Hall, 1976), pp. 34–35.
12. "Seaside News," *Columbia Journalism Review*, September/October 1977, p. 14.
13. This quote and Charles Long's quote following from Hulteng, *The Messenger's Motives*, p. 33.
14. Information on "Private Interest Contests" and "A Statement of Purpose" from Chris Welles, "Business Journalism's Glittering Prizes," *Columbia Journalism Review*, March/April 1979, p. 43.
15. Information on the Wisconsin study from William B. Blankenburg and Richard L. Allen, "The Journalism Contest Thicket: Is It Time for Some Guidelines?" *Ethics and the Press*, John C. Merrill and Ralph D. Barney, eds. (New York: Hastings House, 1975), pp. 303–17.
16. Edwin Diamond, "Checkbook Journalism," *Washington Journalism Review*, January/February 1979, p. 32.
17. "The Statesman from NBC News," *Columbia Journalism Review*, March/April 1978, p. 23.
18. Comments from Anthony Lewis and Donovan Moore following from Warren K. Agee, "Network Checkbooks and Confrontation," The *Quill*, March 1978, p. 29.
19. Hulteng, *Messenger's Motives*, pp. 228–30.
20. "NLRB Supports Paper's Code of Ethics," The *Quill*, September 1977, p. 13.
21. The following opinions from Bill Kirtz, "A Boston Forum on Press Ethics," The *Quill*, January 1978, p. 10.
22. From *The People, Yes* by Carl Sandburg, copyright 1936 by Harcourt Brace Jovanovich, Inc.; renewed by Carl Sandburg. Reprinted by permission of the publisher.

For Further Reading

Agee, Warren K. "Network Checkbooks and Confrontation." The *Quill*, March 1978, p. 29.

Albertson, Mike. "Ethics: In Most Cases, the End Justifies Our Means." *Gannetteer*, July/August 1977, p. 1.

Anderson, Walter. "Lie? Deceive? If You Are Caught, No One Remembers Your Good Intentions." *Gannetteer*, July/August 1977, p. 5.

Diamond, Edwin. "Checkbook Journalism." *Washington Journalism Review*, January/February 1979, p. 32.

Kirtz, Bill. "A Boston Forum on Press Ethics." The *Quill*, January 1978, p. 10.

"NLRB Supports Paper's Code of Ethics." The *Quill*, September 1977, p. 13.

"Seaside News." *Columbia Journalism Review*, September/October 1977, p. 14.

"The Statesman From NBC News." *Columbia Journalism Review*, March/April 1978, p. 23.

Welles, Chris. "Business Journalism's Glittering Prizes." *Columbia Journalism Review*, March/April 1979, p. 43.

"What They Said At the Regionals About Ethics." The *Quill*, June 1978, p. 20.

Williams, Jack. "There's Little in Common on Handling of Errors." The *Quill*, January 1978, p. 12.

News in Pictures

The Business Side 12

Upon completing this chapter you should be able to—

understand the current economic problems of the mass media and the cases cited

explain the basis of increasing competition between morning and evening newspapers and their effects

discuss current employee-management relationships in the news media in terms of the cases provided

relate the state of magazines to modern and future media

recognize the issues and problems of advertising, which provides the basic financial support of the news media

Metro Dailies   Daily newspapers based in metropolitan cities. (p. 365)

Supplements   Special sections added to a newspaper, sometimes dealing with a particular subject (travel, hobbies, etc.). (p. 367)

Demographics   In the media sense, the study of human populations in terms of size, growth, education, income, purchasing power, and other statistical data on which media content and advertising are based. (p. 369)

A.M.s and P.M.s   A.M.s refers to morning daily newspapers and P.M.s to evening dailies. (p. 373)

Suburbs   In the media context, communities located close to metro cities that are served by metro dailies at least partially.

Promotion   Plans and programs to increase print media circulation or broadcasting audiences. (p. 375)

Strike Paper   A temporary newspaper launched in a community whose regular newspaper(s) are not published due to a strike by employees. (p. 381)

The press is undeniably possessed of extensive influence upon government. . . . While society is furnished with so powerful a vehicle of political information [as the press], the conduct of administration will be more cautious and deliberate. . . . Ambition cannot fail to dread that vigilant guardian of public liberty, whose eye can penetrate, and whose voice be heard, in every quarter of the State.

Tunis Wortman, *A Treatise Concerning Political Enquiry, and the Liberty of the Press,* New York, 1800.

Economic Roots of the Mass Media

In the final quarter of the twentieth century, it is clear that the *business* of American newspapers, big-city dailies in particular, may be headed for stormy times. As one analyst puts it, newspapers are threatened by inflation, reader dissatisfaction, unemployment, and population moves away from urban areas that have traditionally supported them. Their existence is also threatened by continued credibility problems, competition from other media, increases in public participation in indoor and outdoor recreational activities, and public absorption in specialized publications that support those interests.

At the close of World War II, total combined circulation for morning and evening newspapers in the United States stood at 50,927,505. By 1978, the total had risen to 61,989,997 for an overall increase of 11,062,492. Over the same span of time, the American population increased by approximately seventy-five million. It is clear, then, that daily newspaper growth is far behind overall population growth. The figures indicate that a greater percentage of the whole read daily newspapers in the late 1940s than do so today. In addition, at war's end Americans had 1,763 morning and evening papers available to them, while today a larger population has 1,756. Hence, statistics indicate that for a variety of compelling reasons the nation has fewer dailies and, more important, fewer *readers* of daily newspapers compared to the total population than it had thirty years ago.[1]

David Shaw is a reporter for the *Los Angeles Times* assigned to keeping tabs on the newspaper industry itself.[2] In that role he has uncovered serious problems in the daily newspaper field. For example, between 1973 and 1975, daily newspaper sales in the United States dropped 4.6 percent and the number of daily newspaper readers declined by more than 7 percent. These were the worst falloffs in forty years. The pains are being felt most noticeably among metropolitan dailies.

Economic Problems of American Newspapers

Then and Now

Slumping Metro Dailies

Since 1970, the three financially solvent metropolitan newspapers in New York City have lost 550,000 readers. The two dailies in Cleveland have lost about 90,000 circulation and the two papers in San Francisco have dropped by more than 80,000. And since 1960, such major American cities as Boston, Chicago, Cleveland, Detroit, Los Angeles, San Francisco, and others have lost newspapers. With such shrinkage in major newspaper markets increasing, one justifiably wonders to what extent the First Amendment will continue to be served.

Some observers suggest that current circulation woes reflect the stagnant state of the nation's economy. It is true that some dailies have recovered a portion of lost circulations and even increased advertising revenues. But dark clouds still gather.

Barry Bingham, editor and publisher of Louisville's *Courier-Journal* and *Times*, remains concerned: "If we're not careful, we could find ourselves in the buggywhip business; we could phase ourselves right out of existence."

Groping for Solutions As indicated in chapter 3, many newspapers have begun looking to market analysts for help in increasing circulations. And some of the techniques recommended, including greater emphasis on entertainment content, have radically altered the traditional content of a large number of newspapers. As Shaw has determined, some of these include short-term promotional gadgetry including "games and sweepstakes, front-page gossip columns, daily soap operas, a sensationalized approach to the news."

Modernization Other media managers have sought fiscally sound means of improving their circumstances, including adoption of new technologies of modern typesetting and printing procedures, improved home delivery systems, and smaller page formats to cut already high newsprint costs. Still others have geared their changes to page layouts and news departmentalization to make finding and reading different kinds of information easier and more physically attractive to consumers.

Roots of the Problems But, as Shaw has found, at the hub of the problem are the readers themselves. Times have indeed changed. For one thing, former "regular" readers now have other interests and activities to occupy their minds, bodies, and *Increasing Costs* leisure time. This change is especially significant in light of the 26 percent *to the Reader* increase in the *cost* of newspapers in the last two years. If papers have not proved vital to readers before a rate increase, why would they prove vital after? Otis Chandler, publisher of the *Los Angeles Times*, expressed doubt that his or any other big daily is "really essential" to as many as 50 percent of those who buy it. "Our readers just aren't a captive audience anymore. They can do without us."

Need to be "Useful" Syndicated columnist James Kilpatrick commented that the daily newspaper has "no intrinsic function. . . . You cannot wear it, drive it, drink it or live in it." The newspaper's function is to provide information, and if modern newspapers are going to survive they must not just enlighten or entertain, but be *useful*.

Tom Winship, editor of the highly regarded *Boston Globe*, agrees. "Most newspapers just pay too little attention to the daily concerns of their readers," he said. "We're out of touch. We have to show them we're aware of their problems. They're low now; we have to give them a little sympathy, a little hope, a little excitement."

To accomplish that, many daily newspapers have turned to alternative forms of information by providing readers with *useful* suggestions on economizing at the grocery store, information on health programs, proper grooming, caring for pets, household and auto repairs, investments, vacationing, and a host of other basic but meaningful concerns reflected in the day-to-day lives of readers. The *Detroit Free Press* has even instituted a "Sound Off" column to which readers may submit their comments and complaints about the paper's content. The comments are then published in the column. Other big dailies have taken to publishing special supplements to guide weekend leisure and entertainment activities for readers. With it all, the problems are far from being solved. Continued application of energy and creativity is essential if big newspapers are to rebuild and again take firm hold of the market.

The economic problems of big-city dailies create upheavals just as other urban problems do. The cost of producing a newspaper has risen dramatically and newsprint, the stock on which the paper is printed, leads the way. If advertising and circulation (especially the former) fall off, the paper is hard put just to break even.

The city of Chicago is a prime example of this, with the passing of the *Chicago Daily News* still a mournful event in the minds of loyal supporters.[3] As in other metro areas, distribution of afternoon papers is expensive in Chicago. Radio and television offer brisk competition to afternoon papers, and the population continues to change as white residents move to the suburbs and blacks and Hispanics remain. Approximately 45 percent of the population of Chicago is comprised of minority groups. And they are, as one analyst terms it, "skimpy newspaper readers." That, in turn, is due to the very real fact that their formal education has not prepared them to ingest and understand fairly complex information carried by metro dailies. In addition, the commercial press does not reflect their personal needs and concerns. Finally, because so many minorities are in low-income brackets, they can ill-afford to support climbing subscription rates of daily newspapers. Due to these and other inner-city problems (including high crime rates, which affect distribution of newspapers in many critical ways), metro dailies try to concentrate on higher-income minority communities where there is reasonable opportunity to gain and maintain sales.

Attempts to Be "Relevant"

Newspaper Supplements

Increasing Production Costs

Newspaper Problems in Chicago

City Papers Do Not Appeal to Minorities

The Last Edition

Chicago Daily News

SATURDAY, MARCH 4, 1978

35¢

So long, Chicago

It took 102 years to finish, and these are the final pages of The Chicago Daily News.

By M. W. Newman

The Chicago Daily News, the writers' newspaper, ends as it began—a momentous Book of Life. It took 102 years to finish, and these are the final pages.

But the story isn't over—just The Daily News' part of it. A newspaper dies, but newspapering goes on. Life goes on. Tomorrow is the sequel, and all the tomorrows after that.

We die knowing we did our job to the utmost and to the very end. To today, in fact, precisely 102 years, 2 months and 12 days after founder Melville E. Stone ran off the first issue on a rickety press rented for $12 a week.

Stone's Daily News burst out of the gaslight age, when Ulysses S. Grant was brooding in the White House and Lincoln was dead just 10 years. It dies in the

Turn to Page 3

The News inside:

- A legend in the making, Page 4
- A farewell editorial and John Fischetti's cartoon, Page 12
- The foreign service, Page 16
- The Pulitzer Prize winners, Page 20
- 102 years of investigating, Page 21
- The Washington bureau, Page 24
- Our last 'Done in a Day,' Page 26
- The last staff, Page 30
- A writer's newspaper, Page 50

A truly great newspaper: Why couldn't it make it?

By Mike Royko

About the only good thing that can be said for working on a newspaper that folds is that it is sort of like reading your own obit.

Since the official announcement was made on Feb. 22 that The Chicago Daily News would cease publication on March 4, the nation's press has been lamenting our demise.

We've been reading about how we were one of America's oldest papers (102 years), rich in tradition and boasting of great staffs, past and present.

Most of the obits point out that The Daily News had the nation's first foreign service. It was a great one. Over the years, it included such star reporters as John Gunther, Edgar Ansel Mowrer, Paul Scott Mowrer, Keyes Beech, George Weller and Bill Stoneman.

This was the paper that once employed Carl Sandburg as a silent movie critic. Ben Hecht worked here and gathered the material for "Front Page," his classic play about the roughhouse days of Chicago journalism. The Daily News invented the daily columnist.

Our 15 Pulitzer Prizes and countless other awards put us right up there with the best of papers.

The Daily News was doing investigative reporting and sending politicians to jail when Woodward and Bernstein were toddlers.

Our Washington bureau, while not big in number, was always respected. The late Ed Lahey was a living Washington legend.

Bureau Chief Peter Lisagor, who died in 1976, was often described by his peers as the best reporter in the capital.

The recent staff was as good as its ancestors. Pulitzers were owned by cartoonist John Fischetti, associate editor Lois Wille and Beech, lately of the Washington staff. More than 50 books have been written by recent Daily News writers.

Well, you read enough glowing obits about yourself, and you can be pardoned for thinking: "Yeah? If we were that good, how come we didn't make it?"

And that is the toughest part of being on a 102-year-old, tradition-laden newspaper that goes under. If it had been a cheap rag, its death would have been easier to take. But The Daily News, while it had some bad days, was still one of the best papers in this country.

The very day publisher Marshall Field stood on a desk in the city room to break the bad news, the paper was notified that Lois Wille had won the William Allen White award, the nation's top honor for excellence in editorial writing.

In recent months it had dominated the city's news coverage, with spectacular front-page exposes of political scandals. The talk in the news room was about which story

Turn to Page 2

A statement from the publisher

With this edition The Chicago Daily News ceases publication. I am saddened that it must be so, for the loss of any great newspaper is a tragedy for the community, its employes, readers and advertisers.

The Daily News has been a Chicago institution for more than a century, and as a winner of 15 Pulitzer Prizes it has been respected throughout the country and the world. The men and women who have worked over the years on this newspaper can be proud of their achievements and the level of excellence attained. I am grateful to them for their talent and devotion and to our readers and advertisers.

Despite all our efforts, the economics of publishing, reader habits and life-styles have changed dramatically in the last two decades, making it impossible for The Daily News to earn the revenues needed for any healthy, sound business operation.

As the publisher and man responsible for The Daily News, I feel this loss very deeply. I feel I owe you, the reader, a personal thank you for your loyalty.

The Chicago Sun-Times, which has been growing steadily, will be expanded greatly and will serve an ever increasing number of readers with vigor and dedication.

Your favorite Daily News columnists, writers and editors will be waiting for you in the new Sun-Times. Now 10 Pulitzer Prize winners on the same team will bring you the finest news coverage. The Chicago Sun-Times can be delivered to your home in the morning or picked up at your newsstand every afternoon—with the latest stock market reports.

I believe you will enjoy this exciting newspaper, and I pledge our continued commitment to journalistic excellence.

Marshall Field
Publisher

Last edition of the *Chicago Daily News*. (Reprinted with permission from Field Enterprises, Inc., March 4, 1978.)

To bring that about, the *Chicago Sun-Times*, for one, has attempted to address some of its content to minority interests. It also hired a black city editor and gave him visibility to other blacks via television appearances and speaking engagements to high school students and other formal groups. The paper also hired a columnist to turn out a regular column in Spanish. The success of the *Sun-Times* in Chicago might well be due to the fact that it is the city's only tabloid paper, a handy size for readers who commute via mass transit systems. In the city itself, the *Sun-Times*, with a circulation of about 351,830, has gained over the rival *Tribune* which, in spite of its overtures to minorities, remains a conservative, establishment newspaper. But in the suburbs, the *Tribune*'s circulation is over 370,000 while that of the *Sun-Times* is only a little over 208,000. Both are morning papers. With the *Tribune* staking its future in the booming Chicago suburbs, it should continue to prosper. But the *Sun-Times*, tied for the most part to the stagnating inner city, will likely realize smaller circulation gains.

The Sun-Times*'s Experiment*

Chicago's newspaper problems have cropped up in other metropolitan areas, Los Angeles being one of them.[4] A large portion of that city's white, middle-class population has moved out. The white middle class has also been the principal target of the advertising content of the *Los Angeles Times*. In order to maintain its appeal, the *Times* has, in a real sense, followed the outflow of people via special editions geared to suburban communities, creation of a new San Diego edition, and other direct appeals to suburban readership.

Dailies in Los Angeles

The Los Angeles Times

Even so, the *Times*'s problems in Los Angeles remain. Nearly 23 percent of the population of Los Angeles County is comprised of Spanish-speaking, black, and Asian-Americans. They are expected to comprise the majority by 1980. Thus, how is the *Times* to define its true audience? How will it appeal, editorially and in advertising, to such diversified groups both geographically and in terms of personal interests and needs? And how well will the First Amendment be served under such circumstances?

Growing Numbers of Minorities

Otis Chandler, publisher of the *Times*, has indicated that the paper still has "a way to go" in its coverage of minorities. He also said that directing the paper's content to low-income readers "would not make financial sense." That is because that audience does not have "the purchasing power and is not responsive to the kind of advertising we carry."

The Crux: Audience Purchasing Power

Chandler also pointed out the difficulties inherent in making the *Times* attractive to minorities in the area. "It's not their kind of newspaper: it's too big, it's too stuffy. If you will, it's too complicated."

To the advertising people, the problem is one of "demographics," or the science of determining who and where the spenders are, and how to appeal to them. The *Times* is a paper "of high demographic profile." That means it has a well-educated, well-to-do, middle-aged readership.

The Role of Demographics

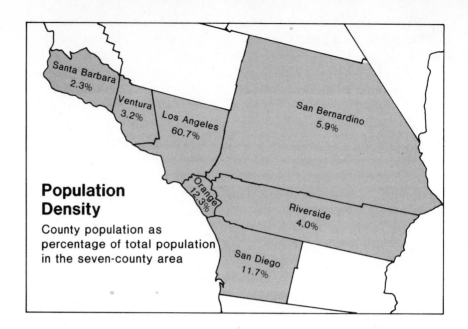

Population Density

County population as percentage of total population in the seven-county area

Santa Barbara 2.3%
Ventura 3.2%
Los Angeles 60.7%
San Bernardino 5.9%
Orange 12.3%
Riverside 4.0%
San Diego 11.7%

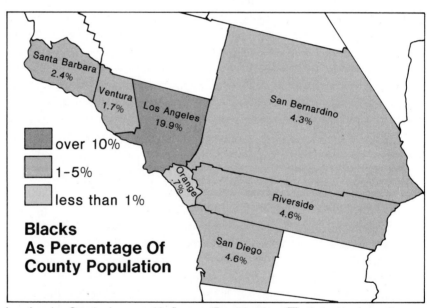

over 10%
1–5%
less than 1%

Blacks As Percentage Of County Population

Santa Barbara 2.4%
Ventura 1.7%
Los Angeles 19.9%
San Bernardino 4.3%
Orange .7%
Riverside 4.6%
San Diego 4.6%

Los Angeles County demographic figures. (Reprinted from the *Columbia Journalism Review*, January/February 1979.)

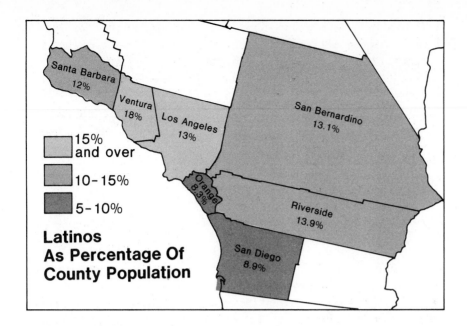

Latinos
As Percentage Of
County Population

Santa Barbara 12%
Ventura 18%
Los Angeles 13%
San Bernardino 13.1%
Orange 8.3%
Riverside 13.9%
San Diego 8.9%

15% and over
10-15%
5-10%

Chandler supports that profile. He reports that his major retail advertisers have told him: "We want a certain class of audience, a certain demographic profile of the reader, whether that person be black, white, or brown, or Chinese or whatever. We don't really care what sex or race they are. But we do care about their income," which enables them to buy what is advertised in the paper. And a sizeable number of minorities in Los Angeles, as in Chicago and other metro areas, are poor, and many are likely to remain so. But, the theory goes, when their standard of living increases so will their reading and buying interests.

Demographics also influence news content. For example, Chandler admits that special inserts in the paper related to minority communities have been rejected by him because of resistance by advertisers. "The advertisers would not support that" because the minorities would not likely buy their goods and services. He added that audience surveys show that nonminority audiences are "not very interested" in reading minority coverage.

Influence of Advertisers on Content

With it all, Chandler said that the *Times* has improved its minority coverage since he became publisher, though some of his staff argue the economic logic of it. For a metro daily anywhere to serve its poor minorities, even when it wants to, is an issue of major proportions as actual experience shows. The hard facts say that newspapers are supported by advertisers, who are tied to demographics. Therefore, to an impressive degree, advertisers in these circumstances certainly help to determine what news content will *not* be. To what extent they determine what it *will* be is a subject to be treated later in this chapter.

Some troubled newspapers are fighting back. The Hearst-owned *Los Angeles Herald Examiner* had been staring financial disaster in both eyes when new management came in to coax it back toward solvency.[5] After a ten-year strike had shattered the paper's 725,000 circulation, management grasped for ways to survive. Executives were reshuffled at the top, including the transfer of former publisher George Hearst, Jr. to the company's real estate division. Then new blood was brought in. In a sea of negativism, two points in particular appeared to favor new life for the paper. First, a survey by the Belden research firm indicated that a sizeable untapped body of readers existed in the Los Angeles area that might be attracted to a good second newspaper, second, that is, to the dominant *Times*. Secondly, many area advertisers had been longing for a workable alternative to the *Times*. Perhaps there was hope for a resurgence of the *Herald*. It was worth a try.

*An Untapped
Body of Readers*

Herald management then brought in Francis Dale as publisher. With a solid reputation earned as head man of the *Cincinnati Enquirer*, Dale took over with a burst of energy and ideas. He lured former *Los Angeles Times* editor James Bellows away from the editorship of the *Washington Star* to take the *Herald*'s editorial helm. Bellows, in turn, hired a deputy, Don Forst, who had been managing editor of *Long Island Newsday*, a thriving daily in the suburbs of New York City.

*New Publisher
and Editor*

One of Bellows's first discoveries, a major find as it turned out, was the *Herald*'s sports section, a special tabloid that enjoyed wide popularity. Surveys indicated that many people read the sports section but threw the rest of the paper away. That was a meaningful plus in the rebuilding plan.

The Sports Section

Then came the editorial staff. It was a mix of old-time Hearst people and young bloods who had gone to the *Herald* because it was the only paper around that would accept inexperienced reporters. The business side of the paper was a wreck. Circulation continued to fall as did national advertising, though the local retail and classified ads picture had improved. And finally, based on the overall financial picture, the corporation told Bellows that no budget increases would be available for the editorial side. He would have to make do by shifting budgetary priorities around to make ends meet. As Bellows commented, the editorial process became one of "Band-Aids" and "patchwork."

Retrenching Begins

Bellows launched the *Herald*'s revival by getting rid of all the deadwood personnel he could under the watchful eyes of the unions. Others he exiled to the paper's library or promotion department. He then informed the staff that any employee accepting a freebie would be fired. He also brought in fresh new talent as he could find it, especially editors who would help steer the paper's new course. Most of the latter were experienced magazine writers, talents that would come to characterize much of the *Herald*'s content.

Next Bellows and Forst revised the physical appearance of the paper. The front page carried a "Q and A" feature, fewer headlines, smaller type, and a "Bottom Line" feature that contained mostly pickups from other news sources. "What we want," Forst said, "is life-styles, trends, humorous things. 'People' stories with an emphasis on details, the unusual, personal touches." The *Herald Examiner* was about to become another "fluff" newspaper.

The first major story, one that would typify the new *Herald*, was about Bubbles, a hippo that had escaped from Lion Country Safari. For three weeks the paper carried a running feature on page one headed "The Hippo Watch." Readers were invited to write in about Bubbles. The feature was an instant success as more than 11,000 letters poured in from readers of every stripe, many of them school children.

Bellows also launched "Page 2," a gossip column that one observer called "irreverent, naughty, punchy," with no real effort at accuracy—more mockery. Much of it was aimed at motion picture personalities in nearby Hollywood.

Other features and featurized news crept into the pages of the *Herald*. Advertising increased, but not yet to prestrike levels, and circulation edged slowly upward. Still, observers agree that the entertainment-type formula, which is certainly not new, might give the rival *Times* a reasonable run for its money. It's a formula that would do William Randolph Hearst proud. Only time will tell if the *Herald* will become a bonafide competitor of the *Times* or merely a lightweight alternative paper. The readers in greater Los Angeles will ultimately decide.

Jim Bellows (*Los Angeles Herald Examiner*).

In the American press system, evening newspaper circulation runs higher than that of morning newspapers. Currently, figures show that of 1,756 daily newspapers in the United States, 1,430 are evening papers and 360 are morning. Circulations for both total 61,989,997 copies per day—34,333,258 for P.M.s and 27,656,739 for A.M.s. Statistics also show that evening papers do well in those large cities where there is no competition among newspapers. Readers will buy the afternoon paper, if that's all there is, even though they might prefer a morning newspaper. That has been the picture, more or less, for many years. But hard facts indicate that the picture is changing.

For example, since 1975, twenty-one new dailies entered the morning field while six evening papers died. Since 1975, overall evening circulation dropped by 831,987 copies as morning circulations rose by 2,166,553.[6] These figures provide no reason for panic in the evening field at this point. But they do indicate, for one thing, that evening newspapers in large cities having heavy competition for readers are facing dark days, or nights, as the case may be.

A classic example of these changes is the 157-year-old *Long Island Press*, an evening daily in New York. In 1969, the *Press* enjoyed a daily circulation of 400,000 readers. But when it folded in 1977, the figure had fallen to 250,000. Reasons include the ferocious competition between the *Press* and the rival *Long Island Newsday*, also an evening paper. Another factor was the competition for readers presented by the *New York Times* and the *Daily News* in the same Long Island suburbs. And new evidence indicates that readers prefer morning papers anyway. Why the change in preference?

Reasons for the Changes

Observers of the competitive scene suggest that the change in reader interest between morning and afternoon papers is due to three basic factors: changes in the economy, continued growth in the suburbs, and competition from evening television. Due to congested commuter conditions, many people in the white-collar "clerks" readership category go to work somewhat later than before and, therefore, have time to pause over their morning papers for longer periods than in earlier times. They also get home somewhat later. But, after a long workday and battling traffic, they prefer watching the evening news on television and the entertainment shows that follow to the physical act of manipulating and ingesting the contents of the evening newspaper.

Table 12.1 Number of U.S. Morning, Evening, and Sunday Newspapers and Their Circulation, 1920–1978

Year	Morning	Evening	Total M & E*	Sunday
1920	437	1,605	2,042	522
1925	427	1,581	2,008	548
1930	388	1,554	1,942	521
1935	390	1,560	1,950	518
1940	380	1,498	1,878	525
1945	330	1,419	1,749	485
1946	334	1,429	1,763	497
1950	322	1,450	1,772	549
1955	316	1,454	1,760	541
1960	312	1,459	1,763	563
1965	320	1,444	1,751	562
1966	324	1,444	1,754	578
1967	327	1,438	1,749	573
1968	328	1,443	1,752	578
1969	333	1,443	1,758	585
1970	334	1,429	1,748	586
1971	339	1,425	1,749	590
1972	337	1,441	1,761	605
1973	343	1,451	1,774	634
1974	340	1,449	1,768	641
1975	339	1,436	1,756	639
1976	346	1,435	1,762	650
1977†	347	1,424	1,753	668
1978†	355	1,419	1,756	696

Source: Editor & Publisher.

*There were twenty "all-day" newspapers in 1977 and 18 in 1978. They are listed in both morning and evening columns but only once in the total.

†Revised figures.

Mass population movement to the suburbs has also hampered the delivery systems of both metro and suburban dailies. Truckloads of evening papers become caught up in traffic jams just as commuters do.* To offset that problem, many P.M.s go to press earlier than before—around noontime—in order to get the trucks rolling earlier. That means that the news is less "newsy" than it once was. At the same time, morning papers continue to go to press around midnight and their delivery trucks move about the suburbs in the early hours of the morning when traffic is minimal. Thus, A.M.s continue to offer fresh information for their readers. So afternoon papers are facing new problems *because* they are afternoon papers. At least in some cases, they could be in serious financial difficulty if workable solutions are not found.

In hopes of turning the tide, the *Miami News*, a P.M., has tried to identify itself with evening television viewing by publishing news "briefs" and more pictures, and creating new graphic designs. The paper's promotion director said of this change:

Special Promotions

> Realistically, the lifestyle of most people each day is dominated by watching TV from 5 P.M. on. Most people refuse to admit it. They choose to battle it. We have chosen to admit it. Yes, people do watch TV from 5 P.M. on, but there are a lot of things that can be done while the TV program or commercial is on—like reading the newspaper.

Establishing satellite printing plants in suburban areas is yet another option for coping with heavy competition. (This development is based on the notion that, if the newspaper is printed closer to the reader, the news is fresher.) The morning *Detroit News* took that road several years ago in a maneuver to beat out its rival, the *Detroit Free Press*, also a morning paper. The *News*'s promotion department beat the drum as having more recent news than the *Free Press* which, of course, it does. The same strategy has been employed in other highly competitive markets. But it is an expensive tactic that not all newspapers can afford.

Satellite Printing Plants

Finally, various specialized magazines catering to particular interests—cross-country skiing, boating, golf, woodworking, hobbies, and other leisure activities—also compete with newspapers for readers' time. Their presence is especially felt by evening papers.

Competition from Specialized Magazines

Laird Anderson, of the American University School of Communication in Washington, D.C., writes of these concerns:

> Newspapers face the same problems all of us face in a rapidly changing society, the problem of adaptation, of finding a role, staying useful. And when papers fail to resolve that problem, they die. It is always a sad occasion. The only thing sadder might be to fail and continue to live.[7]

---

*The American Newspaper Publishers Association estimates that 90,000 vehicles drive some thirty million miles *each week* delivering United States daily newspapers to readers.

Competition between rival papers sometimes takes on volatile characteristics. Consider the recent competition for readers between the *St. Louis Post-Dispatch* and its rival, the *Globe-Democrat*, a throwback to the Hearst-Pulitzer tactics of the 1890s.[8] This one actually reached the editorial pages. The squabble arose when the *Post-Dispatch* published a story that said that the Federal Bureau of Investigation had "fed information and editorial viewpoints" to the *Globe-Democrat* as part of a FBI campaign against "new left" organizations in St. Louis in the late 1960s and early 1970s. The author, a *Post-Dispatch* correspondent in Washington, D.C., reported that the information had come from FBI files. The *Globe-Democrat* responded rapidly and forcefully.

In an editorial titled: "For Hanoi? Or for America?" G. Duncan Bauman, publisher, termed the *Post-Dispatch* story "a cheap shot, a biased and slanted item. In its normally hypocritical manner, the *Post-Dispatch* presented material about the *Globe-Democrat* as a news story, when in fact it was an editorial in a bogeyman's costume." Bauman added that if it had been offered in the form of an editorial, he would not have bothered responding to it.

Bauman continued: "For the *Post-Dispatch* news story to state that the FBI arranged stories in the *Globe-Democrat* through contacts with the publisher of the *Globe-Democrat* is a villainous lie typical of the depraved thinking of a Communist 'Big Lie' technique—designed to undermine the fabric of the country."

Evening television winning out against P.M. newspapers. (Illustration by David Seavey, *Washington Journalism Review*.)

Bauman admitted in print that he had known FBI Director J. Edgar Hoover personally but denied that the bureau had given him any information. Of the action of his rival paper in publishing the story, Bauman said it "emits a barnyard stench . . . which is a measure of that paper's pretense at news coverage: Rot."

The *Post-Dispatch* came back with a page one story that showed how the FBI attempted to keep secret its relationship with the *Globe-Democrat*.

The *Hannibal* (Mo.) *Courier-Post* followed the battle editorially and commented that the *Post-Dispatch*'s revelations had been handled fairly. It also said that Bauman had done himself and his paper a disservice by replying as he had.

Competition, whether in St. Louis, Chicago, New York, or anyplace else, has been traditionally viewed as a means of improving the products of all competitors. And that is very much in the spirit of the First Amendment. To what extent that is actually reflected in the newspaper industry of today is open to question. In many cases, competition has come to mean an economic war waged for the purpose of killing off the competition. It is economic survival and nothing less. And as markets shrink and media diminish in numbers, one may justifiably wonder about the print media's future and the public's right and *need* to know. Who will tell them? (By comparison, broadcast stations must be financially solvent as a condition of licensing. If a radio or television station goes broke and can no longer function, the license is given to somebody else.)

Media Survival and the Public's Right to Know

Union and Employee Relations

High jinks in union negotiations have characterized labor-management relations ever since labor organized and developed bargaining power. In time, unions grew strong in numbers, unity, and internal discipline and arrived at that exhilarating point where they did the dictating while management twirled its thumbs. Labor's lever has been the strike, and when it is applied it is to force management's hand and get labor what it wants. But in the modern newspaper picture, evidence increasingly suggests that the balance may be turning back to management's favor.

A major indication of the change came in late 1978 when Time Incorporated ("Time Inc.," as known in the trade), parent of *Time* magazine among other media properties, purchased the *Washington Star*.[9] It promptly took on the paper's unions.* The company launched its campaign by threatening to close down the *Star* and go back to New York if labor failed to cooperate. In this case, management employed a new tactic based on the knowledge that the employees were concerned about the rickety future of their paper and, therefore, their jobs.

Time Inc. and the Washington Star

*Approximately 48 percent of the more than 406,000 newspaper employees in the United States are production personnel as opposed to editorial, advertising, circulation, and other workers.

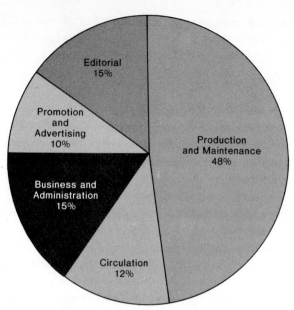

Newspaper work force: distribution of employees at a typical U.S. metropolitan daily newspaper. (Reprinted by permission of the American Newspaper Publishers Association Foundation.)

One of management's first moves was to request that the eleven unions representing the *Star*'s employees enter new contract negotiations immediately. Management did not wish to wait until current contracts expired several months away. The unions agreed to do so.

Negotiate or Close Down!

The pressures came when publisher George Hoyt told union leaders that the company would invest $6 million in the *Star* over the next five years. But that would happen *only* if new five-year contracts were negotiated and ratified by December 31. If not, the company would close the paper down permanently on January 1. "Time [Incorporated] doesn't invest very long in losers," Hoyt warned the labor leaders.

In a formal resolution, the *Star*'s unit of the Newspaper Guild, which represents editorial employees, declared its outrage at management's tactics. The company refused to budge.

As December wore away, the unions became convinced that Time Inc. really meant to close the paper down rather than absorb millions in losses from previous owners. It would close down and all those jobs would be liq-

Union Resolve Weakens

uidated. By the end of the month, nine of the eleven unions had agreed to management's terms. Only the pressmen and the Columbia Typographical Union (CTU) remained out. The CTU took its case to federal court, where it asked the judge to prohibit the *Star*'s closing on the grounds that the old union contracts were still in force. The judge granted an injunction but stayed its enforcement while negotiations continued. Meanwhile, Time Inc. announced that it was preparing a petition of bankruptcy that would close the paper. That did the trick. When that word got out, further resistance by the two holdout unions buckled. Time Inc. had gotten what it had set out to get by applying the force of threat.

The strategy of managers applying pressures to employees as done with the *Star* may be part of a trend. Capital Cities Communication, CapCities for short, recently bought the 70,000-circulation *Wilkes-Barre Times-Leader* in Pennsylvania.[10] The deal ultimately created what one observer called "a battleground in a labor war." The confrontation between the two forces, CapCities and organized labor, climaxed in chaos including broken windows, vandalized trucks, and injured pickets. The confrontation threatened to destroy the newsaper itself.

CapCities Comes to Wilkes-Barre

The CapCities case is another example of increasingly powerful management forces *dictating* working conditions, rather than negotiating them, to unions that had held the upper hand in bargaining for generations. As in the *Washington Star* case, existing contracts in Wilkes-Barre were still in force. Yet the new ownership demanded concessions from labor all the way from job security to sick leave.

Dictation vs. Negotiation

Richard Connor, chief operating officer for CapCities said, "We didn't negotiate the old contract, and we're not going to live by it. If you buy a house and you don't like the wallpaper, you change the wallpaper." The unions disagreed, but management stood firm.

Management's Reasoning

The unions involved in the CapCities dispute included the Newspaper Guild, Printing Pressmen, Stereotypers, and Typographical Union. Their contracts were due to expire the following September. But management demanded the concessions immediately, even before new contracts could be negotiated.

Paul Golias, a *Times-Leader* reporter and secretary of the Council of Newspaper Unions, said, "Working conditions became unbearable as it became clear that Capital Cities was heading for a confrontation." A strike was inevitable. Union people met in local bars and made plans to form a strike newspaper.

Drawing Up Sides

At the same time, CapCities began screening editorial employees from their other newspapers to keep the *Times-Leader* running. To protect them, the company hired uniformed security guards and stationed them throughout the building. Some of them reportedly even followed union members into bathrooms.

Two days before the contracts were to expire, the union voted 185 to 5 to strike if settlements were not reached. When negotiations broke down on October 6, 205 of 225 employees walked off their jobs. In short order the ground-floor windows of the *Times-Leader* building were covered with yellow stickers demanding that "CapCities Go Home!"

Talks Collapse

Security guards face strikers at the *Times-Leader* gate. (*Times-Leader*.)

Confrontation

Violence erupted during the first five days of the strike. At the six-week point, matters had not improved. And, local people noted, CapCities had done little by way of improving the paper's content or style with its imported staff. It was, in the words of one critic, "essentially the same unsophisticated paper—a medium for funeral notices, bowling scores, and supermarket ads."

A Standard Pattern

In most of CapCities's other newspaper holdings, the Newspaper Guild is nonexistent. Therefore, "management is free to dictate conditions as it sees fit." The company has been successful in some of its properties with pushing union members into striking and then bringing in personnel from the outside to replace them. Employees of the *Oakland Press* near Detroit entered negotiations with CapCities and finally walked out. They are still out and the paper is being operated by staff members from other CapCities papers plus new blood hired as permanent replacements. This is possible because the unions keep refusing unacceptable contract proposals.

CapCities Faces a Bastion of Labor

But in the Wilkes-Barre case, management misjudged the dedication of the trade unions. The area has long been a bastion of organized labor, where vigorous opposition to management goes back to the anthracite boom days. The militance of unionists on this occasion knocked CapCities off its corporate feet, Connor testified. The strikers tried to shut the plant down and violence

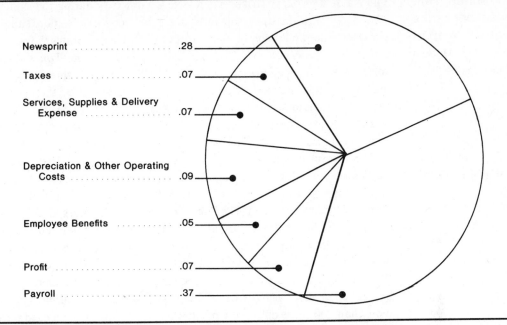

Newsprint	.28
Taxes	.07
Services, Supplies & Delivery Expense	.07
Depreciation & Other Operating Costs	.09
Employee Benefits	.05
Profit	.07
Payroll	.37

Newspaper Expenses: distribution of a revenue dollar at a typical U.S. daily newspaper. (Reprinted by permission of the American Newspaper Publishers Association Foundation.)

resulted: they obstructed traffic at the plant gates and smashed windows. Finally, on October 9, CapCities decided to close the paper down. "We were frightened," Connor said. "Our building was being attacked, our trucks were being demolished, and we couldn't get any police protection."

The paper began publishing again four days later with a court order limiting the number of pickets and enjoining CapCities "from any acts of violence."

Closing the paper down brought a development that management could not have anticipated. The strikers began publication of an alternative news-paper called *Citizens' Voice*, a twenty-four-page tabloid that immediately began reaping local advertising to the point of alarming the CapCities people. And when the *Times-Leader* resumed publishing, they found that "Wilkes-Barre was no longer a one-newspaper town." CapCities had lost its advertising monopoly, a substantial number of readers had fallen away, and they even had trouble getting enough home-delivery carriers. Many citizens, including carriers, had deserted to *Citizens' Voice* because of their union loyalties.

Finally, in his New York office, CapCities president Daniel Burke an-nounced that CapCities was now part of Wilkes-Barre. And, he added, "One way or another, we're going to inflict a paper on the community."

A Strike Newspaper

The New York Newspaper Strike of 1978
Traditional vs. Modern Production Methods

The major newspaper strike that hit New York City during the summer of 1978 portrays dramatically the modern conflict between traditional and modern electronic production of newspapers in the United States.[11] For eighty-eight days, the *New York Post*, the *Daily News*, and the *Times* remained voiceless as Printing Pressman's Union No. 2 struck all three papers. The major issue was the number of pressmen to be employed by the papers at a time when, due to new technological advances, fewer were needed. The issue was of obvious economic concern to the pressmen but also to management, who recognized substantial payroll cuts as vital to survival.

The Crux: Fewer Workers Needed

The pressmen had not struck in New York City since 1923, when the number of on-the-job pressmen was last determined. But the dramatic changes in newspaper production methods in recent years has drastically reduced the need for so many pressmen. The Publishers' Association, the spokesman group for the three papers, let it be known that a new pressman's contract would have to include major reductions in the number of workers employed. The new contract would give management the authority to determine the size of the working crews. It would guarantee jobs for life for those union members having ten or more years with one employer plus a record of having worked more than 200 shifts during the previous year. The union challenged the offer on the grounds that it would oust nearly half of the 1,600 members, particularly those who had previously worked for now-defunct area newspapers before joining one of the three papers presently involved.

Publishers Modify Their Position

The publishers then modified their position, offering immediate salary increases of $23 a week to workers on all three papers and similar increases during each of the next two years. The new offer would permit management determination of the number of pressmen needed to turn out the day's press run. Management would also guarantee five shifts per week for pressmen who had worked for one paper for *three* years. The union rejected the offer and voted to strike. Similarly, the papers would stick together and see matters through. The union then set up a picket line that other unions refused to cross. Thus, approximately 10,000 newspaper employees were out of work and the three newspapers were idle.

More Strike Newspapers

According to the *Washington Post*, Rupert Murdoch, the Australian entrepreneur and owner of the *Post*, took advantage of the news blight by launching the *Daily Metro* and staffing it with *Post* editorial employees. He even called advertisers to personally solicit their business. When word got out, a *Times* spokesman responded, "I don't believe it!" Even so, some *Times* staffers also worked for the *Daily Metro*.

Other new faces appeared as well, the *City News*, headed by a *Daily News* editor, was launched as a temporary venture with a press run of 250,000 copies. It began with 36 pages but to keep pace with news-starved New Yorkers, it eventually expanded to as many as 104 pages daily and even more on Sundays.

Rupert Murdock, publisher of the *New York Post*. (© 1978, photo by Harvey Wang.)

Members of pressman's Local No. 2 picket the *New York Post* during the 1978 newspaper strike. (© 1978, photo by Harvey Wang.)

The *Daily Press* was yet another strike paper. It was published by Gary and Mark Stern, who make a specialty of producing temporary newspapers in strikebound cities. Some established papers in suburban areas put out special editions for New Yorkers.

Other efforts were minor and people turned to newsmagazines, radio, and television for their information. But in general, the major news coming out of the struck city was paltry compared to what readers were accustomed to.

Finally in early November, the contending parties came together and agreed on a new contract. "Each side in the strike can claim some victories," one spokesperson said. The union gained a degree of assurance that it would not be dismembered by the inroads of the new technologies. And the publishers got much of what they had demanded, including reductions in the number of employees in certain work classifications and the right to deal directly with various abuses in pressroom practices. The cost of the strike to the *Times* and the *Daily News* was estimated at $150 million. Losses to the *Post* were proportional. Losses in wages for union members came to about $60 million. The *Times* reported a loss of $16.6 million for the third quarter of the year. As expected, the *Daily News* also lost in the third quarter with a 20 percent drop in income.

Agreement at Last

As Nicholas King, a veteran New York journalist, points out, nobody could really "win" a strike of that magnitude, a strike whose echoes are likely to be felt far into the future. The publishers gained the right to reduce the number of pressroom employees by 30 percent by 1984. The union defended its existence and all its members will continue to work for the time stipulated in the

agreement. But each union member involved lost between $3,000 and $4,000 beyond the income received from strike benefits and unemployment compensation. In addition to the $150 million lost by the *Times* and *Daily News*, the losses in retail trade, business activity, and other categories in the city are beyond calculation.

At the same time, the strike proved that the public wants and will support their newspapers. Circulation figures for the *Daily News* are higher than before the strike and that paper and the *Times* have to turn advertisers away. As King commented: "Nothing is certain in the world or in the newspaper business, but for the present at least, it looks as though the daily printed press in New York City will survive."[12]

**Equality
in the Ranks**
*Sex Discrimination
at the* Times

If the 1978 strike wasn't enough to spin the minds of the three papers involved, three weeks after it ended, a federal court found the *New York Times* guilty of discriminating against women employees on the basis of sex.[13]

In a class action suit, the court ruled that the *Times* had violated Title VII of the Civil Rights Act of 1964. The verdict covered not only the 7 women who filed the suit, but approximately 550 other women employed as of November 7, 1974. The paper agreed to comply with the decision rather than launch an appeal. The settlement required the *Times* to pay $350,000 in annuities and other payments in addition to paying attorneys fees and expenses incurred by the women who had brought the suit. In addition, by 1982, the *Times* must have "at least a stated proportion of women" in each of the various job categories from top executive positions (10 percent) to middle-level office and clerical jobs (70.8 percent). In news departments, the percentages must range from 25 to 30 percent in favor of women journalists. Retroactive salaries and benefits were not included in the order.

The attorney for the women commented: "I hope this settlement will lay to rest forever the ignorant, bigoted notion, asserted by one of the *New York Times*'s experts, that women, particularly those with families, are not really interested in attaining responsible, demanding jobs and are, therefore, less valuable employees."

Other newspapers have worked to counteract sexism without awaiting the force of lawsuits, and some are drawing up data to restructure their employee practices and priorities. In time, those who choose to ignore the matter, or hope to stall indefinitely on their commitments to all employees, are likely to end up in court.

The Glossy World of the Slicks

Magazines in America went "big time" around the turn of this century with the thunder of the Muckrakers, a group of reform-minded men and women journalists who set out to right the nation's wrongs. They chose magazines as the primary vehicle of social and political change. And because of revelations that resulted, many of their publications moved to center stage among other mass media of the time.

The Promise at War's End

By the end of World War II, national gross income from American magazines was an estimated $739 million. In 1947, optimists in the field, and they had every right to be optimistic, anticipated that in a few years' time, total incomes would reach or exceed a billion dollars a year. By the mid-1950s, twenty-three national magazines enjoyed circulations of two million readers or more and fifty-three others more than a million each. More than three-quarters of a billion copies of American magazines were being purchased each year. Between the end of World War II and the mid-fifties, magazine circulation increased 62 percent and more than $653,400,000 was earned in national advertising.[14]

The Shock Wave Strikes

But even as total circulations continued to build, the 1950s began downward trends for many of magazine's superstars. Others would hold on into the sixties and early seventies when the downward trend began to turn upward again. The shock wave that staggered the magazine industry was the almost overnight success of big-time commercial television. Heretofore secure with the vastly successful formula of producing *something* for everyone in each issue, the magazine giants based their content on broad audience appeal. That assured huge readerships, especially in view of the pennies-per-copy cost to the reader. Profits came from charging high rates to advertisers based, in turn, on the high circulation figures. The problem was that, in time, not every reader was attracted to every article in each issue. Nor did each advertisement appeal to each reader. Hence, there was considerable lost exposure in each issue. But that was the formula of the magazine giants and everyone seemed happy with it. Then, with the explosive arrival of commercial television, the formula began to unravel.

Formula for Success

The Impact of Big-time Television

Uniqueness of the New Medium

People under thirty-five might find it difficult to appreciate the tremendous social impact television had on Americans in the 1950s. It was unique, show-biz gadgetry on an immense scale. It invaded the privacy of the home; it was a totally unknown but welcome intruder with unique things to offer—for free, except for the price of the set. It was radio, movies, and the Broadway stage in one magic box. It was world, national, and local news unravelled before one's eyes. Performers sang and danced and cracked jokes *live* and advertisers did the same. The change altered living habits and styles as few changes in history have done. Americans dined in the living room which, in turn, brought about the creation of television tables. People held television parties and invited the neighbors in, giving way to new munch-type snacks, soft drinks, beer, and home popcorn makers. There had never been anything like it.

Social Effects of Television

Major Shift in Advertising

The changes in entertainment habits were many, sudden, and in some cases permanent. Moviegoers stayed home, leaving theater managers to count empty seats: many went out of business. A nation of readers put away their reading. In a very real sense, Americans had become ensnared by television. Those who had been selling their goods and services through the print media looked hard at this new medium. They soon found that not only could television deliver their wares to millions of viewers, many more than magazines could, but it could do so at the same rates charged by the big magazines. Even more, television could aim them directly at *desired* consumers, those who were most likely to want or need the products advertised. Soap flakes, cookery, and beauty products were aimed at housewives during daytime broadcasts that they would most likely be watching; beer, lawn mowers, and sporting goods went out to the men via sportscasts and other male-oriented shows. Television even altered traditional product identities to the point of having attractive women in slithering gowns pushing automobile tires, while dashing Hollywood-type males promoted the latest in cosmetics. So the switches began and magazines gasped as their financial bases began to evaporate. Many were caught with huge circulations and heavy production costs that could no longer be supported due to the advertising drain to television. Some tried rate increases, but the public, now reading less, had become accustomed to "a lot for a little," and per-copy increases seemed to make it "a little for a lot." In time, some of the old giants began to topple.*

Newspapers: The Major Advertising Medium

Newspapers have traditionally led all media in advertising income, due mostly to their virtual monopoly of local advertising. They still do today. Since magazines are a vital arm of the print media, it is interesting to compare ad incomes for each medium from the beginnings of the television industry to the present time. In 1946, newspapers received 34 percent of all advertising expenditures. Magazines took about 13 percent. The coming of television in the 1950s brought impressive changes. By 1955, newspapers were holding at 34 percent but magazines had fallen to 8 percent. At present, newspapers take 29 percent and magazines 5.9 percent. While those changes were developing, television was moving into the market in force. In 1950, television earned 3 percent of all monies spent for advertising. By 1955 it had risen to 11 percent, and today it takes more than 20 percent, second only to daily newspapers.[15]

Increasing Ad Revenues to Television

---

*Not so coincidentally, a major novel of the time was *The View From the Fortieth Floor* about the fruitless, but energetic, struggle to keep a major magazine afloat.

Television was not the only force that jarred big-time magazines. Media consumers had also become better educated and more directly involved in the issues and concerns of society and the world. (The World War II and Korean War education assistance plans, the "G.I. Bill," so-called, had much to do with that, with subsidized educational benefits for millions of veterans.) To support their changing interests, men and women began seeking more specialized publications. In time, publishers sensed this and began juggling content to keep up with changing tastes. Some made it, some did not. *Collier*'s died. The *Saturday Evening Post* died. *Bluebook* died, then *Life* and *Look* went along with others, many of them the staples of the magazine industry. The old formula had gone. Survivors included most of the women's slicks which, in editorial and advertising content, had actually been specialized all along, at least more so than the general circulation publications. Others tried to retrench and hold on.

Major changes in the magazine industry are still going on and, in some significant ways, magazines are coming back. By way of comparison, in 1950, 250 American periodicals sold 140,259,540 total copies. Then circulation began falling. But by 1975, with television less of a novelty, that picture began to change. In 1975, 327 periodicals sold 250,831,209 total copies. New arrivals had replaced the departed old by something like five to one.[16]

How some of the old standards of the industry survived into the present age is significant, especially the women's magazines, which, as mentioned, were more specialized than general anyway. *Cosmopolitan*, formerly a Hearst property, turned new corners under editor Helen Gurley Brown. Geared for career women in the eighteen to thirty-four age group, *Cosmo* currently enjoys a 2,500,000 circulation and a vast assortment and number of advertisements aimed directly at that readership. *Good Housekeeping* also has impressive reader loyalty with 5 million copies per issue while *McCall's* is healthy with 6,500,000. The latter two have solid advertising support directed at specific readers. *Women's Day*, with fourteen issues a year, is the largest of the lot at an 8 million circulation. A wide assortment of new women's magazines have also joined the market with *Ms.* being one of the best known via its association with the women's liberation movement.

The men's magazines generally have not held on the way women's publications have. Traditional magazines like the *Saturday Evening Post* (which has come back as a monthly), *Collier's, Bluebook*, and others fed male interest in adventure and conflict content. But most major circulation magazines currently geared for men are sex-oriented slicks catering to young, urbane, well-educated types. Major representatives of the market are *Playboy, Penthouse, Gallery*, and others of the genre, plus lesser lights of the *Hustler* mold. Yet other magazines for men have been around a while, reflecting male interest in the outdoors, sports, and history. Some are *Argosy, True, Cavalier, Gentle-*

men's *Quarterly*, and *Esquire*. All carry impressive amounts of advertising aimed at their particular readership. Of course men and women readers look to publications beyond these particular identities as other personal interests dictate.

Life
Struggles Back

At its creation, *Life* magazine was almost as unique to the world of mass media as television later became. Not as totally absorbing, as hypnotic, or as radical an entry perhaps, but *Life* had a difference about it that nobody else in the business could match. A brainchild of Henry Luce, head of the Time Incorporated empire, *Life* entered the general magazine field in 1936 on a "run it up and see if it flies" basis. The element that made it different was its

Uniqueness of Life:
Photojournalism

basic "identity": *photojournalism*—to prove that a news picture was indeed worth a thousand words. The idea was to tell the story of America in all its facets, good and bad, through the lens of the camera. Those were depressed

Luce's Formula

times, and Luce's talented staff captured the misery and the fun (what there was of it) constructively and positively at a time when many thought the country had lost its way. Luce hired the best photojournalists he could find and told them to go find the news. They did and the public was awed by it: real-life circumstances sensitively portrayed. In Luce's terms, the purpose of

Table 12.2   Analysis of Content of 14 National Magazines in U.S., by Subject Matter and Proportion of Advertising, 1938–1976

	1938		1946	
	Total Coverage (pages)	Percent of Total Pages	Total Coverage (pages)	Percent of Total Pages
National Affairs	928.5	5.9%	1,196.9	7.1%
Foreign/International	666.7	4.2	1,103.6	6.5
Amusements	504.7	3.2	501.6	3.0
Beauty, Grooming	227.9	1.4	271.0	1.6
Building	885.2	5.6	970.8	5.7
Business and Industry	435.1	2.8	414.4	2.4
Children	501.3	3.2	585.2	3.5
Farming and Gardening	630.5	4.0	504.4	3.0
Food and Nutrition	495.8	3.2	787.8	4.6
Health/Medical Science	159.6	1.0	247.3	1.5
Home Furnishings and Management	1,193.2	7.6	1,496.8	8.8
Sports, Recreation, Hobbies	248.0	1.6	235.5	1.4
Travel and Transportation	376.7	2.4	193.8	1.1
Wearing Apparel and Accessories	1,965.3	12.5	1,934.1	11.4
Cultural Interests	912.6	5.8	1,510.0	8.9
General Interest	1,433.3	9.1	1,131.5	6.7
Miscellaneous	912.6	5.8	580.4	3.4
Fiction	3,256.3	20.7	3,292.5	19.4
Total Editorial Content	**15,733.3**	**100.0%**	**16,957.6**	**100.0%**
Total Editorial Content	15,733.3	57.2%	16,957.6	41.4%
Total Advertising Content	11,753.1	42.8	23,988.4	58.6
Total Magazine Pages	**27,486.4**	**100.0%**	**40,946.0**	**100.0%**

Source: Prepared especially for this volume by the R. Russell Hall Company (1977).

Life was "to see life; to see the world; to eyewitness great events," and to portray them positively. The purpose was to fight the depression gloom and correct journalism's distorted priorities—"That evil makes news and good makes little or no news." Luce would tolerate no negativism in *Life*.[17] But time, television, and changes in public tastes and lifestyles finally brought it down after thirty years in American homes.

In 1978, Time Inc. gave *Life* another shot at recapturing the attention of American readers. It came back as a monthly with a press run of 700,000 (which eventually was raised to 1.2 million). At $1.50 per copy, it was 136 pages thick, 56 of them with advertising. But it wasn't the same publication. As one critic noted, the new product was "a fat, bland, harmless four-color puppy that everyone will love—except those who missed the regular diet of photo-essays in the old weekly *Life*." The problem with it, the critic continued, was that it teemed with "dogs, kids, family reunions, and flocks of celebrities," which made it look like "a swollen Technicolor version of *People*," the publication dedicated to gossip.[18] The guiding hand of Henry Luce was gone. Whether *Life* will make it in the modern world remains to be seen. If it stays with the gossip crowd, it might be a financial success, given the public penchant for eavesdropping. And if it does, the old *Life* (to many the *real Life*) has indeed remained in the grave.

The "New" Life

1956		1966		1976	
Total Coverage (pages)	Percent of Total Pages	Total Coverage (pages)	Percent of Total Pages	Total Coverage (pages)	Percent of Total Pages
1,213.8	6.3%	1,662.0	8.4%	1,885.6	10.9%
947.6	4.9	977.9	5.0	942.3	5.4
634.3	3.3	731.6	3.7	710.2	4.1
341.7	1.8	573.0	2.9	778.5	4.5
1,031.4	5.4	883.1	4.5	545.2	3.1
688.3	3.6	640.2	3.2	555.7	3.2
630.2	3.3	665.5	3.4	338.6	2.0
526.7	2.7	333.7	1.7	237.8	1.4
1,251.4	6.5	1,609.5	8.2	1,671.8	9.6
317.9	1.7	362.0	1.8	529.2	3.0
2,146.5	11.2	2,273.6	11.5	2,164.2	12.5
301.5	1.6	268.4	1.4	273.5	1.6
523.4	2.7	550.7	2.8	355.1	2.0
2,335.4	12.2	2,616.8	13.3	1,546.8	8.9
1,843.0	9.6	2,038.7	10.3	1,856.6	10.7
1,314.7	6.9	1,050.4	5.3	1,040.0	6.0
774.5	4.0	643.8	3.3	650.8	3.7
2,363.6	12.3	1,829.3	9.3	1,284.0	7.4
19,185.9	**100.0%**	**19,710.2**	**100.0%**	**17,365.9**	**100.0%**
19,185.9	48.2%	19,710.2	49.6%	17,365.9	49.0%
20,631.1	51.8	20,052.3	50.4	18,074.8	51.0
39,817.0	**100.0%**	**39,762.5**	**100.0%**	**35,440.7**	**100.0%**

Meanwhile, *Look* magazine, *Life*'s chief rival in the old big-magazine days, has also staged a comeback, but as a semimonthly.[19] As editor and publisher, Jann Wenner, founder of *Rolling Stone*, currently heads *Look*'s revival with an eye to molding it into a more specialized publication than the earlier format provided. "*Look* is going to be a magazine for people about 25 to 40, sophisticated, educated, primarily living in the cities."

Wenner added that the new *Look* will not be a *People*-type gossip magazine, in spite of the fact that early editions seem to contradict that assessment. The first issue carried forty pages of advertising, which is now down to about fifteen pages per issue. The plan is to produce 700,000 copies per issue, since the first two issues sold 1.5 million copies combined. Wenner also indicated that the per-copy price will be raised from $1.25 to $1.50.

The new package is news oriented, but features will be included as well. The main ingredient is *concentration of circulation*, i.e., seeking out and capturing particular kinds of readers. Wenner has no intention of trying to recapture the 6 million readers the magazine had when it left the field. The new audience will be more select with an eventual circulation high of 1.2 million. And emphasis will be on newsstand sales, rather than cut-rate mail subscription sales with advertising taking the brunt of the cost as the old formula dictated. The company also expects to lose $16 million before *Look* begins to pay for itself. Another spokesman indicated his awareness of the gambles involved but remains optimistic: "The trend over the last two or three years has been extremely favorable for magazines."

The Economics of Imagery
Oldies Spruce Up:
The Nation

While some publications are attempting comebacks, other existing publications are sprucing up their images for greater impact in the marketplace. The *Nation*, a premier publication of opinion and commentary for 112 years, recently changed owners and format. But rather than imitating competitors as other magazines have done, the *Nation*'s editors have partially fallen back on tradition. It's new nameplate reflects the style embraced back in 1865 when the publication was founded. And unlike other modern types, its goals are "to capitalize on our most cherished asset, our identity; to underline our commitment to content." In the words of the *Columbia Journalism Review*, the *Nation* is "a constant demonstration that, given publishers' tenacity and generosity, a political weekly can survive without profit."

Victor S. Navasky, the new editor, said: "We intend to continue the *Nation*'s focus on issues. We recognize that this is a radical aspiration at a time when electronic journalism has turned news into entertainment and so many publications seem to be increasingly mired in life styles, gossip and essays on

U.S. News and World Report "before" and "after" covers. (Reprinted by permission of U.S. News and World Report.)

hair spray, upholstery, comparative soups and coping with dandruff." Approximately twenty investors covered the sale price, estimated at $150,000.[20]

On the other side of the coin, what once was a tower of individualism in publishing, *Esquire*, appears to have joined the trend of imitating others as an economic strategy. Once the showcase of major authors of fact, fiction, and commentary, the newly revamped *Esquire* is now heralded as a "new magazine for the new American man," which will "explore new dimensions of success." *Esquire* dropped its traditional stout binding as a cost-saving device and replaced it with staples. It added more features, cartoons, photographs, and drawings along with a classified ads section. All that makes *Esquire* strikingly similar to new owner Clay Felker's old *New York* magazine, which has been described as "the country's most imitated magazine in the seventies." (That was until Australian media baron Rupert Murdoch bought it and made it into something less.)

The first several issues of the new *Esquire* offered a hodgepodge of personal profiles of those who had "made it," along with other assorted goodies. But overall, as one critic commented, the new *Esquire* offers "an exasperatingly shrewd combination of the irresistable and the unsatisfying" that is likely to "discombobulate" those who remember *Esquire*'s former self during its best days. "But if Felker's business instincts hold up, it may succeed anyway, due, again, to the public's appetite for the mundane."[21]

Esquire *Retrenches*

The New Breed of Specialized Magazines

On other fronts, a covey of new magazines have appeared in hopes of attracting readers who have developed special interests. *Penthouse* publisher Bob Guccione recently founded *Omni*, "an original if not controversial mixture of science, fact, fiction, fantasy, and the paranormal." Seeking to cash in on current popular interest in science fiction, *Omni*'s thrust is to present the works, fact and fiction, of the authors prominent in the fields of interest to the magazine. The magazine's first press run—a million copies—contained 178 pages, 49 of which carried full-page advertisements.

Cross-country Skiing

Other magazines are also trying to break into the special-interest market, where competition for readers is keen. For example, as cross-country skiing has come into its own as a leisure-time activity, a number of publications have arrived on the newsstand whose editorial and advertising content is geared explicitly to those interests. How-to-do-it articles dominate and cartoons poke fun at the bumps and the bruises. Color photographs depict the lure of the snowy outdoors, and advertisements for goods and services associated with the sport abound. This reflects the formula for special-interest magazines—to provide the reader with information on all facets of the activity, including the advertising. The same holds true for most do-it-yourself sports for amateurs including tennis, bowling, and scuba diving. Some specialized publications come and go but others stay around to become "must" reading for enthusiasts.

Do-it-yourself Sports

The Jogging Craze

With twenty million Americans now active in jogging and other running programs, magazines geared to those involved have begun to proliferate (in keeping with the vast number of paperback books on the subject). *Runner's World* is something of a giant in the field, but others are closing in. The *Runner*, published by the newsweekly *New Times*, is one of the most attractive in the field. Articles and advertisements depict people running in all sorts of settings from mountains to parks. Other pieces treat associated concerns such as proper conditioning, dieting, rules of the road, proper equipment—presumably everything associated with the activity.[22]

The Formula

With Americans increasingly seeking escape in leisure activities, specialized magazines are vying for their attention in order to contribute to the enjoyment and to turn a profit. In the days of the general magazine giants, advertising content geared to special interests was minimal. But reader participation in leisure activities was limited as well. That was due to longer work days and weeks, shorter vacations, and limited entertainment budgets. Now that recreation in its broadest sense has caught on, the magazines are there, or will be soon, to lend their support. Although circulations are smaller than the larger magazines, these magazines get by via smaller staffs and low overhead. Most important in terms of economic survival, there is a demand for them. It is a highly competitive market and specialized publications come and go. But they do provide essential services to those who buy them.

A sampling of the specialized magazine market. (Reprinted by permission of *Skate Boarder* magazine; *Working Women*, 1980 by HAL Publications, Inc.; and *Racquetball Illustrated*.)

More from the
Specialized Market

Writer's Market, an annual directory of magazines published in the United States, provides one measure of the popularity of special-interest publications. It offers thirty-six pages* of listings geared to "sport and outdoor" reader interest. Some titles in that category include: *Tennis*; the *Water Skier*; *Surfer*; *Skin Diver*; *Archery World*; *Bay & Delta Yachtsman* (for enthusiasts in Northern California); *Canoe Magazine*; *Billiards Digest*; *Bowlers Journal*; *Gambling Times Magazine*; *Country Club Golfer* (one of six periodicals for golfers). Nine publications are geared to guns and shooting, others to karate, backpacking, and so forth. *Writer's Market* also offers thirteen pages of listings in the "teen and young adult" category alone. There are also specialized publications for cooks, ice skaters, star gazers, gardeners, fruit and vegetable canners, and so on. These speak only to recreational and hobby interests; still others are aimed at dieting and health interests, politics and government, the environment, space exploration, nature—again, the possibilities are almost without limit.

City Magazines
*Another Form of
Specialized Magazines*

Another facet of specialization in the magazine field is the impressive development of "city magazines," which have proven immensely successful business ventures in their own right.[23]

City magazines, as such, are not new to American journalism. Some existed early in this century though they were a far cry in quality from today's crop. Some were blatantly promotional vehicles ground out by chambers of commerce (and some still are). They were more dedicated to "selling" the com-

*1979 edition.

munity to new business interests, tourists, or both, than to providing local citizens with meaningful community related content. But in the last fifteen years, between seventy-five and a hundred sharp, slick, highly professional magazines have made their physical and editorial presence felt. Most of them are monthlies put out by independent publishers for consumption *within* their own communities.

A Unique Factor

One unique aspect of this publishing genre is that the city magazine has no direct competition. That fact carries mixed blessings as the individual case may be. For one thing, it means that each can be as highly professional or as horribly unprofessional as the public will take.

The Leaders

Among the best of the city magazines are *Chicago* (155,000 circulation); *Los Angeles* (135,000); *Philadelphia* (130,000); *Boston* (120,000); and the *Washingtonian* (95,000) in the nation's capital. *New York* is also in this class except that it is a weekly publication. Probably the most outstanding of all is *Texas Monthly*. Although its circulation covers the entire state, it is classified, in magazine terms, with city magazines. Its 215,000 circulation serves a market of 12 million people with an editorial budget of about $800,000 per year. High income does not necessarily equate with quality, but in this case it does.

Reasons for Success

One of the basic selling points for city magazines is the "buying guides" they offer. In effect, they tell readers "what to do, how to do it and where." That alone attracts many top advertisers. And since each is supreme in its own city, it does not have to worry about competition. That fact opens the way to mutual business arrangements among them. For example, *Philadelphia* and the *Washingtonian* have a mutual advertising sales program out of a New York advertising agency. Sharing editorial costs is another business advantage. As one editor put it, "If we do a travel article on Canada, why can't it be made available to all city magazines, who would offer a local sidebar to it?" In that fashion, the editor could invest the money saved in a major article that might also be shared by others.

All Part of Social Changes

It is clear that the magazine world has changed as all media have changed. It is not surprising when one considers all the other social changes that have developed since the end of World War II. Transportation has shifted from the railroads, to personal conveyances, to jet airplanes. Women's fashions have gone from padded shoulders and piled hair of the war years, to the miniskirt, and on into the present, while men's fashions have also changed several times. Athletic leagues have expanded from a few choice cities to most of the nation's metropolitan centers. The oil crunch promises further changes, while international developments have created friends of enemies (and vice versa). The mass media have influenced change and have been influenced *by* change. Along the way, some media could not adapt and were lost: others came to take their places. Such is the nature of social change and the modern mass media are aware of it.

Reprinted with permission of *Texas Monthly*, Copyright 1979 by *Texas Monthly*; *Chicago* magazine; photo © Phil Porcella, 1979.

The Issues and Problems of Advertising and the Mass Media

Because advertising provides a substantial portion of mass media income and content, and thus keeps the media free as the Founding Fathers intended, its credibility before the public is of major consequence to the media that carry it.* When the advertisements in a print or broadcast medium are honestly and fairly presented, the media that carry them are viewed positively by readers and viewers. But when advertisements are ethically suspect, the medium that carries them is likely to become ethically suspect as well. Advertisers who genuinely labor in the public interest, and many do, are aware of the pitfalls of the profession. They are also aware of their obligations to the public beyond those forms of government control that say that they *must* be responsible.

Reflections of Advertising in the Mass Media

With varying degrees of success, the advertising industry has attempted to deal with fast-buck hucksters, fraudulent claims, and the pitch for products that are inherently harmful to health or pocketbook. The industry is involved in constant, ferocious competition among a vast number of practitioners over highly competitive products and services. And sometimes in an effort to swamp the opposition, some practitioners go all out to promise the consumer Nirvana at the lowest cost. The consumer might end up with a bargain; he or she might also end up with a faulty guarantee, a mechanical clinker, or upholstery that sags. It is an age-old problem that continues to plague responsible business practice and the media of communication in the democratic order.

The Nature of Advertising

The very presence of advertising in American newspapers is awesome. According to the American Newspaper Publishers Association, daily newspapers earned $885 million *more* in advertising in 1978 than television and

The Presence of Advertising in Public Life

*Other aspects of advertising are covered in chapter 4 (Sexism) and chapter 8 (Controls).

		1977[1]		1978[2]		
		Millions	% of Total	Millions	% of Total	% Change
Daily Newspapers	Total	$11,132	29.2	$12,690	29.0	+14.0
	National	1,677	4.4	1,810	4.1	8.0
	Local	9,455	24.8	10,880	24.9	15.0
Magazines		2,162	5.7	2,595	5.9	20.0
Television	Total	7,612	20.0	8,850	20.2	16.0
	Network	3,460	9.1	3,910	8.9	13.0
	Spot	2,204	5.8	2,600	5.9	18.0
	Local	1,948	5.1	2,340	5.4	20.0
Radio	Total	2,634	6.9	2,955	6.8	12.0
	Network	137	0.4	160	0.4	16.0
	Spot	546	1.4	610	1.4	12.0
	Local	1,951	5.1	2,185	5.0	12.0
Farm Publications		90	0.2	105	0.2	14.0
Direct Mail		5,333	14.0	6,030	13.8	13.0
Business Publications		1,221	3.2	1,420	3.3	16.0
Outdoor	Total	418	1.1	465	1.1	11.0
	National	290	0.8	310	0.7	7.0
	Local	128	0.3	155	0.4	21.0
Miscellaneous	Total	7,518	19.7	8,630	19.7	15.0
	National	3,935	10.3	4,495	10.3	15.0
	Local	3,583	9.4	4,135	9.4	15.0
GRAND TOTAL	National	21,055	55.2	24,045	55.0	14.2
GRAND TOTAL	Local	17,065	44.8	19,695	45.0	15.4
TOTAL—ALL MEDIA		$38,120	100.0	$43,740	100.0	+14.7

[1]Revised figures
[2]Preliminary figures

Breakdown of media advertising revenues, 1977 and 1978 percentages. (McCann-Erickson, Inc.)

radio combined—$12.7 billion total. Projections indicate that it will soon reach $13.9 billion and beyond. Classified advertising enjoyed the largest increase, jumping 21.2 percent to approximately $3.9 billion. Retail advertising went up 12.6 percent to $7 billion and national advertising was up 8.2 percent to $1.8 billion. And the number of special, preprinted advertising inserts carried in daily newspapers is now over 20 billion per year compared to 8 billion in 1970. There can be no doubt about the importance of newspapers to advertising and vice versa.[24]

Creativity in Advertising

The secret of success in ethical advertising seems to lie less in what one is selling than in how one sells it. Bill Bernbach, cofounder of the New York-based advertising agency of Doyle Dane Bernbach—the person who made Volkswagen a household word—tells his clients that creativity is the ingredient essential to successful advertising. It is even more essential than all the charts and graphs that purport to reflect trends. To stay ahead of the competition, he says, new product ideas, new merchandising ideas, and new advertising ideas must be created. "In the coming decade, playing it too safe may be the most dangerous thing you can do," he said.

Bernbach urges advertisers to avoid terminology like "hard-sell" and "soft-sell." The primary ingredient is to touch and move and persuade the audience. No equation or formula anywhere will accomplish that. A formula in communications is death, he said. The advertiser's impact is in direct proportion to the originality of his or her advertising. And a formula is original only the first time it is used. Hence, questionable gimmickry, outlandish techniques or persuasion, and other underhanded selling devices are not needed.[25]

Advertising Self-Regulation Procedures Step-by-Step

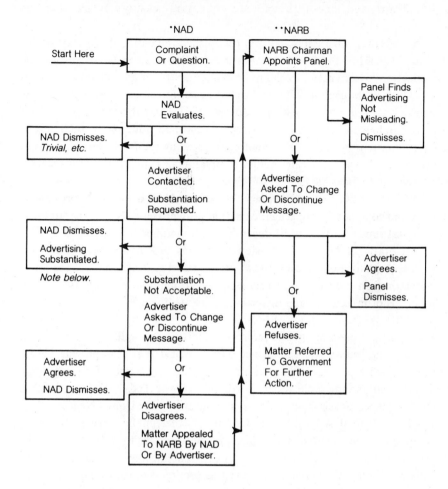

Note: If the original complaint originated outside the system, the outside complainant at this point can appeal to the Chairman of NARB for a panel adjudication. Granting of such appeals is at the Chairman's discretion.

*National Advertising Division, Council of Better Business Bureaus
**National Advertising Review Board

Advertising self-regulation procedures step-by-step. (Reproduced from William Ewen's *The National Advertising Review Board 1971–1975: A Four Year Review and Perspective on Advertising Industry Self-Regulation,* pamphlet published by the National Advertising Review Board, 1975, p. 12.)

Many within the industry are concerned about the morality of the profession and have moved to apply industry controls to insure that the public will be served fairly and honestly. Legitimate advertising executives are showing concern.

The NAD

In 1971, the advertising industry established the National Advertising Division (NAD) of the Council of Better Business Bureaus (CBBB). This organization investigates complaints of shoddy practices and makes judgments on actual cases dealing with charges of deceptive national advertising. The industry also set up the National Advertising Review Board (NARB) to act as a "higher court of appeals" in such cases. In addition, NARB makes determinations in cases that cannot be resolved by the NAD. On local levels, the Better Business Bureau handles complaints of fraudulent and inaccurate advertising in local media.

The NARB

In the first five years of activity, NAD and NARB took on more than a thousand complaints lodged against national advertisers. As a result, hundreds of advertisements found to be deceptive were modified or discontinued.

The National Advertising Review Board has had the greatest visibility of the two organizations and has its share of critics as well. Many of the latter doubt that an industry supported policing group can deal objectively with problems of inaccuracy and distortion by its members.[26]

**The Advertising
Council**

Problems are found in "public-interest" advertising as well. For example, the Advertising Council was established during World War II to provide special advertising support for the war effort via sloganizing, support for scrap metal drives, and innumerable other worthy exertions. Today, the council has switched its emphasis from war to such programs as the United Negro College Fund, the United Way, Savings Bonds, and other public service advertising campaigns. The advertisements are supposed to be free to the sponsor "in the public interest." Ad Council public service announcements (PSAs) are typically wedged between regular broadcasting programs or paid-for commercials in ten-, fifty-, and sixty-second spots. With a multitude of organizations seeking to promote their own particular interests, competition for air time is fierce.

*How the
Ad Council Works*

*Problems of
the Ad Council*

Though founded with a high purpose in mind, the Ad Council has also created a sizable group of highly vocal critics. Deborah Baldwin, an editor of *Environmental Action* magazine, cites one of the problems about public service advertising: "It's the new electronic soapbox and everyone—from gay rights advocates to consumer groups to corporate public relations agencies—wants a piece of the action."[27] As a result, not every qualified group can participate in the program. A basic reason, she says, is that the definition of "public service" is interpreted by television executives in a way not shared by all public-interest groups. Over the years the television industry has come to equate public service advertising the way it does paid commercial advertising: "Say it quickly, say it slickly, and stay away from controversy."

Jane Crowley screens public service announcements for the NBC network. A major guideline to acceptable content, she said, is that "PSAs should deal affirmatively with the causes they advertise, as opposed to those that attack or demean."

John Cowden, who handles PSAs for CBS, has a similar approach to what constitutes acceptable network content. He suggests that a public service message dealing with highway safety could not depict a scene with "bodies all over the highway." His reasoning: "Coming between [regular] programming, it might have a shock value. It'd be out of context. . . . [A PSA] can't be a scare message."

The result of such thinking, according to Deborah Baldwin, is that public service announcements "are at best bland and at worst misleading." What is lacking, she says, is positive recommendations to cope with issues and problems, such as the need for clean, renewable sources of energy. Instead, blame for the nation's ailments falls on the individual: "Only you can prevent forest fires!" "People start pollution!" "America. It only works as well as we do!" and so forth. "No mention of the impact of clearcutting on forest preservation, or the critical cleanup problems posed by industrial dumping in public waterways or the role of the corporation in shaping the economy." The same rules embraced by the networks appear to apply among local stations.

Need to Explain Issues

Asked if she would approve a PSA beginning with "Sugar starts tooth decay," a person in charge of PSAs for a Washington, D.C., affiliate of ABC retorted, "Heavens no. I don't see any reason to attack things." In short, Baldwin says, PSAs can generalize about people but not about products.

The Ad Council seems to have drifted away from its original purpose of serving the public in meaningful ways. For one thing, the council's board of directors contains "85 representatives of the nation's corporate and media giants." No representatives of public-interest groups are included. The council receives direct financial support from vested interests including the National Association of Broadcasters, the Outdoor Advertisers Association, the American Business Press, and the American Association of Advertising Agencies, to the tune of $1 million per year. That helps support a full-time staff of thirty-three persons. To put PSAs together, the organization draws from "the talent of New York's finest advertising agencies." In the original planning, PSAs were to be put together free of charge to the sponsoring public-interest organization other than for out-of-pocket expenses. In fact, however, putting a PSA together can be costly—about three times what private contractors indicate they would charge for the same project. Only the coordination of the campaign and placements in the mass media are free.

Possible Conflict of Interest

Application of the First Amendment to the business of advertising has long been charged with controversy. The constitutional question has been, Should a media message designed to sell commercial goods or services enjoy the same protections as a news story or editorial devised to inform people and thus enable them to participate in the democratic process? On several occasions, the United States Supreme Court has ruled that certain kinds of advertisements do enjoy First Amendment protection. Those narrow exceptions are advertisements that deal with "matters of clear public interest" as opposed to ads related strictly to commerce. The latter may be regulated (and some are) by various government agencies.

A Case in Virginia

A 1975 Supreme Court decision dealt with an advertisement published in a Virginia weekly newspaper that offered detailed information on abortion services in New York City. The Virginia courts found the newspaper to be in violation of Virginia's antiabortion law. The United States Supreme Court overruled that judgment on the grounds that, while the ad in question "had commercial aspects" to it, it also "contained factual material of clear 'public interest.' " Thus, it and other such "informational" advertising do enjoy First Amendment protection. Then in 1976, the high Court upheld an advertiser's right to include the prices of prescription drugs in advertising, which had also been held in violation of Virginia law. The Court interpreted the price listing to be information of interest to "the sick, the aged and the poor."[28]

*Government Controls
of Advertising*

These First Amendment applications to advertising have been in *exceptional cases only*. In the main, commercial advertising of goods and services to the public are monitored, in the public interest, by various government agencies. These include the Federal Communications Commission, the Food and Drug Administration, and the Federal Trade Commission. All three are interested in different aspects of advertising as represented in the mass media.

**The Federal Trade
Commission**
*The FTC Improvement
Act of 1975*

Chief among these agencies is the Federal Trade Commission (FTC). That agency has been given broad new powers to deal with unfair advertising under the FTC Improvement Act of 1975. It now has the authority, for example, to consider what is *implied* in an advertisement along with what is literally stated. In an actual case, as a result of FTC pressures, cigarette manufacturers agreed to carry health hazard warnings in their advertising as well as on their cigarette packages. In addition, the FTC created an order requiring public documentation of advertising claims by manufacturers of certain patent medicines, air conditioners, automobiles, and other specified products. The First Amendment does not protect advertising content from government controls in such cases.

Function of the FTC

Michael Pertschuk, FTC chairman, outlined the function of his agency: "Our role at the Commission is entirely consistent with . . . Supreme Court statements. We seek to promote the dissemination of honest and complete information and to police ads that fail to meet that standard."[29]

It is evident from official announcements by and the action of staff members that the FTC is putting together what one business source terms "an assault on advertising that goes far beyond anything that Washington regulators have tried in the past."[30] A particular target is promotional campaigns that encourage shoppers to make questionable purchases even if the advertisers do not misrepresent what they are selling. For example, there is the question of whether children are "a proper target of advertising" at all. If they are not, commercials aimed at them might be declared unfair according to FTC standards. Then there are advertisements for energy guzzling products like hair dryers, which encourage consumers to waste energy in spite of the government's drive to cut down. One consumer protection lawyer at the FTC underscored the large numbers of ads that urge sales of hair dryers. "What is unfair," he commented, "is that there is not an opportunity for someone to say that if you wait 25 minutes, your hair gets dry anyway."

Increased FTC Activity

Advertising and Children

Energy Using Products

Yet another target area for the FTC is to force food and drug advertisers to "conform to precise rules about health claims," especially those products purchased by the elderly, the poor, and the non-English speaking. As one commission member put it "is overweight a problem among poor women because they are bombarded with advertising for high-calorie foods?"

Health Products

The FTC has other crusades pending and, in sum, they could create considerable upset in the advertising industry.

In late 1975, the FTC filed a complaint against the American Medical Association and the Connecticut State Medical Society and its New Haven chapter. The complaint stated that the societies' collective ban on physicians advertising their services is a violation of antitrust laws. The ban, the FTC went on, discourages competition among physicians, which, in turn, supports arbitrary medical fees charged by doctors. In brief, without advertising, physicians cannot *compete* for patients by charging lower rates than others as other businesses do. The FTC brief stated: "Doctors have very little of the normal free-market pressure on them to lower their prices or offer special services to meet competition." The same measures could apply to dentists and other groups in health-care fields. Finally, in late 1979, the FTC ordered the American Medical Association to end all "ethical" restrictions on advertising by physicians.[31]

Advertising and the Professions: Physicians

The United States Supreme Court has already ruled that attorneys may advertise their services and many practitioners have begun doing so via newspapers, radio and television, and special printed leaflets. One Detroit lawyer has become a familiar figure on local television ads as "the people's attorney." Another who advertises offers to draw up wills for $25 each or two for $45. Yet another, who has twenty-three offices in Detroit, also supports the advertising approach. "I think I'm performing a public service by doing this. Personal bankruptcies used to cost $400 or so to perform. Through advertising, the man in the street knows I can do it for $100, plus costs."

Attorneys

FTC, AMA spar on doctor ads

WASHINGTON (AP)—Depending on whom you listen to, the Federal Trade Commission is considering action that could: (a) Hold down doctors' bills, or (b) Promote medical quackery.

The four commissioners on Wednesday heard final arguments in an antitrust proceeding against the American Medical Association that accuses the doctors' group of an illegal price-fixing conspiracy that has inflated medical bills.

FTC ATTORNEYS contended that the AMA's restrictions on doctors' advertising hurt competition and inflated bills. "We need an order to prevent the AMA from ever again preventing doctors from advertising their prices," FTC staff attorney Barry Costilo said.

But AMA lawyers said such an order could increase shoddy medical care. "If Hippocrates were alive today, he'd have to come to the FTC to get its approval before framing the Hippocratic oath," attorney Newton Minow said.

The Associated Press.

Taymar Legal Services.

But many attorneys take exception to all that. One feels that lawyers who advertise their services "denigrate my profession. We are not hucksters, we're professional people . . . I think the low opinion the public has for us will be further justified."[32]

The Abstainers

The Cereal Commercial Dilemma

The Federal Trade Commission is also girding its loins for a battle against television commercials aimed at children. The controversy isn't new, except that lately the fight is being waged by forces other than Action for Children's Television (ACT). The new opponents are dentists, physicians, and even labor unions, in addition to dietitians and parents. School children have participated in organized school letter-writing projects (at the insistence of teachers, some say) that demand that something be done about television commercials aimed at children. This time the FTC itself will attempt to place enforceable restrictions on such advertising. The main targets are General Foods, Kellogg, and General Mills, all major media advertisers. The FTC is currently holding public hearings on the controversy. One aim is to force manufacturers of sugar-coated cereals to print or broadcast messages on proper nutrition as a public service. The American Dental Association has been outspoken in its support of placing controls on such advertisements.[33]

"Appeals" of Advertising to Children

Critics say that some of the commercial "pitches" aimed at children are as attractively portrayed as regular programming. A sampling: A cartooned fruit peddler asks some elves if they would like some of his fruit. They refuse because they're already eating Keebler cookies. The peddler tastes a cookie, likes it, and then throws the fruit away in preference to peddling cookies. In another, two cartoon-type monsters are terribly agitated because someone has stolen their chocolate cereal. They discover the culprit and the young viewers are then urged to "enjoy a complete breakfast" with Count Chocula. (Count Chocula has 48 percent sugar content.) Other compelling commercials include the $100,000 "chewy, chewy caramel" candy bar from Nestle's; Cookie Crisp cereal that "looks like little chocolate chip cookies"; and Snickers Bars "all covered in delicious milk chocolate."

An ad for sugarless cereal. (Reprinted with permission of Little Crow Foods.)

As many as eight Saturday morning commercials per hour on each of the three networks project the delights of sugared foods, some of them containing as much as 70 percent sugar. Sophisticated advertising techniques make the products an impressive package for young viewers, and sponsors invest more than $600,000 per year to insure that their messages get across.[34]

Opposition to FTC Activities

In the interest of accuracy, it should be noted that *opposition* to FTC action is also visible. Syndicated columnist Louis Rukeyser wrote: "I don't know what they've been putting in their cornflakes in Washington, but this has to be the best example this year of why U.S. businessmen don't have that 'confidence' in the economy that the Carter administration is always urging on them." Economist Phillip Nelson, of the State University of New York at Binghamton, said that, in fact, the FTC is trying to "break up companies that consumers have deemed winners." In addition, many parents have become highly vocal about the federal government "interfering" in the raising of their children, that only they should determine dietary programs for their young.[35]

Either way, the fact of government dealing directly and decisively in the activities of media advertisers is to be reckoned with. Because the matter is highly charged, both sides seek public support and the debate is liable to continue far into the future.

Cigarette Advertising

Positive Aspects of Cigarette Advertising

The United States Department of Health, Education, and Welfare (HEW) spends an incredible $30 million a year on advertising to persuade Americans to stop smoking cigarettes.[36] (At the same time, the United States Department of Agriculture spends twenty times more to support tobacco growth and sales). Most of the funds are aimed at young people, warning them of the risks of cancer, heart disease, and other physical problems linked to cigarette smoking.

Negative Aspects

While HEW works feverishly, the powerful tobacco interests spend many millions in media advertising to push cigarette smoking at American youth as a glamorous, relaxing, sexy pastime that will make them Marlboro men and Virginia Slims women. At this point, the tobacco interests appear to be winning, as surveys reflect increases in smoking among American teenagers, especially young women.

The Imagery of Cigarette Advertising

The Federal Trade Commission has reported that "the association established between attractive lifestyles and cigarette smoking is one influence leading teenagers to smoke cigarettes." According to a recent survey, more than half the teenagers questioned found that the characters depicted in recent cigarette advertising were "attractive," "enjoying themselves," "well-dressed," "sexy," "young," and "healthy." Only 5 percent found the characters unattractive.

Tobacco vs. HEW

Meanwhile, the strong tobacco interests are going after HEW itself. They are attempting to influence Congress into prohibiting that agency from spending the entire $30 million on antismoking activities. In addition, the Tobacco Institute has proclaimed that there is "no scientific evidence that cigarette advertising has any influence on smoking among young people." The tobacco interests seem to have clout on other fronts as well.

Tobacco and Magazine Advertising

R. C. Smith, managing editor of the *Columbia Journalism Review*, explored the practices of magazines that accept cigarette advertising to determine if they also publish articles on the dangers of cigarette smoking.[37] His findings were discouraging in the extreme. Not one of the magazines analyzed carried any articles that would provide readers with "any clear notion of the nature and extent of the medical and social havoc being wreaked by the cigarette-smoking habit." Better records were attained by magazines that accept *no* cigarette advertising.

Leading the pack in the number of pieces on the negative aspects of smoking were *Reader's Digest* and the *New Yorker*. *Consumer Reports*, which accepts no advertising at all, aired its findings on smoking and associated effects on health and called on Congress to prohibit *all* cigarette advertising.

Smith labeled the performance of magazines that do accept cigarette advertising as "dismal." Some have carried innocuous how-to-quit pieces, but only rarely. Even women's service magazines like *Good Housekeeping* (which does not accept cigarette advertising), *Cosmopolitan*, and *Ladies' Home Journal* have not contributed noticeably to familiarizing readers with the health hazards of smoking.

An editor of *Ms.* magazine confessed that she did not run antismoking articles because the magazine is "heavily dependent on cigarette advertising." She admitted that *Ms.* had turned down advertising by Virginia Slims cigarettes but only because the theme ("You've come a long way, baby") is sexist.

Similarly, Smith found that magazines geared for men carry considerable cigarette advertising while avoiding the subject of smoking editorially. *Penthouse* and *Playboy*, for example, have published no articles on the dangers to health caused by smoking. The performances of other biggies, *Time*, *Newsweek*, and *U.S. News & World Report*, have been little better.

Cigarette advertising is an influential force in the editorial process, with production and distribution costs of magazines constantly on the rise and profits from advertising close to marginal. But, as Smith indicates, when, over a seven-year period, not one magazine that accepts cigarette advertising attempts to educate its readers about the hazards of smoking, "one must conclude that advertising revenue can indeed silence the editors of American magazines."

Advertising Pressures on Media Content
Effects of Advertising on Editorial Content

Many persons who comment on the long and the short of mass media performance reflect the view that advertisers are the virtual slaves of media. That position is based on the assumption that, because media competition, print especially, has eroded so much in recent years, advertisers are at a disadvantage and media advertising managers are in the driver's seat. Perhaps so in some cases, but other cases suggest that advertisers still wield considerable clout of their own.[38]

The *Denver Post* got caught in a pressure situation with one of its major advertisers when it agreed to publish 1,820 column inches of "news" about a shopping center simply because the center had purchased thirty pages of advertising. The *Post* had done the same thing for another big advertiser. Even though the quota of editorial space provided had not yet been filled, reporters were complaining that there was nothing further to say about the shopping center "short of repetition."

The *Dallas Times Herald* made a habit of running between two-and-one-half and three pages of what they called business, commercial, and industrial news of greater Dallas. In fact, the space allotted to any business firm was in direct proportion to the amount of advertising it purchased in the paper.

Advertising pressures on the content of television programming, both news and entertainment, are well known in the industry. But its continued influence in the decision-making process of the print media is becoming alarming.

*Media as Critics
of Advertising*

On the other hand, media's willingness to evaluate and criticize the goods and services of some major advertisers is also well known. It is especially so in the case of automotive advertising, one of the major sponsors of the print and broadcast news media. Yet negative reports on automobile performance, company "recalls," and so on are reflected in all the media. The shortcomings of Detroit's newest clinkers, the Ford Pinto and General Motors' X-frame cars, are regularly presented and one is hard pressed to see pressures taking hold in such cases. The same holds for oil companies, also major advertisers, whose image is severely battered these days due to media reportage.[39] Thus, it appears that both media and advertisers have the means to bring certain pressures to bear on each other—advertisers on some forms of content (e.g., entertainment shows on television) and news media evaluating performance of goods and services. But that each supports the other most of the time appears certain.

Application of Themes in Advertising
Advertising "Packaging"

All products that hope to meet or surpass the competition go in heavily for appropriate "packaging"—the window-dressing, the backdrop, whatever will best represent the product or service being offered. The "package" might be palms swaying against an azure sky with fun and games at water's edge, all of it readily available by purchasing the goods or services of the sponsor. Or it might be the macho male, shirt open to the chest, sipping the best of scotch, or the soothing green of a Vermont-type scape breathing health and vigor. The possibilities are unlimited. The point is to create a mood or setting favorable to what is being offered. Automobiles, including those in the low price ranges, are not presented parked before a slum-dwelling backdrop. Smokers do not cough. Drinkers are not shown drunk. Obese persons are reserved for motherly roles or are portrayed as big eaters who require the aid of an Alka Seltzer (if the product works for over-indulgent fatties, it is certain to work for you). Beer is not sold in "Joe the laborer's" kitchen: the advertisers prefer to offer Joe an escape from whatever might plague him, perhaps a fleeting glamorous lifestyle on the gleaming deck of a yacht adrift in a lagoon, its decks populated by beautiful young people with trim, tanned bodies and flashing teeth. "Move up to quality, move up to Schlitz!" "Miller, the champagne of bottled beer." Or the pitch might be rugged individualism portrayed in another Schlitz series: "Take away my *gusto*? Take away my *Schlitz*?"

Highly competitive products—refrigerators, washers, dryers—are sold less on their basic functions than on secondary features and gadgetry that might even be incidental to their basic function. There is really nothing sinister in all this. When company is invited to dinner everyone spruces up and the house is tidied. It's good "packaging." Advertisers present their products in attractive "packaging" as well, but sometimes the packaging creates controversy among the reading and viewing public.

Advertising Competitive Products

Without question, sexual portrayals in advertisments are a major part of packaging. They vary from basic sexist portrayals to the pornographic,* depending on what is being offered, how, and to whom. But overall, sex-oriented advertising is most commonly found in *traditional* forms of advertising, the advertising that most Americans see regularly.

Sexual Portrayals in Advertising

With a good many of the votes in, it is apparent that sex in advertising does sell, or tries hard to, in both male- and female-oriented products and services.[40] Sometimes the sexual association is patently obvious, in others it is subtle. Indeed, sometimes it has little or no direct bearing on the product at all. Many people, many women especially, disapprove of the practice. But, as one observer put it, "Monday night quarterbacks love it." This is reflected when they can "flick their Bic" in the tunnel of love or "get stroked" before leaving for work—with a Bic shaver, that is.

Burt Manning, chief creative officer of the J. Walter Thompson advertising agency said: "That sort of stimulus in advertising is only effective or only gets attention when it shocks. It has a certain adolescent taboo built into it. It only works when you're not supposed to talk that way."

Lois Korey, creative director for Needham, Harper & Steers, commented: "It's like the old mule joke: 'How do you get a mule's attention? First you hit him over the head.' Sex does get the audience's attention."

Perhaps, but indications suggest that, in some cases anyway, the impact may end there. French actress Catherine Deneuve tried it as a television sales gimmick for Lincoln-Mercury's Monarch and it flopped. Tom Westbroom, who heads a group response firm, told why: "Neither men nor women were interested in the Monarch while viewing the commercial. When the camera focused on the dashboard of the car and the announcer spoke of the splendid engineering, the response went down. The very next shot had Catherine Deneuve in the back seat. The response zoomed up." But even then, according to Westbrook, the product was not the focal point of attention. The shift in attention resulted from fantasies of backseat romance. It was attractive, but it did not leave viewers with especially positive impressions of the car which, of course, was the point.

Deneuve and the Monarch

*These extremes have been developed in chapter 4 (Sexism) and chapter 8 (Obscenity).

Not all sexy commercials geared for television can make the grade. CBS's standards department rejected a Muriel cigar project that placed model Susan Anton in a "slithery" gown in a men's locker room. Donn O'Brien, vice president of program practices for the network said, "It was the body language and how they were touching each other that was beyond our speed limit."

The print media also reflect sexual themes and promises in some of their advertisements. They "are just as daring as what interrupts sitcoms on the home screen." The headline for Varsity-Knothe nightware reads, "We're good in bed." The copy then described the positive points about the sponsor's products—pajamas and robes.

Another print ad, this one for European Health Spas, announced: "I want your body."

A colorful magazine ad for Black Velvet Canadian whiskey portrays a dashing, smiling Telly Savalas growling, "Feel the Velvet, baby!"

An advertisement for Southwest Airlines states that its sponsor offers more services to Love Field in Dallas than any other airline. Its tagline goes: "You can't make Love four times a day in your car."

The sex sell (Wide World Photos).

Some ad agency executives see the likelihood of sexy advertisements increasing. Burt Manning, who feels that it could eventually become a bore, believes that sex in advertising will get sexier to keep public attention focused where sponsors want it focused. But Lois Karey feels that people need and want hard facts about what they want or need to buy.

The Impact of Advertising on the Media
The Hartford-Tribune

That advertising has enormous impact on the public is evident in the following examples. The *Hartford-Tribune* in Connecticut demonstrates one of the most short-lived existences in daily newspaper history.[41] The paper came into being on November 14, 1977, and died on January 3, 1978, after twenty-seven issues. The paper was created to fill the void left by the departure of the *Hartford Times*. Yet in a matter of weeks, the *Tribune* left a staff unemployed, unpaid, and severely angered with the people who owned it.

The *Tribune* ran thirty-two pages per issue, offered attractive graphics and page design, along with stories from Reuters and the Associated Press. It also carried dog and horse racing information and considerable local news and features. But advertising proved hard to come by and most of what the *Tribune* got came from a nearby shopping center owned by two of the paper's backers.

By the end of the year, management had missed payrolls, and finances, generally, were far below the $900,000 supposedly supporting the venture. Then the *Tribune*'s circulation was found to be a third of the 20,000 claimed by management. Finally the announcement came: the paper was $120,000 in debt and would have to close. The editor said that the collapse came because of insufficient public support and, especially important, the lack of advertising.

A similar situation occurred in New York City when Leonard Saffir, a believer, tried to give the city a brand new daily that he called simply the *Trib*. A five-day-a-week tabloid, its birth in early 1978 was based on the belief that New Yorkers would support a conservative-bent paper of high quality. In just three months the experiment was over, the paper dead.

The Trib

A leading factor was the reluctance of advertisers in appreciable numbers to buy space in its pages. The *Trib* rarely carried more than five pages of advertising, perhaps due to its meager (for New York City) 75,000 circulation. Compared to the almost two million circulation of the *Daily News*, the *Trib* was barely visible. Yet the paper's backers spent at least $4 million to make it a success. In the end, Saffir indicated that the *Trib* couldn't even pay its bills.[42]

In both of these cases, advertising, by its absence, dramatically portrayed its vital role in the continued existence of the mass media in the United States.

In a more positive vein, *Time* magazine made use of advertising to enhance its public image as well as to aid community improvement programs.[43] In an effort to promote crucial public issues, goals, and projects on local levels, the

Time's *Advertising Campaign*

magazine offered free advertising on its pages to ad agencies in ten American cities who could come up with meaningful ad support geared to constructive community change. Each agency in the cities designated was awarded a free full-page ad in one of the metropolitan editions* to bring public issues and needs to light. *Time* placed no limits on the number of ads to be run but they averaged one per month for a year.

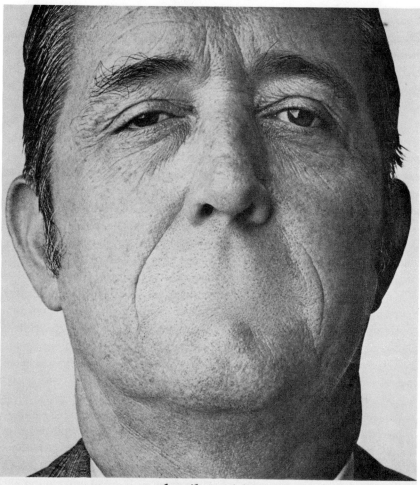

the silent citizen

Students riot. Races clash. Crime grows. Traffic snarls. Cities decay. Millions of people say nothing, do nothing. The silent citizens. Men without mouths.

Other voices are heard. Loud voices, with passionate convictions, crying for action. Whether their causes are good or bad, right or wrong, the silent citizen looks away.

He's often well informed and he has good ideas of his own, but he saves them for his wife and friends and people he meets at cocktail parties. He never bothers to get them across to his congressman or his newspaper or City Hall or the school board. He never comes out in the open to confront the other point of view.

If he stays silent long enough, the other point of view wins out...unless its supporters suddenly become silent too. Then they go nowhere together, silently waiting for time to run out.

DANCER · FITZGERALD · SAMPLE, INC.

"The silent citizen." A winner in *Time*'s community improvement campaign. (Reprinted with permission of Dancer-Fitzgerald-Sample, Inc.)

*Editions published in high population areas that carried some *local* news and advertising as well as national and international content.

In Philadelphia, where some of the ads appeared, agencies focused on a polluted marsh, child abuse, and reasons why Philadelphians should love their city.

A *Time* spokesman said: "The idea behind the campaign is to give agencies the space to say something they want to say, unencumbered by the marketing requirements and goals of a client. It is also very good to do something beneficial for a community. And, by the response the ad gets, it does also indicate the drawing power of a magazine like *Time*."

In an earlier Power of Print effort sponsored by *Time*, an antipollution campaign put together by the Leo Burnett ad agency brought 600,000 requests for reprints. Another project, by Young and Rubicam, solicited $7,000 to create a tiny park in Harlem. Donations amounted to several times the amount requested.

It is clear from these examples just how much authority the advertising industry commands. It is equally clear that the American mass media cannot survive as they are now structured without massive support from advertisers.

Finally, one must consider that advertising, no matter the wealth of creative talent behind it, the almost unlimited resources, the plans and hopes, does not always succeed in what it tries to do, good or bad, positive or negative, wet or dry. It is not magic. It is not even un-American as some would have it. As an institution run by people, it has its highs and lows just as other American institutions do. Sometimes it works and goods and services move about the marketplace. Sometimes it doesn't work. The determining factor in all such ventures is the consumer. As Harvard University Professor Stephen Greyser explains, "The consumer is hardly a helpless pawn manipulated at will by the advertiser. We know, for example, that almost all consumers are very selective in what advertising they pay attention to, perceive, evaluate and remember—let alone act upon."[44] Advertising is highly competitive. If an approach fails, it is abandoned and the investments in money and human involvement are lost with it. Then a new attempt is put together and the gears grind again. In the end, the people decide. And that goes for all the media as well. The people really make or break all of it.

Summary

The dictates of profits and losses are essential parts of the structure of the mass media in America. In many ways they are the most essential part. Without the development and maintenance of earning power there would be no independent mass media as we know them to be. As "free" people, we would have to get by with only what government wanted us to know in order to project and implement its own designs as totalitarian states do. The mass media of the present time are the products of continued economic change over the last 300 years or more. They will continue to change according to new economic demands. And those that fail to keep pace will be lost.

Notes

1. Statistics from "Facts About Newspapers 1979," American Newspaper Publishers Association, April 1979, p. 3.
2. Shaw's comments and findings from David Shaw, "The Newspaper Must Be Fit to Survive," The *Quill*, February 1977, p. 11.
3. Information on "Newspaper Problems in Chicago" from Gene Gilmore, "How Chicago Lost Another Paper," *Columbia Journalism Review*, May/June 1978, p. 37.
4. Information on "Dailies in Los Angeles" from Felix Gutierrez and Clint C. Wilson II, "The Demographic Dilemma," *Columbia Journalism Review*, January/February 1979, p. 53.
5. Information on the *Herald Examiner* from Bob Gottlieb, "Pep Pills for the Herald Examiner," *Columbia Journalism Review*, September/October 1978, p. 68.
6. "Facts About Newspapers 1979," American Newspaper Publishers Association, April 1979.
7. Laird Anderson, "P.M.s: A Day Late & A Dollar Short," *Washington Journalism Review*, April/May 1978, p. 26.
8. Information on these competing papers from "Readers Watch Papers Square Off in St. Louis," The *Quill*, January 1978, p. 7.
9. Information on Time Incorporated and the *Star* from "Waltzing With Oblivion," *Columbia Journalism Review*, March/April 1979, p. 6.
10. Information on CapCities from Robert Friedman, "CapCities Comes to the Coal Country," *Columbia Journalism Review*, January/February 1979, p. 34.
11. Details of the strike from "Strike: New York in Limbo: The Story So Far," *Columbia Journalism Review*, November/December 1978, p. 5; "New York: The Long Anticlimax," *Columbia Journalism Review*, January/February 1979, p. 6.
12. Nicholas King, "Can Print Survive in New York?" *Washington Journalism Review*, January/February 1979, p. 52.
13. Details of the sexism case at the *Times* from "Out of Court," *Columbia Journalism Review*, January/February 1979, p. 9.
14. James Playsted Wood, "Magazine Publishing Today," *Mass Media and Communication*, Charles S. Steinberg, ed., (New York: Hastings House, 1972), p. 172.
15. Christopher H. Sterling and Timothy R. Haight, *The Mass Media: Aspen Institute Guide to Communication Industry Trends* (New York: Praeger Publishers, 1978), pp. 130–31; "Facts About Newspapers 1979."
16. Sterling and Haight, *The Mass Media*, pp. 342–43.
17. Quoted in Charlene J. Brown, Trevor R. Brown, and William L. Rivers, *The Media and the People* (New York: Holt, Rinehart and Winston, 1978), p. 85.
18. "Innovations." *Columbia Journalism Review*, November/December 1978, p. 15.
19. Information on *Look*'s comeback from Mark Potts, "After 8-year Absence, Look Magazine Back on the Stands," The *State Journal* (Associated Press), Lansing, Michigan, April 22, 1979, p. 2-E; Stuart Elliott, "A Revival for Life, Look and the Post," *Detroit Free Press*, May 14, 1979, p. 2-C.
20. "The Survivor," *Columbia Journalism Review*, March/April 1978, p. 9.
21. "Felker's Esquire," *Columbia Journalism Review*, May/June 1978, p. 5.
22. "Innovations," p. 15.
23. Information on city magazines from "City Magazines: Bigger and Better?" *Washington Journalism Review*, September/October 1978, p. 47.
24. "Facts About Newspapers 1979."
25. "Advertising's Bill Bernbach," *Detroit Free Press*, April 3, 1978, p. 6-E.
26. Eric J. Zanot, "The National Advertising Review Board, 1971–1976," *Journalism Monographs* (Minneapolis: Association for Education in Journalism, University of Minnesota, 1979), p. 8.

27. Information on the Ad Council's critics from Deborah Baldwin, "Ad Council Prescription: Public Service Pablum," *Washington Journalism Review*, October 1977, p. 36.
28. Bigelow v. Virginia, 421. U.S. 809 (1975), in *Mass Media and the Supreme Court*, Kenneth S. Devol, ed. (New York: Hastings House, 1976), 2d ed., pp. 337–41.
29. "Crackdown Ahead on Advertising: What the Government Plans Next," *U.S. News & World Report*, October 17, 1977, p. 70.
30. Information on FTC targets from "The FTC Broadens Its Attack on Ads," *Business Week*, June 20, 1977, p. 27.
31. "Dr. Huckster: Advertising by Physicians," *Newsweek*, January 9, 1978, p. 71.
32. "Advertising Guidelines Asked by State Bar," The *State Journal* (Associated Press), Lansing, Michigan, April 23, 1979, p. 9-B.
33. Roger Hedges, "Others Join Kids' Television Advertising Battle," The *State Journal*, Lansing, Michigan, January 3, 1979, p. 3-C.
34. Jack Anderson, "Television Sugar Derby Planning Counterattack," The *State Journal*, Lansing, Michigan, April 15, 1978, p. 6-A.
35. Louis Rukeyser, "FTC Hits Excessive Cereal Choices in U.S.," The *State Journal*, Lansing, Michigan, April 9, 1978, p. 1-E.
36. Information on HEW and cigarette smoking from Jack Anderson, "U.S. Fights Cigarettes, Subsidizes Tobacco," The *State Journal*, Lansing, Michigan, May 17, 1978, p. 10-A.
37. R. C. Smith, "The Magazines' Smoking Habit," *Columbia Journalism Review*, January/February 1978, p. 29.
38. The following cases from John L. Hulteng, *The Messenger's Motives* (Englewood Cliffs, N.J.: Prentice-Hall, 1976), p. 145.
39. "Advertising Pressure," *Columbia Journalism Review*, November/December 1978, p. 18.
40. Information on "Sexual Portrayals in Advertising" from Dolores Barclay, "Sexy Ads—How Well Do They Sell?" *Detroit Free Press*, May 1, 1978, p. 14-B.
41. Information on the *Hartford Tribune* from Keith F. Johnson, "Infant Mortality," *Columbia Journalism Review*, March/April 1978, p. 10.
42. "The Trib Dies at the Age of Three Months," The *Quill*, May 1978, p. 10.
43. Information on the *Time* program from "Time Is Offering Ad Space for Free," *Detroit Free Press*, April 17, 1978, p. 13-B.
44. Leonard L. Sellers and William L. Rivers, *Mass Media Issues* (Englewood Cliffs, N.J.: Prentice-Hall, 1977), p. 357.

"Advertising Pressure." *Columbia Journalism Review,* November/December 1978, p. 18.

Anderson, Laird. "P.M.s: A Day Late & A Dollar Short." *Washington Journalism Review,* April/May 1978, p. 26.

Baldwin, Deborah. "Ad Council Prescription: Public Service Pablum." *Washington Journalism Review,* October 1977, p. 36.

Bigelow v. Virginia, 421. U.S. 809 (1975), *Mass Media and the Supreme Court.* Edited by Kenneth S. Devol. 2d ed., New York: Hastings House, 1976, pp. 337–41.

"City Magazines: Bigger and Better?" *Washington Journalism Review,* September/October 1978, p. 47.

"Crackdown Ahead on Advertising: What the Government Plans Next." *U.S. News & World Report,* October 17, 1977, p. 70.

"Dr. Huckster: Advertising by Physicians." *Newsweek,* January 9, 1978, p. 71.

"Felker's Esquire." *Columbia Journalism Review,* May/June 1978, p. 5.

Friedman, Robert. "CapCities Comes to the Coal Country." *Columbia Journalism Review,* January/February 1979, p. 34.

Gilmore, Gene. "How Chicago Lost Another Paper." *Columbia Journalism Review,* May/June 1978, p. 37.

Gutierrez, Felix, and Wilson, Clint C., II. "The Demographic Dilemma." *Columbia Journalism Review,* January/February 1979, p. 53.

"Innovations." *Columbia Journalism Review,* November/December 1978, p. 15.

For Further Reading

Johnson, Keith F. "Infant Mortality." *Columbia Journalism Review*, March/April 1978, p. 10.

King, Nicholas. "Can Print Survive in New York?" *Washington Journalism Review*, January/February 1979, p. 52.

"New York: The Long Anti-Climax." *Columbia Journalism Review*, January/February 1979, p. 6.

"Out of Court." *Columbia Journalism Review*, January/February 1979, p. 9.

"Readers Watch Papers Square Off in St. Louis." The *Quill*, January 1978, p. 7.

Shaw, David. "The Newspaper Must Be Fit to Survive." The *Quill*, February 1977, p. 11.

Smith, R.C. "The Magazines' Smoking Habit." *Columbia Journalism Review*, January/February 1978, p. 29.

Sterling, Christopher H., and Haight, Timothy R. *The Mass Media: Aspen Institute Guide to Communication Industry Trends.* New York: Praeger Publishers, 1978.

"Strike: New York in Limbo: The Story So Far." *Columbia Journalism Review*, November/December 1978, p. 5.

"The FTC Broadens Its Attack on Ads." *Business Week*, June 20, 1977, p. 27.

"The Survivor." *Columbia Journalism Review*, March/April 1978, p. 9.

"The Trib Dies at the Age of Three Months." The *Quill*, May 1978, p. 10.

"Waltzing With Oblivion." *Columbia Journalism Review*, March/April 1979, p. 6.

Zanot, Eric J. "The National Advertising Review Board, 1971–1976." *Journalism Monographs*. Minneapolis: Association for Education in Journalism, University of Minnesota, 1979.

News in Pictures

Mass Media and Future Shock 13

Upon completing this chapter you should know—

how technological changes affect the production of newspapers and magazines

the workings of present and future home delivery systems and print and electronic media

about recent advances and projected development of electronic cable and satellite systems to aid the mass media

how new technologies influence and will continue to influence pay-television systems, electronic postal deliveries, and videophones

how media technologies plan to use outer space in future developments

details of the "media home" of the future

the future of the First Amendment

Chapter Objectives

Cathode-ray Tube (CRT) or Video Display Terminal (VDT)   An electronic typewriter with a built-in television screen tied into a computer: used to prepare editorial and advertising copy for print media. (p. 420)

Digital Information   Information produced by computers. (p. 422)

Home Delivery Systems   The means of transferring media content from source to consumer. (pp. 423; 426)

Communication Satellites   Electronic conveyances in space that transmit information and pictures from place to place, near and far. (p. 424)

Superstation   A television station that broadcasts far beyond its physical location via satellite to gain new viewers on television cable systems. (p. 426)

Key Terms

The only security of all is in a free press.

Thomas Jefferson to Lafayette,
1823.

New Technologies and the Print Media

An impressive number of technological changes in the newspaper industry have been developed in recent years. These changes have moved newspaper production a long way from the green eyeshade, thick copy pencil, and elongated layout sheet system that embodied the editorial process for so long. In many important ways, newspapers have tended to lag behind their electronic counterparts in the development of modern production and home delivery systems. While radio and television have experimented and grown with machines and techniques essentially new, many in the print media have played it close to the vest, seemingly content with the notion that the old ways have carried them this far and would continue to do so. The difference is that the electronic media, with a considerably shorter past, were the products of modern technological change in the first place and thus have been more receptive to further change.

Media analyst Ben Bagdikian points out that ten years ago, 1 percent of the daily newspapers in the United States utilized computerized production techniques while at least 60 percent do so now. A notable growth picture, to be sure, but that also means that about 40 percent of American dailies still hold to the old ways.[1]

What the new technology has done for the 60 percent is exciting and meaningful. As the cost of sophisticated new systems has dropped to more affordable levels, publishers and editors have shown increasing interest in changing over. Many have been impressed by the new hardware, even better, with how it can improve production methods and the makeup of the product itself. It is also economical. The following is an explanation of how it works in a "typical" newsroom setting.

Changes in Newspaper Production Methods

Electronic Systems in Newspaper Production

Newswriter preparing copy on a video display terminal (VDT). (The Electric Newsroom, James E. Murphy, Vic-Com, Inc., 1978.)

Preparing News Copy

The cathode-ray tube (CRT), or video display terminal (VDT), is an electronic typewriter with a built-in television screen that is tied into a computer. Instead of writing a story on a standard typewriter, a reporter can type it on the CRT and watch it appear on the screen. The screen offers eighteen lines of copy with a twenty-two-point type size. By touching a key labeled SLUG, the reporter tells the computer where in the building to send the story—say, in this case it is local news. After including a few more code symbols, the reporter then writes the story. While writing, the letters and words form on the screen. If a correction or addition to a line or lines is needed, the reporter simply presses certain command keys and the corrections are made and the lines are readjusted. If the story is late breaking, it can be sent to the appropriate editor electronically in segments (called "takes") by pressing a key labeled MORE. When the story is completed, the reporter touches a key marked END, which sends it to the computer. With the new technology, the reporter is able to do the job faster, neater in finished form, and probably tighter and easier to read. The story is available to anyone in the office with the touch of a finger.

Story Selection

At the city desk, the editor types LO (for "local copy") on his keyboard then presses DIRECTORY and the computer slips onto the screen a list of all local stories thus far available for the upcoming issue of the paper. Other departments do the same for stories of interest to them. The editor may receive

Producing A Newspaper

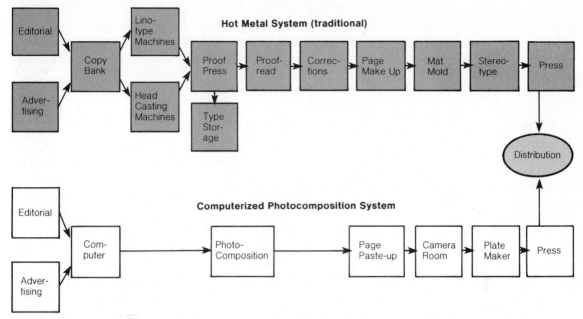

Differences in composition systems—the old and the new. (American Newspaper Publishers Association).

any of the stories by pressing the key labeled NEXT, read the entire story on the screen, and edit it electronically. The editor then types GE and the story is transferred to the news editor.

The news editor checks the story by looking at the length, column width, and body type and makes note of where it is to appear in the paper. Notes on the style and size of the headline to accompany it are also made. Then, by typing CE, the story is transferred to the copy editor, who gives it a final check and adds the headline. After that, the copy editor types GN, and the story goes to a "slotman," who gets a printout of the story on an impact printer, which operates at 200 lines per minute. The slotman then hits the COMP ROOM key, which sends the story to the computer. There the story is automatically put on paper tape at the rate of about 1,000 words per minute. It is next fed into a linecaster, which sets it into print at the rate of 14 lines per minute. It is then placed into the appropriate page in the newspaper.

Printing Procedures

Before these technological marvels entered the newsrooms of American newspapers, all of these procedures were done by humans, with considerable walking about, interoffice telephone calls, discussions, penciling changes on the copy, and all the rest. But with the new technology, a story can be processed as late as ten minutes before the paper goes to press. This new method is a photocomposition process (cold type) rather than the older and slower hot

The New vs. the Old

type system. In addition, the number of steps between writing and printing the story is reduced from eleven to seven, and the entire process requires considerably fewer workers to get the job done.

Copy from the Associated Press and United Press International is also processed electronically without conventional typing or penciling and is fed into subscribing papers ready to be used.

Technology and Magazines

There has been considerably less headway made by the new technologies in magazine production than in newspapers. That is due primarily to the fact that magazine production is more complicated, and printing plants are typically located far from the editorial offices, in some cases, thousands of miles. Therefore, the tidy arrangement of computerized newspaper systems under one roof, described above, has not been as readily applicable to the magazine industry. Still, promising developments in this sector seem to be coming.

U.S. News Takes a Gamble

The news and opinion magazine *U.S. News & World Report* became involved in a gamble with technology that appears to be paying off. Under the auspices of *U.S. News,* technology made possible a computerized technique of "scanning" black and white glossy photographs and reproducing them thousands of miles away without sacrificing any of the visual quality. It is a significant development in that the magazine's regional printing plants are located in California, Illinois, and Connecticut. The system converts photos into the same kind of "digital" information that computers use to produce type as mentioned above. And that permits full pages, headlines, text, and pictures to be sent electronically to editors in Washington, D.C., where completed pages may be checked before being transmitted by satellite to the printing plants. The system is cheaper than earlier methods and considerably faster.

Bugs in the System?

The magazine industry has begun to recognize the value of computerized production methods, and some publishers are attempting to adopt new technologies to their needs. Many editorial offices have already converted to CRTs or VDTs to compose their stories and articles. But others still see bugs in the system. David Jensen is an executive of McGraw-Hill Publishing Company, which produces a line of magazines along with its books. He indicates that the high costs involved in such advances will limit changeovers to the largest magazine companies. "Only the magazines with a real news commitment will spend that kind of money to transfer halftones [photographs]—because you could send them by plane . . . in eight hours." At the same time, Jensen admits that the new electronic page processing for magazines is a profound technological breakthrough.[2] Time alone will tell how widely the technology will be applied to actual production.

As for bringing "electronic newspapers" into the home, the future is already here. In parts of England, Germany, and Japan, people receive printed news on their television sets whenever they wish. They can also select from world, national, and local stories, sports, cooking, classified advertisements, and other forms of information usually provided by newspapers. And in some systems, viewers can simply push a button and receive a printout of anything that appears on the screen.

Indiana University Professor John Alhauser indicates that American newspapers must "consider themselves part of the electronic media" and take advantage of the changes. He points out that electronic home delivery systems for print journalism currently cost up to $1,800 but that mass production will eventually make them available at about $150. Thus, they will be affordable to media consumers. "Newspapers are the logical choices" to provide such news electronically and they should get ready for it, he added.[3]

Home Delivery Systems—Print
Newspapers Go to the "Viewers"

As reflected in chapter 12, technological advances in the production of newspapers have left print-oriented trade unions reeling. Printing unions are among the oldest in organized labor, some of them going back before the Revolutionary War. With electronic devices supplanting traditional typesetting and printing procedures, the power of unions has eroded markedly and is likely to continue doing so.[4] As in the newspaper industry, management in other spheres of the nation's business are certain to challenge labor on broad fronts, taking the upper hand in negotiating such issues as questionable working arrangements that, in past times, were forced on them by the sheer might of the unions. For years, tightly organized unions successfully resisted the advancements of automation, which usually requires fewer workers, by putting together, under the authority of the strike, contracts devised to protect the status quo. Evidence indicates that the reverse is now happening.*

The New Media Technology and Organized Labor
Decline of Media Unions

The toppling of a number of metropolitan dailies by heavy competition from other newspapers and other media, and rising costs (including overstaffing and frequently inefficient work procedures), have dramatically sketched out the need of print media to go for automation. And it appears that now the unions will have little to say about it. Technological advances in the newspaper industry hold considerable promise for longer life spans and increased profits for many papers in spite of the expense of changing over to the new systems.

The Need for Automation

*The Newspaper Guild for editorial employees appears to be the only print media union to have security in a rapidly changing industry. Regardless of how thoroughly automated they become, the print media will always need editors and writers to put the basic product together.
The printers' union, long the wielder of worker power against the designs of management, is staggering under the weight of onrushing automation. Its membership has fallen from 94,500 in 1961 to about 60,000 today.

As new ways are incorporated and workers keyed to older methods are retired, a newspaper stands to save $20,000 to $30,000 for each retiree. And as systems improve with yet newer technology, profits are bound to increase further. Thus, automation is not only the wave of the future but of the present.

New Technologies and the Electronic Media

Home All-purpose Communication Systems

In many ways, the electronic mass media of the future are with us now, at least on the drawing boards. Beyond the fact that much of the future and what it will bring is endlessly beyond the most imaginative current thinking, educated guesses are possible and reasonable. They are also essential. The capabilities of future times have already taken root and some have begun to sprout.

Advanced Cable Systems

Cable television is a technological and commercial fact. And two-way systems by which the public may "talk back" to broadcasters are not far away. That aspect of media technology has many profound implications for the future. It is not farfetched to envision Americans doing at home much of what they now do in business offices. They may transact most or all of their business from communication systems in their living rooms or dens. These electronic cable systems could also deal with basic family needs such as ordering groceries, shoes, or dresses from stores located miles away. People might also dial up (in whatever form that takes) the public library and have the latest bestseller delivered to and read over their home communication systems.

The new technology is applied to the various media in different ways. As we have seen, the print media technology has already changed the manner and means of gathering and disseminating news with the availability of tape recorders and other electronic gadgetry plus new electronic production systems. To broadcast journalism, the new technology means (among other things) providing *more* news *now* rather than later.

Changes in Satellite Availability

Ten years ago, communication satellites high above the earth were available for dispensing news from far away only about twelve minutes a day. Today their involvement in the disseminating process goes on twenty-four hours a day. New and different applications of this aspect of technology are bound to increase in the future. In addition, electronic satellite sentinels provide the media with twenty-four-hour-a-day reports and pictures on weather and atmospheric conditions, which permit communities to prepare in advance for major storms. Other satellites scan the earth for electronic clues to untapped mineral and oil deposits.

Robert Mulholland, vice president of news at NBC in New York, says that "fixed position satellites over the Atlantic, Pacific and Indian oceans, plus nearly 90 earth stations for sending up pictures and sound, make it possible to transmit news to the United States from every continent, 24 hours a day."[5]

There is dramatic evidence of this. When the Allende government was toppled in Chile, the anti-Allende faction closed borders and airports so that reporters couldn't get in and news film couldn't get out. But a Santiago television station filmed all the action and fed it to a satellite in the sky and American viewers witnessed the developments within hours. Had it not been for the presence of the satellite, viewers would have had to wait for days or longer for the film to be flown to New York, processed, and put on the air.

The Santiago Experience

The future promises even faster and better quality broadcast reporting via hand-held electronic cameras to be used for domestic news coverage. NBC News calls its new electronic camera the PCP-90; CBS's is called the *Minicam*. Regardless of the labels, as Mulholland emphasizes, "these new cameras are in the process of changing the way news is covered in this country."

Electronic Cameras

The new cameras do not use film. They record events on magnetic tape similar to that used in audio tape recorders. That means that no processing is required as it is with film. It also means that major events can be covered later in the day than before and still be shown on the evening news. Perhaps even more to the point, the cameras can cover sudden events "live" by plugging into a telephone line or by means of a portable transmitter. Thus, a major breaking story can be shown to home viewers *as it is happening.* The new electronic color cameras are also easier to use than the old film cameras because they weigh as little as 30 pounds, while older models weighed over 200 pounds. In some major television markets, e.g., New York, Chicago, and Los Angeles, the new cameras are now being applied to local news coverage.

Film vs. Magnetic Tape

Mulholland questions how far broadcasting stations should go with new technological advances in the near and distant future. "Do they go all-electronic? Do they go half and half? Or do they continue film as the basis for television news coverage, using electronic cameras only in special situations?"

The answer, if there is one yet, lies in the fact that each system, film and electronic, requires a separate support procedure, one being incompatible with the other. In brief, the film system cannot utilize any procedures used by the electronic system and vice versa: film is film and electronic tape is electronic tape. Using film creates certain problems, including the fact that it takes longer to process from the shooting stage to air time. But many television news producers complain that the new electronic tape cannot be edited as rapidly as film. So while the industry is excited about recent developments in electronic visual taping, technology continues to work on even more sophisticated innovations in film and film cameras. At this point a stalemate reigns. Time, as usual, will likely bring about a final solution.

Separate Support Systems

Another NBC News executive offers a glimpse of what that future might bring: The television reporter will wear a small hearing aid device, actually a microminiaturized satellite receiver that will provide constant contact with the office. In addition, the reporter will have a small electronic camera, about the size of today's home movie cameras, and a small videotape recorder as

The Future in Broadcast Reporting

small as today's audio tape recorder. To get the story on the air, the reporter will open his briefcase, flip a switch, and push a button on a recorder. The briefcase will hold a satellite transmission terminal that will provide on-the-air access from any location.

Home Delivery Systems— Broadcasting

Changes in Broadcast News Content

Methods of delivering broadcast news to American homes will also change with the advancement of technology. Development of communication satellites and low cost, ground level receiving stations will enable the broadcast news media to create regional networks, as opposed to strictly national networks. Those changes, in turn, will provide specialized services and more programming for consumers. An important development extending from *that* will be telecommunications recording systems in private homes. They will be required hardware when broadcasting expands to a twenty-four-hour-per-day format. When that happens, home viewers will record late-night broadcasts for viewing at more convenient hours.

Bill Daniels is a pioneer in the development of cable television. He indicates that further growth in the cable industry will create outlets for expanded specialized programs to include news content. Current cable systems now serve more than twelve million homes and development of two-way cable and cable printouts will help the industry to grow even more.

According to John Quinn, director of the News Service for the Gannett group, the new electronic technologies should be accepted by news companies as an opportunity to provide information geared for special-interest audiences. He adds that the news industries "must forget the way we have always done it" and embrace change in the interest of doing a better job of providing information to the public. And that is directly in the interest of First Amendment provisions. In the matter of who should "own" the news delivery system, Quinn says: "Whoever owns it is not as important as how it is owned. The coverage of news must be isolated from the owners and regulators of the channels."[6]

Going Super with Turner

Ted Turner is not only the multimillionaire owner of two major league sports teams in Atlanta, he is also a mass media entrepreneur who prefers that his investments pay off.[7] It is not so much that other owners have a fondness for losses, but the unique way that Turner solved his problem is what media observers are excited about.

The Superstation

Irked that his Atlanta television station, WTBS-TV, was losing $50,000 a month, Turner decided to do something about it. He decided to beam his programs, particularly his sports coverage, via satellite to cable television systems in other parts of the country. That decision not only quadrupled his audience to three million homes in forty-five states, but it created a startling new broadcasting concept—the "superstation."

Ted Turner (Courtesy WTBS, Atlanta, Ga.).

Increased Advertising

The experiment proved so successful that Turner eventually opened an advertising sales office in New York among the network giants. It quickly won WTBS-TV a number of national advertising accounts including Panasonic, Miller beer, and Toyota. In total, about 505 cable systems serving 2.5 million homes receive WTBS-TV programming via a Satcom II satellite.

Program Content

Turner's experiment now offers badly-needed program alternatives to existing network content. In this case, the alternatives include large doses of exposure to his Atlanta-based sports specials—the Atlanta Braves of the National League in baseball and the Atlanta Hawks of the National Basketball Association. The enthusiastic cable audience is comprised of small-town Americans whose only chance of viewing big-time athletes in action is via the weekly offerings of network television. Turner's station also has a well-stocked film library of 3,000 titles, far more than most independent stations can offer.

In time, other stations began following Turner's lead. WOR, New York City; WGN, Chicago; KTTV, Los Angeles; and KTVU out of Oakland-San Francisco are now broadcasting their offerings nationally via satellite. Other big-city stations are planning to do the same.

Superstations Compete with the Networks

The real concern of the established networks is that the superstations might cut deeply into the audiences and advertising incomes of local network-allied stations. John Summers, an official of the National Association of Broadcasters, commented: "It might be that the locals will lose so much revenue that they will go down the drain." And Turner manages to beat the networks in the advertising revenue game. WTBS charges about $30,000 for a 30-second commercial. The going network rate is $48,000.

While networks show their concern, the Federal Communications Commission likes what the superstations are doing. One spokesman said: "We find it hard to accept the argument that a development should be stopped because it might provide too good service."

Ted Turner is more direct: "Broadcasters who are part of the old technology are trying to hold back the new technology. They just don't want the competition."

Turner is now considering setting up a live news-by-satellite operation that will function twenty-four hours a day. The system would be staffed by reporters in regional bureaus around the country, and news programs would offer as many as fifty on-camera personalities. But to support news programming of that magnitude would require about 7.5 million home subscribers, more than double the number that Turner now has.

With the superstations currently in operation representing different sections of the nation, and with FCC approval, they could join forces and become a fourth network with front-line programming of its own. Financing would come from advertisers disillusioned with staggering ad rates now charged by the existing networks. To Ted Turner, all that is not out of a dream world. "We look upon the other stations as rivals," he said. "We intend to have a fourth network of our own."

Growth of Pay-television Systems

The growth of pay-television in recent years has been impressive.[8] Some 13 million homes are tied into cable pay-TV systems as various firms compete energetically to reap viewers willing to pay for one service over another on the basis of what is being offered in programming. Home Box Office (HBO), owned by Time, Incorporated, offers a monthly package of movies, sports, and special entertainment programs, each of which is shown several times a month during varying evening hours. If a subscriber misses something the first time shown, he or she can pick it up on another evening. HBO goes into about 1.5 million homes at a cost of approximately seven dollars per month per home.

HBO is in heavy competition with other pay-TV companies, notably Viacom International's Showtime Entertainment, Incorporated, which managed to manipulate 250,000 subscribers away from HBO in one swoop. Viacom, which boasts that its programming and marketing techniques are superior to HBO's, moved to the front ranks of the pay-TV industry when it began transmitting its programs via satellite (at a cost of $1.2 million a year) rather than via videocassettes as others were doing.

One of the problems faced by competitors in this field is that the United States has some 3,900 cable-TV systems, each with an average of about 3,100 subscribers. Thus, selling programming by HBO versus Showtime has proven to be a slow process as each vies for customers among the cable companies.

The pitch is based on low subscription rates and quality program offerings. How low the rate can go while maintaining the high costs of producing quality programming is the nub of the issue.

Basis for Sales

An HBO executive indicated that the production of comedy specials and other original programs designed to attract new subscribers must increase. It is essential if the companies are to ask for, and get, eight to ten dollars per month per subscriber. "Such shows cost money to make," he said.

Showtime has also begun part-time pay-TV service for viewers in rural areas who cannot afford the full programming rates. Called "Front Row," the service provides a variety of older movies, shows for children, and other family-oriented programming for five dollars per month. HBO has since announced that it will provide similar programming to its cable outlets via a separate "family-oriented, lower-priced service."

Part-time Services

As HBO and Showtime compete for business across the nation, other pay-TV operators are active on a regional basis. Warner Cable offers its "Star Channel" programming over sixteen of its systems. And the 20th Century-Fox Film Corporation and United Artists Corporation jointly provide programs to Philadelphia and to systems in the Southwest.

Other Pay-TV Systems

Other Aspects of Applied Technologies

Another critical factor in the ever-changing communications picture is the rapid decrease in the *costs* of technology, with reductions from 20 to 25 percent each year, as well as in the costs of *transmission* of communications matter.

For example, the United States Postal Service will likely give way to a computerized mail service that will eventually permit people to pay their bills by means of electronic funds transfer systems. The Congressional House Committee on the Post Office and Civil Service has already opened the way for such changes.

Computerized Postal Services

Citizens band and mobile radio are expected to grow substantially in numbers and quality. And by the year 2000, cordless portable telephones will be available at the same cost as wired telephones today. In the near future, video recorders, certain to increase in numbers, may well change the nature of both television and cable-TV broadcasting. All these developments will impact heavily on the means of person-to-person and small group communications as well as on the mass media themselves.

Changes in Other Media

Harry M. Shooshan is staff director and general legal counsel for the United States House of Representatives Subcommittee of the Committee on Interstate and Foreign Commerce, which oversees the actions of the Federal Communications Commission. He indicates that all such changes will require much more sophisticated official policies to guide media into the future than

Need to Modernize Government Policies

what the current Communications Act provides. "We have a clear choice confronting us right now," he warns. "Will we be the masters *or* the servants of the communications revolution in which we find ourselves?"[9]

The application of communications satellites to the dissemination of information generally has been positive, especially as related to major media. But it also offers auxiliary benefits certain to increase in the future.

Marisat and Mariners

Marisat is a satellite system developed to update international communications for ships at sea. While that, in itself, might appear to have little bearing on technologies affecting the mass media, it does dramatically portray the level of sophistication that international communication systems have achieved. Marisat has contributed substantially to the saving of lives and shipping properties in the brief time it has been in operation. In 1974, an American oil tanker developed engine trouble at sea and began drifting toward a reef in the Indian Ocean. It sent out frantic SOS calls but, due to atmospheric disturbances, the SOS was delayed for thirty-one hours. Meanwhile, the ship ran onto the reef and tore a gash in its hull, which resulted in a spill of more than three million gallons of oil. It would not have happened had Marisat been available. With its availability, ship captains at sea anyplace in the world can, for the first time, be in direct telephone touch with New York in minutes. The call is transmitted by one of three Marisat satellites stationed 22,240 miles above the oceans. The system has saved the lives of seamen injured at sea and has brought immediate help to ships in trouble where older radio systems might have been inadequate. As the United States comes to depend more and more on the sea for oil, gas, and minerals, it is certain that Marisat will take on even greater meaning than at present.[10]

Satellites and Safety at Sea

Videophones

In another sector, the promise of videophones—telephones attached to television screens—could be a boon to current conference-call capabilities as individuals in a community or in various parts of the country could see as well as hear each other. They could also share graphical and statistical materials and hold formal discussions though many miles apart from each other. For the news media, videophones could advance individual newsgathering with newsworthy persons all over the globe. This form of technology is well on its way. But even without the visual aspect, technology has already carried individual communication far beyond international boundaries. This is also a boon for the mass media.

Computerized Personal Communications

For example, a professor in Los Angeles had prepared a scholarly paper for submission to a professional journal. It was to be reviewed by an editor who lived in Montreal. But the author wanted to make last-minute changes before the deadline and have them checked by the editor. Rather than send the manuscript to Montreal by mail, he "sent it" to a computer terminal in Montreal. It so happened that the editor had gone to London, England. So the editor's assistant entered a new address in the computer and transmitted the entire text of the article to a London terminal where the editor received it, made notations, and sent the edited copy back to the author in Los Angeles. The author then made the suggested changes and sent the final draft back to Montreal where it was prepared for publication in the journal. All that movement and activity required less than forty-eight hours from start to finish.[11] The same system promises the news media much by shortening the time now needed to transmit news copy from media bureaus situated all over the globe and thus make foreign news more immediate than it traditionally has been.

The National Aeronautics and Space Administration (NASA) has plans on the drawing board for utilizing earth's outer space.[12] If NASA has its way, which appears likely, the space near earth will eventually become populated by a variety of Buck Rogers-like equipment, including a parasol antenna measuring about 100 feet across that will pop open in orbit as part of an elegant communications system on earth. The system will include pocket-size telephones and robot craft, called space gliders, which will help create structures in space out of extremely thin aluminum. Workers in space suits will float about, pushing into place creations as heavy as freight cars on earth but feather-light in weightless space. And because of the weight factor, humans will be able to steer the structures in all directions.

The largest of the space structures will be solar-powered satellites, each of them about the size of Manhattan Island. Each satellite will be an expensive package at a cost of between $2 and $20 billion. About a hundred would be needed to provide 30 percent of the nation's energy needs.

In practical terms, most of the activity in the near future will be with communication satellites, already a going business in itself. Each space shuttle will house a mechanical "arm," which can place satellites in place and, as needed, pick them up for repairs. The shuttle will be able to carry up to 65,000 pounds of equipment into orbit. The shuttle is also prepared to be part of the launching of a $600 million space laboratory, a cylinderlike structure crammed with sophisticated equipment. As the demands of communication systems increase, satellites will become larger and stronger. At present, the United States Air Force has in the works a "dish" antenna for radar that could be collapsed for transport aboard a space shuttle and then snapped open after it is launched into space.

In time more sophisticated systems will be required, including what NASA calls an "antenna farm." A metal structure about 700 feet long, it would carry as many as thirty dish antennae and would be towed into orbit and put to work. Practical application of the antenna farm would include handling of electronic mail, which is already growing in volume. The antenna farm would also be able to handle the demands of five national television networks. Because of the power required, each receiving station on earth would be a much simpler mechanism than at present, probably about the same as a pocket telephone.

The "Far-out" Future

Communications via Outer Space

The Antenna Farm

The farm would also service as many as 45,000 private television channels that would have the capability of handling the calls from millions of pocket telephones. The calls, in turn, would cost about twenty cents each. Construction of antenna farms is expected to begin around 1985.

Industry in space: the antenna farm in action. (Illustration by Nicholas Solovioff, *Fortune* Magazine, February 26, 1979.)

Media scholar John Hulteng, of the University of Oregon, admits, with some misgivings, that the media-oriented home of the future is a major possibility.[13] Ultimately, he says, Americans will be able to bring communication systems into their homes in a style and manner now inconceivable to all but the most dedicated of dreamers. The mechanism will be the complete home information-entertainment center, which will offer untold volume and variety of news and feature programming along with drama, musical presentations (high- and low-brow), and all the rest. Newspapers and magazines will, at the touch of a button, be magnified on a wall screen to be read when and as the reader wishes. And an attached printout mechanism will give readers permanent copies of anything they wish to keep.

In Hulteng's opinion, other print forms—books and magazines—will become extinct. Central data banks will store information that may be called up instantly by punching code numbers in the terminal computer systems. Banks will shift funds about electronically (as they are now doing) and physicians will treat patients by television.

The education of children will move from the schoolroom into the home via technological innovation. Originating from centralized locations, instruction will be distributed into the home by means of the family television screen. Hulteng opines that all the sitting and staring by children might eventually change people into "pear-shaped blobs" with "bulging, thick-lensed eyes."

He concludes:

> It is an appalling prospect, simply from as aesthetic point of view. If one contemplates as well the problem of sustaining ethical (media) standards in a world where, to all intents and purposes, there will be a single medium of communication—very likely under some form of governmental control—the view is even bleaker. Orwell* may have been conservative.

Others are equally uneasy about the technological future of the mass media, particularly as it applies to press freedoms. Bruce M. Owen, professor of economics at Stanford University and a fellow of the Aspen Program on Communications and Society, expresses concern over the growing technological association of electronics and print.[14] He warns that the connection "may lead to government regulation of the press, with attendant dangers to our civil liberties."

*Reference is to George Orwell's futuristic novel *1984* about the horrors of a totally technological society in which the mass media are used to enslave the people rather than to enlighten them.

The Media-oriented Home

The Home as Schoolhouse

Shortcomings

The First Amendment and Future Shock

If the electronic development of newspapers reaches the point where the product is more electronic than print on paper, regulators of electronic media might move to control newspapers as part of the electronic spectrum. What that would do to the First Amendment guarantees of free press makes many shudder.

Electronic Newspapers

It is not beyond possibility, Owen points out, that a fundamental part of "newspaper" distribution in the future will be by small-screen cassette players placed in American homes just as radio and television sets are today. Current indicators imply that such alternatives to current print methods are technologically and economically possible. That notion is further supported by increasing costs of postal service and of paper on which newspapers, magazines, and books are printed.

Lessons from Gutenberg

Johann Gutenberg's invention of movable type around the year 1440 revolutionized the "media" of his time. It did so by removing information from the single dominance of the church and placing it in the open marketplace of ideas. Instead of having to undergo the laborious process of lettering information by hand (usually done by monks) and carving the message, word-by-word, page-by-page, on blocks of wood for printing, movable type provided the means of much more rapid composition and printing. Because this was "mass" production (though primitive) it made information available to many people. Gutenberg has thus been credited with, in time, making it technologically feasible to spread basic literacy about Europe to a degree greater than ever before in human history.

The knowledge circulated over the years, the opinions formed, and the lessons learned because of that technological development are, in turn, credited with toppling thrones, starting wars, and, perhaps most significant for its time, bringing on the Protestant Reformation. Essentially, this was an intellectual-ideological revolution fed by the printed word. From that evolved philosophical concepts of freedom of thought and actions based on libertarian, humanistic principles. Thus, Gutenberg's invention ultimately resulted in wiping out a technology of information that was conducive to authoritarian control by the church. And, as Owen indicates, "electronic technology, by contrast, destroys a technology (print) characterized by a tradition of freedom" and replaces it with another that is readily open to authoritarian control by the state.

Expansion of Media Regulation?

Certain forms of electronic media channels, such as communication satellites, are now regulated by the federal government and it is likely that computer technology will be as well. In Owen's words, "when this happens, the dependence of print technology on electronics will mean that print is regulated." Americans will then be faced with such issues as whether people ought to be allowed to pay for printed communication, whether there is too much from the political right or left, too much violence, or too much "skin," and how many people—and *which* people—should be allowed the privilege of printing. When these factors come together, he says, a crucial element of freedom becomes the tool of social engineering designed for the purpose of pursuing ill-formed social goals of questionable meaning and value.

It is also possible that the print media of the future may escape the Orwellian nightmare of total state controls by utilizing technologies that do not lend themselves to regulation. Even so, the possibility of government eventually controlling all mass media requires serious consideration. Consider that the Federal Communications Commission currently regulates cable television much more studiously than it regulates the telephone industry. In this aspect of the issue, Owen says that enforcement of the FCC's pay-television rules required the commission to extend its authority to cover the *persons* holding cable channel licenses. "From the point of view of freedom of expression, this is the worst of all possible worlds."

Options to Government Regulation

The question basic to the debate is whether electronic printing will mean more or less freedom of expression both by those who have things to say through the mass media and those who wish to listen. The new technologies themselves allow at least as much freedom as we now have, perhaps even more. The degree and scope of freedom in the future will depend on the policies established by government. The solution might lie in a suggestion by Owen: "The lesson is that in order to avoid regulating the content of the print media we may have to start now to deregulate the electronic media."

Case for Deregulation of Media

Future Issues of Deregulation

What Professor Owen suggests about deregulating the electronic media has already sprung roots in Washington D.C. A House subcommittee chaired by Congressman Lionel Van Deerlin (D-Calif.) has come up with official recommendations for revising the Communication Act of 1934, the act that created the Federal Communications Commission and under whose auspices the commission functions.

The projected revisions have produced, in the words of one print editorialist, "a slick, political package that promises relief for the complaints of all the industry segments involved while demanding some fairly tough concessions in return." It also resulted in a proposed bill that would change the structure of the commission. The FCC has guided the electronic media for almost fifty years according to measures enacted before the advent of commercial television.

Revision of the Communications Act of 1934

The proposed bill would move in the electronic media stream of the times—*deregulation*. Under the recommendations, the government's authority over electronic media would be limited to those aspects of industry activities in which "marketplace forces are deficient." In brief, the plan is to give greater freedom to the broadcasting industry to function on its own in a mature marketplace.

Recommendations include altering the membership of the FCC from the present seven members to a five-person panel. The panel's responsibilities would be carefully defined and more technical in function and purpose than the law presently requires. The functions of establishing official policy and overseeing research activities would be done by a new agency under the executive branch of government.

These and other changes in the structure of the FCC must, of course, gain the approval of both houses of Congress. It is unlikely that that will happen without considerable jockeying by special interests, including the broadcast industry and the American Telephone and Telegraph Company (ATT), which virtually controls the nation's telephone industry.

Among other changes in regulations would be that station licensees would ultimately be able to run their stations on a permanent basis rather than being required to stand FCC inspection every three years. In addition, license periods would be extended from three to five years with permanent ownership possible after ten years. Perhaps of greater importance nationwide, the proposed bill would also limit ownership of broadcast stations to five per owner, thus cutting a mighty swath in the conglomerate media power structure of the nation.

Congressional opponents of the bill see no critical reasons for change. Telephone service works as it stands, they say, and the broadcast industries offer a balance of programming. But others, especially from within the industry, complain that the commission is the outmoded watchdog of a technology long since surpassed by increasingly sophisticated thinking and capability.

Business Week commented that the proposed act succeeds in "prying open a tightly regulated environment and exposing it to the more dynamic and uncertain forces of the 'information age.' "[15]

What will happen to the proposals, how they will be cut and shaped in debate, what will emerge, and what will be lost all remain to be seen. At the center stands the First Amendment to the United States Constitution, its supporters wondering if it will survive. The political forces involved, confronted by the presence of powerful lobbies, will make for interesting and highly vocal exchanges of facts and viewpoints. And that can only serve "the public interest," which is what all this is really about. The future will determine the size, shape, content, and controls of the mass media. For now we must wait—and watch.

Summary

Although some communications media, within the print sector mostly, resist, for whatever the reasons, the advances of the new technology, it is clear that radical changes in the gathering and disseminating of information are already at work. They will advance even further in times to come giving way to even more notable changes. It also appears likely that those who continue to resist are apt to fall behind and ultimately disappear from the competitive market.

Americans have always cherished a fondness for the past and properly so, particularly as applied to their mass media. Radio shows and original music from the Big Band era of the 1930s and 40s are preserved on 33⅓ rpm records, singles, and albums, which enjoy steady sales. Book publishers produce volumes and sets of volumes that recreate in words and pictures the nostalgia of the good old days. Even newspapers publish anniversary editions in which old stories, etchings, photographs, and assorted other materials reflect the delights, even agonies, of times long gone. Many newspapers also include as regular features resurrected local news highlights of decades past. All of these vehicles are obviously meaningful to sufficient numbers to make the investments worthwhile.

These vehicles are living records of how generations have created change, more or less, depending on the needs and resources available at different times. With the dawn of the 1980s now upon us, it is apparent that coming changes will thrust yet new ways upon the world, more dramatic and in shorter time spans than ever before. The main movers of the new technologies will utilize inner and outer space the way the frontiersmen utilized the Great Plains. The changes already created have had profound impact on associated fields of American life—medical advances, explorations of ocean depths to fulfill human needs in food and energy, educational systems and methods, modes of entertainment, the preparation and cooking of food—the applications are virtually endless.

History also emphasizes that those who resist change of the kinds enumerated here are doomed to reside in the good old days by themselves. It also seems clear that if the mass media in America are to be part of the future, they will need to accept the new in preference to the old. Current media issues, First Amendment freedoms chief among them, will have to be dealt with as they arise. And freedom, when appropriately applied, has always encouraged constructive change. If new advances in media technology mean curtailing freedom, nothing will have been gained and much will have been lost. The time is now.

Notes

1. The figures, along with a description of the new technology from Ben H. Bagdikian, "Publishing's Quiet Revolution," in *Readings in Mass Communication,* Michael C. Emery and Ted Curtis Smythe, eds. (Dubuque, Iowa: Wm. C. Brown Company Publishers, 1977), p. 159.
2. "Printing by Computer: A USN&WR Gamble Pays Off," *U.S. News & World Report,* September 5, 1977, p. 56.
3. "Electronic Home Delivery Here Now," The *Quill,* December 1977, p. 24.
4. Information on the unions from A. H. Raskin, "The Big Squeeze on Labor Unions," The *Atlantic,* October 1978, p. 41.
5. This and further comments by Mulholland from Robert Mulholland, "Toward Totally Electronic TV News," in *Readings in Mass Communication,* Michael C. Emery and Ted Curtis Smythe, eds. (Dubuque, Iowa: Wm. C. Brown Company Publishers, 1977), p. 170.
6. "Electronic Home Delivery Here Now," p. 24.
7. Information on Ted Turner from "Going Super with Ted," *Newsweek,* January 1, 1979, p. 16.
8. Information on the growth of pay-television from "The Race to Dominate the Pay-TV Market," *Business Week,* October 2, 1978, p. 33.
9. Harry M. Shooshan III, "What Communications Future? What Role for the Federal Government?" *Current,* May/June 1978, p. 27.
10. Irwin Ross, "Marisat: Deep-Space Switchboard for Ship-to-Shore Calls," *Popular Science,* February 1979, p. 73.
11. Walter S. Baer, "Telecommunications Technology in the 1980s," *Communications for Tomorrow,* Glen O. Robinson, ed. (New York: Praeger Publishers, 1978), p. 79.
12. Information on "The 'Far-Out' Future" from Gene Bylinsky, "Space Will Be the Next Big Construction Site," *Fortune,* February 26, 1979, p. 63.
13. Hulteng's comments from John L. Hulteng, *The Messenger's Motives* (Englewood Cliffs, N.J.: Prentice-Hall, 1976), p. 243.
14. Owen's comments from Bruce M. Owen, "The Role of Print in an Electronic Society," *Communications for Tomorrow,* p. 229.
15. Theodore B. Merrill, Jr., "A Slick, Thoughtful Overhaul of the Communications Industry," *Business Week,* July 10, 1978, p. 86.

For Further Reading

Bagdikian, Ben H. "Publishing's Quiet Revolution." *Readings in Mass Communication.* Edited by Michael C. Emery and Ted Curtis Smythe. Dubuque, Iowa: Wm. C. Brown Company Publishers, 1977, p. 159.

Bylinski, Gene. "Space Will Be the Next Big Construction Site." *Fortune,* February 26, 1979, p. 63.

"Electronic Home Delivery Here Now." The *Quill,* December 1977, p. 24.

"Going Super With Ted." *Newsweek,* January 1, 1979, p. 16.

Merrill, Theodore B., Jr. "A Slick, Thoughtful Overhaul of the Communications Industry." *Business Week,* July 10, 1978, p. 86.

Mulholland, Robert. "Toward Totally Electronic TV News." *Readings in Mass Communication.* Edited by Michael C. Emery and Ted Curtis Smythe. Dubuque, Iowa: Wm. C. Brown Company Publishers, 1977, p. 170.

"Printing by Computer: A USN&WR Gamble Pays Off." *U.S. News & World Report,* September 5, 1977, p. 56.

Raskin, A.H. "The Big Squeeze on Labor Unions." *Atlantic,* October 1978, p. 41.

Ross, Irwin. "Marisat: Deep-Space Switchboard Ship-to-Shore Calls." *Popular Science,* February 1979, p. 73.

Shooshan, Harry M., III. "What Communications Future? What Role for the Federal Government?" *Current,* May/June 1978, p. 27.

"The Race to Dominate the Pay-TV Market." *Business Week,* October 2, 1978, p. 33.

Conclusion

The struggle for freedom of expression in America has gone on continuously in one form or another since the earliest colonial settlements. The early American colonies were generally antagonistic toward any who vocalized dissenting viewpoints. They had jails for criminals—and dissenters.

In the time since then, the American media as dissenters have performed well, even heroically, in many aspects of performance, but certainly not in all. That has been due to many things, including professional dereliction and other human failings. But much of it has been due to the size and composition of the population and significant editorial and popular differences about what is important and what is not. It is also due to geographical, ethnic, racial, educational, and economic differences among the general population of the nation and the degree of their participation in the public business.

The American press has become a major power in the kingdom of big business. As with all corporate enterprises, it sometimes succumbs to advancing its own interests above the common good. As big business, the mass media are also sometimes guilty of applying great dedication to beating out (or down) the competition or killing it off altogether. That frequently means that information content is geared to the most emotionally charged failings of our society: what is most bawdy, most violent, most titillating.

In our system, the public's right to know is often as difficult to pin down as the media's obligation to tell them. Hence, the compelling question posed by those who think kindly of Jeffersonian principles: Is the press required to give the people what they want or what they need even if what they want is not what they need? Some media executives, embroiled in the jolt and jar of the competitive marketplace, charge that giving the public what they need even if it is not what they want could bring economic disaster. Yet Jefferson's call to service contains a gnawing ingredient of timeless truth: "Cherish, therefore, the spirit of our people. And keep alive their attentions." At the same time, Jefferson also recognized how difficult it was to "reach, galvanize, vitalize, organize this great widely scattered mass" of human beings. The media of his day had to cope with the whimsies of about four million widely-scattered citizens. Today the mass media, though more numerous, varied, and sophisticated, must keep up with the needs and wants of some 220 million people spread over a vastly larger country. So the mass media of the 1980s must cope with the same realities—and more—as the press in Jefferson's time. How to "reach, galvanize, vitalize, organize this great widely scattered mass" is a significantly more complex problem. It is little wonder that many issues extend from it.

In the interest of economic survival, many modern media have become more dedicated to *reaching* the massive population than in *galvanizing, vitalizing* or *organizing* them. In many cases, *reaching* has become an economic panacea that places its emphasis on frothy or seamy entertainment matter rather than on meaningful information vital to the democratic process.

In balance, a vast, if mostly unheralded, segment of the press have endured honorably because they have ground out the day's news, informing their people of the ups and downs of living costs and what they mean to current human existence, the ailments of local education, the availability and quality of health care, the dealings of the bogeymen and women in public life, and other matters designed to generate public involvement in the governmental process. Some members of the press have even given their lives for it. And in most cases, their work is barely noticed, if at all, by the donors of prestigious awards and professional prizes. Public officials frequently bully them and judges sometimes jail them. It's a job, and those who prefer to do it well are honorable, if unhonored, men and women who take pride in what they do.

Others are in it for what it might do for them, to make themselves shine. These types might strike hard at persons and institutions in the public light without first doing their homework. We have libel and privacy laws to cope with their excesses. In turn, libel and privacy actions, and threats of actions, are also used to club responsible media into inaction.

Massive changes in the mass media have arrived in recent years and more are on the way. How they will impact on the role of the media as a free and meaningful social-political force can only be supposed. The shape, weight, and substance of the First Amendment might well change with the onslaught of new technologies and different ways of doing things. The changes might be for the better or they might bring new restrictions and some in our midst would cheer "Hooray to that!" Serious independent studies have warned that much will be at stake. The question to be decided by each citizen is, Is the First Amendment worth it?

Index